TRADING WITH ASIA

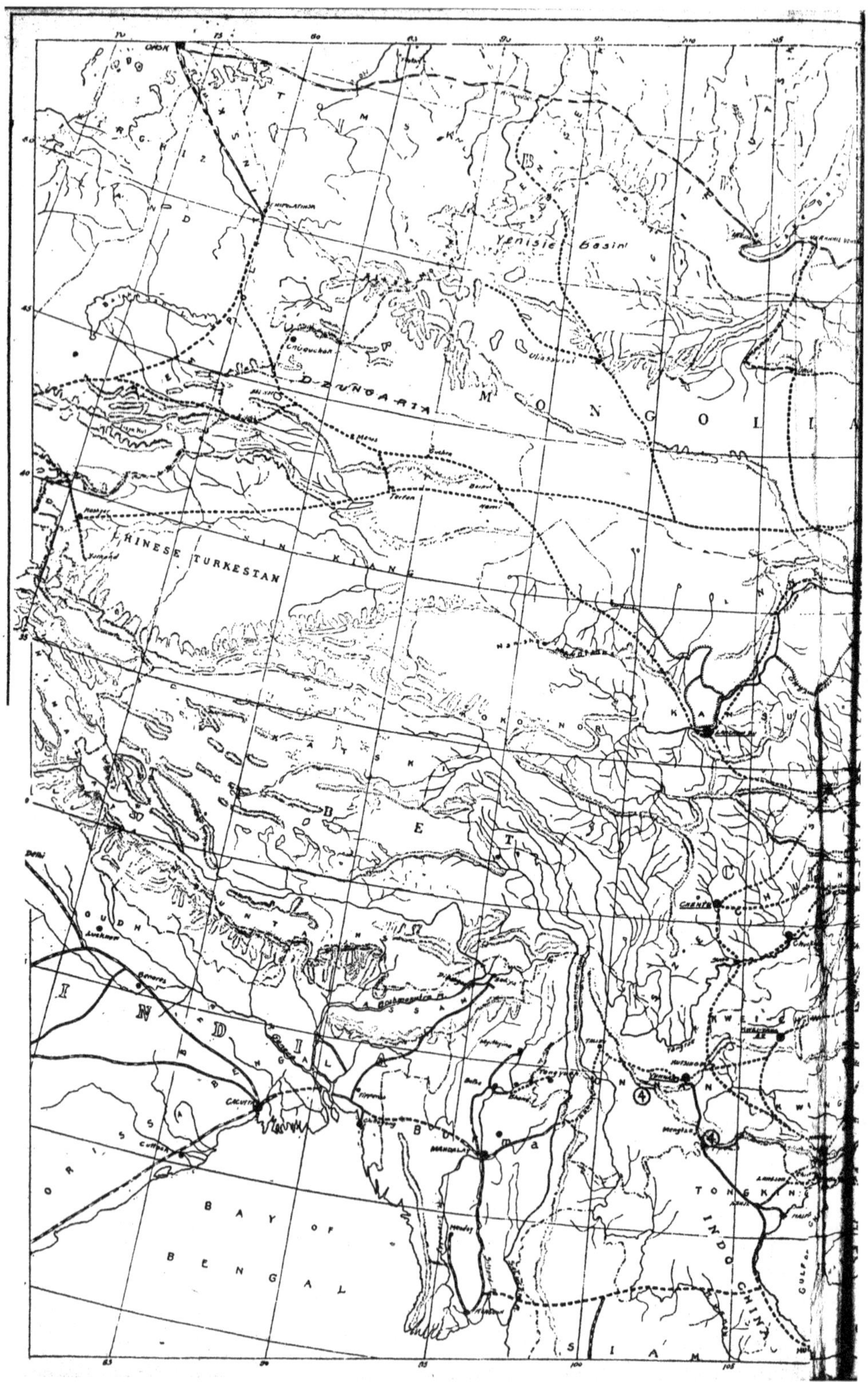

Yenisie Basin
DZUNGARIA
MONGOLIA
CHINESE TURKESTAN
KOKO NOR
KANSU
TIBET
OUDH
INDIA
BENGAL
ASSAM
BURMA
TONGKIN
INDO CHINA
SIAM
BAY OF BENGAL
ORISSA
Calcutta
Mandalay
Chengtu

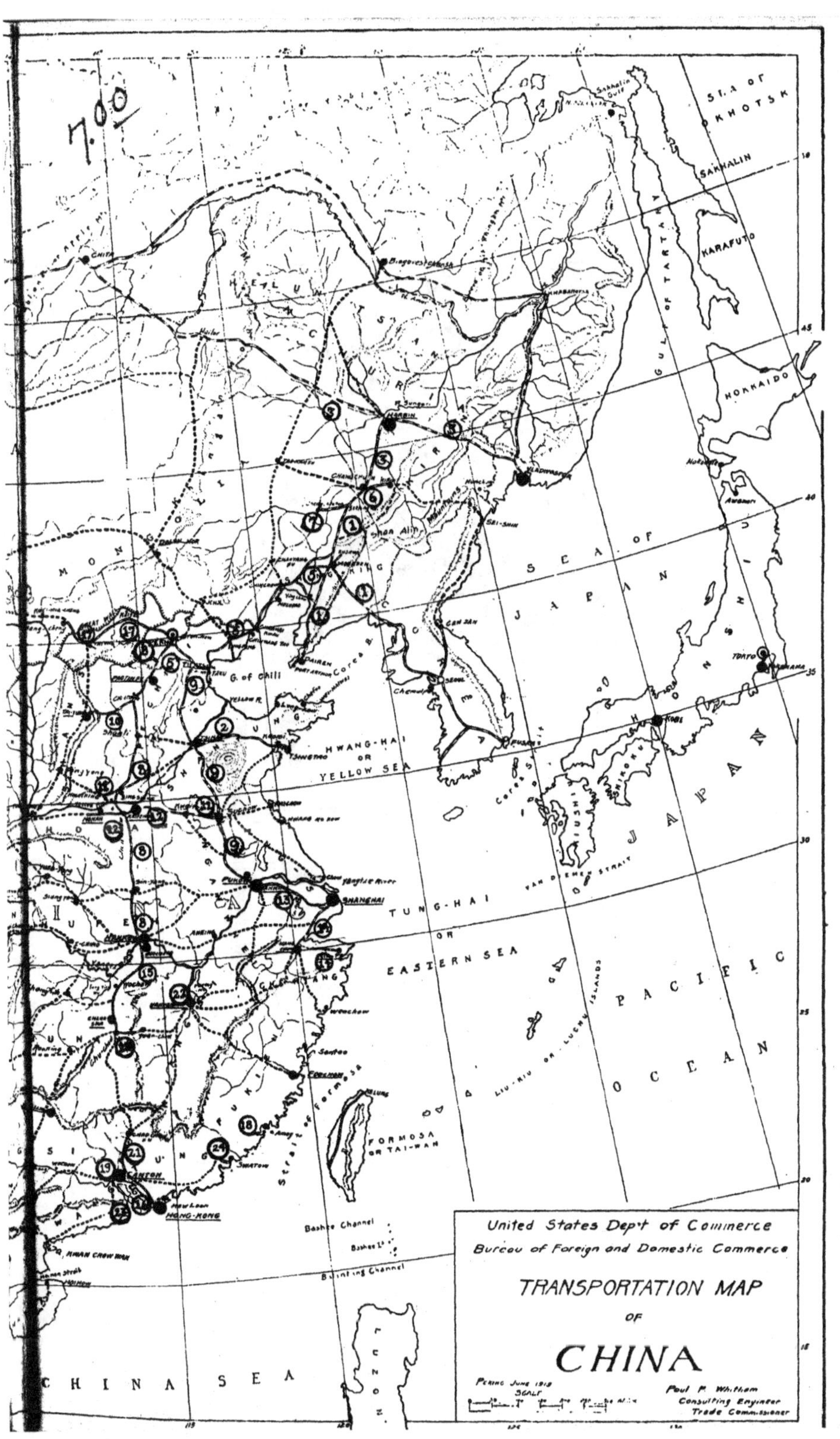

United States Dep't of Commerce
Bureau of Foreign and Domestic Commerce
TRANSPORTATION MAP
OF
CHINA
Peking June 1918
SCALE
Paul P. Whitham
Consulting Engineer
Trade Commissioner
SEA OF OKHOTSK
SAKHALIN
KARAFUTO
HOKKAIDO
SEA OF JAPAN
HWANG-HAI OR YELLOW SEA
TUNG-HAI OR EASTERN SEA
PACIFIC OCEAN
CHINA SEA
FORMOSA OR TAI-WAN
LUZON
SHANGHAI
CANTON
HONG-KONG
HARBIN
Yangtze River
G. of Chili
Bashee Channel
Balintang Channel

TRADING WITH ASIA

BY

FRANK R. ELDRIDGE, Jr.

CHIEF OF THE FAR EASTERN DIVISION OF THE UNITED STATES
BUREAU OF FOREIGN AND DOMESTIC COMMERCE; LECTURER
ON FAR EASTERN ECONOMIC SURVEY IN THE SCHOOL
OF FOREIGN SERVICE OF GEORGETOWN UNIVERSITY

MAPS

D. APPLETON AND COMPANY
NEW YORK LONDON
1921

PRINTED IN THE UNITED STATES OF AMERICA

PREFACE

This book is intended to serve as a primer on Far Eastern trade. It is designed for the student, but it will be found useful by that large class of business men who have felt that they were approaching the great markets of the Orient without a proper knowledge of the fundamental facts concerning the history, government, and commerce of the Oriental peoples. It is designed to be informative rather than opinionative, and subjects of a controversial nature have been purposely omitted. I have striven to make it more a compact handbook than a descriptive or didactic treatise, and for that reason I have included only such references to habits and customs as were absolutely necessary to bring out important economic facts. The book is built upon the theory that a knowledge of commerce is essentially a knowledge of the reasons why certain commodities dominate the trade of certain regions. Predictions as to the possible growth of the import trade of the various countries are indulged in only sparingly as it is realized that such growth is dependent in the last analysis upon individual enterprise which is guided only by profitable return. To encourage unwise or fitful development of these Far Eastern markets is the last thing to be desired by those who have the ultimate growth of our foreign trade at heart. The present development, however, is analyzed fully with a view to pointing out the lines of permanent and profitable growth. Many works on the Far East have been consulted freely, and special mention of these is made at the close of each part of the text, where they are given special consideration in the bibliographical notes. The appendix is considered by no means the least important part of the book; an attempt has been made to render it particularly concrete and valuable for reference purposes.

It is of vital importance to the continued prosperity of the United States that new markets be developed to replace those of the countries with whom we formerly traded but whose effective buying capacity has been reduced by the consequences of war. American manufacturers must export greater quantities of their products than at present in order to keep running at full capacity the plants which have been enlarged to meet the demands of the last seven years and to continue to employ all American workmen at wages that will enable them to maintain unimpaired the American standard of living of which we are so justly proud. The Far East offers the great possibilities of an unexploited field, especially as the 600,000,000 souls of China and India alone are rapidly developing industrially already need large quantities of American machines and metal goods of various types, and accept readily the products of American inventive genius and technical skill.

The domestic market of the United States has hitherto been of such supreme importance that it has not been necessary for American merchants to familiarize themselves with the markets of Asia, but the present commercial depression demands prompt action. The representatives of American concerns who have investigated on the spot the opportunities of the Orient report that satisfactory outlets for our products exist even now, and are capable of unlimited development along certain lines. Knowledge of existing political, economic, and commercial conditions is evidently necessary for an intelligent study of marketing methods.

The Far Eastern problems that will be discussed at the Disarmament Conference are primarily all economic problems. The "battle of concessions" has its present-day aftermath in a jockeying for position in the coming race for commercial supremacy in China. The market belongs to the adventurous and the well informed. With enormous capital ready for investment, we must sooner or later make a definite decision as to whether or not we wish to participate in the development of Asia. We are handicapped in many ways, but most severely by a timid investing public and a lack of trained men. In the last analysis, our bankers can only reflect the courage and confidence of their clients. If we deliberately decide to neglect the investment opportunities in the Orient, we must content ourselves with a restricted foreign trade, a lower production at home, and ultimately more difficult economic conditions in this country. If we face the situation intelligently, study our field, invest judiciously and wisely, there can be no doubt about the ultimate outcome. It will mean wider foreign commerce, greater production and greater prosperity at home. The choice is with the American people.

F. R. Eldridge, Jr.

CONTENTS

PART I

CHINA AND JAPAN

PART II

THE PHILIPPINES AND THE DUTCH EAST INDIES

PART III

BRITISH INDIA, BURMA, AND CEYLON

APPENDICES

MAPS

TRADING WITH ASIA

CHAPTER I

INTRODUCTION

The people of that part of the world known as the Far East have been in more or less constant contact with the people of Europe and America since the early part of the sixteenth century. During that period they have watched the Western world develop a civilization by means of a series of epoch-making inventions, in which steam, electricity, and lately the internal-combustion engine, played the principal rôles. Because some of them have failed to realize the value of these new discoveries, they have been termed backward. They have more recently witnessed the logical result of what they have probably considered a mad struggle to overcome time and space in a world-destroying conflict which has left these same "advanced" nations economically paralyzed. For centuries they have been urged to adopt the new civilization of the West, to abandon their own customs and adopt "higher" standards, and some of these things they have done. They have readily acquired Western knowledge of sanitation, medicine, and hygiene. By successive stages they have evolved from oil lamps to electric lights, from oil-paper to glass windows, from thatched roofs to galvanized iron, from mud and straw houses to stone and brick. But by adopting these more useful evidences of Western civilization, they have by no means abandoned all the ancient customs and habits that long centuries of economic necessity have inculcated in them. The dense population of most of the Far Eastern countries has long kept the people of many large territories dependent solely upon the food which they produce for immediate consumption, and has permitted no great accumulation of wealth in goods on the part of the individual.

Causes of Oriental Backwardness.—By the use of labor-saving devices the Western producer has for many years been steadily increasing his store of wealth. His standards have risen because he has been less and less dependent upon his own and others' labor and to a greater extent upon the more efficient work of mechanical devices. The capital which he has thus accumulated has been seeking new lands to develop, and the United States and Latin America have reached a high stage of development through the investment of this accumulated wealth. When the Western investor turns toward the Far East, he finds few fertile tracts of land which are not already supporting the limit of population. He finds these peoples in an economic rut, keeping just ahead of starvation by the greatest manual exertion. In what way may his capital be invested in these countries so that a return commensurate with the risk may be earned? In the case of the tropical peoples the more aggressive white settler has seized the reins of government and with one exception intends to keep them. In the Philippines alone a new and daring experiment has been tried with results which bid fair to upset the established theories of colonization. The northern peoples have been found less tractable. In one case, that of Japan, a warlike and virile people have adopted so energetically the best that the West has had to offer that they stand to-day as one of the recognized powers of the world. The vast reaches of China have perhaps been saved from dismemberment only because of the mutual jealousies and greed of the Western powers. These powers China's rulers have desperately played the one against the other, in an effort to forestall complete agreement on division of her territory.

Difficulties Confronting the Prospective Trader.—Such is the situation that confronts the American seeking to extend the sales of his goods to Far Eastern markets. He may have enjoyed a certain sale of his product in parts of Europe, where he found, before the World War, conditions somewhat similar to those at home. In Latin America he has perhaps been less successful because of his unfamiliarity with the Latin civilization which has been transplanted there. But in the Far East he is confronted with a civilization so remote from anything he has encountered heretofore that he is discouraged at the start. The distance is great, the shipping facilities are unsatisfactory, and business is conducted in a manner which requires more time and patience than he believes it is worth.

Character of the Market.—But no market is so remote and so intricate in its complexities that it is beyond the reach of the well informed and the adventurous. No market, moreover, compares with the Far East in its absolute call for both of these characteristics in the make-up of those who would capture it. Our lack of interest in Asia has been important in its effect of discouraging original research and presentation of the basic economic facts concerning Asia to the American public. Nevertheless, certain historical, legal, and economic background is absolutely essential if we are to embark upon a permanent commercial career in the Orient.

Area of Asia.—Comprising all of the territory extending from the southern and southwestern borders of Siberia to the Indian Ocean, Asia proper, as included within the scope of this book, is divided from Asia Minor by the Indian-Afghanistan and Indian-Persian borders, and includes the homes of all but the white races of Siberia and Australasia. Were a map of North America superimposed upon a map of this vast area at like latitudes, the Canadian border of the United States would correspond roughly with the Chinese-Siberian border, with the State of Washington and part of Oregon extending into Siberia. The Pacific coast of the United States would reach to the Himalaya Mountains, while Mexico and Central America would overlap Burma, French Indo-China, Siam, and Malaya. The whole extent of India, except Burma, would represent additional territory falling outside this area, while southwest China with approximately 300,000 square miles, including the provinces of Kweichow, Kwangsi, Hunan, Kwantung, Kiangsi, and part of Fukien, would fall within the Gulf of Mexico. The tip of Florida would extend over to Foochow, China, opposite Formosa; Charleston would touch the China coast above Shanghai; Norfolk would hit Tsing-tao; and New York City would touch on the Korean border west of Mukden, Manchuria. Maine would extend almost to the Amur River border of Siberia, and the Great Lakes would stretch north from Peking to Urga in Mongolia, leaving a stretch in Manchuria of 300,000 square miles extending over Ontario and Quebec. Korea, Japan, the Dutch East Indies, the Philippines, and India would, of course, fall entirely outside the area covered by such a superimposed map of North America. The comparisons in area between North America (excluding Canada) and Asia are shown statistically in square miles on the next page.

Population of Asia.—When population is considered, the comparison between these two regions of the world as shown on page 5 is even more remarkable and brings home in a very striking manner the vast potentialities of Asia. Were each one of these population units as favorably situated, from an economic standpoint, in Asia as they are in North America, these comparative figures would have much more force than they now actually possess. The effect on civilization of such economic development as would bring

COMPARATIVE AREAS OF ASIA AND NORTH AMERICA

Asia			North America (excluding Canada)		
Country		Square miles	Country		Square miles
China		4,278,352	United States (Including Alaska, Hawaii and Porto Rico)		3,627,557
Burma	230,839				
Siam	195,000				
French Indo-China	256,000				
Malaya	46,992	728,831	Mexico		767,323
			Costa Rica	18,691	
Sub-total		5,007,183	Guatemala	48,290	
British India		1,571,353	Honduras	46,250	
Dutch East Indies		736,400	Nicaragua	49,552	
Philippines		115,026	Panama	32,380	
Japanese Empire		245,551	Salvador	13,176	208,339
Total		7,675,513	Total		4,603,219

COMPARATIVE POPULATIONS OF ASIA AND NORTH AMERICA

Asia			North America (excluding Canada)	
Country		Population 1918 or latest	Country	1918 or latest Population
China (estimated)		325,000,000	United States	108,291,000
Burma	12,115,217			
Siam	8,149,467			
French Indo-China	16,990,000			
Malaya	1,036,999	39,291,683	Mexico	15,502,000
			Costa Rica	455,000
Sub-total		363,291,683	Guatemala	2,119,000
British India		303,041,179	Honduras	562,000
Dutch East Indies		47,204,000	Nicaragua	800,000
Philippines		10,000,000	Panama	450,000
Japanese Empire		78,708,000	Salvador	1,288,000
Total		802,244,862	Total	129,467,000

these two factors into comparable similarity can hardly be estimated.

Climate of Asia.—Those familiar with the climate of North and Central America will have no difficulty in gaining, from the description of the comparative area of Asia and North America, some idea as to the similarity of climatic conditions between the two continents. So close is the comparison that the wheat belt of Ontario, Minnesota, and the Dakotas corresponds in climate and temperature with the great plains of Manchuria and inner Mongolia; the desert of Takla-Makan is in the same latitude as Nevada, and the great wastes of Gobi and West China are comparable with the Rocky Mountain region of the United States. It is in the south that the analogy is weakened by the incomparably greater heights of the Himalayas than those of any mountain range of northern Mexico, while the plains of Texas, falling within the mountainous regions of Yunnan and West Thibet, present widely different climatic characteristics although in the same latitudes. The one fundamental difference of great economic significance is the lack of a western "coast" to China, depriving the Chinese of the lure of the ocean, without which many a prairie schooner would never have braved the wilds of western America.

There is little essential difference in climate between the tropics of Dutch and British India and the tropics of South America, while the similarity between the Malay Peninsula and Central America is more marked in climate than in topography. The seacoast of China is similar to the Atlantic coast of the United States in the same latitudes. Asia thus presents a diversity of climate as varied as the climates of Canada and the Amazon, with an added element of the highest mountain ranges in the world located in a position analogous to northern Mexico. It is this Himalaya range which produces the "monsoon" of India by chilling the moist winds from the Indian Ocean, thus affecting climatically all of southern Asia.

Races and Languages of Asia.—Three predominant strains run through the peoples of all Asia. The Ayrian race forms the nucleus of the people of India and merges with the Malay in Burma, reaching a decidedly Malay-

Mongolian strain in Siam and French Indo-China. In the vast area of China the races vary from a pure Mongol, in the northwest, to variations in the Manchus, the Chinese of central China, and the southern Chinese, the latter being closely akin to the natives of French Indo-China and Siam. The natives of the Dutch East Indies, the Philippines, and Malaya are Malay with a mixture of Arab and Chinese. The race of the Japanese has long been a matter of conjecture and dispute, the claim that they are a Malay-Mongolian mixture perhaps coming nearest the truth.

Following the racial strains, the languages show a decided tendency to vary directly with the race mixture. Hindustani is as basically different from Siamese as Siamese is from some south-China dialects, yet each has influenced the other. Nothing has shown the independent provincial growth of China so markedly as the difference in dialects. The superimposed Mandarin is the only common language that can be used by all the official classes, so that next to inadequate transportation, if not because of it, the language difficulty is the greatest bar to any hope for a unified, homogeneous China. Quite distinct from the Chinese spoken language, but using the ideograph, borrowed from China, in the written language, Japanese is by far the most difficult language of the East for the foreigner to master. Malay, on the other hand, is comparatively simple and serves as a basis for most of the dialects of the Island tropics. Spanish is useful in the Philippines, but more Filipinos speak English now than ever spoke Spanish. The commercial language in the East is English, and its use is becoming more widespread among the educated natives every year.

Economic Interdependence of Asiatic Countries.—The diversities in climate and resulting diversities in production have brought about a certain economic interdependence among the several countries of Asia. Thus, the rich agricultural lands of the tropics and India, particularly the rich rice fields of Burma and French Indo-China, help to feed the less favored portions of China and Japan and receive in exchange manufactured goods and certain commodities that cannot be raised in the tropics. The great trade routes, therefore, lay overland from India and Burma to northern China and by water around the China coast and the Malay Peninsula to India. This economic self-sufficiency of Asia was, perhaps, never more noticeable than during the war, when trade readjustments on a strictly inter-Asiatic basis were necessary and were accomplished with little, if any, economic upheavals.

Relation of History and Laws to Commerce.—The history of China and Japan presents an amazing variety of contrasts and similarities, contrasts in the manner in which historical lessons have been accepted by the two peoples, and similarities in the development of the two peoples under like circumstances, albeit the development has not been contemporaneous because of geographical, racial, and other conditions. On the other hand, the history of the tropical Far Eastern people of the Philippines, Dutch East Indies, French Indo-China, Malaya, Siam, and British India is very similar in many respects, varying only with the peculiar characteristics of the European nations that have imposed their own determinations upon them. The buffer state of Siam stands alone as the one tropical Oriental country that has escaped foreign domination, and the history of its development is surprisingly similar to that of Japan, leading to the presumption that perhaps the relative "backwardness" of the European colonies is not in spite of, but because of, foreign control. The development of the commercial laws of these Far Eastern countries reflects very closely their political history. Japan has followed European, particularly German, codes in her commercial laws, perhaps from choice and because of their easy adaptability to native codes, but not without some desire to placate the most exacting of those foreign nations, without whose consent extraterritoriality could not have been abolished. China showed a tendency to adopt the same tactics until the war in Europe and her entrance into the League of Nations immeasurably advanced her chances for undictated legal autonomy. The tropical countries, except Siam, have all adopted modified systems based upon the home laws, and any development must necessarily follow, rather than precede, greater economic independence. The American system in the Philippines, with modifications dictated from time to time by the policy of gradual aspiration to independence, may prove the forerunner of like changes in the other tropical countries.

Potentialities and Actualities of China.— The temptation to consider Asiatic resources in their potentialities rather than in their actualities eventually has done much to discourage and dishearten the prospective trader and investor. An overstatement of the facts is in all respects as undesirable as an understatement, and there is no way to give the exact picture except to recite the actual extent of the present production in each of the principal commodities. While such a method of presentation is not conducive to imaginative flights, and its chief drawback lies in the rather dry and precise statements which exactness dictates, we have sought to sacrifice style to staidness only when precision could be attained in no other way. In the face of all that has been said about the potentialities of China it is feared that the export figures during the past five years, representing the only true index to production, show a rather depressing condition. The inordinate rise in prices had so far concealed the true condition that many will be loath to believe that the volume of China's export trade was much smaller in 1919 than in 1914.

Japanese Trade and the War.—What China lost through the dislocation and withdrawal of shipping due to the war and the high price of silver—the medium in which her products were valued for sale to countries on a correspondingly lowered gold basis—Japan gained by becoming the *entrepot* for Far Eastern shipping through her control of practically all the merchant vessels left on the Pacific. In a large measure Japan's industrial growth was predicated upon this control. As a result, Japan's trade increased remarkably, not only in value, but in volume as well. The character of Japan's development was well illustrated by the heavy imports of raw materials from America and India and the large exports of manufactured goods to China and the South Seas. In this way Japan catered to the starving markets of the Far East at a time when all European markets were closed and America's lack of ships and preoccupation with furnishing supplies to Europe permitted only casual participation in the trade. The war trade which Japan built upon the ruins of European commerce with the Orient bids fair to be only a temporary structure erected upon the sands of Japan's economic unfitness in many lines of industry.

Effect of War on Far Eastern Colonial Trade Policies.—Not the least interesting studies of commercial history during the war are those of the colonial trade developments in the Far East. The Dutch East Indies, cut off from their usual markets, turned instinctively to Japan and the United States, and in the latter case many of our traders discovered for the first time the source of many of their imports from Germany and Holland. The growth of the "Dutch Colonial" sentiment in the colony's population during the war, demanding as it did free markets for its products without the necessity of paying tribute by transshipment through Holland, gave an added impetus to the growth of direct trade which commercial and economic considerations had already dictated. In the British colonies, however, a somewhat different development took place. Realizing her inability to control India's exports of raw materials as in the past, Great Britain, rather than encourage an outlet through direct channels, adopted the policy of encouraging industrial growth, although such a policy was directly inimical to British markets for manufactured goods in India and the Far East. The long view was taken, however, that prosperous, industrial India was a greater asset to the Empire than an agricultural India weaned from Imperial economic control. The policy, while not carried out in its entirety, has had a profound effect upon Indian economics, and the industrialization of India has carried in its train a score of social and political consequences. The effect upon other countries in the Orient whose pre-war trade with India was important has been equally farreaching. British Malaya, on the other hand, producing three commodities of immense significance in the war—rubber, tin, and coconuts, has been encouraged in extensive production as an agricultural and mining asset to the Empire. In the same manner the French have sought to utilize French Indo-China, with, however, only indifferent success, due primarily to the disabilities of the French as colonizers and also to the relatively restricted resources of the colony. Our own experience in the Philippines has been decidedly more encouraging, and the handsome profits made in coconut oil have only been partially counterbalanced by the losses incurred from too hasty and ill advised expansion of the oil-mill industry. In their steady and patient industry during a period of turmoil in Europe, the native colonials have displayed in every instance the real economic potentiality of the East—frugal and industrious labor.

In the face of such a diversity of conditions, it has been no small task to collect from a number of sources all of the pertinent facts relating to the history, government, resources, and trade of Asia. Brevity and conciseness have been striven for, and the aim in writing the following chapters has been to present in the fewest possible words all that is worth while on every important phase of each subject. The arrangement of the material on resources and trade has been by commodities, so that the reference value of the book would be enhanced. No attempt has been made to cover any subject exhaustively, and the bibliographies are intended as a guide to further reading for the student whose interest has been aroused in any particular part of the work. The files of the Far Eastern Division of the Bureau of Foreign and Domestic Commerce have furnished much of the economic material, and these are always at the disposal of those seeking further enlightenment.

PART I

CHINA AND JAPAN

CHAPTER II

HISTORY OF CHINA AND JAPAN DURING FOREIGN INTERCOURSE

The Attitude of China and Japan to Foreign Intercourse.—There is nothing more significant in the modern history of the Orient than the manner in which the two great nations, China and Japan, accepted the coming of the foreigner. Greeted wholeheartedly by Japan in 1542, the foreigner, by an undue zeal in spreading the Gospel, paved the way to his own expulsion in 1640, setting up a barrier against the West which was only removed by the influence of the American Admiral Perry's big guns in Tokyo Bay in 1854. China accepted the coming of the foreigner grudgingly, confined his activities to narrow precincts in the larger ports, and after a series of unsuccessful wars was compelled to recognize in 1842 the claims of the "foreign devils" to rights of residence and trade. What Japan yielded as the inevitable had to be wrested from China, but this fact would not have been of great consequence had it not been the origin of the attitudes toward the West in the two countries, attitudes fundamentally different and which profoundly affected the history of the succeeding century. When Japan resolved to throw open her doors and accept the foreigner, she decided at the same time to admit that the marvelous inventions that Perry had demonstrated before the awestruck Shogun on the shores of Tokyo Bay were evidences of a superior civilization. From that time (1854) onward, it became the resolve of the thinking Japanese to master this new civilization before it mastered them. China showed no such fixity of purpose. The only thought in the Chinese official mind from 1842 until 1911 was to seek every means to check the foreigner in his purpose of opening up the country to Western intercourse. Whether this was accomplished by intrigue or by open obstruction mattered little so long as the net result was to offset the efforts which the West was making to bring China into line with Western nations. China formerly had been successful in assimilating her conquerors by the simple process of passive resistance, but the flood of Western civilization which beat against her shores was too great to be overcome in this manner. The outcome was that China, almost completely dismembered and hopelessly stifled, sought to express in revolution her purpose to conciliate Western knowledge, fifty-seven years after Japan, foreseeing the inevitable, had gracefully bowed to, and very nearly mastered, it. Any other reading of Oriental history during the period of foreign intercourse fails to account satisfactorily for the present wide differences in the condition and general advancement of the Empire of Japan and of the present Republic of China.

Opening of China.—Early in the sixteenth century China's loosely knit administration under the Ming Emperor Chêng-te had come in contact with the first foreigners who approached China from the sea, an expedition under the Portuguese D'Andrade, which arrived off Canton in 1511. The leader of this expedition went to Peking, where he was received as a *quasi* ambassador, but the outrageous acts of his followers at Ningpo and elsewhere led to his banishment and death. Soon after, in 1535, a massacre of Portuguese took place at Foochow. After much negotiation the Canton officials permitted the Portuguese to settle on the Macao Peninsula, just south of Canton, in return for an annual rental. Although in constant conflict with pirates and others, the trade was so lucrative that five or six hundred Portuguese adventurers soon made this settlement their headquarters.

Because of the acts of these early European settlers, the missionary Xavier was refused permission to land on Chinese soil. He took up his residence on an island outside Canton but died in 1552 without achieving his desire to carry a message of peace and goodwill to the Chinese. The missionary Ricci was more successful in 1582, having prepared the way by a study of the language and of the religious beliefs of the people. He was received at Peking, where his scientific knowledge opened the way for some real accomplishments. Among other things he translated six books of Euclid into Chinese and also wrote a work in Chinese on the character and attributes of God. This early idea of Ricci has now been revived, and to reach the hearts of the Chinese through propagation of scientific and general knowledge is the task of the modern missionary.

The First Invasion from Japan.—The years which followed were marked by a foreign invasion of a quite different character. The Japanese had obtained in 1552 a footing on the coast of Chekiang Province, had fortified their position, and defended it successfully. From this vantage point Nanking on the Yangtse was besieged unsuccessfully, but the presence of the invaders reduced the central provinces to a chronic state of disorder. In 1592 the Japanese invaded Korea, reached Seoul, the capital, and were met by a Chinese force, sent in response to an appeal from the Korean Emperor, on the Yalu near Pingslang, at almost the same spot where three hundred years later (1894) they were to meet another Chinese army. Although defeated by the Chinese, Hideyoshi was so incensed by the action of China in sending low-ranking ambassadors to negotiate peace that he had nearly gathered together his exhausted resources for a fresh attack when he was overtaken by death. This put an end to the war.

The Opposition to Western Influence and Its Decline. —The evident esteem with which foreign missionaries were held by the first Manchu Emperor, Sun-chi, whose dynasty had finally succeeded the tottering Ming dynasty, was given a new meaning when he advised his people in his sixteen maxims "to avoid strange sects." It became evident from this time that the missionaries who had been received with such effusion by the Manchu Court were more honored for their scientific knowledge than for their religious belief. Until his death in 1710 the famous Manchu Emperor was in constant conflict with the missionaries, attempting to thwart their efforts in every manner except actual banishment. This probably would have been impracticable, for the Manchus exercised only a precarious and largely nominal control over China in the face of many attempts to restore the Mings.

An attempt to banish the missionaries was made early in the reign of the next Emperor, K'ang-hi, and over 300 churches were destroyed in an effort to compel all foreigners to retire to Macao, but the possibility of a Mongol invasion soon engaged the attention of the Manchus elsewhere. Chinese sentiment, however, was against Christians in particular and foreigners in general and not until 1727 was a foreign emissary successful in approaching the Court. The Russian embassy, then received, accomplished two things. By arranging for the despatch of Russian youths to study Chinese, a firm footing was established in Peking by Russia; and by designating a number of persons to attend and supervise these youths, valuable diplomatic agents and constant intercourse between the Russian and Chinese capitals were instituted. The Russian emissary, by insisting upon dealing directly with the Emperor and handing his credentials to him instead of depositing them on a table, as had formerly been the custom with foreign embassies, emphasized the beginning of direct personal relations between foreign sovereigns and the Emperor himself. One result of this stand was a reconciliation between the missionaries and the Court.

The next Manchu Emperor, Yung-cheng, ascended the throne in 1735 and soon started upon a military career which was to enlarge his empire and enrich his treasury to an extent unknown to his predecessors. His principal conquests extended along the western frontier and eastern Turkestan. The inroads of the northern chief, Galdan, had led to an exodus of the more peaceful Tourgots of this region to the Russian Volga region, where they were permitted to remain for half a century, until the return of their native land to Chinese control created an irresistible impulse for repatriation. This started 600,000 on a fateful journey which ended in disaster, those not drowned in Lake Tenghis in a mad attempt to quench their long-enduring thirst being massacred by wild tribes. The conquest of Burma was next undertaken and led to the payment of tribute to China by that country until some years after it was nominally under British rule. By similar conquest Cochin China became a tributary state, while Tibet, after many campaigns and much intrigue, recognized the suzerainty of China.

England's Entrance into China.—Although England had attempted many times during the reign of Chienlung to open diplomatic intercourse, the efforts had not been successful, and privileges of trade at Canton, Amoy, and Ningpo had only been obtained by force. The greed of the local mandarins had tended to make profitable trade impossible, and burdens were heaped upon a trade which would have enriched both native officials and merchants had they been content with a nominal gain. In 1792 Lord Macartney was sent as a special ambassador to the Chinese court. He was received at Tientsin with great pomp, although the boats which bore his party to Tungchow, the port of Peking on the Peiho River, bore the Chinese inscription, unknown to the Englishmen at the time, "Tribute bearers from England." Upon reaching the royal presence every effort was made to compel the British Ambassador to do the "kowtow," or ceremonial bow, but he refused. He brought, however, presents ranging from matches to carriages, which required the services of 3,000 coolies in conveying them from the boat to the palace. The results of this first formal mission are typical of the Chinese attitude toward the West. Though every courtesy and good will was displayed toward the person of the ambassador, no commercial privileges except permission to trade at Canton were gained, and the exclusiveness of the Chinese court was not broken down in the least.

Meanwhile the first American clipper ships had arrived in Canton in 1784, and by 1805 thirty-seven American clippers had carried nearly six million dollars worth of American goods to China, bringing back an equal amount of Chinese products. In 1834 Lord Napier was appointed by the British government to take over the trading rights heretofore exercised by the East India Company at Canton. The opposition which he experienced was largely due to the opium trade which the East India Company had built up between India and China. The trade had been declared illegal by the Emperor, Kia-K'ing, K'ien-lung's successor, who thereby lost a good revenue from customs duty, while the local mandarin was enriched by permitting illicit smuggling of the drug. In the face of many vexations and persecutions Lord Napier continued to hold out for the single principle of the right to trade. After his death in 1834, the British merchants at Canton petitioned the British government to take effective steps to open the Chinese empire to trade. Captain Elliott, the successor of Lord Napier, was quite as unsuccessful in asserting his position as a representative of the British government. Meanwhile the opium question was becoming a prominent one in the empire. Although the local mandarins professed their horror at the wide use of the drug, they continued to enrich themselves by permitting illicit smuggling all along the coast and illegal cultivation of the poppy in the interior. The Peking court, where Tao-kwang had begun his reign in 1820, continued to excite feeling against the foreigner by stirring up the anti-opium Chinese. The climax of the situation was reached when a specially appointed commissioner of the Peking court, named Lin, demanded that the British merchants at Canton deliver up all opium in their possession. After bitter negotiations, some 20,000 chests were handed over to the Chinese authorities. Encouraged by his success, the Chinese Commissioner further demanded the right to punish Europeans who committed crimes on Chinese soil, and upon the refusal of the British, called upon his countrymen to arm themselves against the foreigners. The first battle in the First Opium War between the British and Chinese was a naval engagement at Chuanpi, in which many Chinese junks were destroyed. In the summer of 1841 Admiral Bremer blockaded Canton, took Ningpo, and soon arrived at Taku, near Tientsin. Here the expedition was met by the Governor General of Chihli, who, fearful of the effect of the foreigners upon the court and his own position, succeeded by all of his Oriental wiles in persuading the English to return to Canton for negotiation. Upon the return to Canton, the seriousness of the situation was fully realized. A native army had been raised and dispersed by a British force near Macao, but with the British fleet no longer menacing Peking, it required the taking of several forts leading to Canton to bring the Chinese to terms. These terms, proposed early in 1841, were the cession of the Island of Hongkong to the British Crown, the payment of an indemnity of six million dollars for opium destroyed, and the opening of official intercourse between

English and Chinese officials on terms of international equality, as well as the resumption of British trade at Canton. But the Emperor showed no disposition to accept this decision, and issued numerous edicts offering rewards for Captain Elliott, Admiral Bremer, and other English leaders of the expedition. By May, 1851, 50,000 Chinese troops, unarmed, had gathered in the neighborhood of Canton, and after the British fleet off Canton had been attacked at night the war was formally resumed. Realizing that the only sure results could be obtained from the Emperor at Peking, the British fleet again sailed north, took Amoy, and after capturing Chenhai pushed on to Ningpo, Shanghai, and Chenkiang. In all of these engagements little resistance was encountered by the superiorly armed British. Peace was finally concluded in 1842 at Nanking on the terms demanded at Canton, with the additional demands of fifteen million dollars and the opening of the ports of Amoy, Foochow, Foo, Ningpo, and Shanghai to trade.

The Taiping Rebellion in China.—With the signing of the Nanking treaty in 1842, China showed no tendency to bow to the inevitable. Difficulties continued to be experienced at Canton which, because of its distance from the actual seat of the war, was not impressed by the results. Secret societies fanned the fire of rebellion, which the Emperor had sought to turn against the foreigner with such disaster. By 1853 organized raids on Manchu garrisons, resulting in the ruthless extermination of the whole force, were common occurrences along the Yangtze. The rebels, or Taipings, had now become firmly intrenched along the Yangtze and in March, 1853, under the leadership of Tienwang, began to march northward toward Peking. The reputation of these rebels for cruelty had become so terrible that their march was practically unimpeded by the flight of whole Manchu garrisons before them. In six months they had captured twenty-six cities and finally intrenched themselves near Tientsin, within a hundred miles of the capital. Being dependent upon plunder for their supplies, movement was essential to the life of the expedition, and when the fortification of Tientsin withstood their attack, the failure to reach Peking had to be realized. The way back to Nanking was now barred by Imperial troops, but the rebel chief managed to cut his way through. Li Hung-chang, who was destined to fill a large place in the later history of China, was one of those who headed independent bodies of loyal troops to harass the retreating rebels.

The rule which the Taipings now set up at Nanking was a veritable reign of terror, and this condition affected their field forces who gradually relinquished all of the cities they had held, except Nanking and Anking on the Yangtze, both of which were besieged.

In the meantime the British were demanding the right to trade at Canton, and the local Governor was obstinately refusing. In October, 1856, Admiral Seymour bombarded the city but only brought forth a proclamation calling on the people to exterminate the English. Unfortunately the British force was insufficient to occupy the city effectively and he withdrew and appealed to London for reinforcements. Lord Elgin was at once despatched with the necessary force, but was delayed in India by the mutiny. During the interval Admiral Seymour had attacked a number of Chinese junks, but his withdrawal only heartened the Chinese to renewed vigor. Finally on Christmas Day, 1857, Lord Elgin, who had finally arrived, despatched an ultimatum to the Governor and, after taking steps to warn the inhabitants, stormed and took Canton and captured the obstinate Governor Yeh.

Lord Elgin thereupon attempted to open peaceful negotiations with Peking but to no avail. An expedition against the Taku forts therefore was despatched, and, after the capture of these, Lord Elgin proceeded to Tientsin.

After much discussion a treaty was signed on June 26th, 1857, which provided for the appointment of a British Resident Minister at Peking, the opening of five additional ports to trade, and the legalizing of the opium traffic.

When in 1859 the British emissary entrusted with the exchange of ratification of this treaty attempted to reach Peking, his path was blocked and a British fleet sent against the Taku forts was severely defeated at Peiho. This called forth an ultimatum from the British emissary, Bruce, which was ignored and the next year an allied French and British force stormed and took the Taku forts. After the obstructions at the mouth of the Peiho River were cleared away, the party sailed up the river to Tientsin, where commissioners from the Emperor demanded the terms of peace. These were laid down by Lord Elgin as first, an apology for the attack at Peiho; second, ratification and execution of the treaty of Tientsin; and, third, the payment of an indemnity to cover the cost of the military preparations. After some delay and much negotiation, including a great deal of treachery and the actual capture of two British envoys, Parks and Loch, the treaty was signed with much ceremony on October 24, 1860. This treaty has guided China's relations with the West until the present time.

Meanwhile the diversion of Imperial troops to meet the threatened foreign invasion in the north had encouraged the Taipings to renewed activity under the "Faithful Prince." City after city was taken until the whole country on the north side the Yangtze opposite Nanking passed into their hands. Hangchow was soon captured and Soochow threatened, when an Imperial attack on Nanking saved that city. At Li Hung-chang's request, an American named Ward assembled an army formed of Europeans, Filipinos, and Chinese and opposed the Taipings at Tsingpu, but was unsuccessful. By an agreement with Admiral Hope of the British Navy, the Taipings had agreed not to attack Shanghai for a year, but on the expiration of that time besieged Shanghai. The allied forces which had lately opposed the Imperial forces near Peking now attacked their foes and drove them from the neighborhood of Shanghai. Ward's forces, now known as the "Ever Victorious Army," had grown to number 5,000, but in an attack on Tsuki, Ward was fatally wounded. After several failures, a successor was chosen in Major Gordon. Fushan and Changshu fell easily before him. After many vicissitudes, during which Gordon nearly resigned his command due to the parsimony of Li Hung-chang, Soochow was captured and a crushing blow dealt the Taiping cause. Hangchow was captured and finally Nanking, the last stronghold of the rebels, was taken together with the Faithful Prince, who, with the heir of the already self-poisoned "Heavenly King" (the high sounding title of the Taiping leader), was beheaded.

Turmoil at the End of the 19th Century in China.— The period between 1860 and 1894 was marked by a series of rebellions, massacres, and local disorders, with which the unorganized administration of the Manchus was only partially able to cope. It was during this period that the French, in 1884, after a military campaign in Cochin-China, established a protectorate over the country south of Tongking. In their relations with the foreigners, the Chinese continued to assume the same supercilious hauteur and practice the same deception and deceit which experience should have taught them was in the long run of little avail. This attitude was assumed by the Manchus largely as a matter of self-preservation, for by fostering the myth that the foreign ambassadors were tribute bearers, their hold upon the Chinese was strengthened. It was during the later years of the Taiping rebellion that the collection of the Shanghai customs was placed under the control of three foreign officials, and a few years later the entire custom administration was by treaty placed under a British Directorate on the basis of Great Britain's predominant trade interests. American trade had developed until by 1860 fifty per cent of the foreign shipping of Shanghai was under the American flag. During this period the first railroad in China was constructed by foreign merchants for a distance of twelve miles between Shanghai and Wusung, while by 1887 extensive telegraph lines had been established throughout the Empire.

In 1894 the King of Korea appealed to Peking for help in putting down a rebellion in his domains. Without consulting Japan, whose relations with Korea were equally intimate, China landed troops on Korean soil. The Japanese likewise despatched troops and, although hostilities did not immediately break out, the Chinese insisted upon Japan's entire withdrawal, which was agreed to by the Japanese on condition that no further Chinese troops be sent. China failed to live up to this agreement and war was declared by both sides. The first battle of Asan in southwest Korea resulted in the rout of the Chinese. At Pingyang on the Yalu the Chinese were reinforced by Manchurian troops, but the city was taken by the Japanese, and in a subsequent naval battle on the Yalu River the Chinese were defeated. The Chinese were pursued across Manchuria, defeated at Hushan, and concentrated upon the defense of Port Arthur. This was captured by the Japanese who continued their victorious march across Manchuria. Peking now sued for peace and by the terms of the treaty of 1895 Japan exacted recognition of her equality with Western nations in China and the independence of Korea. As indemnity, the Island of Formosa, the Liaotung Peninsula surrounding Port Arthur, and two hundred million taels were exacted. Upon joint representation of Germany, France, and Russia, however, Japan waived her claims to Liaotung upon payment of an additional thirty million taels.

After the China-Japanese war the break-up of China was

generally expected by European powers. Each, therefore, determined to seize the most advantageous ports possible for trading purpose and in 1897 Germany, as compensation for the murder of two missionaries, secured a lease to the harbor and port of Kiaochow and certain economic privileges including the building of a railroad and the working of certain mines in Shantung Province. Russia exacted a similar lease of Port Arthur, which had so lately been withheld from Japan, while Great Britain leased Weiheiwai on the opposite side of Shantung from Kiaochow and France secured Kwangchow in the extreme south. Aroused by these encroachments and determined to remove the cause which was ostensibly the inability of China to rule her own domains, the Emperor Kwang-su published in 1898 his famous reform edicts, providing for modern education, the building of railways, and a general program of Western development. The reactionaries opposed this plan, however, and the Emperor lost his power and his plans were nullified.

The reactionary program now rapidly developed and took definite form in the Boxer uprising, which, though really aimed at the Manchus, was skillfully diverted by them to the "foreign devils." Peking was besieged, the German minister Von Kettler and several other foreigners were murdered, and upon relief of the foreign legations by an allied force in the summer of 1900 an indemnity of 333 million dollars was exacted by the foreign powers. It was due to the efforts of the American Secretary of State, John Hay, that the inability of China to pay this huge sum did not result in the partition of China at this time. By a circular note to the powers he elicited their support to an "open door" policy of equal opportunity and this policy, with some variations, holds China intact to-day.

The Russo-Japanese War.—In the meantime Russian aggression on South Manchuria had precipitated the Russo-

Japanese war in 1904–5, Japan not being willing to permit Russian influence to encroach upon Korea. By the terms of the treaty of Portsmouth, New Hampshire, Japan succeeded to Russia's lease on Port Arthur and the Liaotung Peninsula and this was further strengthened by the famous "twenty-one demands" of 1915 whereby China agreed to an extension of this lease from 1923 for a period of ninety years, including the leases of the South Manchurian and Antung Mukden Railways, as well as important concessions to Japanese subjects in Manchuria and eastern inner Mongolia.

The Fall of the Manchus.—On October 10, 1911, the Manchu régime, its usefulness long outlived, was overthrown and a republic established. Thus ended the rule of the dynasty which had so blindly sought, by all the Oriental diplomacy at its command, to stay the hand of progress. Unwilling to learn by experience, and maintaining an impossible attitude toward the West until the very end, this régime, itself foreign to the Chinese people, imposed useless and unnecessary suffering upon the Chinese, deprived them of a Western enlightenment which would have placed them abreast of Japan as an enlightened state and in the last analysis contributed nothing to the sum total of human usefulness and knowledge. Had China, or the Manchus, in 1842, or in 1860, read the handwriting on the wall, and entered upon the course adopted by Japan, the effects upon the civilization of the Far East and of the world would have been far reaching and potent.

Early Intercourse of Japan with the West.—Little need be said of the first unsuccessful effort at foreign intercourse with Japan, extending from 1542 to 1640, except that it ended in the general persecution of 300,000 native Christians and the confining of foreign trade, which the Dutch had inaugurated in 1600, to the single port of Nagasaki.

The large monopolistic profit realized from this trade by the Shogun was largely influential in obtaining greater tolerance for the missionaries after 1603, but a Japanese emissary sent to Europe brought back such reports of religious strife in Europe at this period that the Shogun Iyeyasu published in 1614 an edict banishing all missionaries. After long persecutions, which were not tamely submitted to by the Christians, a Christian revolt in 1637 resulted in a general massacre and the final expulsion by 1640 of all foreigners except the Chinese and Dutch, both of whom were willing to confine their activities to trade. Thus Japan remained with but one small window looking out upon the world at Nagasaki, a hermit nation until 1854.

The Opening of Japan.—The history of Japan since 1854 has been one of continuous growth. The reopening of the country by the peaceful mission of Perry, led to the restoration of the Emperor to the power which had been exercised in his name for centuries by his chief military representative, or Shogun. The treaty signed by the Shogun and the American Consul-General, Townsend Harris, in 1858 provided for diplomatic intercourse, residence of consuls at open ports, the right of Americans to be tried by their own laws for offenses committed in Japanese territory, the right of Americans to reside in Tokyo and the open ports, freedom of commerce, except for a low *ad valorem* duty, the prohibition of the opium trade, and the guarantee of the same treatment in other respects as may be accorded any other nation in the future. This last was the "most favored nation" clause. The seventy-one Japanese emissaries, sent to Washington in 1860 for the ratification of the Harris treaty, were the vanguard of a host of students and others whom Japan sent to Europe and America during the next half century in an effort to absorb quickly the science of the West. The unwillingness on the part of the Satsuma and Choshu clans to recognize the treaty led to the bombardment of Shimonoseki by American and European vessels and the collection of three million dollars indemnity, the American share of which was returned twenty years later. The reaction on these clans was complete and they soon became the leaders in the race for Western culture.

In 1868 the Shogun practically voluntarily turned over the temporal power to the Emperor Mutsuhito, who had succeeded his father on the throne the year before. This was not finally accomplished, however, without a struggle between the followers of the Shogun and a few clans who were not satisfied with a restoration which they considered only nominal. The defeat of the Shogun placed the Emperor in full control.

The introduction of the telegraph and railroad soon followed and the first newspaper appeared in 1871. Education along Western lines was next inaugurated and in a famous rescript the Emperor exhorted his subjects to study the Western civilization.

The Development of Japan in the 19th Century.— Japan's insistence on the revision of the Harris treaty was acceded to by the United States in 1878, but it was not until the promulgation of the Constitution and the election of the first Diet that the other powers agreed to treaty revision in 1894. By 1897 all the powers had revised their treaties whereby they surrendered extra-territorial jurisdiction or the right to try their own nationals, and relinquished control over the tariff, subject to an agreement that certain rates should remain fixed for twelve years. In return Japan opened the whole country to foreign residence. Thus in the remarkably short period of forty years Japan had emerged from absolute seclusion to the full rank of a world power. Since 1880 the merchant marine has grown under government subsidy until in 1914 Japan stood sixth in merchant tonnage with a total of 1,700,000 tons. A thoroughly established educational system requires the elementary education of every boy and girl for six years, with high schools and universities for those who wish to pursue their studies.

The banking system has been completely transformed and the gold standard adopted, while the currency system has proved to be sound. State revenues had increased sixteen fold within the twenty years preceding the war, but due to the Russo-Japanese war and subsequent heavy armaments, the expenditures have grown to an even greater degree, with an increasing burden of taxation. From every standpoint Japan has demonstrated a remarkable ability to attain her desired goal and the goal itself has seemed worthy of attainment.

Questions

1. Contrast the manner in which China and Japan accepted foreign intercourse.
2. Why were the first efforts to open Japan unsuccessful?
3. What methods were followed by early missionaries in China to spread the Gospel?
4. Describe the opening of diplomatic intercourse by Lord McCartney. What were the results?
5. What were the causes of the First Opium War? Outline the terms of peace and the date.
6. How was Japan finally opened to foreign intercourse? Outline the terms of the Harris treaty and date.
7. Describe the progress of Japan since 1868.
8. What were the principal events in the Taiping Rebellion?
9. What was the cause of the China-Japanese war in 1894? What were the terms of peace?
10. Enumerate the concessions granted European powers in 1897 and 1898. Describe the causes and result of the Boxer Rebellion. What was the result of the Russo-Japanese war?

CHAPTER III

THE CONSTITUTIONS AND POLITICAL PARTIES OF CHINA AND JAPAN

CHINA

The End of the Chinese Empire.—The tortuous history of Chinese Imperial duplicity and diplomacy ended with the Manchus in 1911. Sudden changes in dynasty had been the rule in China, where twenty-six changes in the ruling family had occurred in 4,000 years. Contrasted to this was the Japanese dynasty which it is claimed has continually reigned for 2,500 years. Chinese philosophy had contributed to the firmly held belief that a ruler should hold the throne only so long as he governs well, with the result that revolution had come in China at irregular intervals of about 200 years. The prestige of the Manchus had never quite recovered from the Taiping Rebellion, when, but for foreign aid, the rebels would have defeated the Imperialists. Moreover, the steady aggression of the West could not be effectively checked by the Manchus, who were unable to adapt themselves to the new conditions and so only emphasized the weakness of the country. The failure of the Boxer Rebellion and the fixing of the huge indemnity of $333,000,000 strengthened the forces conspiring against the Manchus, especially in the provinces south of the Yangtze. The belated reforms of the Empress Dowager led to the meeting of the first National Assembly in 1910, two years after her death, and although designed to be merely a deliberative body, it assumed further authority, formulated a budget, and demanded the establishment of a cabinet.

After the Assembly had adjourned, the Imperial Government established a cabinet, nine of whose thirteen members were Manchus under the leadership of Prince Ching, a conservative and corrupt Manchu of the royal family who was responsible to the throne alone. This body embarked upon a policy of further centralizing the governmental power and was opposed by a newer and more progressive element which demanded provincial autonomy, especially in matters of railroad construction and loans. Concessions for the construction of railroads in the Empire had, after 1898, been granted England, France, Germany and Belgium and these concessions were only granted in return for funds furnished the Peking Government. One American loan for the construction of a railroad between Canton and Hankow had fared rather badly, the stock in the corporation formed to construct it being bought up by Belgian interests in spite of the terms of the loan agreement which stipulated that it should not leave American control. After steps had been taken to regain American control the concession was sold back to the Chinese Government and the railroad remains unconstructed. Meanwhile, the German and English banking institutions in China in 1895 had an agreement to share equally all business which either might obtain. In 1905 France entered into this financial alliance and when three years later China desired a loan to build a railroad from Hankow to Chengtu, the United States was admitted into the alliance after personal intervention by President Taft and the Four Powers. Loans thus negotiated in the spring of 1911 were for the purpose of building the Hukuang railways up the Yangtze and for currency reform. The provinces through which the Hukuang railways were to pass, however, objected strenuously to the Imperial scheme and announced that they would build the railroads within their borders for and by themselves.

The first warning of the Revolution came in the revolt of

the province of Szechuen and while first Manchu and later Chinese officials were being hurried thither to pacify the people a bomb exploded by accident in the Russian concession at Hankow disclosing a widespread revolutionary plot. This had been timed for the next year but the accidental discovery caused the Revolution to take place six months ahead of time. Local forces seized Hankow and Wuchang and the Viceroy became a fugitive. The leaders in the revolt were Sun Yat-sen and Huang Hsing, both of whom had been exiles and had formed societies and collected funds from Chinese abroad for years. The Manchus now reinstated one of their ablest Chinese officials, Yuan Shi-kai, whom they had dismissed in 1909 and gave him complete authority to put down the rebellion. Within two months the rebels had taken the strategic city of Nanking and Yuan Shi-kai, foreseeing a long and expensive civil war, responded to the invitation of Dr. Wu Ting-fang, twice Minister to the United States and now rebel leader, for an armistice and a discussion of peace terms. Meanwhile, Dr. Sun Yat-sen had arrived in China and had been made President of the Southern Confederacy and the arrangement now agreed upon was that the Manchus should abdicate in favor of Yuan Shi-kai and Sun Yat-sen should turn over his power to the latter, who was to act as Provisional President until a regular government was established. The revolution was primarily negative and aimed against the Manchus and only succeeded in making China a republic because of the deep hostility toward the monarchy and a desire to establish an entirely different form of government.

The Structure of the Chinese Imperial Government.—The Imperial Government which was thus overthrown was one of the most ancient known to recorded history. The Duke of Chou, on founding the Chou Dynasty 3,000 years before, had revised and codified the laws which formed the basis of the system of government down to the Revolution.

Thirteen hundred years later feudalism had been abolished and the government greatly centralized, but until the period of foreign intercourse there were few if any changes in the form of government. During the fifty years between 1861 and 1911 most of these changes took place and the government which was overthrown in 1911 was largely the result of an unsuccessful attempt on the part of the Manchus to meet foreign conditions. In 1860 the Emperor stood at the head as an absolute monarch, surrounded by an imperial clan. The Grand Secretariat and the Grand Council were directly responsible to the Emperor for administration and these functioned through six boards or departments, which corresponded somewhat with modern ministries abroad in their range and scope of administrative duties. Under these departments were bureaus and this constituted the central or Peking Government. Each of the eighteen provinces of what was known as the Middle Kingdom was ruled by a Viceroy, or Governor, appointed by the Emperor, under whom were provincial treasurers and provincial judges as well as numerous salt controllers and grain intendants in certain areas. After the Manchu conquest, they established garrisons in twelve provinces over which they placed Tartar-generals, or generalissimos. These military officials were always Manchus, ranking the civil Viceroy, and they constituted a very effective check upon his authority. The provinces were divided into *taos,* or circuits, over each of which was a *taotai,* or intendant. These *taos* were in turn divided into *fus,* or prefectures, over each of which was a prefect. There were also in this grade independent *chows* and *tings* who reported directly to the provincial authorities. The lowest administrative areas were *hsiens,* corresponding to American counties, over which magistrates presided and reported to intermediate officials. There were also dependent *chows* and *tings* who reported to intermediate officials instead of directly to the provincial authorities. All of these officials were appointed theoretically by the Emperor, but in practice the recommendations of the superior provincial officials were nearly always accepted.

This organization extended only to the eighteen Provinces. Manchuria was organized somewhat like China proper while Mongolia had a separate and independent organization subject to a Mongolian Superintendent with headquarters at Peking. Eastern Turkestan was a dependency of the Viceroy of Kansu and Shensi Provinces. Tibet was divided into two parts, one ruled by the Viceroy of Szechuan Province, and the other under a special district Governor who resided at Siningfu in Kansu Province.

In 1861 a foreign office, or Tsung-li Yamen, was added to the original six boards of Civil Appointment, Revenue, Ceremonies, War, Justice, and Works. This department was abolished in 1901 when the Wai-wupu, or Board of Foreign Affairs, was established. In 1903 a Board of Commerce and a Board of Education were added. In 1906, after the return of the Imperial Commission sent abroad to study foreign governments, a Board of Posts and Communications was added and the Board of War reorganized as a Board of Military Affairs. A Board of Dependencies and a Board of Navy were next added, making twelve Ministries in all in existence in 1911. Meanwhile the Grand Council had superseded gradually the Grand Secretariat and the latter had assumed a more formal and honorific importance. The Grand Council, on the other hand, assumed the function of Privy Council, Imperial Chancery, and Court of Appeals. It was composed usually of six heads of Boards and a number of Secretaries. In 1906 it was designated Privy Council. In 1907 an Advisory Council, including all members of the Grand Secretariat, the Grand Council, and the heads of all Boards, was created, but in 1911 these three councils were abolished and a new Privy Council was formed. The Boards became Ministries and their heads the Cabinet.

The National Assembly of 1910.—The National Assembly which the edict of August 27, 1908, promised to convene in the ninth year from that date, was hurried in its organization by the death of the Empress Dowager, who was the leader of the reactionaries and it actually convened October 3, 1910, at Peking. It consisted of 200 members divided into eight classes, one hundred being appointed from the newly created provincial assemblies.

The Emperor, although absolute and ruling by divine right, was under obligations imposed by Confucian and Mencian philosophy to govern justly before the people who were obliged to reciprocate by obeying loyally. The peculiar Chinese institution of the Censorate helped to accentuate this relation. This body, consisting of two presidents, twenty-four supervisors, and fifty-six censors, was supposed to be the eyes and ears of the Emperor and reflected public opinion for the benefit of the Court. The officers composing this body were also privileged to watch and criticize officials and even the Emperor himself. They naturally held an important place in the scheme of government. In actual practice the Emperor, being by custom closely confined to the precincts of the palace, was largely influenced by his immediate personal following. His every word and act was recorded and this served as a check against ill advised use of power. Although all appointments were made by the Emperor, most of the officials under the old régime were holders of degrees obtained purely for excellence in literary composition. Official positions were also frequently purchased. This purely literary examination was abolished in 1905 and an examination of officials in modern and practical subjects replaced it.

The Provinces and Duties of the Officials.—The authority of the fourteen governors and eight viceroys—distinguished from the governors in that they ruled over two provinces—was very broad. As long as they paid a certain specified sum as tribute, which they in turn collected from the people as taxes, and followed the general policy of the administration, they were left free to administer their own affairs in detail. Thus the character of the individual and the distance of his province from Peking were often determining factors in the amount of independent authority he wielded. Some of these rulers organized their own armies and conducted negotiations with foreigners. With all of the authority given them, there was nothing to compel them to coöperate with Peking for the common weal. This, more than any other factor, has accounted for the lack of such practical, coöperative work as river conservancy, the lack of which alone has caused the flooding and destruction by erosion of vast areas of rich agricutural land. Compared with American institutions, the province was a more independent and more widely separated administrative area than one of our states; it more closely resembled a territory.

The duties of the *Hsien,* or prefectural magistrate, were manifold and exacting. Though assisted by many secretaries, collectors, clerks, sheriffs, etc., the district magistrate was personally responsible for every governmental function. He was the court in civil cases and in some criminal cases; he was tax collector; registrar of land; famine commissioner; custodian of official buildings, temples, walls, prisons, bridges, roads, and schools; he was postmaster, in that he maintained the courier service; and in short he was the connecting link between the prince and the peasant. The town and village organizations under him were nothing more than enlarged family groups which were practically self-governing, and in these institutions the essential democracy of the people was retained through centuries of autocratic rule. This loosely knit governmental organization sufficed as long as China was isolated, but contact with the foreigner brought the necessity of a central government, controlling the provinces and their people and uniting them for common defense against Western aggression. Then the inherent weakness of the situation became apparent and a belated attempt to centralize authority only precipitated revolution.

The Provisional Government of 1912.—When in February, 1912, Yuan Shi-kai was unanimously elected Provisional President by the National Assembly at Nanking, a Provisional Constitution was also adopted. This instrument placed many restrictions upon the President against his wishes and resulted in a conflict between the executive and the legislature, which lasted for two years and resulted in the dissolution of the opposing Assembly, in which southern sympathizers were predominant. Before this occurred, however, Yuan had been immeasurably strengthened by the $25,000,000 reorganization loan which was concluded with the bankers of England, Germany, France, Russia, and Japan, the United States group, upon the pronouncement of President Wilson, having withdrawn. Strengthened by this outside aid in his fight against the southern leaders, who were now conspiring to rebel, Yuan ordered the military governor of Kiangsi Province to give up his office and sent troops into that Province who met armed opposition. Huang Hsing and Sun Yat-sen denounced Yuan as a traitor to the republican cause and organized a force with which to punish the Provisional President. But the rebellion was premature and badly staged and when Yuan's general took Nanking the rebellion collapsed. The leader took refuge in Japan and began to plan a third rebellion. The question of whether a permanent President should be chosen before the adoption of a constitution had already become an issue, the northerners contending that the first thing to do was to choose a President and the southerners maintaining that the President's office must be created by and his duties defined in the constitution. In October, 1913, the President's supporters, by a coalition with one of the minor parties in the Assembly, succeeded in passing the Election law, which provided that the President should be elected by the National Assembly by a two-thirds majority of a three-fourths quorum for a period of five years and should be ineligible for two successive terms. This law was to remain in force until the adoption of a constitution. On October 6, Yuan Shi-kai was elected President and the next day Li Yuan-hung, Vice-President, and the Chinese Republic, which had already been recognized by the United States, was promptly recognized by Japan and the European powers. The Kwo Ming party, which had consistently sought to tie the hands of the Executive, now submitted a draft of a constitution which was extremely obnoxious to Yuan. The theory of the drafted constitution was that of a cabinet government, modeled on the French Government, but avoiding the French centralization. Yuan appealed to the country for a decision and in return received a flood of telegrams denouncing the drafted constitution. Assured of the strength of his position, Yuan on November 4th declared the Kwo Ming party members expelled from the Assembly, which, thus lacking a quorum, became incapable of action, and Yuan became the Government to all intents and purposes. The dissolution of the National Assembly as well as that of the provincial assemblies now followed and the President, advised only by an administrative conference which he had called together, ruled alone.

The Administrative Conference of 1913–14.—With the Assembly disposed of, Yuan proceeded to put into effect his own ideas of a constitution, and a draft prepared by Professor Goodnow of Johns Hopkins University, who had become constitutional adviser, was circulated throughout the country. This provided for a gradual evolution into a parliamentary system. The Administrative Conference called together at the end of 1913 had been requested to render advice on the matter of formally dissolving the Assembly and the creation of a special conference to amend the provisional constitution. This conference continued to function until June, 1914, when a Council of State was created to supersede it. The conference upheld the dissolution of the Assembly as the only way to end an "incompetent and obstructionistic" legislature which had squandered millions of dollars. The Conference also advised Yuan to take steps to revise the provisional constitution, rather than draft a new one. A constitutional compact conference was elected, therefore, by a qualified suffrage and proceeded in March, 1914, to make such changes in the Provisional Constitution as the President considered necessary to relieve his embarrassment. These changes released the President from subjection to the Assembly; made Cabinet members dependent on the President; and gave him power to issue urgent orders to deal efficiently with financial questions. The problem of ultimately drafting a constitution was also to be kept in mind. A revised provisional constitution along these lines was submitted and promulgated on May 1, 1914. In addition to the changes outlined, it provided for a single House in the Assembly, and gave the President the right, with the consent of the Council of State when the Assembly was not in session, to make treaties, to make war and peace, to confer titles of nobility, to grant amnesties and pardons, and to refuse to promulgate an act of the Assembly even though twice passed. The Council of State was to consist of 70 members appointed by the President, with the Vice-President as speaker. It was to rule on doubtful points in the provisional constitution, and to act as a special reference body for the President. In many respects it resembled the early United States Senate.

The first act of the Council of State, when it assembled in June, 1914, was to pass on a new presidential election law presented by the President and made necessary by the changes in the Constitution which had combined both houses of Parliament into one, and eliminated the Premier as a successor to the President in event of his and the Vice-President's incapacity. The new law, promulgated December 26, 1914, provided that male citizens 40 years of age and of 20 years' residence should be eligible for the Presidency for a term of ten years, subject to extension at the discretion of the Council of State, and should be elected from three candidates nominated by the former President by an electoral college of 100 members, half from the Council of State, and half from the Legislative. This law was defended on the plea of the necessity, in the early stages of development, for a continuity of policy which could only be had by the President nominating his successor. The organization of the new legislature was next considered by the conference, and these regulations, issued in March, 1915, provided for a House of 275 members, with a term of four years, forty to be elected from the central electoral college, 202 from the provincial electoral colleges, apportioned according to population, nine from special administrative districts, sixteen from Mongolia, six from Tibet, and two from Shanghai. One session each year shall extend from September 1 to December 31, with extension by the President for not more than two months. Ministers of State have a right to attend the sessions and speak. The qualification for a voter is that he own $10,000 worth of property in Peking or $5,000 worth in the provinces, or that he has rendered meritorious service, or is a high official, or recognized scholar, or graduate of a college, or teacher in a college. The qualifications for candidates were the same except the $30,000 and $10,000 qualification in Peking and the provinces, respectively. These qualifications are peculiar to China and are designed to suit the stage of political development which China had attained, rather than to follow blindly the standards set up by Western nations more advanced in the art of self-government. After providing for the organization of a

National Constitutional Convention to meet the next year to draft a permanent constitution, the Constitutional Compact Conference was adjourned.

The Growth of Chinese Political Parties.—Until 1912 there had been no organization in China calling itself a political party. A number of political associations had existed since 1898, some planning reform and others revolution, and before that there had been many secret societies. One of these, the Tung-meng Hui (Alliance Society), had been organized as openly in favor of revolution. It had headquarters in Japan, and Dr. Sun Yat-sen was its leader. After the compromise which led to Sun Yat-sen's resignation, this society became a political party in 1912, almost entirely southern in its composition and character. Five of its members were appointed to Yuan's first cabinet, including the premier. Yuan's determination to overshadow the Cabinet led to their resignation in June, 1912, and from that time the rupture between this party and Yuan and his successors has been complete. The formation of several conservative parties followed in quick succession, including one less radical formed by the military Governor of Yunnan named Tsai Ao, and three others formed by influential citizens in Wuchang and Peking. These last three parties attracted many scholars and officials and soon became amalgamated into the Kung-ho Tang (Republican Party) and became the supporters of the President. The strength of this new conservative party just about balanced that of the southern party, or Tung-meng Hui, and the Tsai Ao party, therefore held the balance of power in the Assembly for some months until its members split and joined the two major parties. Another party, the Tung-yi Tang (Coalition Party) was formed in March, 1912, as an offspring of the Tung-meng Hui, while at the same time the Ming-chu Tang (Democratic Party) sprang up as the advocate of a strong centralized government. In August, 1912, the amalgamation of several smaller radical parties with the Tung-meng Hui brought about the formation of a new Nationalist Party, the Kwo-ming Tang, which was thoroughly organized with a declared policy to maintain the union of north and south, to develop local government, and to encourage the adoption of socialistic principles. This strengthening of its chief opponent led the Kung-ho Tang, or Republican Party, to organize more formally and it became the backbone of opposition to the Kwo-ming Tang by amalgamation with the Tung-yi and Ming Chu under the name of the Chin-pu Tang, or Progressive Party, continuing to support the President. China, however, is not ready for party government, nor is any party qualified to assume such responsibility.

The Movement to Restore the Monarchy.—In May, 1915, the famous twenty-one demands were made by Japan and these will be discussed in detail later. Suffice to say they left the one-man government of Yuan Shi-kai deplorably weak and steps were immediately taken to call the Constitutional Convention and elect a new National Assembly. At this juncture the movement to restore the monarchy under Yuan as Emperor began. The authorship of the movement is variously attributed to Yuan himself and to those conservatives who were fearful that unless a strong government were quickly set up disintegration would result. To whatever source the movement may be traced it soon took definite form in the organization of a "Peace Planning Society," conspicuous among whose charter members were close friends and supporters of Yuan Shi-kai. This society made adroit use of Dr. Goodnow's utterances on the strong points of a monarchical government, and used Mexico as an example of a weak government under a republic. Soon after this Dr. Goodnow made a statement denying the words attributed to him, but setting forth that a restoration to monarchy would only be justified if accepted by the thinking people of China and the powers, if the succession to the throne were made indisputable, and the monarchy were limited by a constitution, with provision for the development of a more popular government. These opinions were also embodied by Dr. Goodnow in a long memorandum to President Yuan. Among the most violent attacks on the proposed change was one by Liang Chi-chao, the one-time leader of the Chin-pu Tang, who proclaimed that the wish to reform the conduct of government by a change in its form was nonsense. In October, 1916, the Council of State decided upon the election of citizens to a convention to decide upon the form of government. Meanwhile the militants urged Yuan to proclaim a monarchy, but he steadfastly refused until he had heard the "voice of the people." Just at this time the Japanese Charge d'Affaires at Peking, backed by the Russian and British Minister and supported by the French, made representations to the President that in view of the unsettled conditions in the south consideration of this question should perhaps be postponed. The United States Government was now appealed to but refused to express an opinion. The Chinese Government thanked the foreign governments for their interest, but stated that it was an internal question and was already before the people and could not be withdrawn. They likewise guaranteed to maintain order. In the meantime the vote was being taken on the basis of the electoral census and resulted in all but 50 of the 2,043 electors declaring for a constitutional monarchy, and many of them specifying Yuan Shi-kai. Yuan, therefore, announced on December 11, 1916, that "in deference to the will of the people" he would become Emperor, the formal coronation to be held the following year after the Constitutional Convention had framed a permanent constitution. On the following day Yunnan Province in the south had revolted and formed what was to be the nucleus of the Southern Confederacy.

The "Twenty-one Demands" by Japan.—In the meanwhile, on August 15, 1914, Japan had demanded the withdrawal of Germany from Kiachow, and meeting with their refusal proceeded to expel Germany by force. This brought the Great War to China's door in a forceful manner, but as Japan's ultimatum to Germany had called specifically for the delivery of the leased territory, "with a view to the eventual restoration of the same to China," China had no official cause to complain. Considerable uneasiness was felt throughout the Orient, however, at this time as to Japan's ultimate intentions. To allay these suspicions Count Okuma declared to the American public "Japan has no territorial ambitions and hopes to stand as the protector of the peace of the Orient. I state to the people of America that Japan has no ulterior motive, no desire to secure more territory, no thought of depriving China or other peoples of anything which they now possess." By the end of 1914 the immediate end of the war was not in sight and unequalled opportunity presented itself, in the preoccupation of the powers in Europe, for Japan to satisfy various territorial and economic ambitions in China. These ambitions came under five general heads, first, to succeed Germany in Shantung; second, to consolidate the Manchurian territory obtained as a result of the Russo-Japanese war and add parts of inner Mongolia; third, to control the iron output of China; fourth, to render a military menace to Japan from the coasts of China impossible by preventing the lease of any of China's ports and coastal islands; and fifth, to obtain, if possible, such economic, military, and political domination over China as to make it practically a tributary to Japan. These five aims were contained in the famous Twenty-one Demands served on China on January 18, 1915. Absolute secrecy was imposed upon President Yuan, but despite every precaution, including official denials from Japan, the text of the demands became known and after much maneuvering Japan presented an ultimatum on May 7, demanding immediate acceptance of the first four groups of a new set of twenty-four demands, similar to the old, and threatening force if a favorable answer were not received. Groups one to four of the new demands were consequently acceded to in 14 specific notes covering briefly the first four points mentioned above.[1] The fifth group of seven articles calculated to encroach very seriously upon China's sovereignty and internal administrative control was "reserved for future consideration."

Death of Yuan Shi-kai and War with Germany.—This action on the part of Japan was the real impetus toward the movement to restore the monarchy under Yuan which has already been outlined. The excuse for this movement was that China was slowly disintegrating because of a lack of strong, unified control. Despite the uprising in Yunnan, the promoters of the monarchist movement, encouraged by the unanimous votes of the provincial electors in favor of the monarchy, decided to continue on their course. The revolt of Kweichow Province adjoining Yunnan in the south now took place, followed in March, 1917, by Kuangsi, and within a month by Chekiang and Kwantung Provinces. Yuan tried in vain to conciliate the southern leader, Wu Ting-fang, but the southern position was consistent in demanding that he resign from the position he had taken. In May, Szechuan Province revolted and two days later Yuan publicly announced his intention to retire, but before he could carry out his purpose he died on June 6, 1917. Vice-President Li Yuan-hung, immediately entered upon the duties of President and the new government sought

1 This action was never ratified by any Chinese Assembly as required by the Constitution.

to establish a Parliament according to the Provisional Constitution adopted at Nanking in 1912. The Constitutional Compact was discarded; Parliament reconvened on August 1, a Cabinet headed by Tuan Chi-jui as Premier was formed, and Feng Kwo-chang was elected Vice-President. The Republic of China thus had been preserved. On September 15, Parliament began drafting the permanent constitution, and for eight months China progressed satisfactorily as a Republic. The action of the United States in severing relations with Germany, and calling upon all neutrals to do likewise, had a far reaching effect upon China, which had also made the subject of the sinking of 500 Chinese laborers on a French transport, and the indiscriminate sinking of shipping in general, the basis for a note of protest to the German Government. On March 14, 1917, diplomatic relations with Germany were broken, and on August 14, 1917, China declared war against her. This decision was not reached, however, without a struggle which shook the new Republic to its foundations, and made indirectly possible the restoration of the Manchus for a brief period. This move was abortive, however, and as it implicated President Li, he having been captured by the Manchu leader and held prisoner for a short time, he resigned on July 17th in favor of Vice-President Feng, who had early repudiated the Manchu movement and had become Acting President at Nanking. The new President came into office at Peking on August 1, 1917, and ten days later war was declared.

The Lansing-Ishii Agreement.—On November 2, 1917, the Lansing-Ishii Agreement between America and Japan was signed at Washington. This contained two important clauses, namely, that the United States recognized Japan's "special interests" in China, and that both countries repledged themselves to observe the principle of the "open door" and territorial integrity of China. The reasons for this agreement were three in number. First, the apprehension in America and the world regarding Japan's intentions in China; second, Japan's apprehensions regarding America's intentions in China; and third, the need of the allies for a definite understanding with Japan in view of the loss of Russia from their ranks.

The Military Agreement of 1918.—With the abdication of the Czar of Russia in March, 1917, German penetration into China along the many thousands of miles of border was feared by China and the Allies, but Japan could take no steps along this line without an agreement with China. The military agreement signed on May 16, 1918, therefore, was designed to remedy this situation and an exchange of notes between Chang and Viscount Motono on March 25, 1918, gave no definite details regarding the arrangement. These were said to be contained in twelve articles undertaking, in brief, to form a military alliance between China and Japan for mutual defense against Russia.[2]

Effects of China's Entrance into the World War.—An immediate effect of China's entrance into the World War was the temporary suspension of payment of the Boxer indemnity, and an increase in tariff rates to an effective 5 per cent, but the Chinese still feel that their full recognition as a sovereign power is the goal to be striven for.

The Election of President Hsu.—In 1918 the country was divided into a progressive south, with headquarters at Canton; a conservative north, with Peking as capital, and a neutral zone along the Yangtze River, of which Nanking is the chief center, but over which there was no definite government. Until September, 1918, this territory was in control of the north and the neutrals, with Tuan Chi-jui as Premier leading the first group, and President Feng, the second. On September 4th, 1918, Hsu Shih-chang, the present President, was elected to succeed President Feng, by

[2] The agreement was cancelled by mutual consent January 28, 1921.

a Parliament convened at Peking on August 14, against which the south protested. This Parliament had been selected after the national council, succeeding the Parliament dissolved on June 12, 1917, had passed new laws providing for its organization and election. Elections under these laws were held in the spring and summer, and a reduced membership of 573 was elected as the five revolting provinces abstained from any participation. At first hope was held out that the new President would command the support of the south, but the several negotiations toward internal peace have been unsuccessful.

JAPAN

The Constitution and Political Parties of Japan.—As early as 1881 the first step towards a constitution had been taken in Japan, when an Imperial Edict was issued promising a constitution providing for a national assembly, which was to be called ten years later. While this act had long been advocated by many constitutional societies, it was not exactly an involuntary act on the part of the Emperor. The Restoration Government organized in 1868 had provided for the creation of a deliberative assembly, the Gisei, with Lower House members chosen by the Emperor, one from each Diamiate, who were empowered to discuss certain matters under an Upper House of Nobles. In 1871 this was replaced by the Sain or Left College, also composed entirely of Imperial nominees, but with wider deliberative powers. At the same time a commission sent to Europe and America reported in favor of a constitutional form of government so adapted as to provide for a gradual increase in popular government as the capacity of the people increased. In 1875, after the establishment of a deliberative assembly of local authorities, the Sain was abolished and its legislative authority delegated to the Genro or Elder Statesmen, who have ever since determined the personnel and policies of the various governments and, as a privy council and Imperial mouthpiece, are really the Government of Japan. A constitutional Investigation Bureau was established in 1884 with (later Prince) Ito at its head and in the same year the European system of nobility was adopted, followed the next year by the establishment of the cabinet system, and in 1888 by the Privy Council. On February 11, 1889, the constitution was promulgated. This instrument which was the crowning work of Ito's career, was a step toward self-government, and did not destroy the Imperial control over the Government, but furnished a foundation on which popular institutions could later be set up. The power of the Emperor is supreme and is derived by inheritance from divine origins. He exercises the legislative power with the consent of the Imperial Diet, which also has permission to initiate proposed laws that may be withdrawn, however, and amended by the crown, as well as vetoed absolutely. Constitutional amendments may be proposed by the Emperor alone. The session of the Diet is limited to three months and during the remainder of the year the ordinances of the Emperor have all the force of law, but they must not conflict with law and must be approved when the Diet assembles. All officials, including Cabinet Ministers, are appointed by and responsible to him, and he has supreme command of the military forces, declares war, makes peace, and concludes treaties.

Structure and Powers of the Japanese Diet.—The Diet consists of a House of Peers and a House of Representatives. The first has 374 members and consists of princes of the blood, nobles, and Imperial nominees. Nobles below the rank of marquis are empowered to elect representatives to the Upper House for a term of seven years. Imperial nominees consist of persons rendering exceptional services to the State, who sit for life, and those elected one from each city and prefecture from among the highest taxpayers, who sit for seven years. Specific provision is made that noble members shall always be in the majority. The House of Representatives is composed of 381 members chosen by male electors over 25 years of age and paying at least $5.00 in direct taxes. Any male citizen of the age of 30 years may become a candidate for the Lower House. Under the present restriction there are but 1,500,000 qualified electors out of a population of 54,000,000. The constitution safeguards the right of free speech to the members of the House, who hold office for four years. The Japanese Lower House possesses only a power of resistance against what could become an arbitrary exercise of authority by the Emperor who still retains the sovereign rights.

The legislative power of the House consists in the right to initiate ordinary laws and in the final right to approve all laws. The control of the finances of the Empire is lodged in the Diet and the budget must be introduced into the Lower House. While the Diet has control over taxes and loans, administrative fees and charges comprising one-third the entire revenue are beyond the control of the Diet. The same is true of expenditures already fixed, or arising from the effect of law, or those dealing with the legal obligations of the Government. These comprise the expenses connected with the various departments, the army and navy, expenses of all officials, including salaries and pensions, obligations arising from treaties, and obligations arising from the national debt, all of which are beyond the control of the Diet. The Government is carried on in case of the dissolution of the Diet before it has acted on the budget by a provision empowering it to carry out the budget of the preceding year. The popular support of the Diet, therefore, is the only factor which makes it of essential importance in the financial scheme of the Government, which, but for fear of popular disapproval, could operate practically independently.

The right of interpellation of Cabinet Ministers is the chief weapon now utilized by the minority parties, who have practically no other method of registering their interest in national affairs. The uncertainty of party allegiance has made this a particularly significant method of registering individual sentiment in lieu of speechmaking, although there is no necessity for a reply from an irresponsible Cabinet. When the Cabinet thus proves obdurate to the majority in control, an address to the throne is sometimes resorted to, and sublime justice from the fountainhead of justice is consistently expected in such cases.

With no real representative government there is little public debate in the Diet, and most of the real work is done in committees, where bribery has had an opportunity to greatly weaken the effectiveness of the Lower House, and leaves the Upper House a strong, conservative factor in exerting what influence the Diet possesses.

The Genro and the Cabinet.—The Genro has already been described as the real government of Japan. Its position is no less remarkable in that it is extra-legal. During the difficult period of transition since 1868 it has been a wonderful sustaining force charting the course for the new nation and—in short—a continuous and effective control over cabinets and policies. The place of the Cabinet is simply set forth in the provision in the Constitution that "Ministers of State shall give their advice to the Emperor and be responsible for it." The Privy Council is empowered to deliberate, when consulted by the Emperor, upon matters of state. Comprising *ex-officio* the members of the Cabinet, its decisions reflect, theoretically, the will of that body, and the approval of the Emperor gives them an unquestionable sanction. Because of this peculiar arrangement of power, the Cabinet may escape the results of many of its acts and avoid interpellation by incorporating ministerial policies with those of the Privy Council. The premier of the Cabinet is appointed by the Emperor and chooses the nine department heads, who from expediency have come to include the leaders of the dominant groups in the Lower House, with the exception of the Ministers of War and the Navy, who must be Army and Navy officers. These ministers sit and speak in either House and have free access to all committees. They may introduce, amend, or withdraw bills, and these have precedence over those of private members. The Cabinet may prorogue the House for 15 days in order to concentrate attention upon its own bills, and by this weapon, which shortens the brief space allotted to legislation, its wishes are often carried out. Dissolution of the Diet signifies that the peoples' representatives are at variance with the Imperial Government and that the Emperor wishes others elected.

The Organization of the Judiciary.—The judiciary is organized according to law and the courts exercise their power under the same sanction. The judges have life tenure unless dismissed for cause. But since "according to law" practically means "according to the wish of the Government," the legal safeguards surrounding the judiciary in cases affecting the official hierarchy have small force.

The Real Character of the Japanese Constitution.—The Japanese Constitution is skillfully drawn to apparently establish many new and democratic forms, but in fact it retains the old forms. In this respect it is a splendid instrument of transitional reform. This condition has been accepted in a matter of fact way by the people who are apparently content to leave the power where it can be exercised with greatest discretion. With a coming conception of greater political freedom, the manner in which a new situation, marking the end of this transitional period, will be met, is of interest.

The Evolution of Japanese Political Parties.—Emerging in sixty years from a state of feudalism to the position of a modern state, Japan, whose first elections for an Imperial Diet were held only 26 years ago, presents a political party situation somewhat puzzling to the average observer. It must first be realized, however, that four distinct factors constitute the Government, the Emperor, the Genro, or Elder Statesmen, the clans, and the bureaucracy. The official class has been controlled by the clans through the Genro, and while the Choshu clan, for example, has gotten control of the Army, the Satsuma clan has succeeded in dominating the Navy. For the past 25 years the Genro has made and unmade Cabinets, always selecting the majority of the personnel from one of these two clans. This condition explains the real movements in Japanese politics. Champions of representative government have contended from the first against this absolute control, and also against the division of spoils, which has developed a jealousy between these two powerful clans that has greatly weakened their power. Finally the people have discovered that the burden of taxation under which they are staggering only furnishes money which goes eventually to one or both of these clans, and so to the support of either the Army or the Navy, and they are objecting to heavy expenditure in either. The first political party was founded in 1880 by Itogaki and was called the Jiyu-to, or Liberal Party, and was an outgrowth of several organizations for the study of political science. Okuma, two years later, organized the Kaishin-to, or Reform Party, which later became the Shimpo-to, or Progressive Party. This party stood for internal reform as a necessary precedent to the obtaining of tariff autonomy and the abolishment of the rights of foreigners to exercise legal authority over their own subjects in Japan. In the same year the Taisei-to, or Imperial Party, was organized by Government supporters and advocated absolute obedience to the Emperor and the reforms promised by the Emperor with the Constitution. Until 1889, when the Constitution went into effect, these three parties, the Liberal representing the radicals or doctrinaires, the Progressive advocating reforms, and the Imperialists bent upon thwarting any movement toward democracy, dominated Japanese politics.

Count Ito and Count Okuma.—The first national election under the Constitution in 1890 returned 300 members divided into ten groups. The Independents with sixty-nine members headed the list. These ten groups finally coalesced into four, the Liberal and Progressive groups becoming the leaders, and these two parties finally alternated as the party in office and the opposition until 1900. Meanwhile a law prohibiting branches of political parties being established in the provinces was replaced in 1893, and greatly strengthened party government as it existed. It was not until 1895 that Count Ito obtained the first government majority in the House of Representatives by a coalition of the Liberal, Nationalist, and Official parties. By opposing a party measure of this Government granting more responsibility to the Cabinet, the House of Peers caused Ito's resignation. After a short term of office in which he vainly endeavored to separate Okuma from his party, the Progressives, Count Matsukata, the next Premier, resigned and was succeeded by his predecessor, Count Ito, who, rejecting the offers of the Liberals for their support attempted to establish party government by winning over the Progressives, but this was opposed by the Genro who held that party government was unconstitutional. Thus in 1898 a coalition of the Liberals and Progressives resulted in the formation of a new Constitutional Party, which was charged with important duties in connection with the going into effect of the new commercial treaties in 1899, and the resulting necessity for domestic reforms and a strengthening of national rights and prestige. This attempt at party government proved immature and the coalition went out of office in four months. Marquis Yamagata now attempted to hold office with the support of the Liberals, but Count Ito formed a new party, the Seiyu-kai, from the dissolved Liberal Party and took over the Government. At the same time the Progressive Party was reorganized under Count Okuma. Ito now received opposition from the Upper House which resented his having become a leader of a political party, and he was forced to resign. The Elder Statesmen now decided to take no active part in the parliamentary Government, but to rule through younger men.

The Choshu Clan and Seiyu-kai Party.—A Choshu follower of Yamagata, named Katsura, was selected for Premier in 1900, and held office under clan protection for four and one-half years. The parties had now decided to coöperate with, rather than oppose, the clan government of the Elder Statesmen, and the belief that party government could not prevail in Japan was predominant. During his tenure of office the militaristic program of the Choshu clans to "make Japan the predominant country in the Far East" was greatly strengthened, first, by the Anglo-Japanese alliance, and then by the successful war against Russia. Japan's preëminence as a military power is, therefore, in no small measure due to England. The disappointment over the terms of the Portsmouth Treaty, ending the war with Russia, led to Katsura's downfall, and on his recommendation the Seiyu-kai leader, Saionji, succeeded him. The new Premier held office for three years and, although he had the support of his party throughout, made no attempt to found party government. In 1908 Katsura again assumed office and retained the support of the Seiyu-kai, principally because the nation as a whole was pleased with the Government's Manchurian and Korean policy. In 1911 popular feeling against the Katsura military group caused Saionji to again be summoned to form a Cabinet.

The Kokumin-to and Count Okuma.—The year before this the Progressives had formed themselves into a new party, the Kokumin-to or Constitutional Nationalists, also under Okuma's guidance. This group sought to break up the Seiyu-kai by advocating some policy to which the several small independent parties could rally. Throughout Saionji's second ministry the question of finances was uppermost, the Choshu men insisting upon creating two new divisions of the Army, or 40,000 additional men for Korea, which had now been annexed. Upon the death of the Emperor in 1912, a reaction against the absolute power of the throne was feared and Katsura was called upon for the third time. In his new government he showed no signs of alleviation from the same bureaucratic principles and soon lost the support of the two great parties and popular confidence which he attempted to regain by creating a new party, the Rikken Doshi-kai, or Constitution Friends Society. Upon his failure he was succeeded by Admiral Yamamoto, who, as a member of the opposing, or Satsuma, clan, received the support of the Seiyu-kai. In 1914 disclosures were made of a great scandal in the Navy, and several Japanese naval officers were indicted in Berlin for graft. This lead to the downfall of the Yamamoto Cabinet, and Count Okuma was called from his retirement to organize a Cabinet. The policy of this new Cabinet was largely influenced by the Great War, which soon broke out and resulted in the active participation of Japan in the capture of German possessions in Shantung and the resulting twenty-one demands upon the Chinese Government. These were designed greatly to strengthen Japan's influence in China, if not actually to usurp Chinese sovereignty. Such action called forth a vote of censure by the Diet which, while not carried, was significant in obtaining a one-third support of the House. This was followed in 1915 by disclosures of corruption in the election held the previous March in which Viscount Oura, the Home Minister, was implicated, and Count Okuma offered the resignation of the whole Cabinet.

After canvassing the situation and finding no other available candidate the Elder Statesmen commanded Count Okuma to remain in office and select a new Cabinet. This Cabinet continued to struggle with the popular demands for retrenchment, and the military demands for a larger Army and Navy and finally gave way in 1918 to the present Premier Hara who, as leader of the Seiyu-kai, has again established a semblance of party government.

Questions

1. What is the fundamental difference between the Chinese and Japanese in conception and form of government?
2. Outline the structure of the old Imperial Government of China.
3. How did Yuan Shi-kai undermine the power of the first Assembly?
4. Outline the form of government in China under the revised provisional constitution.
5. Outline the growth of Chinese political parties.
6. What outside pressure led Yuan to assume the title of Emperor?
7. What is the Lansing-Ishii Agreement?
8. What is the form of the Japanese Government under the Constitution?
9. Describe the position and power of the Japanese Emperor. Of the Genro. Of the Cabinet.
10. Outline the growth of political parties in Japan.

CHAPTER IV

TARIFFS, TREATIES AND COMMERCIAL LAWS IN CHINA AND JAPAN

China

The outstanding feature of the treaties which have been negotiated between China and Western powers is the granting to foreign subjects of the right of extraterritoriality. The ordinary doctrine of international law holds that a sovereign state has jurisdiction over the person and property of foreigners within its confines, but China has partially surrendered this right by treaty with the West. Under these treaties the person and property of the foreigner in China does not come under Chinese jurisdiction at all, but under the protection of his own flag, and it is by his own officials that the foreigner is tried, except under certain conditions to be described later. By waiving her rights to try foreigners China does not evade her responsibility to protect them and this obligation is fully imposed by treaty.

Extraterritoriality in China.—This situation of responsibility without right of trial has long been complained of by China, who maintains that it was forced upon her against her will. While this contention is technically just, historically and practically China has long allowed foreigners to be governed according to their own laws. This is due to some extent perhaps to the large administrative area, and the unwillingness of early Chinese provincial governors to assume any responsibilities with reference to the foreigners, or to have any intercourse with them except trade for profit. As early as the ninth century the Arabs were granted extraterritorial rights at Canton, and in the sixteenth century the Portuguese at Macao were granted the same privileges. The treaty which the American Minister Caleb Cushing negotiated with China in 1844, therefore, simply carried out the tradition thus established, and the grant of extraterritorial rights was obtained from China as a matter of course. This treaty was the basis upon which all disputes with foreigners, of whatever nationality, were settled up to 1858–60, when the treaty of 1842 between China and Great Britain was revised. This treaty provided several distinct things:

1. That Chinese committing crimes against British shall be tried and punished by Chinese authorities and law.

2. That British subjects committing any crime in China shall be tried and punished by British authorities and law.

In order to carry out the provision of this treaty the British Government established in 1860 a Supreme Court at Shanghai. The Chinese Government established a mixed court in whose proceedings the case was tried by the official of the defendant's nationality, the official of the plaintiff's nationality merely attending to watch the proceedings in the interest of justice. The officer so attending could protest against the proceedings in detail if he were dissatisfied. The law administered was the law of the officer trying the case. The British Supreme Court at Shanghai is presided over by a chief justice before whom personal and property rights of British subjects in China are heard and determined. Complaints against British subjects residing outside Shanghai in China are tried before the nearest British consular officer, subject to appeal. The mixed court established by the Chinese Government likewise has jurisdiction over all matters in which a subject of China, residing at Shanghai, may be the defendant and a foreigner the plaintiff. Under the most favored nation clause in the treaties of other nations, whereby they enjoy all rights and privileges granted by China to the "most favored nation," the provisions of this treaty with Great Britain apply to other foreign nations, and the United States now has its own court at Shanghai, which also holds circuit sessions in other treaty ports. In other districts where the American court does not sit the American Consul exercises judicial power, presiding over what are known as Consular Courts.

The International Settlement at Shanghai.—Although the Chinese magistrate in the Mixed Court has jurisdiction over cases in which the plaintiff is a foreigner, he cannot arrest even a Chinese in that territory in the city of Shanghai, known as the International Settlement, except through the agency of foreign police. This International Settlement is the direct outgrowth of the theory of extraterritoriality in China. After this theory had been accepted by the Chinese, provision was made in the treaties with various foreign powers for certain specified areas in Chinese ports where foreigners were permitted to reside, which should be ceded to the foreign power for a long period of years, and which should form a sort of legal oasis where foreign law reigned supreme not only over foreigners, who, of course, remain under their own laws wherever they go in China, but over such Chinese as choose to reside in these areas. Such a concession was given to the French in Shanghai and, adjoining it, similar areas were granted to Great Britain and the United States, who, the concessions not being separate and independent as was the French, united their interests in what is now known as the International Settlement. This Settlement has a regular foreign government, under the control of the foreign consular representatives at Shanghai, and a municipal council of nine members elected by the payers of taxes up to a certain amount. These taxes are assessed by the taxpayers at a yearly meeting at which an annual fiscal budget is approved. Regulations for police and fiscal government are drawn up by the consular body and approved by the foreign minister at Peking. The taxes consist of a small land and house tax and are levied entirely independently of the Chinese Government. The police force is under the Municipal Council, and consists of foreigners, Chinese, and Indian Sihks. Arrests can be made only upon warrant by the proper consular officers, or conditionally, by the Mixed Court subject to approval of the senior consular representative. If the Chinese, for whose arrest the Mixed Court makes application, is employed by a foreigner, the order must first be signed by the Consul of the foreigner, and countersigned by the senior consular officer, and such offenders may also claim the right to be tried by a foreign consular officer sitting with the magistrate in the Mixed Court. These rules simply mean that all foreigners and natives residing in the International Settlement at Shanghai shall not be subject to interference on the part of the Chinese Government, which Government exercises no control over a foreigner, whatever, and its control over a native is exercised under the supervision of a foreign official. There are International Settlements at Shanghai and Amoy. In the former, British interests are predominant, while American, Japanese, and Russian interests are represented on the Municipal Council. The term "treaty port" does not necessarily imply foreign political control, although most of them have regular reserved areas. At others, like Cheefoo, the foreigners have for a long time conducted an informal international municipal government. At some of the newly opened treaty ports special arrangements for foreign self-government have been made, while at others Chinese municipal administrations have been provided for the areas reserved for foreigners.

Foreign Concessions.—In addition to these foreign concessions and international settlements in the treaty ports, certain areas in China are wholly under foreign control by treaty. The most important of these areas are the Japanese leased territories of Kwantung, situated on the

Liaotung Peninsula of South Manchuria, in which Dairen (Dalny) and Port Arthur are situated; the former German leased territory, Kiachow, in Shantung Province, which contains the port of Tsingtau; and the British leased territory of Kowloon on the mainland opposite the British Island of Victoria, on which the city of Hongkong is located. Dairen is a Chinese treaty port, but is also a free port, while Tsingtau in addition to being a treaty port contains a free zone. Chinese customs are levied on goods passing from these ports to the interior. In addition to leased territories, China has also granted certain concessions to foreign powers in the shape of railway areas, which are narrow strips of territory through which foreign railways are built. These railways are known as concession railways and the railway areas also included settlements near the stations along the route. The concession railroads are the South Manchurian Railroad running from Chanchung to Dairen; the Shantung Railway running from Tsinan to Tsingtau, both under Japanese control; and the Chinese Eastern Railway, which runs across North Manchuria to Vladivostok and which is an important connecting link in the trans-Siberian Railroad, including a branch from Harbin to Changchun to join the South Manchurian Railroad. The status of this road is now uncertain. The Japanese maintain railway settlements at Mukden, Changchun, and Antung, although the Chinese have resumed administrative control in the former Russian area at Harbin.

Chinese Tariff.—The Chinese tariff as it affects foreigners is entirely conventional, that is, provided for by treaty or convention with foreign governments. The tariff is administered by the Maritime Customs Administration. No complete revision of the original treaty of Tientsin of 1858 has ever been made, although revisions in rates have taken place on two occasions. The conventional rate of duty is five per cent *ad valorem* on imports and exports, but to simplify collections these duties were converted into specific duties on the basis of prices in 1858, and the revisions which have been granted have not affected this rate, but merely the prices of the articles concerned, as these have risen year by year and have yielded a smaller and smaller proportion of the five per cent nominal value of imports intended. The prices on imports fixed in 1858 were revised in 1902 on a basis of prices in 1897–99, but export prices remained unchanged. The latest adjustment was in 1918, when a five-year average of prices from 1912–1916 was struck as a basis for an effective five per cent *ad valorem* conversion to specific rates. All these adjustments, however, had to be made with the consent of the signatory powers to the 1858 treaty. By similar consent, export duties on certain exports have been removed, or reduced, in order to stimulate Chinese industry. These include such articles as tea, strawbraid, lace, hair nets, preserved fruit, and ginger.

Maritime Customs Administration.—Maritime customs duties are also levied on articles passing from one Chinese treaty port to another. An article produced in Shanghai, and sent to Tientsin, must pay not only the export duty from Shanghai, but an additional two and one-half per cent *ad valorem* import duty at Tientsin. This is known as a "coast trade" duty. On the other hand, an article imported from abroad into Shanghai, on which an import duty is levied, may be exported to any other treaty port within three years without extra tax. This is an important right, and of much more importance is the provision whereby such imported articles may be protected from all native customs charges, and what is known as *likin,* or barrier tax, arbitrarily imposed en route to a non-treaty port or city, by the payment of additional "transit dues" amounting to an extra two and one-half per cent. All goods transported by steam vessels and what are termed "chartered junks" come under the Maritime Customs Administration, are subject to the above rules. Goods transported in other ways, no matter of what origin, are subject to the "regular" or Chinese native customs, and likewise to the *likin,* or barrier tax. Railroad freight is not classed under maritime customs rules, and foreign goods so transported to the interior, unless protected by a "transit dues customs pass" showing that an extra half duty has been paid, are subject to either native customs charges or *likin* or both. These "transit dues" on imported articles, therefore, compensate for the obvious burden on native goods imposed by the "coast trade duty" on shipments from one treaty port to another, and this apparent hardship on goods of native production is further modified by a second provision, whereby Chinese domestic factory products, including those manufactured with foreign capital, may be sent to any part of China free from all further taxation upon the payment of what is termed an "excise," equal to the original import duty on foreign goods of the same class. A duty quite unique is the Peking *octroi,* which is a duty of three per cent *ad valorem* levied at the gate of Peking on all goods entering that city, and is distinct from both native customs and *likin.* Trade with China is open to all classes of goods except salt, a government monopoly, opium, firearms and explosives, only under special permit, and industrial explosives. The prohibition of the latter is a serious handicap upon mining and construction work.

Japan

Early Commercial Treaties with Japan.—The early Japanese trade became a Dutch monopoly after the expulsion of the foreigners in 1638, and remained so until 1858, when the first commercial treaty was signed with the United States. In the same year a commercial treaty with Great

Britain was also signed. By these early treaties Japan granted extraterritorial jurisdiction to foreign powers just as China had done, and notwithstanding a growing resentment on the part of the Japanese Government, the powers, led by Great Britain, steadfastly refused to grant Japan any more recognition than was granted China until 1894. By that time the Constitution had gone into effect, the first Diet had assembled, and Japan was considered by the powers to have reached her majority. Consequently by treaty with Great Britain, followed by treaties with France, Germany, Russia, and Italy—the United States having already signed a treaty of recognition several years earlier conditional upon similar action by the other powers—Japan was granted full judicial autonomy and restored the tariff autonomy which she had given up in the treaties of 1858 with the West, although the latter treaties did not have full effect until 1911. A few days later the war with China was declared, and when France, Germany, and Russia demanded the return of Port Arthur, Great Britain refused to join in the protest. This led to a mutual *rapprochement* between Great Britain and Japan, whose interests in the Far East were in many respects identical, and, as a consequence, the Anglo-Japanese Alliance was signed in 1902 for the purpose of maintaining the independence of China and Korea. By the terms of this Alliance both parties disavowed any aggressive policy in the Far East, and each promised to come to the aid of the other if they became involved with more than one power in the defense of these principles. Two years later the Alliance was renewed and extended to include India and Asia generally, and it was furthermore provided that if either party were attacked in the defense of these rights the other would come to their aid. The renewed treaty was announced toward the end of the Russo-Japanese War and was destined to maintain peace in the Far East. Again renewed for a period of ten years in 1911, this Alliance contained a clause practically excluding the United States from its provisions. In 1907 France and Russia both signed treaties with Japan agreeing to recognize the independence of China, to mutually maintain order there, and to defend the "open door" principle of equal opportunity for all. The early effects of the commercial treaties between Japan and Great Britain and the United States, under the terms of which both nationals are free to travel and reside in the territory of the other, were to arouse opposition on the part of white inhabitants of British Columbia and of California, where Japanese immigrants, it was claimed, competed with the original settlers, and were driving them out because of a lower standard of living. In order to remedy a situation which was full of serious possibilities, the Japanese Government voluntarily agreed to restrict emigration of laborers and workmen of certain classes to these countries, at the same time formally maintaining their full rights under the treaty. These "gentlemen's agreements" have been in effect since 1908.

The Japanese Statutory Tariff.—It was not until 1911 that Japan received full tariff autonomy. By the terms of the revised commercial treaties of 1899 a general Japanese statutory tariff was established, but certain tariff conventions with foreign countries were by the most favored nation clause extended to all countries until 1911. The customs tariff during this period, therefore, was a combined conventional and statutory tariff. The rates up until 1899 had not averaged over five per cent, and the total receipts in any one year had never been over five million dollars. By 1900 the average rate of duty had increased to eight and one-half per cent, and by 1911 it had reached an annual average of fifteen per cent. In the same year $18,000,000 in revenue was realized from the tariff.

The Effect of Tariff Changes on Industry.—The immediate effect of the lapsing of the conventional tariffs in

1911 was to put into effect certain rates, which had been written into the statutory tariff years before, but had been a dead letter up until that time. The rates so framed had been fixed with due consideration for the economic effects upon Japan, and in every case Japanese industries were well protected, although every attempt was made to conserve good relations with foreign countries by interfering as little as possible with established trade. Japanese industries were not ready at this time to meet the full home demands for manufactured goods, which the new tariff would give them the opportunity to supply, so that the policy was adopted of simply adhering to the statutory rates fixed some years before with the view to revising them as circumstances demanded.

The Opposition of England to an Effective Statutory Tariff.—This attitude on the part of Japan of merely putting into effect the statutory rates long inoperative, aroused no little opposition from British manufacturers and merchants, who took the view that in as much as these statutory rates were higher than the old conventional rates, Japan was taking an unwarranted advantage of the situation. But this was finally adjusted and Japan, long bound by unilateral conventional tariffs, was allowed to formulate and put into force an industrial policy which would meet her economic needs. As a matter of fact, the statutory tariff had yielded 89 per cent of the total customs revenue, and Japan was well within her rights in demanding such an increase in rates as would yield a revenue commensurate with her needs and even foster certain industries which were still in their infancy.

The Effect of Tariff Reform on Revenue.—This question of revenue was just at this time a very pressing one for the Japanese Government. The interest on the enormous debt, incurred by the war with Russia, had to be paid, and loans made prior to that time were coming due and had to be redeemed. A substantial source of revenue had to be found and this was only possible from two sources, internal revenue and customs tariff. Realizing this situation, Great Britain reached certain reciprocal agreements with Japan which were satisfactory and substantial reductions in the duties on textiles, iron, and steel formed the basis for similar negotiations with other powers. These reductions in the Japanese statutory tariff amounted to from 20 to 33 per cent of the original rates. In return Great Britain agreed to continue to admit free of duty certain Japanese specialties, such as silk cloth, copper, straw goods, camphor, etc., into England, but not into her dominions or colonies without their consent. This reciprocal agreement with Great Britain was after all entirely gratuitous on the part of Japan, because of Great Britain's free trade policy, and it evinced a strong desire on the part of Japan to placate and conciliate the British nation. These concessions and like concessions to other powers were all applicable to every treaty power with Japan under the "most favored nation" clause in the commercial treaties. As a whole, therefore, they constituted a very liberal reduction in the moderate rates which Japan had determined upon as necessary to insure sound industrial advance, but in spite of that fact Japan has gradually developed many industries such as the textile, paper, chemical, and glass, and during the last war the shoe and leather, dyestuff, and iron and steel industries. In many, as in the iron and steel industry, Japan is tremendously handicapped by a lack of natural resources, but despite this handicap she has created an enviable record in industrial advance and has succeeded not only in supplying her own markets in many lines formerly imported, but in furnishing other markets, especially in the Far East, Australia, South Africa, and South America, with many lines of manufactured goods formerly supplied by Western nations.

The Revision of Codified Law.—In order to obtain judicial autonomy it became necessary for Japan so to revise her codified law so as to conform and harmonize with European and American law. It is not strange, therefore, to note strong foreign influence in the present day Japanese laws. In this adaptation Japan showed no partiality, but sought the best that could be obtained. After much study the French penal codes and criminal codes were taken as a basis for the new Japanese laws on these subjects, while German influence was strongly noticeable in the civil and commercial codes. The latter is divided into five books which deal briefly with (1) fundamental rules, (2) methods of doing business by companies, (3) commercial acts, (4) commercial paper, and (5) maritime law. The law of bankruptcy, formerly under the commercial code, has now been made a separate branch of the law.

The Judicial System.—The Japanese judicial system operates without juries, and the judges and public procurators, corresponding to our district attorneys, are appointed after examination. There are four classes of courts, district or lower courts presided over by one judge, who decides small civil and criminal cases; local courts, which are courts of first instance in more important civil and criminal cases, and are presided over by three judges; courts of appeal, hearing appeals from local courts; and the Court of Cassation, or Supreme Court, presided over by seven judges in each of its two sections, and hearing appeals from both the court of appeals and the lower courts.

Patent Laws and Trade-Mark Regulations.—The Japanese patent laws are applied indiscriminately to foreigners and Japanese. Any citizen of a country which is a party to the International Convention for the Protection of Industrial Property is granted on application for a patent or invention, a right of priority good for one year in the case of a patent, and four months in that of a design or trade-mark. A Japanese patent runs for 15 years and may be extended under certain conditions. A design runs for 10 years, and a utility model three years with a right of extension for another three years. Trade-marks are protected for 20 years with rights of extension. Right of appeal to the courts for these rights is granted unsuccessful applicants through the Patent Bureau. The application fees are $165 for a patent, $8.50 for a design, $10.00 for a trade-mark, and $7.50 for a utility model.

Land Tenure by Foreigners.—The legal status of foreigners in Japan is similar to that of foreigners in most European countries. They are not permitted to own land, however, and are subject to income, business, and customs taxation on a par with Japanese. On the whole, the administration of the law is fair in regard to foreigners, and compares favorably with that of any other country.

Questions

1. What is extraterritoriality?
2. Describe the administration of justice in China, as relating to foreigners.
3. What is a Mixed Court?
4. What is the nature of the Chinese tariff, and how is it levied?
5. Name the foreign concessions and describe their extent.
6. What was the attitude of Japan in putting into effect her statutory tariff, and how was the situation met?
7. What was the effect of the financial condition of Japan on tariff revision?
8. Outline the principal features of the Japanese commercial code.
9. Describe the judicial system of Japan.
10. What is the status of foreigners under Japanese patent laws?

CHAPTER V

AGRICULTURE, MINES, AND MANUFACTURING INDUSTRIES OF CHINA

The total area of China, including Mongolia, Turkistan, and Tibet, is 4,278,352 square miles. The exact population is unknown, but estimates vary from 325,000,000 to 400,000,000. In China proper there are 18 provinces whose average population is 174 to the square mile, the most populous province being Shantung with 528 to the square mile, and the least populous being Kansu with only 40 to the square mile. China is one-third the size of the whole British Empire, and one-fifth larger than the United States in area, while in population it is exceeded only by the population of the British Empire.

For commercial purposes, China proper may be divided into three main trade zones. The northern, having for its outlet the port of Tientsin, covers the large fertile valley of the Yellow River, and extends to the low plains of Manchuria. The central consists of the basin of the Yangtze River, and extends from the far interior of Szechwan Province to the ocean at Shanghai, which is the chief port. The southern concentrates, at Canton, the trade originating in the valley of the West River and its tributaries. Fully 70 per cent of the population is concentrated along the banks of these main rivers and their tributaries, the densest population being found in the low delta regions.

Agricultural Industry

The principal agricultural products of China are silk, vegetable oils and oil seeds, rice, tea, cotton, tobacco, cereals, fibers, and vegetable wax. Official production statistics are lacking, and export figures furnish the only clue to the volume of Chinese production.

Silk.—The silk crop is the most valuable crop which China exports, and is raised mainly in the Canton district, 46 per cent of all silk products being attributed to the southern trade area. Silk is raised, however, all over China, and especially in the provinces of Szechwan, Shantung, and Yunnan. Wild silk has recently become more popular, owing to the belief that it is stronger in texture than the cultivated. The silk industry as a whole, however, has steadily declined, due to the lack of scientific care in eliminating diseased worms. This decline is best shown in the Chinese export statistics, from which it will be noticed that the exports of steam filature silk, that is, standard raw silk for foreign manufacture, have decreased from nine million pounds in 1913 to eight million pounds in 1918, although the export value has nearly doubled; on the other hand waste silk, which is largely the product of unskilful reelers, increased from fifteen million pounds in 1913 to seventeen million pounds in 1918. This increase accounts for the total increase in Chinese silk exports from forty-six million pounds in 1913 to forty-eight million pounds in 1918. The value of these exports has risen from $75,000,000 in 1913 to $127,000,000 in 1918, due to the rise in the price of silk throughout the world.

Oils and Oilseeds.—This second great article of export has attained a wide market during the war because of its glycerine content. Soya bean oil is produced in small mills throughout the entire country, but particularly in the neighborhood of Shanghai and in Manchuria.

The soya bean oil exports have risen from 32,500 tons in 1913 to 151,000 tons in 1918, or about 370 per cent. Together with this increase in soya bean oil exports has come a decrease in the export of soya beans from 688,000 tons in

1913 to 588,000 tons in 1918, which, nevertheless, considering the oil exports, denotes a considerable increase in soya bean production during this period, and, of course, a great development in the oil crushing industry. A million tons of bean cake were exported in 1918, valued at $35,000,000, compared with 700,000 tons in 1913. This is used largely for fertilizer in Japan.

The export of peanut oil has shown a less momentous gain of from 17,000 tons in 1913 to 39,000 tons in 1918. Peanut growing was introduced by American missionaries in Shantung Province some decades ago, and the product now holds a commanding place in the exports of China. In the case of peanut kernels and peanuts in the shell, the export has also declined from 82,000 tons in 1913 to 43,000 tons in 1918.

China wood oil, made from the seed pod of the Aleurtes tree, attained an export volume of 32,500 tons in 1918, there being no separate statistics for the 1913 exports. Cottonseed oil amounting to 8,000 tons was exported in 1918, and furnishes an interesting commentary upon the growth of cotton production in China. In the same year 11,000 tons of cottonseed were shipped abroad. Other vegetable oils exported in smaller amounts included tea oil and sesame seed oil. The export of sesame seeds has fallen off considerably in the past five years. In 1913, 135,000 tons were shipped against only 15,000 tons in 1918. Rape seed exports, on the other hand, increased somewhat from 41,000 tons in 1913 to 45,000 tons in 1918. An important new oil seed in the Chinese export market is linseed of which 6,000 tons were exported in 1918. The export of rape and sesame seed cake declined from 87,000 tons in 1913 to 76,000 tons in 1918.

Rice.—Rice is grown universally on small garden farms not exceeding in size more than three or four acres. Due to the lack of official Chinese statistics, there is no definite knowledge of the production, but it is estimated at about 4,000,000 tons. Chinese foreign trade in rice is large, but the exports almost balance the imports. The great variety of rice plants produce many different grades which find a ready market in various parts of the Far East. As a rule the export of the Chinese rice is of the higher and the import of the lower grade. The export has fallen in recent years, due to lack of shipping facilities, and only 2,000 tons went out in 1918.

Tea.—The consumption of tea in China is estimated at five pounds per head of the population. The origin of tea as a beverage is found in the sixth century A. D., and is supposed to result from an effort to make boiled water, which it is necessary to use for the prevention of disease, more palatable. The tea industry is carried on in millions of small homesteads throughout China, there being no plantations as in India and the Dutch East Indies. The leaves are picked by the members of the families and dried in the sun, then turned over to middlemen who subject them to the process of firing. Green tea leaves are roasted almost immediately after they are gathered. There are usually three pickings of tea, one early in April, one in May, and a later one in August. Brick tea is manufactured in China for the Russian market by pressing the damp tea leaves in a mould eight inches by twelve inches and one inch thick, and marketed principally at Hankow.

The foreign markets for Chinese tea have been seriously affected by the growth of the industry in Ceylon and Java, where more scientific methods have lowered production costs. Only 11,000 tons of black and 10,000 tons of green tea were exported from China in 1918, compared with 36,000 tons of black and 18,000 tons of green tea exported in 1913. The brick tea exports have suffered even more severely because of the chaotic conditions in Russia, China's principal brick tea market. Forty thousand tons of black and green brick tea were exported in 1913, and, in 1918 this had fallen to 5,000 tons.

Cotton.—The cotton plant grows best in the Yangtze Delta and in the two provinces to the north of the Yangtze. The native cotton is short staple, but American cotton seed has lately been introduced, which furnishes satisfactory material for the woof, and the cotton spinning industry has in the last two years made enormous headway. There are now about 50 cotton mills in China with over 2,000,000 spindles. The bulk of these mills are located in Shanghai. The majority are British owned, although there are a number of Japanese owned mills as well. Practically all of the mills run day and night on a 23-hour schedule. The annual production of yarn is estimated at 250,000,000 pounds, and of cotton cloth 50,000,000 yards, practically all of which is consumed at home. About 10,000,000 pounds of nankeens and cotton yarns were exported in 1918.

The exports of raw cotton have increased from 50,000 tons in 1913 to 86,000 tons in 1918. It is estimated that there are 9,000,000 acres of land in China capable of producing cotton, and a tremendous development in this industry is looked forward to in the near future. Heavy demands for cotton-spinning and weaving machinery are now being filled by American factories.

Tobacco.—The production of tobacco is about 70,000,000 pounds annually and it is cultivated in large quantities in every province of China. Aside from this enormous production, tobacco still remains the second largest import into China, the first being cotton goods. Cigarettes are almost the universal form in which tobacco is used. The exports of leaf tobacco have increased from 10,000 tons in 1913 to 12,000 tons in 1918, and in addition 4,000 tons of prepared tobacco were sent abroad in the latter year.

Cereals.—Wheat is the principal cereal entering into the export trade, and 120,000 tons were exported both in 1913 and 1918. Millet and sorghum to the amount of 61,000 tons were also exported in 1918. Other cereals entering the export trade include maize, barley, and oats.

Fibers.—Ramie, hemp, and jute are the three most important fibers in point of production in China. Ramie, or China grass, is produced mainly in Hupeh and Szechwan, and exported to the extent of about 18,000 tons annually. Hemp is more widely distributed, and in some provinces is harvested three times a year. The export amounts to about 10,000 tons per year. Jute is grown principally in Chihli Province and exported to the extent of 6,000 tons annually.

Vegetable Wax.—Vegetable wax is a product of the tallow, or *rhus,* tree. It is a wax-like substance formed between the kernel and the outer skin of the seed. About 10,000 tons are exported annually, and the export has fallen off about 50 per cent in five years. White wax is also grown in Szechwan. This is produced by wax insects, which are placed on dwarf ash trees and cover themselves and the branches with a thick coating of wax.

Vegetables.—Fresh, dried, and salted vegetables to the amount of about 35,000 tons were exported in 1918, but these exports had declined from 78,000 tons exported in 1913.

Pastoral Industries.—The Chinese are primarily agriculturists, pastoral lands only being used when unfit for cultivation. Cattle breeding has not yet been engaged in to any great extent, although experimental stations have been established recently, and the export of livestock has consequently been increased. The dairying industry has not been carried on except in a small way, as the Chinese do not use dairy products. About 3,000,000 poultry and 850 tons of fresh and preserved eggs, together with 19,000 tons of egg albumen and yolk were exported in 1918. These eggs are gathered from individual farms all over

China, and form a most important source of income to the people. Trade in undressed skins of both cows and water buffalos is centered in Hankow, 26,000 tons being shipped in 1918, which is 7,000 tons less than in 1913. Goat skins untanned are exported chiefly from Tientsin, which draws on the sheep herds and goat herds of Manchuria and inner Mongolia for its product. About 8,000,000 pieces were exported in 1918. Fifteen hundred tons of horse and mule rawhides were also shipped abroad in 1918, Five thousand tons of pig bristles were exported mainly to Japan, for the manufacture of brushes, during the same year. Sheep raising, centered in Mongolia, furnished 21,000 tons of wool for export in 1918. Twenty-five hundred tons of camel's hair and 800 tons of goat's hair were also sent abroad.

Forests.—Wholesale deforestation has depleted China of a large portion of its forests, and timber must now be imported for the construction of railroads and for other purposes. The only large forest reserves in China are in the Yalu region of Manchuria, which supplied about 32,000,000 square feet of soft wood for export in 1918. A Bureau of Forestry has been created, and a definite attempt has been made to reforest the bare hills of China.

Mines and Minerals

Coal.—The production of coal in China is estimated at about 20,000,000 tons, the richest production being that of the Kailan mines in Honan Province, under joint British and Chinese control, whose annual output is about 13,000,000 tons. The Fushun collieries, under Japanese control, contain deposits of unparallelled thickness. The coal mines of Shantung, developed by German capital and now in the hands of Japanese, are the three largest coal mines in estimated size of deposits. Coal mining is now carried on by foreign concessions, joint Chinese and foreign concessions, and by purely Chinese mines. The operation of new mining laws, which came into effect in 1912, has distributed the investment of foreign capital equally with Chinese capital in Chinese mining projects, and there has been little tendency on the part of the Chinese to develop the properties themselves. The result has been a steady increase in the import of coal for industrial purposes, although the potential production is probably the largest in the world. The development of Chinese coal mines depends largely upon better transportation, and secondly upon Chinese and foreign coöperation. In 1918 1,700,000 tons of coal were exported from China.

Iron.—The largest known deposits of iron ore are near Hankow on the Yangtze and near Hanking lower down on the same river, although large deposits are known to exist in Shansi, Shensi, and in Manchuria. The Hanyeping Iron and Coal Company at Hankow controls the Tayeh iron mines and, while this company is nominally Chinese, Japanese have invested heavily in it, and, by the Treaty of 1915 with Japan, the outcome of the famous 21 demands, the Chinese Government promises not to convert the company into a state owned concern nor to compel it to borrow money from other than Japanese sources. The output of this company is about 200,000 tons annually of pig iron, practically all of which goes to Japan. Steel rails, plates, and nails are now being manufactured for domestic use. The only other iron mine in China is the Penhsihu, which is said to be the equivalent of the mine at Hankow. It is entirely controlled by Japanese capital, and the product is all sent to Japan. In 1918 China exported 417,000 tons of iron ore, 186,000 tons of pig iron, and 23,000 tons of bars, rods, plates, sheets and rails, against 300,000 tons of iron ore, 71,000 tons of pig iron, and 1,000 tons of iron manufactures in 1913.

Copper.—Yunnan Province is one of the richest copper districts in the world, although, due to antiquated methods of working the deposits, the production has never been over 2,000 tons. Copper is also produced in Kansu, where a plant has been established by the British for producing the ore. There are also government copper mines in Kiangsi, Szechwan, and Hupeh. These are still in the experimental stage and the production is small. In 1918 3,000 tons were exported from all China. Copper is largely used in China for the manufacture of bronze, brass, and copper art objects, and for coins which are in daily use. The production of copper does not nearly meet the local demand and nearly 9,000 short tons of copper materials were imported in 1918. This had increased to 14,583 short tons in the first nine months of 1919. The bulk of these imports come from Japan. From 1915 to 1917 Japan bought and shipped much copper from China in the form of copper coins. These were refined and sold at high war prices by the Japanese, but a resulting shortage in copper coin in China is now causing her to import copper ingots and slabs from Japan for minting.

Gold.—Gold is found in small quantities throughout China, but is most plentiful in northern Manchuria on the border of Siberia where it is recovered by primitive washing methods. The best gold mine in China is in Shantung Province. Gold mining in China is carried on almost entirely by individuals who gain a very mean livelihood from their occupation. Many thousands of gold washers prefer to gain a bare living in this manner, rather than engage in a more lucrative occupation, being constantly drawn by the lure at some time of an exceedingly rich find which, however, fails to materialize.

Silver, Quicksilver, Antimony, and Other Minerals.—Silver, quicksilver, and antimony are found in numerous provinces of China, and are mined to some extent by foreign and Chinese-foreign concessions, established before the present mining laws came into effect. About 16,000 tons of regulus and 2,300 tons of crude antimony and ore were exported in 1918. Yunnan Province is the largest producer of tin ore, 10,000 tons being exported in 1918. Tungsten ore has recently been found in great quantities in the provinces tributary to the Canton district, and about 6,000 tons were exported in 1918 principally to the United States.

Chinese salt wells produced 350,000 tons of salt for export in 1918, the sun drying process being almost exclusively used. Rich deposits of asbestos have been located near Antung in Manchuria. Three mines are now in operation, mostly by farmers who devote their spare time to gathering asbestos which lies near the surface. Valuable deposits of lead, zinc, and nickel are found in the territory between the Kwangsi and Yunnan Provinces of South China. The German firms which were predominant in the lead industry before the war have lately been superseded by Chinese. In 1918 1,500 tons of lead and lead ore were exported. China produces much alum, and exported 2,700 tons in 1918.

Petroleum.—Petroleum has been found in the four northern provinces and also in Szechwan. The wells are worked with rudimentary machinery and the production is small. The Standard Oil Company was given an option in 1914 for the exploitation of certain oil resources, but, due to the doubtful value of the prospects in the locations allotted, the options were allowed to expire without being taken up. On the expiration of the options, the Standard Oil Company proposed a joint monopoly with the Chinese Government for the refining and transportation of all crude oil produced in China, but this was rejected.

Manufacturing Industries

The two great problems which must be solved before the fullest realization of China's potentialities can be reached, are transportation and unification of foreign interests. In a sense, the latter is the keynote to the present Chinese situation. Jealousies and fears of rival interests operate to neutralize all effort to affect any substantial reforms looking toward greater production and higher standards for the people. The resulting backwardness in providing suitable means of transportation continues to divide China into provincial water-tight compartments. Some plan must be determined upon for consolidating these rival interests and subordinating their ambitions to the greater benefit of China.

The manufacture of articles for home consumption in China made rapid strides during the war due to the cutting off of the Orient from foreign sources of supply by the dislocation of shipping, but the same causes have interfered to a great extent with China's foreign markets for manufactured articles, so that the net result has been a rather drastic change in China's industrial activities.

The Strawbraid Industry.—The strawbraid industry yielded, however, only 7,000,000 pounds for export in 1918 as against 13,000,000 pounds in 1913; nevertheless, the exports showed an increase in value of from $3,500,000 to $5,000,000. Shantung is the greatest strawbraid district in China.

The Preparation of Proprietary Medicines.—Medicines, mostly of the proprietary variety for Chinese use abroad, totaled almost $4,000,000 in value of exports for 1918 against only $2,500,000 worth in 1913.

Paper Manufacture.—About $3,500,000 worth of paper of Chinese manufacture, representing 30,000,000 pounds, was exported in 1918. Some of this paper was made by crude native methods, although modern paper mills at Hankow and in Hunan Province contribute largely to the total production. China is normally a large importer of news print paper, and the development of the mill paper industry has been steadily carried on. The principal varieties exported, however, are for various domestic uses and "joss" paper for Chinese abroad.

Firecrackers and Fireworks.—The manufacture of firecrackers and fireworks, of which 20,000,000 pounds were exported in 1913, has declined to a volume of 9,000,000 pounds in 1918, due principally to the adoption of the "safe and sane" Fourth of July in the United States, although the value of the exports has remained practically at about $2,500,000.

Earthenware, Pottery, and Chinaware.—Sixty-five million pounds of Chinese earthenware and pottery were exported in 1913, and by 1918 the character of this export had entirely changed to chinaware, of which 12,000,000 pounds were exported, valued at about $1,500,000 or the same as the earthenware exports of five years before.

Grass Cloth.—Grass cloth used in the manufacture of grass rugs reached a total export value of $2,250,000 in 1918, or about double the value in 1913, although in quantity there was a slight decline in the five years.

Cigarettes.—The manufacture of cigarettes has made substantial gains since 1913, increasing the exports from one million to four million pounds, while the value has increased ten times to $2,500,000. Modern cigarette manufacturing machinery is in use, and the principal cigarette importing firms are interested in the manufacture. As cigarettes have long ranked next to cotton goods as the principal item of import the full development of the industry is not entirely reflected in the export statistics, but will be rather clearly indicated in the lessened imports in the near future as the Chinese factories are able to fill the home demand.

Vermicelli and Macaroni.—The manufacture of vermicelli and macaroni for domestic use has steadily increased, although the exports in 1918 were slightly under those of

1913 in value, and only three-fifths of the earlier year's in quantity, the 1918 figure being 12,000 tons.

Mats.—The exportation of mats has remained steadily at 20 million pieces in 1913 and 1918, and the value has also remained unchanged at $1,300,000.

Leather Goods.—On the other hand, leather manufactures have jumped both in quantity and value of exports from 2,500,000 pounds, valued at $500,000, in 1913 to 3,500,000 pounds, valued at $1,333,000, in 1918.

Varnishes.—Varnish exports have also experienced a decided impetus in the five-year period, the quantity increasing from 1,800,000 pounds to 2,300,000 pounds, and the value from $600,000 to $1,200,000.

Questions

1. How does China's area and population compare with that of the British Empire, and the United States? Name the three trade zones and the rivers draining each.
2. Discuss the Chinese silk trade, and state the reasons for its decline. Name three important vegetable oils exported.
3. Discuss China's tea trade and reason for decline. Discuss rice production and trade.
4. What is the present extent of China's cotton industry and future possibilities? Name three cereals and three fibers produced in China.
5. What is the importance of China's egg exports? Name three exports of pastoral industries.
6. Name the principal Chinese coal mines, and indicate those under foreign control. Where are the chief iron ore deposits and by whom are they controlled?
7. What are the prospects for copper mining in China? How is gold mined and where?
8. Name three other mineral products, indicating the location of the principal deposits.
9. What two problems must be solved before China may be fully developed?
10. Name five manufacturing industries of China, and comment on the growth or decline of each as evidenced by exports.

CHAPTER VI

AGRICULTURE, MINING AND MANUFACTURING INDUSTRIES OF JAPAN

The Empire of Japan consists of six large islands, the peninsula of Korea, and about 600 smaller islands. The total area of the Empire is about 142,000 square miles, 33 per cent of which is in the main island of Hondo, 33 per cent in Korea, and 11 per cent in the northern island of Hokkaido, and the balance distributed among the smaller islands. Two chains of mountains form the most distinctive physical feature of Japan, one extending from the far north in Saghalien, and the other extending from the mainland of China through Formosa and being evident in the chain of islands leading to the island of Kyushu. These two mountain chains combine in the center of the main island and rugged ranges divide the main island into two natural geographical divisions of southern and northern Japan, presenting strict contrasts both geographically and politically. The outer, or Pacific, coast, is far more rugged in outline than the inner, or Japan Sea, coast, due to the proximity of the mountains to the coast. The sea on the Pacific side is very deep, while that on the Japan Sea coast only gradually attains to a medium depth. The inland sea is in communication with the outer ocean by only four narrow straits. There are many excellent harbors on the Pacific sea coast, but good harbors are rare on the Japan Sea coast. The same is true of the islands of Hokkaido and Formosa, the harbors in Hokkaido being characterized by the presence of sand dunes, while the coast of Formosa presents a sharp contrast between the eastern and western shores, the former ending abruptly in deep water and the shore facing on China terminating in a shelving bottom with many shoals. There are 60 harbors open to foreign trade, the most important being Yokohama, Kobe, and Osaka on the Pacific Coast of the main island, and Niigata on the Japan Sea Coast, which is the port of transshipment for Vladivostock. Nagasaki, on Kyushu Island, Tamsui, in Formosa, and Fusan, in Korea, are the important ports. The population of Japan proper in 1916 was 55,000,000, or a population of 387 per square mile, as compared with 33 per square mile in the United States.

Agriculture

Intensive cultivation of the land by human labor with the use of crude and simple implements are the outstanding features of Japanese agricultural methods. Horses and oxen are rarely seen, and most of the burden bearing is done by men and women. Eighty per cent of the population is agricultural and the average size of the farm is two and one-half acres. Every available acre of land is under cultivation, the hillsides being terraced so that the water may be drained from the top fields to the lower fields and in this way used many times over in accordance with regulations which are strictly adhered to. Japan has no special legislation on land holding, the average length of tenancy being 10 or 12 years. The migration of the rural population toward the city is making it more and more difficult for the landlords to find tenants on any terms and rural reorganization has become an important economic problem. The difficulty has been that, under the present system, only a bare subsistence is allowed the farmer, leaving no surplus with which to elevate the standard of living or to contribute to their general culture. As a result, the national wealth is still comparatively low. But, with the high prices of silk abroad, the farmers who also raise their own food prospered greatly in the recent past, so that new capital has flooded Japan and started many new enterprises. The agrarian policy of Japan, may be said to be that of increasing the area of land *per capita* without decreasing its average yield.

Rice.—There are about 4,000 varieties of rice plants cultivated in Japan which are divided into three main varieties; those maturing in the early spring, those in the middle summer, and those in the late fall. The average yield of rice, which is the staple crop and foodstuff, is 33 bushels per acre, although, with intensive methods in sections, this has been raised to 40 and sometimes to 60 bushels. The success of the small farmer in Japan depends largely upon the use of all waste material, and the intensive system of cultivation has not been able to keep pace with the increasing population. Japan is each year more dependent upon her rice imports. The *per capita* consumption of rice in Japan is seven bushels per year, or a total consumption of 371,000,000 bushels. The normal rice yield for the past seven years has been little over 265,000,000 bushels per year, to which Korea's production of 50,000,000 bushels and Formosa's 22,000,000 bushels must be added, making a total rice production for the Japanese Empire of 337,000,000 bushels, so that Japan is already dependent upon Siam and French Indo-China for a large share of her most important and necessary foodstuff.

Barley and Wheat.—In addition to the production of rice, Japan normally produces 88,000,000 bushels of barley and 26,500,000 bushels of wheat. These crops constitute the staple crops in the upland farms where the nature of the land makes rice cultivation impracticable. Barley is now very generally mixed with the rice throughout Japan because of the prevalence of beri-beri, or dropsy, which is caused by a diet of pure rice. Barley is extensively cultivated in the northern island of Hokkaido for brewing beer.

The stalks are also used in the making of strawbraids which are exported extensively. Wheat is used in Japan largely as a subsidiary foodstuff in the manufacture of macaroni and confectionery and practically no bread is used by the majority of the people.

Other Grains.—Fifteen million bushels of millet, 5,000,000 bushels of buckwheat, and 3,000,000 bushels of maize are also normally produced. The millets are raised in mountainous districts either as a substitute for rice or in rice producing districts after the planting season has passed, or if rice has not been planted because of adverse weather conditions. Millet and buckwheat are also the ordinary articles of diet for the poorer classes in rural districts. Buckwheat flour is used extensively in the manufacture of buckwheat macaroni, an article of popular diet in Japan. Maize is used rarely as an article of human food, but is grown extensively in Hokkaido for cattle food.

Beans and Potatoes.—Japan annually produced 18,000,000 bushels of soya beans, 4,000,000 bushels of red beans, 2,000,000 bushels of horse beans, and 2,000,000 bushels of peas. The soya bean plays a very important part in the Japanese dietary, daily articles of diet for all classes being *soy*, a sauce brewed from the soya bean; *miso*, a paste used in soup making; and *tofu*, or bean curd, which is used in place of butter. The soya bean cake is a very valuable fertilizer and horse food. The demand for soya bean in Japan has long outstripped the supply, and an immense quantity of beans are being raised by the Chinese in South Manchuria and sent to Japan for oil extraction and shipment abroad. Hokkaido is the principal center of soya bean production in Japan. The red beans are used principally for making Japanese confectionery, and are considered a great delicacy when boiled with rice. Each year 8,000,000 pounds of sweet potatoes and 2,000,000 pounds of white potatoes are produced in Japan. Sweet potatoes occupy an important place in supplying a cheap substitute for rice for the poorer folk. They are also used for making starch and in the manufacture of alcoholic drinks.

Other Crops.—Annually 37,000,000 pounds of leaf indigo, 100,000,000 pounds of leaf tobacco, 16,000,000 pounds of hemp, 6,000,000 pounds of rape seed, and 5,000,000 pounds of cotton are among the other leading productions of Japan proper. Indigo is used in the newly developed dye industry for dying cotton piece goods for export. The tobacco cultivation is under the protection of the government tobacco monopoly, which supervises production and regulates the import and export of tobacco.

Silk.—Sericulture plays almost as important a part as rice in the economic scheme of Japan, and, indeed, were it not for the profit derived from this subsidiary occupation, the average Japanese farmer would be barely able to maintain himself. By rearing the silk worms in spring and autumn, the income of the farmer is doubled. Sericulture is essentially a household industry and has seldom succeeded when conducted on a basis of large-scale operations, and the cheap labor of Japan has been the underlying element of its successful development. Through strict regulation on the part of the Government, the diseases of the silk worm, which have caused such havoc in the Chinese industry, have been practically eradicated. About 80 per cent of the Japanese raw silk production is designed for coarse yarns for the American market. The Japanese cocoons are as yet lacking in uniformity and cannot produce the finer filaments which are at present supplied by France and Italy. The Shinshu district in Nagano prefecture is the leading silk district in Japan, although Koshu and Joshu are noted for hand reeling. In the larger districts 31 families usually form a group which is provided with a common reeling shop where silk produced by each family is combined into one large hank or reel and sent to the head establishment of the district where they are carefully graded according to luster, number of defects, and strength and sent to Yokohama for sale. Japanese women are much more skilful reelers than Chinese and produce much less waste silk. Japanese total production of raw silk for 1917 was 56,000,000 pounds, and of waste silk 24,000,000 pounds. In the same year 257,000 bales of silk were exported, about 90 per cent to the United States. The silk culture in Japan has been afforded the fullest and most scientific encouragement on the part of the Government, which has established experiment stations for investigating every phase of silk culture from the growing of the mulberry trees to the testing of the finished product for export. Under the stimulus of this encouragement, the demand for Japanese silk has increased tremendously and, as the price has kept pace with the price of other textiles in their upward trend during the war, the result was an unprecedented profit for the producer of Japanese silk.

Tea.—In contrast with the development of silk culture in Japan, the tea industry has remained almost stationary, principally because of the formidable rivalry of Ceylon and Chinese teas. The cost of production is higher in Japan than in India, due to the lack of labor saving appliances but, because of their peculiar flavor, Japanese teas still retain a strong hold on the American market. The main tea producing district of Japan is Shizuoka, although the recuring is carried on in Yokohama, from which port and from Shimizu most of the tea is shipped. In 1917 87,000,000 pounds of tea were produced, practically all of which were confined to four grades of green tea.

Pastoral Industry.—The native stocks of horses in Japan were of Mongolian breed, and these were cross-bred with Persian horses some three centuries ago. In 1917 there were 1,500,000 horses in Japan, about 50 per cent of which were of native breeds. The native breeding horses are usually most numerous in the northern part of the main island where the climate makes rice culture impossible. In Hokkaido, where agricultural conditions resemble those of Canada and the United States, horses are most numerous.

Cattle.—Cattle were originally used in Japan solely as beasts of burden but, as in the case of horses, the native breed is gradually disappearing and is being replaced by imported cattle, mainly from Australia and from England. The raising of cattle is being encouraged by the Government largely for the purpose of developing the tanning industry. The total number of cattle in Japan in 1917 was 1,300,000.

Sheep.—The great difficulty experienced in getting a sufficient supply of wool from Australia during the war has strongly impressed the Japanese Government with the necessity of encouraging sheep raising at home. In 1918 a fund was provided for the importation of 1,500 sheep from England and the United States, which were to be distributed among the Government stations and in private pastures. It was further provided to import 1,000 sheep every year thereafter and to take steps to popularize the sheep raising industry among the native farmers as a subsidiary trade. The program contemplates making Japan self-supporting in wool in 10 years. In 1917 there were only 3,300 sheep in all Japan.

Poultry Farming.—Poultry farming has not attained any particular development and Japan has been dependent largely upon China for a supply of eggs. Only 1,150,000 eggs are produced annually. An import tariff on eggs was placed in 1902, and this has gradually been raised to 50 per cent. The Government has established an experiment station near Tokyo where imported fowls are raised and eggs sold at cost in an endeavor to encourage the home industry.

Dairying and Meat Preserving.—Dairying is insignificant in Japan, as the Japanese use very little milk, the soya bean providing a substitute for cooking purposes and bean curd a substitute for butter. With the advent of the European some fifty years ago, the use of butter was introduced, and its manufacture is now carried on in Hokkaido for foreigners, but the use of dairy products and meat among the Japanese is small.

Fruits.—Fruit culture has recently shown a marked activity in Japan. Formerly there was no great need felt for fruits because the people abstained from the use of meat. With the increase in meat eating the demand for fruit is growing and orchards have been planted adjacent to many large towns and on hillsides not suitable for rice culture. The principal fruits are persimmons, which are grown extensively, though seldom in orchards; plums, which are used for pickling in conjunction with native foods; and peaches. The famous cherry trees of Japan bear no fruit, and are famed only for their flowers. Fruit bearing cherry trees are being cultivated in some sections.

Mines and Mining.—The principal mineral production of Japan is copper, which is found in the central mountains of the main island. The production in 1916 was about 120,000 tons. In 1917 494,000 tons of iron were mined and 26,000,000 tons of coal. Also 225,000 troy ounces of gold were produced and 7,500 tons of antimony. Other minerals are silver, lead, manganese, and sulphur. The present coal producing districts in Japan are the northern corner of the island of Formosa and the northern and southwestern section of Kyushu. Korea is also a very important coal producing state. The principal coal fields besides these are in Hokkaido. The future development of the iron mining industry in Japan must take place in Manchuria and in Korea, as the iron resources of the islands are very limited. Petroleum is found in Echigo Province, although the supply does not exceed more than half of the total demand of the Empire.

Fisheries.—The fisheries of Japan have long been one of the most important industries. The principal marine products are herring, sardines, cuttle fish, and mackerel, while the cultivation of oyster beds has been given great attention in recent years. Seal fishing, which was formerly a leading industry of Hokkaido and Saghalien, has recently been prohibited by international agreement. The canning of crabs and other shell fish has in recent years formed an important part of the industrial life of the northern islands. In addition to the fishing in Japanese waters, much revenue has been obtained from fishing in neighboring waters, and this is particularly true of Russian territory, Canada, and California. The noted whaling grounds along the coast of Japan, which were formerly monopolized by Russian and Korean whalers, are now almost entirely in the hands of Japanese. The regulation of the whaling industry by the Government and the limiting of any single undertaking to thirty boats has had the effect of encouraging the industry among a large class of individuals. The use of motor boats and steam trawlers has been a great boon to the development of the Japanese fishing industry.

Forests.—Fifty-four per cent of the total area of Japan proper is covered with forests. Trees grow unusually well, favored by a temperate climate and a plentiful supply of moisture. The islands of Formosa and Kyushu provide both tropical and subtropical species. The yield of Japanese forests in 1915 was valued at $18,000,000, of which $7,500,000 worth was cryptomerias' lumber, $4,500,000 worth, pine, and $1,500,000 worth, cypress. The main use of forest products in industry is as boards for tea chests, railway cross ties, and match sticks. Japan also uses 200,000 tons of wood pulp annually in the manufacture of paper which is now practically all provided by the forests of Hokkaido and Saghalien. Formosa is the world's supplier of camphor, the annual yield being 10,000,000 pounds.

Manufacturing Industries

The principal manufacturing industries of Japan in point of capital employed are (1) the electrical industry, (2) the cotton spinning, (3) the gas industry, (4) shipbuilding, (5) machine manufacturing, (6), the paper industry, (7) chemicals, (8) dyestuffs, (9) brewing, (10) arts and crafts, (11) pottery, (12) lacquer, (13) celluloid, (14) glass, (15) matches, (16) sugar, and (17) miscellaneous industries. The total capital invested in manufacturing at the end of 1917 was $535,000,000.

The Electrical Industry.—The presence of enormous horse power for hydro-electric developments in the short, swift streams of Japan has led to the growth of the electrical industry, and electricity is now in use throughout most of the communities in the island. In 1916, 472 separate electrical enterprises were supplying power with a total kilowatt capacity of 420,000. The surplus capital which has flowed to Japan from high silk prices, high freight rates and war production has led to a boom in hydro-electric development and in 1917 497 enterprises were listed with 475,000 kilowatt capacity, and 82 others with 460,000 kilowatt capacity were contemplated.

The Cotton Spinning Industry.—The raw cotton used in the cotton spinning industry comes chiefly from India, the United States, and from China, the short staple cotton of India and China being mixed with the long staple of the United States. The yarns produced are generally of the coarser grades, due to the low standard of living in Japan and China, the principal markets. About half the 3,165,000 spindles are producing counts of 28 and below, while a third are producing from 38–60 counts. The lack of uniformity in Japanese spinning is gradually disappearing with the formation of larger mills by amalgamation. Five large companies practically control the cotton spinning business of Japan, and the export of their products is in the hands of three or four large selling agencies.

The Gas Industry.—The growth of hydro-electric development has gradually encroached upon the gas industry, and with the sharp advance in the price of gas-making materials, with rates under strict Government control and consequently inelastic, the result has been a gradual decline of the industry. The growing importance of the by-products of the industry such as coal tar, coke and ammonia have tended to encourage investors somewhat, but on the whole the outlook for the industry is not bright.

Shipbuilding.—The war was a great boon to Japanese shipowners and gave a decided impetus to the shipbuilding industry. Even the scarcity of steel plates, for which Japan was dependent upon the United States, did not discourage Japanese shipbuilders. From 1913 to 1917 the steamer tonnage increased from 1,513,000 gross to 1,827,000 gross, and the sailing tonnage from 487,000 gross to 696,000 gross. About half of this tonnage was home built and half foreign built. Of the steamer tonnage 1,700,000 tons was of steel and iron construction. Under a five-year subsidy plan $4,000,000 has been appropriated for European steamship lines, $6,500,000 for North American lines, and $700,000 for South American lines. In 1918 there were 57 shipyards capable of building ships of 1,000 tons or over operating on a total paid-up capital of $54,000,000. In the four years ending in 1918 these yards built 233 vessels, representing a million gross tons of steamers on domestic and foreign orders. In 1919 alone 137 vessels totalling 627,000 tons were scheduled to be built.

Cotton, Silk, and Woolen Weaving.—Considerable advance has been made in the weaving of silk goods and also in the manufacture of cotton braids and piece goods. The woven silk goods manufactured in Japan are known as *habutae,* and a large business is now being done in silk and cotton fabrics, which are produced annually to the amount of about $18,000,000, chiefly for consumption at home. The woolen industry gained an impetus during the war because the Japanese factories were called upon to supply the Russian army with uniforms. The manufacture of muslin and hemp fabrics is also carried on to a large extent.

Machine Manufacturing.—The Japanese are not naturally skilled mechanics, and their delicate physique also acts as a bar to their complete development as a nation of machine builders. In the manufacture of practically every kind of modern machinery some progress has been made, particularly in dynamos, water wheels, telephone apparatus, weaving machines, cars and locomotives, etc. The development of the industry is hampered by an insufficient supply of iron, lack of skilled labor, and an infant industry striving to hold its own against strong competition from the West. With no foreign markets for Japanese-made machines as yet, its production cannot be undertaken on a large scale, and the cost of production is consequently high.

The Manufacture of Paper.—The manufacture of paper, both news print and Japanese native paper, is of particular importance since paper is used in Japan for a great many purposes to which cloth is put in this country. The use of paper handkerchiefs, napkins, and in some rural districts, paper windows, and paper doors in all houses, lend significance to this industry. The large amount of pulp formerly imported has been two-thirds superseded by Japanese pulp produced in Saghalien.

The Chemical and Dyestuff Industries.—The development of the chemical industry has gone hand in hand with the development of the gas industry, and the by-products such as coal tar, which has been used in the manufacture of dyes, have furnished a valuable source of raw material. Aside from sulphur, which has been produced in large quantity, the chemical industry in Japan has been mostly dependent upon imports of crude chemicals from abroad. Many new chemical factories were started during the war for the manufacture of glycerine, sulphuric acid, and bromine. Phosphorus and potassium chlorate for matches, supplied from foreign countries until a few years ago, are now made in Japan. Important developments in electrochemical industries have taken place. In 1917 2,500 factories employing 141,700 persons were engaged in chemical manufacture.

Brewing.—The brewing of Japanese wine, *sake,* and beer and the manufacture of *soy* have been carried on for some years in Japan and four large breweries now supply the total demand for beer. *Soy* and *sake,* made from rice, are manufactured practically throughout the islands, although the manufacture of beer is centered principally at Hokkaido.

Arts and Crafts.—The introduction of Buddhism and its wide diffusion marks the real dawn of arts and crafts in Japan at about 610 A. D. Wood carving had attained a very high level of perfection in 700 A. D. and metal casting had also made remarkable progress at this same date, as attested by the Buddhist image at Nara. Printing on silk, largely an imitation of Chinese style, was introduced in 800 A. D. The effect which this early familiarity with wood carving and painting has had upon the industrial development of Japan is quite remarkable. Even the introduction of Western painting since 1868 and the attempt of the Japanese artists to adapt the Western style to suit the native conditions has not lessened the effect which this long intimacy with these arts has had upon the deftness and artistic sense of the Japanese.

Pottery.—Since ancient times Japan has excelled in the manufacture of pottery, but with the demand for cheaper grades from abroad the ancient skill of Japanese pottery manufacturers has been sacrificed to the commercialization of the industry. The production of pottery in Japan in 1916 was valued at $13,000,000, and the exports at $7,000,000.

Lacquer Wares.—The manufacture of lacquered wares has increased in late years, due to the large demand from abroad. Trays, cake baskets, cigarette boxes, and bowls are among the principal articles of production of this industry. Lacquered wares were made to the value of $5,000,000 in 1916.

The Manufacture of Celluloid.—The manufacture of celluloid from camphor has gained prominence in very recent years and the demand of the celluloid manufacturers upon the Japanese camphor supply has led to serious embarrassment of celluloid manufacturers in this country who depend entirely upon Japan for their supply of camphor. The manufacture of celluloid toys to replace those formerly supplied by Germany has gained great headway during the war.

The Glass Industry.—The glass industry has reached important proportions during the war and much of the glass trade of the South Seas and Far Eastern tropics has been diverted from Europe to Japan. The output of this industry was worth $8,000,000 in 1916. The center of the industry is in Osaka. Sheet glass and plate glass and glass tableware are the chief products.

Matches.—Matches were produced in 1916 to the extent of 50,000,000 gross, 41,000,000 of which were exported. The plentiful supply of wood and sulphur makes the match industry of Japan a particularly profitable one.

The Refining of Sugar.—The refining of sugar has reached important dimensions in Japan, the sugar of Formosa being brought to the main island for refining and shipment to the Chinese markets.

Other Industries.—Flour milling, rubber manufacture, the manufacture of vegetable oils, straw and chip braid, are all developments of the last few years, while the matting industry, in which Japan formerly excelled, has fallen off somewhat, due to Chinese competition. The manufacture of brushes has undergone rapid development, the bristles coming from China, and the product selling in the United States and Europe.

The Future of Japanese Industry.—In the present economic development of Japan the necessity for developing her manufacturing industries is becoming more and more apparent. It is realized that, with a population growing at the rate of 600,000 per year and with no suitable lands to which this population may emigrate, the only economic salvation of Japan is in becoming a strong manufacturing nation. While the low standard of living of the people would seem to act favorably toward this development by supplying a large quantity of cheap labor, the net efficiency of the average Japanese laborer is estimated to be from one-fourth to one-sixth of that of the foreign laborer. This is especially true in those newer industries which have sprung up in recent years and in which the Japanese are not favored by the accumulated knowledge of technique and the use of machinery of past generations. It seems probable, therefore, that the development of Japanese industries will be merely along such lines as require deft and skilful individual work, and not in such industries as the iron and steel industry which depends for its success upon large-scale production and heavy manual labor. While efforts are being made to make Japan self-sufficient in many lines of industrial enterprise and while the war, by shutting off the Far East from the normal channels of trade, had a tendency to foster this development, it is thought that with the return to normal conditions many of the industries which have sprung up in Japan during this period will give way to foreign competition, especially in those lines where the foreign manufacturers are favored by long experience and a laboring class peculiarly adapted to the industry in question. Japan has a distinct place to fill in the industrial world, but that place is decidedly not in competition with large-scale industries which have been successfully continued for many years in Europe and in the United States.

Korea

Korea was annexed to Japan in 1910 by treaty between the two nations. It is now administered by a Japanese Governor General. The total population of Korea is 14,000,000, of which only 210,000 are Japanese and 12,000 foreigners. Korea, therefore, has not proven an outlet for the surplus Japanese population, the standard of living being lower than that of the Japanese. The peninsula, therefore, is not offering an attractive field for colonization, Agriculture furnishes occupation for 80 per cent of the people. The rudimentary cultivation, the absence of drainage and irrigation, and the natural indolence of the natives are the main drawbacks to the agricultural development of the peninsula. But 56 per cent of the total area is fit for cultivation, leaving 44 per cent which is designated as waste land. These waste lands are the direct result of deforestation, which has been recklessly carried on for many years, up to the time of Japanese possession. Under Japanese control experimental stations have been established and better qualities of seeds have been distributed, and better methods of agriculture have been introduced by the establishment of model farms. Livestock farming has been introduced also, and cotton planting has been carried on on a large scale. There is also a government horticultural garden, and numerous sericulture stations for the improvement of the silk crop.

The principal products are rice, wheat, soya beans, ginseng, cotton, hemp, and tobacco. The raising of silk and the pastoral industry are still in process of development.

Rice.—The yield of rice is about 50,000,000 bushels annually, and that of soya beans about 10,000,000 bushels. These products supply the domestic consumption, and leave about $3,000,000 worth of rice and $2,000,000 worth of beans for export. Annually 25,000,000 bushels of wheat and barley are also produced. Among the other crops are 10,000,000 bushels of millet and 3,000,000 bushels of small red beans.

Cotton Cultivation.—Since 1906 the Japanese Government has made every effort to increase the production of American upland cotton, and seeds have been distributed broadcast to cultivators since 1910. The results have been highly satisfactory, and in 1918 250,000 bales of cotton out of 102,000,000 pounds production, were exported to Japan. Attempts have also been made to increase the cultivation of tobacco. Tobacco growing in Korea is largely in the hands of Japanese agriculturists.

Fruits and Vegetables.—The native Koreans have paid very little attention in the past to the cultivation of fruits and vegetables, but the Japanese have recently introduced pears, apples, and grapes, as well as chestnuts and persimmons. These fruits find a ready market in Japan proper, and the less intensive cultivation of Korean soil for rice as well as the cooler climate add to the growing importance of this industry. Ginseng is produced in large quantities in Korea for the Chinese market. The value of this product, which, among the Chinese, is supposed to have great medicinal value, reaches about $1,500,000 annually; the word ginseng meaning "form of man," and is derived from the resemblance of the root to the human body. This fact undoubtedly led to its popularity among the Chinese, although its medicinal value is nil. Beekeeping is carried on throughout Korea, and honey as a substitute for sugar has been in use for many years.

Silk Culture.—Sericulture is still in a very backward state, and the domestic production does not meet the demand, a great amount of silk being imported from China. Formerly very little attention was paid to the choice of eggs, and little improvement in the methods of rearing was noted. Since 1910 improved methods have been introduced by the Japanese, and spinning reels and looms have been distributed by the Government in an effort to stimulate the production of silk. The total cocoon crop, however, amounts to only 100,000 bushels, while the number of families engaged is only 111,000.

Pastoral Enterprise.—Stock farming is carried on as a subsidiary enterprise by a great number of farms, the cattle being particularly well known for their large size and good quality, a great many of them being exported to Japan and Siberia. Annually 5,000,000 pounds of hides are also exported. There are now in Korea about 900,000 cattle, 600,000 swine, 40,000 horses, and 3,000,000 fowls. A model stock farm receives an annual subsidy from the Government and is constantly undertaking to improve the breed of cattle. The Oriental Development Company was formed in Japan in 1908 for the purpose of engaging in agriculture, undertaking the colonization of Korea by Japanese emigrants. The operations of this company have been fairly successful, although not on a scale anticipated by its organizers.

Mining.—The total mineral production of Korea amounts to about $6,000,000, of which gold is valued at $5,000,000. The other minerals of importance are coal and iron ores. Gold is now mined by American companies, British, and Japanese. Both alluvial and quartz deposits are worked, the introduction of the land dredge in the American mines being particularly successful.

Fisheries.—The seas adjacent to the Graham Peninsula abound in marine products, which are exploited mainly by Japanese fishermen. Sardines, sharks, herring, cod, salmon, and mackerel are the principal food fish. The whale industry is carried on entirely by Japanese fishermen from the first of October to the end of April. About 400 seals were captured yearly. A marine product of much importance is salt, which is produced to the extent of about 150,000 tons annually, furnishing a livelihood to about 7,000 people. The climate of Korea being dry and favorable to rapid evaporation, the industry is particularly important. The brine is pumped from wells near the coast and allowed to evaporate in the sun. Until quite recently salt was obtained exclusively in Korea by the boiling process, but the salt produced in China by evaporation soon made it necessary to adopt this process in Korea also.

Forests.—The marked difference in temperature between the north and south of the peninsula leads to a wide variation in forest products. In the extreme south box trees, oak, and bamboo are the principal products; in the northern forests, larch and pine trees. The results of indiscriminate deforestation have been noticed in the frequency of floods and the bare hillsides, but since 1911 seeds and young trees have been planted in certain districts by the Japanese Government, and extensive plans have been made for reforestation in many of the worst districts.

Manufacturing Industries.—Several hundred years ago Korean pewter and copper goods were of very high quality and enjoyed a well deserved reputation, but in recent years these industries have virtually ceased to exist. Some of the industries which have been undertaken under Japanese rule are printing, brick manufacture, and brewing. At the present time, however, the industrial development of Korea is largely in the household or domestic stage, and many families still carry on crude weaving and the manufacture of earthenware. There are 600 households engaged in earthenware manufacture, but their products do not enter into the exports of the peninsula. Colored paper for export to China is one of the important products of Korea. This is made according to native methods. Metal products such as pots, pans, and braziers, and iron tools for agriculture and building are produced in small quantities. The hand weaving of cotton, hemp, and silk, amounting to about 2,000,000 dollars, is a subsidiary occupation of the farmers. Tissue manufacture, however, is crude and the product does not enter into the export trade, since the production is not enough to supply the home demand. The custom which requires long periods of mourning and that the mourners dress in white cotton has led to a very great demand for white cotton fabric, and this is imported from Japan and England to the amount of about $3,000,000 annually.

The occupation of Korea by Japan has had the effect of emphasizing certain very fundamental economic laws. In the first place, Japanese emigrants have had no desire to compete with the lower standard of living which they have encountered in Korea, and have turned their attention to South America and Mexico, where there is more opportunity for them to improve their condition. In the second place, the Koreans themselves have shown little disposition to be improved by Japanese governmental regulations, and their past history as a hermit nation, shut off from foreign intercourse, has made them, as a people, peculiarly impervious to suggestions or innovations from outside. The economic reforms and progress which have been made under Japanese rule, therefore, are largely on the surface and do not extend very far into the economic structure of the people. In a way this experiment in colonization has taught the Japanese that it is sometimes more difficult to conquer a passively inactive people than to undersell and underbid the labor of a higher civilization than their own.

Formosa

The Island of Formosa was ceded to Japan by China in 1895, together with the Pescadores, a chain of 64 islands extending from the mainland to Formosa. The climate of Formosa though tropical is somewhat more temperate than most districts in this same latitude; its chief characteristic being a comparatively long, hot season from May to October, with a very plentiful rainfall during the summer and autumn and many severe storms. In 1910 the population numbered 3,300,000, of which 14,000 were foreigners. This is an increase of not quite 50 per cent over the total population in 1900. There are 11 large cities in Formosa, each with a population of over 10,000, the largest being Taihoku, and the second Tainan. The chief port is Tamsui. The soil of Formosa is extremely fertile, and rice, sugar cane, tea, sweet potatoes, indigo, and jute are produced in great abundance, particularly in the western section of the Island. The eastern and central sections of the Island are still undeveloped, the latter being still inhabited by several thousand head-hunters, whom Japan has made every effort to bring under control.

Rice.—Fifty-five per cent of the entire land under cultivation is planted in rice, and two harvests are the rule where proper irrigation is afforded. The production of rice had increased from 15,000,000 bushels in 1900 to 22,000,000 bushels in 1911; an increase of about 46 per cent. Formerly Formosan rice was exported to foreign countries, but the demand from Japan proper has been so great in recent years that this trade has practically ceased.

Sugar.—The raising of sugar in Formosa dates from the sixteenth century, when the Island was under the influence of the Dutch, and the manufacture of sugar was carried on in a crude way. Sugar has grown best in the southern half of Formosa, and since the cession of the island to Japan the manufacture of sugar has become a very promising industry. The production of sugar increased from 800,000 tons in 1902 to 2,600,000 tons in 1911. Practically all of the sugar is exported to Japan in crude form and there refined.

Tea.—Tea is chiefly grown in the northern part of the Island of Formosa, about 66,000 tons being produced annually. It is exported principally from the port of Tamsui. The famous Oolong tea is the product of Formosa. About $12,000,000 worth is exported annually. There are four grades of tea, maturing in the spring, summer, autumn, and winter. The most important of these are the grades maturing in the spring and summer, constituting over two-thirds of the total product.

Other Crops.—Sweet potatoes are the most important foodstuff next to rice in Formosa. The annual yield of the two crops amounts to 500,000 tons. Beans are cultivated in large quantities for oil extracting purposes, the yield amounting to 800,000 bushels. Soya beans, peas, and pulse are grown generally. Over 15,000 tons of indigo have been produced, but due to the rapid growth of the coal tar dye industry the production of indigo has fallen off. China grass and jute for weaving purposes are other important crops, the former being used in the manufacture of grass rugs, and the latter for the making of burlap. Numerous kinds of rushes are also grown for various weaving purposes.

The Pastoral Industry.—Stock farming is still in a very undeveloped state. The chief domestic animals are the water buffalo and the zebu, both of which are used for tilling the soil and as beasts of burden. In recent years superior breeds of cattle and swine have been imported from abroad, and the Government has endeavored to encourage stock farming. There are practically no horses in Formosa and very little poultry.

Forestry.—About 64 per cent of the entire area of the Island is covered with a luxuriant growth of conifers, broad-leaved trees, and bamboos. In the mountainous districts, which extend through the center of the Island from north to south, there are large virgin forests. In some sections deforestation under Chinese rule has caused much damage, but the Japanese Government is endeavoring to remedy this evil by wide spread planting of trees. Camphor trees abound in all sections of the Island, and camphor oil is manufactured in the northern districts. In order to protect the camphor trees from rapid exhaustion, the purchase and sale of camphor and camphor oil was made a government monopoly in 1899, and the reforestation of camphor forests is now being undertaken by the Government. About 6,000,000 pounds of camphor and 7,000,000 pounds of camphor oil are produced annually, the great bulk of which is now manufactured into celluloid in Osaka, although about 30 per cent of the total output is allotted to celluloid manufacturers in the United States by the Government. During the period of the war the value of all food crops increased to such an extent that the cutting of camphor became unprofitable and a great many of the natives abandoned the industry. The result was a decided decrease in production, and in the proportion allotted to manufacturers in this country.

Fisheries.—Fisheries are located principally on the western, or Pacific, coast, and are not of an important nature. The principal catches are sardines, mullet, and shark, the shark fins being a great delicacy in the Chinese market. Salt is produced by a natural evaporation of sea water at a very small cost, and, under favorable climatic conditions, the production of salt on the southern and western coasts is quite large. Annually 75,000 tons are produced.

Coal, Gold, Sulphur and Other Minerals.—The principal mineral production is coal. Petroleum also promises to become an important product in the future. Sulphur deposits are located along the volcanic beds of mountains in the north. Gold occurs in veins and in alluvial deposits.

Manufacturing.—Manufacturing is confined almost entirely to the making of domestic utensils and agricultural implements of a crude nature. Practically all of the manufactured goods required are imported from Japan proper.

SAGHALIEN

The southern half of the Island of Saghalien was ceded to Japan by Russia after the Russian-Japanese war in 1905. High cliffs compose the whole coast line and good anchorages are rare. The port of Odomari presents the best anchorage on the Island. The seas are frozen from November to April, and coasting service is almost entirely suspended during those months. The Island is also frequently enveloped in dense fogs. The population is 30,000, of which 28,000 are Japanese and 2,000 Russians. About one-half of the population is engaged in fishery and one-half in agriculture, which are the only important industries. The herring fisheries are the most profitable. The greatest catches occur far off the western coast. The use of nets is not allowed within certain distances from the mainland, and stringent regulations are enforced to protect the fishing grounds. Trout and salmon are next in importance to herring, while cod fishing has reached a very profitable basis in the last few years. About 26,000 cans of crabs are shipped annually from Saghalien through Japan proper to the United States. The total value of the catch of all fish amounts to about $3,000,000. The larger quantity of herring is sent to Japan as fertilizer.

Forestry.—Rich forests cover about 80 per cent of the area of Japanese Saghalien, and most of these have never been touched by man. The conifers are used mainly for building purposes and mining. They are also an important contribution to the pulp supply for Japanese paper manufacture. The broad-leaved trees are used in Japan proper for the manufacture of wood shavings and matches. Turpentine, resin, wood spirit, tar, and pitch are also obtained from these forests.

Since the occupation of Saghalien by Japan, the production of agricultural crops has greatly increased. The sparse population of Russian exiles had done little toward agricultural improvement of the land. Annually 45,000 bushels of oats and 15,000 bushels of barley, together with 4,000 tons of potatoes and 400 tons of hay are now produced. There are about 1,000 horses, 1,000 cattle, and about 500 swine on the Island.

Fisheries and Mining.—Herring fishing is the principal industry of the Island. The principal mineral product of Saghalien is coal of a very good quality and in great abundance, the seams being not only regular but very thick, extending for some 60 miles in the northern part of the Island, and from one to three miles wide. Alluvial gold is found in the beds of some of the rivers, but not in very great abundance. Limestone is obtained in large quantities, as well as granite and marble. Iron pyrites and gold are of minor importance.

Questions

1. What is the agrarian policy of Japan? How has the development of industries affected this policy?
2. Discuss Japan's rice production. How are wheat and barley used?
3. Describe the place of the soya bean in the Japanese diet.
4. Discuss the Japanese silk industry giving reasons for its success.
5. What are the principal mineral productions of Japan?
6. What part do Japanese fisheries play in national economy? Forests?

7. Name the five principal industries in order of their importance.
8. Where does Japan obtain her raw cotton and where are the principal markets for Japanese cotton yarn?
9. Discuss the Japanese shipbuilding development during the war.
10. What general considerations affect the development of Japan as a manufacturing nation?
11. Describe the agricultural development of Korea.
12. Discuss three principal agricultural products.
13. Why has Japanese colonization of Korea been unsuccessful?
14. Discuss the three principal crops of Formosa.
15. What are the resources of Saghalien?

CHAPTER VII

CREDIT METHODS AND MARKET ANALYSIS OF CHINA AND JAPAN

China

The general manner of trading with China is the same as that employed in other parts of the world, but the chief distinction between the China trade and that of other countries lies in the details and methods used in the local distribution of goods and the financing involved. The foreign merchant never comes in contact with the real purchaser of the goods, partly because of the language difficulty and partly because of the strongly organized guild and compradore system of merchandising. Until early in the nineteenth century all foreign trade was carried on through 13 *hong* merchants at Canton, who were nothing more than brokers. Their transactions extended to both the selling of Chinese products to the foreigner and the purchase of foreign goods for the interior merchants. Their monopoly of the trade was obtained by bribing the local officials at Canton. When trade was opened with other ports by treaty, the foreign merchants who had established connections with these *hong* merchants, and who had no way of judging the standing of the individual interior merchants, continued to deal through brokers of other ports such as Shanghai, Foochow, Amoy, and Tientsin, whom they employed to handle the credit end of their businesses and to whom they gave the responsibility of guaranteeing and enforcing payments on sales of foreign merchandise and of enforcing delivery of Chinese produce which they had bought. These men came to be known as compradores, and the compradore system is in effect in China to the present day.

Exchange and the Compradore System.—The real necessity for the compradore system in Chinese merchandising is bound up in the subject of exchange. The local dealer buys his goods on a silver basis. The foreign importer wishes to sell his goods on a gold basis in order to be relieved of exchange considerations. Of course, the local foreign banks in China perform a useful function here in selling exchange "forward" and their expert knowledge of finance and the silver market permits them to do so with considerable profit, but occasional loss. But the exchange factor permits the broker to perform a very valuable part in the transaction. S. R. Wagel in his *Finance in China* describes the following transaction as a case in point:

> The (local Chinese) merchant says to the dealer (broker) in the treaty ports that he wants to buy so many pieces of cloth at so much per piece. The dealer goes to the foreign merchant and makes inquiries. The foreign merchant gives his price in sterling, *i.e.,* a total of the manufacturer's cost, freight, insurance, and other costs together with a certain profit for himself. The dealer calculates on selling the Chinese merchant's silver at a certain exchange quotation of a rate being furnished by the bank at the period when the goods will be delivered, and arrives at the amount of silver he will have to pay. If this price is less than the price offered by the merchant who wants that quantity of goods, he at once settles the bargain with the foreign merchant and tells the Chinese merchant that such and such goods will be delivered to him on payment of a certain amount (in silver) at the due date.

In some instances the dealer in the large port may have different ideas about how silver will react in the next four months required for delivery of the goods than has the bank and may desire to take a chance on silver being higher (and gold being lower, consequently) than the rate quoted by the bank. In such a case he will close the deal without selling forward the silver which the local Chinese merchant contracts to turn over in exchange for the goods, and if he is lucky and silver goes up, he makes an additional profit, which the bank otherwise would have taken for assuming a similar risk. The reason the banks can "speculate" in this way is because they both buy and sell silver forward in large quantities every day to cover import and export transactions, and the only real risk they assume is on the difference between their total purchases and their total sales, which combined with their superior knowledge of the general financial situation makes them assume less risk than is assumed by a dealer who perhaps stakes his fortune on a single gamble in the future price of silver.

Guilds in Export and Import Trade.—Guilds in China play a greater part in the export trade than they do in the import trade. The silk and tea guilds, for instance, are effective bodies for regulating the quality, quantity, and price of these commodities, and while their rules apply principally to domestic affairs, their influence upon foreign trade is very potent. This is especially true in the regulation which the guilds maintain over the commercial morals of their members. Much of the proverbial honesty of the Chinese merchant is due more to rigid guild supervision which he cannot evade than to any inherent qualities, for Chinese are only human. But even at that there is nothing in guild control which prevents a member from taking full advantage of any contract which he may have been successful in persuading the other party to sign, and the rule of *caveat emptor* is perhaps more eloquently applied in China than in any other part of the world.

Cotton Goods.—China's principal import is cotton goods, and in 1918 $180,000,000 worth of this commodity, representing 27 per cent of China's total import trade of $662,000,000, was brought through the Maritime Customs. While this showed a gain of $28,000,000 in value over the cotton goods imports of 1913, in actual volume there was a decrease of from 50 per cent to 75 per cent. This was due largely to the establishment of looms in China. In the single item of Indian cotton yarns the volume fell off from 177,000,000 pounds to 48,000,000 pounds in the five years, while the value decreased only from $26,000,000 to $19,000,000. In Japanese yarns the volume decreased from 173,000,000 pounds to 99,000,000 pounds, but the value actually rose from $23,000,000 to $42,000,000. Japanese cotton cloth showed a large gain during the five-year period from 13,000,000 yards to 83,000,000 yards and a corresponding increase in value from $600,000 to $7,000,000. Japanese plain, gray shirtings showed an actual decrease in volume from 3,000,000 to 2,000,000 pieces, and a doubling in value from $7,000,000 to $13,000,000. The war cut the import of English white shirtings from 4,500,000 pieces to 1,500,000 pieces, although high prices held the actual value decrease to about $3,000,000 under the 1915 figure of $14,000,000. Although Japanese jeans increased from 86,000 pieces to 1,900,000 pieces, the value increased in even greater proportion, from $200,000 to $10,000,000. English plain, gray shirtings were reduced from 4,000,000 pieces to 690,000 pieces, and the value reduced from $9,000,000 to $4,000,000, while Japanese plain, gray shirtings increased five times in volume to 940,000 pieces, while the value increased ten times to $5,000,000.

Metals and Minerals.—The total imports under this head more than doubled in value from 1913 to 1918, the figures for the two dates being $21,000,000 and $45,000,000, respectively. Copper ingots and slabs represented $5,000,000 of the 1918 total, a gain of $1,000,000 during the period. This, however, represented a falling off of about 10,000,000 pounds from the 1913 figure of 26,000,000 pounds. Tinned plates, which also decreased in volume from 48,000,000 pounds to 42,000,000 pounds, increased in value almost threefold, or from $1,700,000 to $5,000,000. The imports of new iron and mild steel bars and sheets and plates were each worth $3,800,000, a threefold increase in value and they also showed a one-third decrease in volume, falling from 79,000,000 pounds to 51,000,000 pounds, and from 47,000,000 pounds to 30,000,000 pounds, respectively. In the case of pipes and tubes, of which the value was also $3,800,000 in 1918, there was a fivefold increase in volume over 1913, from 8,000,000 to 38,000,000 pounds, and a 12 times increase in value. The imports of bamboo steel, steel bars, hoops, sheets, and plates showed a substantial increase in volume from 18,000,000 pounds to 25,000,000 pounds and an even greater increase in value from $500,000 to $3,000,000. Nails and rivets doubled in value from $1,000,000 to $2,000,000, while the volume of 44,000,000 pounds imported in 1913 dropped 25 per cent. Rails showed an increase in volume from 39,000,000 pounds to 44,000,000 pounds and a fourfold increase in value from $600,000 to $2,400,000. Tin in slabs fell from 7,000,000 pounds to half that but rose in value from $1,700,000 to $2,000,000. Galvanized iron sheets fell from 30,000,000 pounds to 9,000,000 pounds, but the value remained steady at $1,000,000, while galvanized wire increased from 8,000,000 to 10,000,000 pounds and the value rose four times to $1,000,000. Other important items were brass bars, sheets and wire, lead pigs and bars, iron hoops, and pig iron.

Sundries.—The largest item under this head was refined sugar whose import rose from 350,000,000 pounds in 1913 to 550,000,000 pounds in 1918, with an increase in value of from $10,000,000 to $42,000,000. In addition to this, white sugar remained stationary in volume of imports at 250,000,000 pounds, but doubled in value to $14,000,000, and brown sugar also remained the same at 300,000,000 pounds, but increased in value from $6,000,000 to $11,000,000.

Cigarettes.—Cigarettes rose in number from 6,000,000

thousands to 9,000,000 thousands, and increased in value from $9,000,000 to $28,000,000.

Rice.—Rice and paddy imports increased in volume from 700,000,000 pounds to 900,000,000 pounds, while the value more than doubled, going from $13,000,000 to $27,000,000.

Munitions.—Arms and munitions showed a gain during the period of from $5,000,000 to $16,000,000.

Coal.—Coal imports jumped in value from $7,000,000 to $15,000,000, although the volume actually decreased from 1,700,000 tons to 1,000,000 tons.

Fish.—Fish and fishery products remained about the same in volume although in value they increased from $9,000,000 to $14,000,000.

Kerosene.—Kerosene oil from the United States showed a falling off of from 112,000,000 to 48,000,000 gallons, but an increase in value of $10,000,000 to $15,000,000, while that from Sumatra increased in volume from 41,000,000 to 48,000,000 gallons and in value from $4,000,000 to $14,000,000.

Leather.—Leather imports ranked next with an increase of 2,000,000 pounds over the 14,000,000 pounds imported in 1913, but rose in value from $5,000,000 to $11,000,000.

Paper.—Paper imports fell from 129,000,000 pounds to 72,000,000 pounds, but increased in value from $4,000,000 to $7,000,000.

Other important imports in 1918 were raw cotton, clothing, tobacco, medicines (including cocaine and morphia), sewing machines, match-making materials, bags of all kinds, and emery and corundum.

The Decline in the Volume of Imports.—An analysis of these figures shows that China's trade during the five years ending December 31, 1918, had fallen off materially in the volume of many important lines of goods brought in. Had shipping facilities and conditions abroad enabled the same amount of goods to be shipped in 1918 as in 1913, it is quite probable that the same conditions would have enabled China to dispose of large quantities of raw materials at high gold prices and an enormous foreign commerce in values, but representing little increase over normal volume would have resulted. But as a result of the war China's commerce has been ingrown, and enormous quantities of home produce, which usually found its way to foreign markets, have been kept at home to replace the food and other commodities which could not be had from abroad. Under these circumstances, with a return to normal conditions, a certain amount of revival of foreign commerce may be expected, but in some lines, such as cotton yarns, with an ever increasing cotton production at home, a steady decline in imports must be expected. As these industries are built up they must gradually and surely raise the standard of living, and instead of China's imports being 27 per cent cotton goods, as in 1918, such goods will be made at home. Then China's every increasing exports of raw materials will purchase semi-luxuries for which there is now no market because of the necessity of importing at high prices from abroad goods to fill the most primitive wants.

Japan

Japan has become so thoroughly Westernized that her methods of financing trade are almost identical with those of Europe, more closely resembling the German financial structure than that of the United States. Moreover, the day of the foreign import merchant in Japan is past, except in a few technical and specialized lines and many strong Japanese combinations, such as Mitsui & Company, now maintain buying agencies of their own in the leading markets of the world. These companies are closely affiliated with the one or two strong banks, particularly the Yokohama Specie Bank, and the Mistui Ginko, whose branches extend to all the principal trade centers. The inter-relation between these great corporations, the banks, and the Japanese Government, is so close that an exceptionally strong position has been gained and held by Japan, especially during the World War.

Raw Materials.—About half of Japan's billion dollar import trade of 1919 was raw materials and the same ratio held good in 1918, when the imports totaled $800,000,000. Of this half a billion dollar import of raw materials 66 per cent or about $333,000,000, was raw cotton which showed an increase of $75,000,000 over 1918. This commodity furnished the greatest single item of Japan's imports.

Oil Cake.—Oil cake for fertilizer represented 13 per cent of the raw material imports, or $67,000,000, an increase of $21,000,000 over 1918.

Wool.—Wool filled six per cent of the raw material imports, or $30,000,000, although the actual increase over 1918 was only $500,000.

Sulphate of Ammonia.—Crude sulphate of ammonia, used for fertilizer manufacture, showed a most phenomenal increase in 1919, going to $13,500,000 from $150,000 in 1918, and covering two and one-half per cent of Japan's raw material imports.

Iron Ore.—Ores, principally iron ore from the Japanese controlled Hanyang iron mines near Hankow in China, showed two per cent of the total raw material imports of $10,000,000, a very slight increase over 1918.

Coal.—Coal imports increased from one and one-half per cent to 1.8 per cent of the raw material imports, the 1919 imports totaling $9,000,000 or almost $2,000,000 more than in 1918. Japan's exports of coal jumped from a value of $16,000,000 in 1918 to $18,900,000 in 1919, or nearly 18 per cent, mostly due to the increase in prices.

Rubber.—Imports of crude India rubber and gutta percha used in the manufacture of rubber goods and insulating materials amounted to 1.7 per cent of the raw material imports, or $8,500,000, showing an increase of $2,000,000 over 1918.

Fibers.—Flax, hemp, jute, etc., suffered a falling off of almost $3,000,000 in 1919, but still represented 1.6 per cent of the imports of raw materials in 1919, or $8,000,000.

Hides.—Hides and skins showed a $1,800,000 gain in 1919 over 1918, the import figures being $7,500,000 the last year or one and one-half per cent of the group figures.

Saltpeter.—Chile saltpeter accounted for 1.3 per cent, or $7,000,000, of the group imports, showing a gain of over a million dollars.

All other raw materials represented a trifle less than 10 per cent of the total raw material imports, or $98,000,000.

Partly Manufactured Materials.—Twenty-three per cent of Japan's total trade in 1919 was in materials for further use in manufacturing, and 33 per cent of this represented iron bars, rods, plates, and sheets which decreased in value from $102,000,000 in 1918 to $78,000,000 in 1919. These were used principally in shipbuilding.

Pig Iron.—Pig iron, ingots, and slabs were 12 per cent of the total imports in this group, also showing a decrease, falling from $32,000,000 in 1918 to $29,000,000 in 1919.

Building Materials.—Construction materials were five per cent of the group imports and showed a gain from $8,000,000 in 1918 to $12,000,000 in 1919. This reflects not only the normal increase in construction incidental to an increasing population and a wider adoption of Western architecture, but an impetus lent to building by the increase in wealth and the establishment of industries.

Caustic Soda.—Caustic soda and soda used for soap and paper manufacture remained normal at $7,000,000 for both 1918 and 1919, being about three per cent of the total group imports.

Iron Pipe.—The same was true of iron pipes and tubes

which showed no great variation in 1919 from the $6,500,000 import value of 1918. These were about three per cent of the total group imports.

Dyes.—Coal tar dye imports showed a slight decrease in 1919 having a value of $5,000,000, or two per cent of the total. The demand had increased but the manufacture of domestic dyes had been more than able to take care of it.

Paper Pulp.—Paper pulp imports increased from $3,000,000 in 1918 to $5,000,000 in 1919 absorbing two per cent of the import trade of this group.

Lead Ingots.—Lead ingots and slabs fell off considerably from $7,000,000 to $5,000,000, and composed only two per cent of the group imports.

Other important imports in this group were tin ingots and slabs, leather, nickel ingots, and grain.

Foodstuffs—Rice, Sugar, and Beans.—Articles classed as food, drink, and tobacco accounted for 16 per cent of Japan's imports and covered a wide variety of foodstuffs, comestibles and semi-luxuries for which Japan's rising standard of living and increasing population provided a larger market than heretofore. The 1919 imports in this group increased exactly 100 per cent over 1918, the total figures for 1919 being $175,000,000.

Rice imports were 46 per cent of the total foodstuff imports, amounting in value to $81,000,000, an increase of $36,000,000 over the preceding year.

Sugar represented 16 per cent of the foodstuff imports with an increased valuation of $12,000,000 over the $17,000,000 of 1918.

Beans and peas, representing 10 per cent of the import total, showed an increase of $7,000,000 over the $10,000,000 of 1918.

Japan's growing dependence upon imported foodstuffs is the natural result of her development as a manufacturing nation, but the Government is giving serious attention to the question of increasing home food production by the more intensive use of fertilizer and other agricultural methods.

Manufactured Goods.—Representing but 11 per cent of the total imports, Japan's 1919 imports of wholly manufactured goods, nevertheless, show a $46,000,000 increase over the $85,000,000 imports in this group for 1918. This is largely accounted for by the large purchases abroad of spinning and other machinery, which is necessary in order to make it possible for Japan to adopt a shorter work day in accordance with the decision of the International Labor Conference. This will entail changing from two shifts of 12 hours each, as in most factories at present, to three shifts of eight hours each.

Machinery.—The machinery imports account for 35 per cent of the total imports of manufactured goods, or $44,000,000 worth, an increase of $15,000,000 over those of 1918.

Kerosene.—Kerosene imports are included in this group and represent eight per cent of the group imports and they increase $7,000,000 over the $4,000,000 worth imported in 1918. The falling off of Japan's oil production, due to failure of many wells to yield, accounts for much of this increased import.

Paper.—Paper imports represent seven per cent of the imports in this group, or $9,000,000, an increase of $4,000,000 over 1918.

Woolen Goods.—Woolen tissue amounts to five per cent of the group imports, or $6,000,000, a very slight increase over 1918.

Other important items in this group are cotton tissues, $4,000,000, and iron nails, $2,500,000, the latter showing a slight decrease under the 1918 imports.

A variety of minor manufactured goods in the semiluxury and luxury class represented 40 per cent of the manufactured goods imports of 1919, or about $52,000,000, an increase of $20,000,000 over the imports of the year preceding.

The Future of Japanese Import Trade.—The development of Japan indicates to some extent the development which may be expected to take place in China. With a limitless supply of cheap labor the West cannot hope to continue to supply these two countries with many of the staples and necessities of life, but by supplying the machinery with which these may be manufactured at home, thus conserving to the domestic population a large amount of "goods wealth" which would have to be sent abroad as profit to the Western manufacturer of these staples, we automatically raise the standard of living to a point where all the raw materials produced do not have to be exported to pay for the manufactured goods brought in, but a considerable proportion may be retained at home and form a surplus through which the *per capita* wealth will be raised. When this takes place we will have an opportunity of creating desires for luxuries and semi-luxuries which cannot be manufactured by the crude, untrained labor of the East and in this way the standard of living again rises. This, in short, is the development which has taken place in Japan and the one which may be looked forward to in China.

Questions

1. Discuss the compradore system in China.
2. Why have China's imports of cotton goods decreased?
3. Name some of the principal metal imports of China and describe their uses.
4. Name five imports designated as sundries and comment on each.
5. Why has the volume of China's import trade fallen off?
6. How is trade financed in Japan?
7. What are five of Japan's principal imports of raw materials and describe the use made of each?

8. What part do semi-manufactured goods play in Japan's import trade? Name five commodities.
9. Comment on Japan's imports of manufactured goods, giving five articles.
10. How has the import of machinery increased the import trade in other lines in Japan?

CHAPTER VIII

CHINESE FINANCE AND TRANSPORTATION DEVELOPMENT

The Effect of the Boxer Indemnity on Chinese Finance.—It is, perhaps, not too much to say that the Boxer Rebellion and the resulting indemnities, amounting to 450,000,000 Haikwan taels ($333,000,000), were deciding factors in China's economic development, for without this drain upon the Treasury and the consequent financial embarrassment in official circles, foreign loans would not have been resorted to, and the transportation and industrial development which followed the "Battle of Concessions" would have been postponed. It is undoubtedly true that other factors hastened the construction of railroads, not the least important of which was the desire of the Manchus, who had read the warning in the Sino-Japanese war, to centralize their control over the outlying provinces by better transportation facilities, and the eagerness of rival European interests to grasp at any opportunity to obtain an economic foothold in what was thought to be a disintegrating empire. Whatever the causes, the fact remains that in 1917 China was paying about £174,000 (about $700,000) monthly to the Great Powers as installments of the indemnity, which payments were divided approximately between Russia, 29 per cent, France, 16 per cent, Great Britain, 11 per cent, Japan, 8 per cent, United States, 7 per cent (dedicated in part to education of Chinese students in the United States), and Italy, 6 per cent. The remaining 23 per cent represented the cancelled shares of Germany, Austria, and smaller powers. In consideration of China's entrance into the war all the powers agreed in December, 1917, to permit China to defer payment of an amount equalling nine and one-half per cent of the total which was the average of eight powers in the total of 77 per cent being paid them. The remaining 19½ per cent of Russia's share was thereafter to be deposited in the Russo-Asiatic Bank, as custodian, with the understanding that a certain proportion should be allotted for the maintenance of the Kerensky régime's Russian Legation at Peking.[1] At the same time the revision of the Chinese tariff to an effective five per cent and the rise in the exchange value of silver, resulting in an equivalent reduction in the amount of silver required to pay the gold indemnity payments remaining, strengthened considerably the finances of the Chinese Government.

The Condition of the Chinese Treasury.—The condition of the Chinese Treasury in the early part of 1920 was, nevertheless, in a traditional state of deficit, placed by conservative estimates, at $2,700,000 per month, which was being borrowed from native banks against security of future revenue, piling up a steadily increasing debt. This was due to the fact that in the budget of the Peking Government alone for February, 1920, $2,200,000, out of a total of $4,000,000 expended, was for the maintenance of the military establishment directly under Peking. The cost of the military establishment under the provincial governments cannot be accurately estimated. To meet this deficit, borrowing from foreign countries, especially Japan, was freely engaged in during 1917 and 1918 and about $150,000,000 was obtained in this way for administrative expenses during these two years for which national mines, forests, telegraph property, and railways (existing or proposed) were pledged as security. Domestic loans on the security of the deferred Boxer Indemnity and future reve-

[1] This agreement was discontinued in 1920.

nues of the Native Customs, treasury bills issued in payment for military and other unproductive supplies, and overdrafts by the Government on the Bank of China, the Bank of Communications, the Salt Industrial Bank, and other Chinese institutions only add to the long list of liabilities of the Chinese Government, definite knowledge as[2] to the amount of which, it is almost impossible to ascertain. Rough estimates, however, at the close of 1919 placed the monthly expenditure at $9,000,000 and the monthly revenue at $6,300,000. Of the income $2,700,000 was contributed as surplus from salt revenue not otherwise hypothecated; $1,800,000 came from the Maritime Customs surplus; $900,000 from wine and tobacco tax; and $900,000 from sundry receipts. No revenue was being received from the provinces by the Peking Government.

The Unmobilized Credit of China.—As a result of this hand to mouth financial policy periodical crises arise, especially on settlement day early in February, or Chinese New Year, and in the spring when crop credits are necessary, and to meet these crises further borrowing is necessary. But although the central Government of China is undoubtedly bankrupt, the credit of China as a whole is largely unmobilized and fundamentally sound, resting as it does, upon the immense productive value of the soil and people of China. The total indebtedness of China, accumulated since the first foreign loan in 1895, raised to pay the indemnity resulting from the Sino-Japanese war, to-day amounts to about $1,500,000,000, or a little under $4.00 *per capita*. As security for the foreign loans the Maritime Customs yielded $48,600,000 in 1918, the Salt Revenue, $62,000,000, and the Wine and Tobacco Revenue, $10,800,000, or a total of $121,400,000. This is a total 1918 *per capita* revenue yield of 30 cents per annum, which is over seven per cent on the indebtedness. The 1919 estimated

[2] See appendix VII.

yields of these three revenues are Maritime Customs, $58,-500,000; Salt Revenue, $77,400,000; and Wine and Tobacco Revenue, $27,000,000, or a total of $162,900,000 for 1919 and a *per capita* revenue yield of over 40 cents per annum or over 10 per cent on the indebtedness. This increased revenue yield has permitted the paying off of old debts to keep pace with the heavy borrowings in 1917 and 1918 so that the *per capita* debt has not increased since 1914.

The New Consortium.—The importance of the new Consortium agreement, therefore, between Great Britain, America, France, and Japan, lies in the fact that with the abolition of military expenses the Chinese Government can be easily brought to a solvent position. The whole idea of the Consortium is the safeguarding of funds for productive expenditure only and especially for the construction of railways, which would help China politically by ensuring a rapid extension of the central Government's authority and make a representative government possible. Financially it would provide a national asset in the shape of railways which would produce a rapid and certain return on foreign investments, while commercially, transportation is the one thing needed to bring China's inland products to the sea and convey the manufactured goods of the Western nations to a people whose purchasing power would be enormously enhanced by finding a world market for their products.

Under present conditions the extension of further credit by any single power would be destructive of China's credit and unjust to existing foreign investors. Funds provided on a sound basis of audit and control, on the other hand, such as is proposed by the Consortium, can be used to strengthen the Government in constructive enterprise and improve its financial position. China's national credit is sound and requires only mobilization under a sound policy on the part of foreign lenders.

Present Railroad Development.—The present Chinese railroads built by foreign loans form a mere skeleton of north and south trunk lines extending from Mukden to Peking—the Peking-Mukden Railroad (5) [3] (British Loan, 535 miles)—and then branching in two directions, one due south to Hankow on the Yangtze, the Peking-Hankow Railroad (8) (Belgian-French Loan, Chinese management, 755 miles), thence to Changsha, the Canton-Hankow-Changsha section (15) (British Loan, 295 miles), and one southeast to Tientsin and Pukow on the Yangtze, the Tientsin-Pukow Railroad (9) (British Loan, 628 miles). Across the Yangtze from Pukow at Nanking the Shanghai-Nanking Railroad (13) (British Loan, 193 miles), makes connection with the sea. From Shanghai another road, the Shanghai-Hangchow-Ningpo Railroad (14) (British Loan, 176 miles) makes a detour around Hangchow Bay to the south. Attached to this skeleton are six short feeder lines at various points. One extending from Changchun, the junction of the Chinese Eastern and South Manchurian Railroads, to Kirin in Manchuria, the Changchun-Kirin Railroad (6) (Japanese Loan, 81 miles) and another, the Shipingkai-Liaoyun Railroad (7) (Japanese Loan, 55 miles) extending from the South Manchurian Railroad below Changchun westward toward the Mongolian border, form the feeders to the Japanese concession road, the South Manchurian Railroad. Farther down on the Peking-Hankow line the Cheng-Tai Railroad (10) (Belgian-French Loan, 151 miles) connects Chenting in Chihli Province with Taiyuan in Shansi Province to the west, while the Taokow-Chinghua Railroad (11) (British Loan, 81 miles) connects cities of those names in Honan Province, crossing the Peking-Hankow line at Singsiang. South of this the Penlo Railroad and the completed portion of the Lunghai Railroad (12) (Belgian-French Loan, 287 miles) connects Kaifeng

[3] Numbers in parentheses refer to key map lining front cover.

on the Peking-Hankow line with Suchow on the Tientsin-Pukow line. The only other railroad built with foreign loans in China is the Canton-Kowloon Railroad (16) (British Loan, 89 miles) extending from Canton down the West River delta to Kowloon opposite the island of Hongkong. There have been built in China with foreign loans 3,326 miles of railroad at a total estimated cost of $428,939,000.

The Concession Lines.—In addition to these railways there are four lines known as concession lines, which are the property of foreign countries or their nationals and while built on Chinese territory are located on rights of way, which to all intents and purposes are foreign territory. The Chinese Eastern Railway (3) (Russian Concession, 1,069 miles) extends across northern Manchuria from the Siberian border to Vladivostok and from Harbin to Changchun, where it connects with the South Manchurian Railroad (1) (Japanese concession, 714 miles) extending from Changchun to Dairen, with a branch at Mukden to Antung on the Yalu River border of Korea. The Shantung Railroad (2) (German concession, occupied by Japanese, 306 miles) connects Tsinanfu on the Tientsin-Pukow Railroad with the port of Tsingtao on the Shantung Peninsula. The Indo-China Yunnan Railway (4) (French concession, 289 miles) crosses the Chinese border from French Indo-China below Mengtze and runs on into Yunnan Province to the city of Yunnan. The total cost of these 2,378 miles of concession road is estimated at $288,000,000.

Chinese Government Railways.—Chinese Government railways built with Chinese Government funds and operated by the Chinese Department of Communications form the next largest group of railroad properties in China. The Peking-Suiyuan Railroad (17) (Chinese Government, 266 miles) runs due west from Peking connecting with Kalgan and Tatung and piercing the Great Wall northwest of that place. The Chuchow-Pingsiang (20) (Chinese

Government, 60 miles) runs eastward from the southern terminus of the Changsha section of the Canton-Hankow line. The Canton-Samshui (19) (Chinese Government, 31 miles) extends from Canton up the West River, while the Amoy-Changchow Railroad (18) (Chinese Government, 17 miles) runs west from Amoy. In all the Chinese Government has built, largely from profits made above stipulated returns on the loan railways, 374 miles of railroad at a cost of $37,177,000.

Chinese Private Railroads.—The Chinese private railroads, built with private capital, form the last group. The Canton-Shuchowfu Railroad (21) (Private, 140 miles) is the beginning of the southern end of the Canton-Hankow line. The Kiukiang-Nanchang Railroad (22) (Private, 80 miles) extends from the Yangtze south to Nanchang. The Sunning Railway (23) (Private, 68 miles) runs from a point south of Canton to the coast, while the Swatow-Chaochowfu Railroad (24) (Private, 26 miles) extends inland from the port of Swatow.

Railroads Contracted For.—This total development of 6,740 miles of railroad does not begin to serve adequately the Chinese people either commercially or politically. The additional mileage already contracted for on a loan basis amounts to 8,429 miles and runs in the main from east to west. In general these contracts call for the construction of a huge circle of railroads beginning at Pukow on the Yangtze and running due west to Chengtu in Szechuen Province, and from there south and southeast, skirting Yunnan to Pakhoi on the Gulf of Tonkin, thence northeast through Kwangsi and Hunan Provinces to connect with the Canton-Hankow line and on through Kiangsi and Anhwei Provinces to Pukow. Inside this great circle is a smaller circle beginning at Hankow and running southwest, meeting the larger circle above Nanning in Kwangsi. Another great circle of contracted railroads begins at the terminus of the Taokow-Chinghua Railroad in Honan running northwest to Pingyang, thence due north to Tatung connecting with the Peking-Suiyuan, from the western terminus of which at Tengcheng it runs due west, skirting the Yellow River through inner Mongolia and running southwest to Lanchow in Kangsu Province. From here on east and west lines connect with the Penlo Railroad now running to Suchow from which place a projected line to Haichow on the coast would form the Lanchow-Haichow (or Lunghai) Railroad or Great East and West Trunk line. Other lines in this region are the Tsinan-Shunteh connecting the Peking-Hankow and the Tientsin-Pukow lines, the line connecting Tsinan with the Taokow-Chinghua Railroad and the line connecting Kaomi on the Shantung Railroad with Suchow on the Tientsin-Pukow line.

Manchurian Railroads Contracted For.—The group of roads contracted for in Manchuria and Mongolia consist of a road from Aigun on the Amur south to Chinchow on the Gulf of Chihli; a road west from Changchun to Taonanfu on this proposed Chinchow-Aigun Railroad; a road northwest from Harbin to meet the same road; and a road, the Taonanfu-Jehol, running from the Chinchow-Aigun southwest towards Peking. To the east one road from Kirin would run southwest meeting the South Manchurian road above Mukden and another from Kirin would run due east to the Korean border and on to the coast at Seishin. Work on these contracts has been suspended during the war and little construction has been done. Under the terms of the Consortium agreement, loans for all future construction, upon which no substantial progress has been made, must first be offered to the Consortium and if not taken up by them may be floated by any single power. Under this interpretation the financing of practically all of these roads will be offered to the Consortium, and their construction would mean the real commercial awakening of China.

BIBLIOGRAPHY TO PART I

CHINA AND JAPAN

HISTORY

China

BERESFORD, Lord C. W.:
The Breakup of China. New York, 1899.

BRINKLEY, Frank:
China, Its History, Arts and Literature (4 vols.). Boston, 1910.

CHING, Yen Wei:
The United States and China. American Association of International Conciliation, 1909.

CORNABY, W. Arthur:
A String of Chinese Peach Stones. London.

CURZON, Rt. Hon. Geo. N.:
Problems of the Far East. London, 1896.

DOUGLAS, Sir Robert K., and JENKS, J. W.:
China (Ghent Edition). New York, 1916.

KRAUSSE, Alexis:
China in Decay. London.

LATOURETTE, K. S.:
The Development of China. New York, 1917.

MARTIN, W. A. P.:
The Chinese, Their Education, Philosophy and Letters. New York.

MAYERS, Wm. F.:
Treaties Between the Empire of China and Foreign Powers. Shanghai.

MCGOWAN, James:
A History of China. Presbyterian Mission Press.

MILLARD, T. F.:
Our Eastern Question. New York, 1916.

SMITH, A. H.:
China and America To-day. New York, 1907.

WILLIAMS, S. W.:
Middle Kingdom. New York.

Japan

ABBOTT, J. F.:
Japanese Expansion and American Policies. New York, 1916.
ASAKAWA, K.:
Japan (Ghent Edition). New York, 1916.
BLAKESLEE, George H.:
Japan and Japanese-American Relations. New York, 1912.
BRINKLEY, Frank:
A History of the Japanese People. New York, 1914.
CLEMENT, E. W.:
Constitutional Imperialism in Japan. Colorado University, 1916.
COLEMAN, Frederic:
Japan or Germany in Siberia. New York, 1918.
DAVIS, F. Hadland:
Japan. New York.
D'AUTREMER, Joseph:
The Japanese Empire and Its Economic Conditions. London, 1910.
GRIFFIS, W. E.:
The Mikado. Princeton, 1915.
HILLARY, C. W.:
England's Earliest Intercourse with Japan. London, 1905.
HOLLAND, Clive:
Old and New Japan. New York, 1907.
Japanese Department of Education:
Japan from Government History. New York, 1916.
LATOURETTE, K. S.:
The Development of Japan. New York, 1918.
LONGFORD, Joseph H.:
Evolution of New Japan. New York, 1913.
MCLAREN, W. W.:
A Political History of Japan. New York, 1916.
MILLARD, Thomas F.:
Our Eastern Question. New York, 1916.
MIYAOKA, T.:
Growth of Internationalism in Japan. Washington, D. C., 1915.
PORTER, Robert P.:
Japan, The Rise of a Modern Power. Oxford, 1918.

PORTER, Robert P.:
The Full Recognition of Japan. New York, 1911.

CONSTITUTION AND POLITICAL PARTIES

China and Japan

HORNBECK, Stanley E.:
Contemporary Politics in the Far East. New York, 1916.

China

BLAKESLEE, S. H.:
China and the Far East. New York, 1910.
BROWN, A. J.:
New Forces in Old China. New York, 1904.
CLEMENTS, P. H.:
The Boxer Rebellion. Columbia University Press, 1915.
MILLARD, T. F.:
Our Eastern Question. New York, 1916.

Japan

CROW, Carl:
Japan and America. New York, 1916.
ELIOT, C. W.:
Some Roads Toward Peace. Washington, D. C., 1914.
IYENAGA, T.:
Constitutional Development of Japan. Johns Hopkins University, 1891.
IYENAGA, T.:
Japan's Real Attitude toward America. New York, 1916.
KAWAKAMI, K. K. L.:
Japan in World Politics. New York, 1917.
LAWTON, G. Richards:
Empires of the Far East. London, 1912.
MABIE, H. W.:
Japan To-day and To-morrow. New York, 1914.
NASAOKA, N.:
Japan's Message to America. Tokyo, 1914.
POOLEY, A. M.:
Japan at the Crossroads. London, 1917.

SCHERER, T.:
The Japanese Crisis. New York, 1916.

TARIFFS, TREATIES, *and* COMMERCIAL LAWS

China and Japan

Chinese Maritime Customs:
Treaties Between China and Foreign States, two volumes. New York.
Far Eastern Review:
"China's Corporation Regulations," translation of 1914 Mandate. Shanghai.
HERTSLET, G.:
China Treaties. London, 1908.
JERNIGAN, T. R.:
China in Law and Commerce. New York, 1905.
LOENHOLM, Dr. L. N.:
The Commercial Code of Japan, translated by Dr. Loenholm. Tokyo.
PORTER, Robert P.:
The Full Recognition of Japan. Oxford University Press, 1911.
RUTTER, Frank R.:
The Customs Tariff of Japan. Washington, D. C.
ROCKHILL, W. W.:
Treaties and Conventions—China and Korea (1904). Government Printing Office, Washington, D. C.
WILLOUGHBY, W. W.:
Foreign Rights and Interests in China. Johns Hopkins Press, 1920.

GEOGRAPHY—COMMERCIAL, POLITICAL, AND PHYSICAL, AND TRANSPORTATION

China and Japan

Bank of Japan:
The Recent Economic Development of Japan (1915). Tokyo.
COLLINS, William F.:
Mineral Enterprise in China. London, 1918.
JERNIGAN, T. R.:
China in Law and Commerce. New York.

KING, F. H.:
Farmers of Forty Centuries. New York, 1911.
MORSE, H. B.:
Trade and Administration of China. New York, 1908.
PORTER, Robert P.:
The Full Recognition of Japan. Oxford University Press, 1911.

China

Annals of the American Academy of Political and Social Science: "China, Social and Economic Condition (1917)." Philadelphia.
ARNOLD, Julean:
Commercial Handbook of China. Bureau of Foreign and Domestic Commerce, Washington, D. C.
COLQUHOUN, A. R.:
Overland to China. New York, 1900.
CROW, Carl:
Handbook for China. San Francisco News Co., San Francisco.
DINGLE, Edwin J.:
Across China on Foot. New York, 1911.
DOUGLAS, Sir R. K., and JENKS, J. W.:
China. New York, 1916.
GIBSON, R. N.:
Forces Mining and Undermining China. New York, 1914.
GILES, H. A.:
The Civilization of China. London, 1911.
MOULE, A. E.:
The Chinese People, A Handbook with Maps (1914). London.
WHITHAM, Paul P.:
Special Reports of U. S. Trade Commissioner Paul P. Whitham, Bureau of Foreign and Domestic Commerce, Washington.

Japan

BEAULIEU, P. Leroy:
The Awakening of the East. New York, 1900.
CHAMBERLAIN, B. H., and MASON, W. B.:
Murray's *Handbook for Japan.* London, 1899.

CLARKE, J. I. C.:
Japan at First Hand. New York, 1918.
COLQUHOUN, A. R.:
Mastery of the Pacific. New York, 1904.
Japanese Government Railways:
Official Guide of Eastern Asia, five volumes. Tokyo.
LITTLE, A. J.:
The Far East. Oxford, 1905.
NICHOLSON, Sir F. A.:
Fisheries in Japan. Madras, India, 1907.
NITOBE, Inazo:
The Japanese Nation. New York, 1912.
NUTFORD, E. B.:
Japan's Inheritance. New York, 1914.
OKUMA, Count S.:
Fifty Years of New Japan. London, 1910.

COMMERCIAL METHODS AND MARKET ANALYSIS

China and Japan

Bank of Japan:
The Recent Economic Development of Japan. Tokyo, 1915.
Bureau of Foreign and Domestic Commerce:
Conduct of Business with China. Washington, D. C., 1919.
JERNIGAN, T. R.:
China in Law and Commerce. New York, 1905.
LOENHOLM, Dr. L. H.:
Commercial Code of Japan. Tokyo, 1906.
MORSE, H. B.:
Trade and Administration of Chinese Empire. New York, 1908.
SPALDING, W. F.:
Eastern Exchange, Currency and Finance. New York, 1917.

China

CARUS, Paul:
Chinese Life and Customs. Chicago, 1907.
CHEN HUAN-CHANG:
Economic Principles of Confucius. New York, 1911.

Bureau of Foreign and Domestic Commerce:
Miscellaneous Series, No. 10, "Advertising Mediums." Washington, D. C., 1913.
Special Consular Reports, No. 43, "Agricultural Machinery." Washington, D. C., 1910.
Special Agents Series; No. 107, "Cotton Goods in China." Washington, D. C., 1916; No. 170, "Motor Vehicles in China." Washington, D. C., 1918; No. 172, "Electrical Goods in China." Washington, D. C., 1918; No. 173, "Shoe and Leather Trade of China." Washington, D. C., 1918; No. 180, "Railway Materials and Supplies." Washington, D. C., 1919; No. 104, "Lumber." Washington, D. C., 1915.
Miscellaneous Series, No. 50, "Hardware." Washington, D. C., 1917; No. 92, "Canned Goods." Washington, D. C., 1915.
GOODRICH, J. E.:
Our Neighbors the Chinese. London, 1913.
HOLDICH, T. H.:
Tibet the Mysterious. New York, 1906.
JERNIGAN, T. R.:
Chinese Business Methods and Policy. London, 1904.
LIANG, Y.:
Village and Town Life in China. London, 1915.
MORSE, H. B.:
Guilds of China. New York, 1909.
THOMPSON, J. S.:
China Revolutioned. London, 1913.
WAGEL, S. R.:
Finance in China. Shanghai, 1914.
Chinese Currency and Banking. Shanghai, 1915.

Japan

ANGIER, A.:
Far East Revisited. London, 1908.
Bureau of Foreign and Domestic Commerce:
Miscellaneous Series, No. 10, "Advertising Mediums." Washington, D. C., 1913; No. 50, "Hardware." Washington, D. C., 1912.
Special Agents Series, No. 170, "Automobiles." Washington, D. C., 1918; No. 92, "Canned Goods." Washington, D.

C., 1915; No. 86, "Cotton Goods." Washington, D. C., 1914; No. 62, "Foreign Credits." Washington, D. C., 1913; No. 28, "Customs Tariff." Washington, D. C., 1912; No. 172, "Electrical Goods." Washington, D. C., 1918; No. 173, "Shoe and Leather Goods." Washington, D. C., 1918; No. 180, "Railway Equipment." Washington, D. C., 1919.

DAUTROMER, J.:
Economic Conditions. New York, 1910.

DE BRUNOFF, M.:
General View of Commerce and Industry. Tokyo, 1900.

FOX, Frank:
Problems of the Pacific. New York, 1913.

HITCHCOCK, F. H.:
Our Trade with Japan. Government Printing Office, Washington, D. C., 1900.

HOSIE, A.:
Manchuria. New York, 1904.

KAKUZO, Okakura:
The Awakening of Japan. New York, 1904.

KINOSHITA, Y.:
Past and Present of Japanese Commerce. Boulder, Colorado, 1900.

MILLARD, T. F.:
Our Eastern Question. New York, 1916.

NITROBE, I. O.:
Bushido, The Soul of Japan. Philadelphia, 1900.

WEALE, Putnam:
Reshaping of the Far East. New York, 1905.

WHIGHAM, W.:
Manchuria and Korea. New York, 1904.

PART II

THE PHILIPPINES AND THE DUTCH EAST INDIES

CHAPTER IX

HISTORY OF THE PHILIPPINES AND THE DUTCH EAST INDIES DURING FOREIGN OCCUPATION

The early adventurers from Europe who sought trading privileges with the people of China and Japan had already learned that they could demand them successfully from the peoples of the tropical and semi-tropical islands to the south. These island people, possessing none of the warlike proclivities of the Japanese, nor being favored by a vast unconquerable territory like the Chinese, were subdued with comparative ease and soon sank into the subservient condition of a subject people. This was not accomplished, of course, without some difficulty, but once the different island tribes were pacified, it only remained for their conquerors to play off the jealousies, natural to isolated island people, one against the other in order to protect themselves from unified revolt.

The Philippine Islands

Discovery of the Philippines by Magellan.—Magellan, in search of a western route to the Moluccas, or Spice Islands, had already persuaded King Charles of Spain that Spanish rights of exploration lay in the western hemisphere, leaving the Portuguese their claims to the eastern hemisphere by right of prior discovery. Pope Alexander VI, appealed to as arbitrator by Spain and Portugal, had created an artificial dividing meridian in the Atlantic and had granted Spain the right to explore west of this line and Portugal east of it. This was due to an erroneous idea that the world was much smaller than it really was and that Columbus' discoveries were merely the most eastern reaches of a vast archipelago extending westward to the Malay peninsula. Magellan had visited the Malay peninsula in 1511 and had there heard of the rich islands to the east, which he determined to approach from the west in order to avoid all claims on the part of Portugal. His voyage, begun in 1519, landed him in 1521, after many vicissitudes, at Cebu in the Philippines. Here Magellan was so deceived by the good feeling displayed by the natives that he ventured to another island with too small a force and he and his party were killed. The rest of the expedition escaped and returned to Spain in 1522, having accomplished the first circumnavigation of the globe.

The Work of Legaspi.—Several explorers followed Magellan to the islands, one of whom named one of the islands "Filipina" in honor of Prince Philip of Spain. This name was afterward extended to include the whole group which were thereafter known as the "Philippines." In 1564 Legaspi was commissioned by the now King Philip II of Spain to settle and subdue the islands named in his honor. After encountering little opposition on the islands of Leyte, Bohol, and Mendanao, Cebu had to be taken by force but peace was soon established. Unfortunately the decision of Pope Alexander had made no provision for an eastern limit to the territories which he had divided between Spain and Portugal in the Atlantic and although Portugal continued to lay claim to the Philippines, Spain refused to recognize the claim. In 1569 Legaspi transferred the seat of his government from Cebu to Iloilo and continued to explore and pacify the islands, founding Manila in 1571. In his process of pacification Legaspi depended largely upon the industry of the monks, but resorted, when necessary, to force. Provincial governors were appointed from among his followers who levied tribute at a rate fixed by him and annual voyages were made to Mexico for supplies. In this way the Philippines were really governed from Mexico rather than from Spain directly. When Legaspi died in 1574 the conversion of the natives to Christianity had steadily progressed and the subjugation of the islands to Spanish rule was nearly complete.

Events of the Latter 16th Century in the Philippines.—After the death of Legaspi, the Spanish in the Philippines were almost immediately engaged in resisting in 1574 an invasion headed by a Chinese buccaneer commanding over sixty war junks. Encouraged by the ease with which the Islands had been subdued by the Spanish this expedition of some 4,000 warriors, including 1,500 women, and abundant supplies, landed on the northern coast of Luzon and started toward Manila. After two unsuccessful attacks, during which the small Spanish garrison fought valiantly, the pirates sailed away to the mouth of the Agno River in what is now Pangasinan Province and made all preparations to settle permanently. The following year a Spanish detachment aided by a war junk sent by the Emperor of China routed the buccaneers and drove a remnant of them to the mountains where their descendants, a Chinese-Filipino race, still exist. During the next two decades the only important events were the arrival of the first body of Franciscans, Jesuits, and Dominicans and a Spanish expedition to Borneo and to the Moluccas against the Dutch. It was during this time that the disadvantages of the arrangement whereby the Philippines were governed indirectly from Mexico first became apparent. The conditions and people of Mexico were quite different from those of the Philippines and the Mexican laws grafted upon the Oriental colony were naturally unsuitable. Legaspi had left a large degree of self-government to the local native communes, but his successors gradually abolished this and a greater centralization of authority took place in Spanish hands. Friction between the church and the civil government soon appeared and in response to an appeal from the Bishop of Manila the King of Spain in 1589 defined the activities of church and state in the Islands, abolished slavery, provided proportionate tribute to civil, military, and ecclesiastical establishments and initiated several other reforms. At about this time the Emperor of Japan sent an ambassador to the Spanish rulers of the Philippines demanding allegiance to his throne. After much parley the ambassador was so impressed with the tales of the greatness of Spain and her people that he invited a return embassy to Japan to negotiate a treaty on a basis of equality. This was successfully accomplished but the returning envoys were shipwrecked and the treaty lost. A second treaty signed in 1593 was the beginning of Franciscan intercourse with Japan.

The Developments of the Early 17th Century.—The history of the next seventy years is one of numerous threatened invasions from without or ambitious expeditions on the part of the Spanish to bring the neighboring islands under their control. Thus Viscaya, Isabela, and Agayan were subjugated in 1595 but an expedition to Cambodia and to Mindanao was not so successful. A massacre of Spanish priests in Japan in 1597 put an end to plans for Christianizing Japan from Manila. During this period the royal Spanish court of justice was established with jurisdiction over Mindanao, Sulu, Cambodia, and parts of the Moluccas and the College of San José was founded in 1600. But the attention of the colonists was frequently distracted from internal improvement by threats from without. The source of supplies from Mexico was being constantly threatened by Dutch hostility and many Spanish supply boats were seized and the colonists thus reduced to sore straits. This enmity between the two rival colonizing nations was not finally averted until the restoration of peace between the two countries in Europe in 1763. To add to these difficulties a series of native uprisings occurred in the first half of the seventeenth century which necessitated a strengthening of the armed force, although the economic condition resulting from a number of crop failures and subsequent famines during this period may account for these to some degree. Compulsory military service led to a revolt in Samar in 1649 which was only put down by much show of force. The Moros were a constant source of trouble during this and later periods and their truculence continued under American rule. With all these disturbances religious activity continued to increase and the double mission of the friars, that of education and conversion, was becoming constantly a more successful one.

The same supervision of Mexico which had been found so unsuited to the Philippines politically had extended also to trade and the restrictions of free trade with China and Japan did much to hold back the economic development of the Islands. Yet unsatisfactory as this arrangement was, it continued until the beginning of the nineteenth century.

The period between 1664 and 1764 was perhaps the least eventful in the history of the Islands. A steady improvement in internal administration, coupled with a highly satisfactory advance of the Christian faith, was only occasionally marred by crop failures, epidemics, and Mohammedan and Chinese attacks.

Manila Occupied by the English.—The outbreak of the war between England and France and Spain in 1762 was the occasion of British attacks upon all Spanish colonies and a squadron of thirteen ships was sent against Manila, which was captured after a short siege, and the Philippines remained under British sovereignty until 1764 when the Peace of Paris restored them to Spain. With the restoration of the Islands, Spain began to inaugurate a systematic agricultural development of the Islands. In 1781 tobacco growing had become such an important industry that it was made a government monopoly which it remained for a century.

Insurrections against Spain.—Meanwhile insurrections and uprisings were becoming more and more serious. These occurred in 1807, 1814, and 1823 and finally a formidable uprising in Cavite in 1872 proved to be a most daring and well laid plan to throw off the Spanish yoke. The origin of this revolt was the native opposition to the practice of Spanish friars retaining parochial benefices to the exclusion of native priests. Although the revolt was stamped out the cause and spirit remained and only awaited the psychological moment to burst into flame again.

The Character of Spanish Rule.—The character of Spanish rule did much to aggravate this condition, for it was not of the most tactful and appropriate nature, and provided no representation of the Islands in the Spanish legislature, except during a brief period, and when this was revoked it only increased discontent. Toward the end of the nineteenth century certain reforms were attempted, such as the substitution of an identification paper for the payment of the hated tribute, but the spirit of independence which sought autonomy was not easily appeased. The Spanish rule in the Philippines, however, was not without its good results. Through the efforts of the church the elevation of the people from a state of barbarism to a condition of comparative civilization was effected. Schools were established and the natives were admitted to a small share in the government, while advances in the domestic arts led to the adoption of the customs of living of their rulers. Contrasted with the studied subjugation of the Javanese by the Dutch and the churlish reserve of the British toward their colonies, the Spanish régime was actually benevolent. This arose from the conception of colonization held by the Spanish which was different from that held by the English and Dutch. Primarily a Spanish colony was a field for missionary endeavor and not for commercial exploitation. Yet, notwithstanding this primary purpose, conditions developed which tended to foster militarism, ecclesiasticism, and officialism, and where these are allowed to develop they hamper real economic or social advance. The return of young Filipinos who had studied in Europe was the signal for an organized attempt to bring about reforms in the Government. Alarmed by the success of the revolution of Spanish colonies in America, the revolts which occurred early in the nineteenth century now caused the Spanish to enact half-way reforms. Agriculture was encouraged, a mint was established, roads and bridges were constructed, officials were prohibited from engaging in commerce, usury was suppressed, and the tobacco monopoly established, yet these belated efforts could not ameliorate the narrow, harsh, tyrannical, and unprogressive rule, which discouraged learning, did not tolerate freedom of opinion, prohibited the printing of books and was reactionary in every sense. In 1860 many secret societies, including political affiliations of freemasons, were organized and the aims of these societies, among which was "La Liga Filipino" later founded by Dr. José Rizal, were, briefly, the expulsion of the friars and the confiscation of their estates, the same political autonomy which had been granted Cuba, a just division of civil and military posts, the return to the owners of land seized by the friars, the prevention of insults to natives, and economy in expenditures. Burgos, Joena, and Rizal were the leading advocates of these reforms. Rizal's ideas and ideals were presented in several novels, among which *Noli Me Tangere* was a poetic description of his people's faults, aspirations, and wrongs.

The Revolt at Cavite.—Within a few years after the publication of this book, in 1896, the revolt at Cavite took place, in which Aguinaldo, a young Filipino school teacher, took a prominent part. The success of the revolt was due to the well organized secret societies, as well as to the sending of a large number of Spanish troops to Cuba which was also in revolt. Unable to subdue the *insurrectos,* amnesty was offered to all who would lay down their arms, and the spirit of the revolt had been well spent, when an edict was issued in 1897 placing severe restrictions upon the movements of the people. This fanned the dying embers into flame. In April, 1898, 5,000 natives drove the Spanish from Cebu and took possession of Manila, but were a few days later crushingly defeated and driven to the mountains. The United States soon after declared war on Spain and the Spanish fleet was destroyed at Cavite and Manila captured.

Acquisition of the Philippines by the United States.— By the Treaty of Paris, Spain ceded the Philippines to the United States. Before the arrival of the first Philippine Commission Aguinaldo had started in to organize an army and a government under the protection of American gunboats, in the belief conveyed to him by the Hongkong Junta that our Government would aid him. However, neither Admiral Dewey nor General Anderson made any such promise. To the Americans Aguinaldo was the head of the army coöperating with the American forces. To the Filipinos he was dictator and head of the organized Government. His position was strengthened by a series of edicts and a military expedition against the Spanish in Luzon, although the United States was still negotiating peace with Spain. The establishment of the "Filipino Republic" followed with Aguinaldo as President. Aguinaldo's haste and unwillingness to follow American leadership made a sympathetic or conciliatory attitude impossible. The Americans were unconvinced that the Filipinos were possessed of a sufficient degree of civilization to govern themselves. Six days before the ratification of the Treaty of Paris in February, 1899, hostilities broke out between the Americans and the Filipinos, due to the shooting of a native soldier who attempted to cross over the American lines after darkness and after a campaign of two years all organized opposition had been destroyed, but guerilla warfare continued until the capture of Aguinaldo in April, 1901. The insurrection was declared at an end on July 1, 1901, and Judge Taft, president of the Commission, was made Governor.

The Dutch East Indies

Early Dutch Ventures in the East Indies.—The war of liberation which in 1574 had just been fought in the Netherlands had been, to a large extent, an economic war and its successful culmination resulted in a great expansion of Dutch commerce. Unlike the royal expeditions of Spain, the first Dutch undertakings were the adventures of individuals in search of profit, and the East, as the source of untold wealth was their natural goal. For better protection these individuals sent their ships together in fleets and the first venture of this kind to Java in 1595 resulted in losses in ships, men, and money. But the enormous profits of successful ventures were so alluring that a second trial was made and in 1598 a fleet of twenty-two ships made a successful return voyage from the East Indies yielding a profit in spices alone of four hundred per cent. The rush which ensued to participate in this trade resulted in these individual ventures suffering many handicaps. Competition raised prices of the products in the East and lowered them at home, and although the Dutch Government counselled harmony, the greed for individual profit outweighed all other considerations. In 1602 the States General of Holland formed by law the Dutch East India Company, which not only incorporated the traders who were engaged in the East Indian trade into a single corporation, but gave them and their successors a monopoly of the trade and powers of government in the East Indies which were practically sovereign. The tendency of individual ship captains to compete for trade led to the appointment of a Governor General in 1609 who was to reside in the East and direct the forces of the Company. A center of operations was selected, therefore, near modern Batavia, to serve not only as a base of supplies for the long inter-island cruisers which were necessary to collect products, but also as a good harbor, fortified from attack, and with possibilities as a base for military operations. Thus the ambitions of a few independent Dutch traders had led in twenty years to the establishment of a thriving Dutch colony.

The Dutch East India Company.—The small proportion of the territory of the island of Java under Dutch control, however, was flanked by native states whose constant bickerings led to a condition of continual unrest. Moreover, other European competition entered into the trade with these independent native states, and the protests from the Dutch only led to embargoes placed on the trade with the Dutch by the native princes. The products of these independent states were monopolized by the princes, and high prices as well as high export duties were the rule. The desire of the Dutch to extend their political influence was largely due, therefore, to a desire to overcome these restrictions which the independent states imposed. The Dutch soon developed in their colonial career from mere traders to politicians, and from politicians to warriors, each step being induced by the desire to control larger areas of fertile soil and cheap labor in order to obtain greater quantities of products at a cheaper price. These territorial expansions were, nevertheless, largely at variance with the instructions from Holland which followed a consistent policy of cultivating the peace and friendship of the native states as far as possible. But this policy the local governor found difficult to follow, it being misinterpreted by the natives as a policy actuated by fear. Throughout the seventeenth century, therefore, the history of the Company was a history of petty wars, which, however, only increased the profit to the officials and not to the Company, inasmuch as they were not wars of conquest but wars fought on behalf of one native prince against another, the incommensurate territorial gains only coming to the Company from the victor whom they had helped, while the more concrete profits and spoils went to the officials themselves. To their credit be it said, however, that the Dutch sought to aid always the legitimate ruler against usurpers, and to put down rebellion.

The "Council of Defence."—The remarkable trade which the Company built up during the 150 years between 1650 and 1800 was based purely on the principle of monopoly. Despite numerous attempts at modification of this policy, it remained the bulwark of the Dutch struggle against both Portuguese and English trade in the East Indies. The struggle with the former ended in 1641 with the capture of Malacca, but the struggle with the British was more severe. These two powers, though normally at peace in Europe, were practically continually at war in the East. By 1618 the British had besieged Batavia four times without success. In 1619 an encounter between Dutch and English ships led to the formation by treaty of a "Council of Defence" consisting of an equal number of representatives from the British and Dutch East India Companies. This Council was to maintain a fair division of the East Indian trade. In 1622 a combined fleet under the Council attacked Manila, but this expedition ended in a quarrel and the break-up of the Council. The vague provisions of the treaty were impossible of execution in the face of a policy of monopoly which guided the course of both nations. The Dutch governor declared in 1622 that friendship with the English meant ruin for the Company. In 1628 the English president of the Council removed from Batavia to a neighboring independent state of Bantam, from which, after conquest by the Dutch, the English were forced to withdraw. Thereafter the English carried on an illicit trade with Dutch possessions which the Dutch were never able to stop.

Theories of Colonization and Free Trade.—In 1623 a theory of colonizing the Dutch possessions in the Indies with permanent Dutch residents, who would take the place of the mercenary armies which then garrisoned the Dutch stronghold, was put into practical effect by permitting the Dutch citizens of Batavia to trade on their own account in the adjoining districts but the policy was vetoed by the Colonial authorities after a few years. The old evils of the monopoly system were again in evidence, deterring colonization, and diverting a rich inter-island trade into the hands of other nationals and natives, and in stimulating smuggling by all. This question of monopoly *versus* Dutch colonization and free trade is one which has agitated the colony until the present time, finding its present parallel in the contrast between the aims of the Little Hollander, who may be said to have inherited the monopolistic idea, and the Colonial who is strongly in favor of economic and political autonomy for the Colony.

Policies of the Dutch East India Company.—Some other policies of the Dutch East India Company reflected the mercantilist theories then popular in Europe. Thus purchases were made as far as possible only with goods from Holland rather than with specie. The carrying trade was conducted in outbound groups generally of three vessels, which assembled in the East and returned home in one great fleet, annually, in order to lessen the danger of attack upon their valuable cargoes. The cargoes were based on a few easily grown staples which found a ready market in Europe as well as upon products collected from other nearby territories. These consisted, during the eighteenth century, of tea from China, pepper, mace, nutmegs, and cloves from the Moluccas, and coffee, sugar, camphor, indigo, and cutch from Java. The policy was strictly to regulate the supply and to fix the prices in Europe in this manner. The cargoes from Holland consisted mainly of textiles.

Trade Control Methods of the Company.—At first the Company maintained "factories," or trading posts, where its agents collected the products for shipment but as this trade dwindled toward the end of the eighteenth century, the Company became almost entirely dependent for its trade upon products received as tribute contingents or forced deliveries of subject natives. The first of these sources of supply required no return at all, the second required only a nominal return for fixed amounts of products delivered by the natives annually, while the forced deliveries theoretically resembled contracts to deliver certain products to the Company at a fixed price, but in practice there was little difference between them and contingents.

The Contingent System.—The contingent system originated in the older provinces under the political control of the Company, which appointed certain native princes regents over large districts on condition that they furnish certain amounts of products annually, some free and some at a fixed price, and also perform certain military services and supply armed men in case of need. These regents in turn farmed out the land to Javanese laborers who paid their rent in products to the regents in such quantities as to render a profit for the regent over and above his obligations to the Company. Thus the Dutch showed rare tact in adapting their rule to the native organization as they found it, for in addition to paying prices far below the market, they transferred the actual work of administration to the native officials. This system, however, only imposed greater hardships upon the common farmers who were thus subject to a double exploitation. Naturally the profits of the Company under this system were handsome, ranging from twelve and a half per cent to fifty per cent annually over a period of two hundred years.

The Decline of the Company and Its Fall.—The company, which had begun under such favorable circumstances as a trading corporation, gradually declined as its character changed to that of a political ruler. This change was due largely to the fact that with growing competition it was unable to make large enough profits in the open market to cover the cost of its commercial and military establishment and still pay dividends. So recourse was finally had almost entirely to forced deliveries which, while seemingly cheaper for a time, simply overburdened the Company more and more with the debt of its military establishment. This decline began toward the end of the seventeenth century and by the middle of the eighteenth century the Company's business was entirely on a political basis. At the same time the contingent and forced delivery systems were limiting the markets in the Islands for Dutch wares, there being practically no exchange of commodities, although their commercial rivals, the English, French, Danes, and the Arabs, were finding a ready market for their smuggled wares. This commercial competition was the real cause of the decline, for while the Company stifled Dutch competition, it was unable to protect itself in its monopolistic position against outsiders. The strengthening of the English in India was no small factor in increasing this competition, the nature of which was not monopolistic but practically in the hands of individual traders. With an organization top-heavy with routine, the Company was unable to withstand the effect of the European wars of 1780 and 1795. Futile attempts were made to reform through state commissions but to no avail, and finally in 1798 the Dutch East India Company was abolished and its debts of about sixty-seven million dollars assumed by the Dutch Government.

Java after the Fall of the Dutch East India Company.—With the downfall of the Dutch East India Company in 1798, the history of the Dutch in Java takes a remarkable turn. The French Revolution was soon succeeded by the rule of the Emperor Napoleon and the Dutch colonies now came under French influence as dependencies of the Batavian Republic and so, by the fortunes of war, were made the goal of British conquest. During the era directly preceding British rule there was little change in the Dutch policy and the sole aim of the Government seemed to be the greatest benefit to the mother country with no thought of reforms in the Islands. The principal effect of the change from Company to Government rule was to increase the solidarity and lessen the ultimate responsibility of the rulers. The question of the Government maintaining the trade monopoly or creating another Company to handle the trade independently of the Government was paramount. If the latter course were adopted, should the contingents be abolished and the Government assume active rulership of the masses direct, instead of ruling through the regents? These questions were the subject of public discussion in Holland for several years. It was clearly a parting of the ways and a form of the old system had either to be adopted by the Government or an entirely new system of taxation and free cultivation inaugurated. There was a strong argument in favor of the latter system in the example of the Chinese districts where the Chinese exercised practically the rights of regents over a prosperous group of farmers, unburdened with contingents or forced deliveries, and where, although the taxation was high, it was at a fixed rate and after its payment there remained the incentive to produce more, which added to the general prosperity. The conditions were so favorable in these districts that they were crowded with immigrants from all the surrounding country. With this system was advocated the policy of "free trade" with Holland in all commodities except spices, which alone were to remain a Government monopoly.

The Attempted Reforms of 1803.—Although reform in Java was recognized as necessary the time was not ripe for so drastic a change and the advocates of the plan were not successful. One great difficulty in its practical application was that of redistribution of the land. A Commission appointed in 1803 returned a report unfavorable to a change as striving toward something impossible of achievement. The contingent system was continued as being best calculated to retain the coöperation of the native rulers. The Government in thus succeeding the Company was to undertake to regulate abuses, improve the condition of the people, and abolish all but regular taxes. The Commission, however, recommended abandonment of all monopolies except coffee, pepper, and spices and ships of friendly powers were welcomed to trade. The powers of the Asiatic Council, which succeeded the Dutch East India Company, were also considerably restricted, and improvement in fiscal administration and control were provided for.

The Work of Governor General Daendels.—In 1806 the Asiastic Council was dissolved by King Louis Napoleon, who had ascended to the throne in Holland, and a new Governor General named Daendels was appointed who had gained his appointment solely as a reward for military service under the French in Holland. Due to difficulties of communication he received no instructions from home for two years and being left to his own resources proceeded in a rough and ready fashion to right what wrong conditions he saw. Among other things he sought to reform not only the scheme of administration but also the system of promotions and pay of the Dutch officials so as to make honest government possible. The judiciary was also overhauled and important changes in the relations of the native regents to the Government instituted.

British Occupation and Reforms of Raffles.—Batavia had been blockaded by a British squadron in 1800 and at intervals of several years after that hostile demonstrations by British fleets had been made off the coast. Finally in 1811 a joint expedition on the part of the British Government and the British East India Company was successful in driving out the Dutch and from then until 1816 it was ruled as part of British India. The British Governor, Sir Stamford Raffles, now began a career which was most successful and fruitful. Although some of his plans were not carefully executed, he displayed a wonderful energy and established high ideals of service. His notable reforms were:

1. The entire abolition of forced delivery and the establishment of perfect freedom in cultivation and trade.
2. The assumption by the Government of the direct superintendence of lands and their revenues and the designation of the native regents merely as public officials instead of dependent rulers of districts.
3. The renting out of such lands in large and small estates on leases for a moderate term.

This constituted a most sweeping change in the Government of the Islands. The native regents were deprived of the opportunity of squeezing the native farmers, and European officials were to replace them and administer a new fiscal system. Government taxes were based strictly upon the rental value of lands, instead of on private agreements between farmers and regents. Finally, the Government abolished indirect taxation in the shape of internal tolls and transport duties and instead of farming out the customs took them under its own administration. In Raffles's system the land tax was the principal feature and it absorbed all the many dues and services under native rule. The practical difficulties to be met and overcome were very great and a beginning had only been made by the time the Dutch régime was restored in 1816.

The Restoration of Dutch Rule; the Dutch Trading Company.—The period of British rule marks a turning point in the history of the Dutch East Indies and, although the Dutch inherited an undesirable mixture of the old and new system, they proceeded to straighten out their difficulties with celerity. The first correction to be effected was that of the land tax which was found difficult to collect and insufficient for administration needs. After an investigation in the best method to pursue, the Dutch commissioners decided to depend primarily upon taxes for revenues and especially upon an improved land tax. The provincial administrative system established by Raffles was retained and further reforms in the European civil service inaugurated. During this period trade was jealously guarded by the Dutch who looked with displeasure upon the increasing participation of English and American shipping in the commerce with the Islands.

In 1824 the Dutch Trading Company was established in order to strengthen the hold of the individual Dutch merchants upon the growing trade of the Islands by amalgamating their interests, without adding any monopolistic features or rights to impose forced culture.

The Culture System and Its Failure.—The culture system was introduced in 1830 and provided, briefly, that the natives put at the disposal of the Government a certain proportion of their land and labor time and their taxes should be paid in products for export grown under the direction of the Government, which agreed to bear the losses of crop failures not due to the fault of the cultivators, and also pay a small price for the products furnished.

Where this system was applied to parts of Java especially suited to the cultivation of the required products, such as coffee, pepper, spices, etc., the natives gained by it, but in its general application it was oppressive. Notwithstanding this drawback, the Islands became very prosperous during the period from 1830 to 1870. By 1851 most of the very oppressive cultures had been removed and the Government adopted the principle of limiting its culture crop to one-fifth of the natives' land. In 1860 parliamentary attention in Holland was first directed against the culture system and, after a long struggle during which the fates of several Ministries were involved, the culture system was abolished in 1870. With the abolishment of the culture system the modern era of Dutch rule in the East Indies may be said to have begun.

Questions

1. Describe the settlement and pacification of the Philippines.
2. Why was it necessary to form and extend the political power of a monopolistic company in order to carry on the early trade of the Dutch East Indies?
3. Why was the "Council of Defence" formed and why did it fail?
4. Describe the contingent system.
5. What caused the decline of the Dutch East India Company?
6. What were the advantages and disadvantages of Spanish rule in the Philippines in the nineteenth century?
7. What caused the rupture between Aguinaldo and the United States? Describe the results.
8. What reforms were contemplated by the Dutch after the downfall of the Dutch East India Company?
9. What three reforms did the British under Raffles institute?
10. Describe the culture system.

CHAPTER X

MODERN GOVERNMENT POLICIES IN THE DUTCH EAST INDIES AND THE PHILIPPINES

THE DUTCH INDIES

The Government of the Dutch East Indies.—The Dutch East Indies government is divided into three distinct parts. The general legislative branch is located at The Hague, in Holland. The central colonial government at Batavia, Java, legislates and administers the details of the general policies formulated in Holland, while provincial and local administrations are confronted with the task of actually administering the laws thus formulated. The legislative power which was exercised in the early nineteenth century by the Governor General has been almost entirely transferred to the Dutch Legislature and the Dutch monarch. The Legislature has not entirely superseded the exclusive power formerly exercised by the monarch in the early part of the nineteenth century and, the Queen, acting through her Minister, is still the most influential organ of colonial government. The Minister is responsible, of course, to the Dutch Legislature which, however, seldom makes use of its prerogative to control colonial policy, and most of the important laws affecting the colony are fiat laws of the Minister. He also appoints colonial officials and performs necessary executive acts. The disadvantage in thus vesting legislative power in a single official, whose position is dependent upon political conditions at home and who holds office for only a comparatively short time, as a rule, is the obvious one of a lack of consistent colonial policy, and a remedy for this condition has been sought in the proposal to establish an advisory council, permanently appointed, who would form the basis of a stable policy.

It is only through its control of the finances that the Dutch Legislature has exercised any considerable control over the Indian colonies. But it has been repeatedly held that, because of the lack of interest and knowledge of colonial affairs on the part of Dutch legislators, the financial control of the colony from Holland is disadvantageous. This would seem a reasonable attitude, inasmuch as the Dutch legislators are expected to have only a knowledge of Dutch domestic affairs, and the number of colonial specialists among them are very few. From every point of view there seems no valid reason why colonial autonomy in financial and other important legislative control is not dictated both by reason and by considerations of good government. Several proposals for remedying the situation such as the establishment of local self-government in Dutch India, and the establishment of a special "imperial" Parliament, with colonial representatives, have been advanced, but there is little likelihood of their immediate adoption.

The Power of the Governor.—The principal feature of the Dutch Government in India is the great power wielded by the Dutch Colonial Governor, who is responsible directly to the Crown. Without any serious limitation to his powers, either legislative, or administrative, in India, the only checks upon his exercise of enormous and arbitrary power have come from the home Government, which has shown a tendency to supersede him in many ways. The improvement in means of communication, in recent years, has only seemed to emphasize this tendency, although the Governor General still maintains an important position, and his advice certainly influences the determination of Dutch colonial policy. A council of five members appointed by the home Government assists the Governor General in legislating and decides upon all projects of law, subject to his approval, which in turn must be upheld by the home Government. With a few exceptions, however, the Governor General is the only responsible colonial official in both legislation and administration. Under him, and entirely subordinate to him, are five departments, the heads of which, however, lack the responsibility and independence of ministers in a parliamentary government. The General Secretariat of the Governor General conducts his correspondence and publishes his orders, and the position of this body is peculiarly important, in that it acts independently in giving form and substance to the expression of his will.

The Provincial Administration of the Colonial Government.—The provincial administration of the Dutch Indian Government is the branch which has been developed with greatest difficulty. Through it a distinctly European administration seeks to control a great native organization, whose very nature is so primitive as to be far behind that of the West. The provincial officials, therefore, must remain European in ideal and purpose, but become native in practice and performance. Through them the two peoples, the Dutch and Javanese, are interpreted to each other, and Javanese problems are translated into Dutch legislation, which in turn must be administered according to native rules. These officials include 22 residents, 78 assistant residents, 165 controleurs of three classes, 72 regents, 434 district heads, and 1,033 under district heads of two classes. A residency is the size of a New England county, and the resident, who rules over about a million people, compares somewhat with the French prefect in his many duties. These are administrative, legislative of a minor nature, judicial, fiscal, political, and diplomatic. He must protect the natives from oppression, maintain peace, encourage agriculture and education, and guard religion. His assistants rule over subdivisions of the regency, performing all his duties except that of legislating, and establish contact with the native officials, the regents. The controleurs are the lowest European officials in the actual administration under the regent and his assistants. Their position is theoretically perfunctory, but, actually, by coming in daily contact with the native regents, they occupy positions of much local importance, and exercise much influence upon affairs. The native regents who exercise the immediate rule over the natives are of princely rank, and are responsible for the conduct of their subjects. Their hereditary succession is maintained and the Government thereby gains the prestige and influence of the old native rulers. The district heads are appointed by the regent and, being in close contact with the lower Dutch officials, are directly subject to Dutch administration rather than to the regent, much of whose authority they exercise. Below these officials are heads of village groups whose principal point of contact is the district head. These village officials are important in apportioning the land tax, but otherwise exercise little influence.

Evils of Dutch East Indian Government.—There are many evils in the centralized form of Dutch administration in India. By concentrating all collections and all payments of revenue in one central office, extravagant demands are made by local officials out of all proportion to their contributions, and great difficulty is experienced in making a wise apportionment of expenditure. Due to the press of business upon the central Government, local matters of much importance are left unattended to, resulting in dissatisfaction and discord. A general reorganization of the central Government seems necessary, which would restrict the influence and power of the Secretariat, and place greater emphasis upon more independent coöperation between the Governor General and the heads of his departments. With a view to giving greater rights to the local inhabitants, provincial councils have been suggested which are to be composed of European and native officials, and private European and native individuals designated by the Governor General. They should pass upon matters of public works, agriculture, and industry, and for these purposes should be allowed to expend about a third of their revenue. Under the present system many misuses of power by European officials are noted. Improper gains from auctions and notarial functions, receiving of presents, and misuse of natives for personal service have attracted the attention of the central Government. The chief result of too great centralization is the fact that minor faults of the central administration become greatly intensified as they pass down the scale of authority. Although schools have been formed to train native officials, many of them are without such training. As a result many faults are observable in them, such as the willingness to take advantage of opportunities for abuse of power, and the lack of independence in seeking to placate the Dutch superiors. These weaknesses only call for European officials of qualities above the average, whose training should be specialized in the social and political organizations of the East. The Dutch have exhibited several good sides in their colonial administration, and not the least of these has been a studied attempt to further close and confidential relations between European and native officials, rather than maintain an imposing aloofness and reserve which smacks of terrorism. In order to obtain officials who will further these ends a well established system of education and selection, coupled with a satisfactory arrangement for pay and promotion, has rendered the provincial government service attractive to good men.

Considerations Affecting Colonial Government in the Tropics.—The prime consideration underlying the modern development of the Far Eastern tropics is the fact that nature is so bountiful in supplying so full a satisfaction of the wants of the native that the trader or employer has little hold upon him. It was for this reason, rather than because of any undue greed or selfishness on the part of the Dutch, that the culture system was so long maintained. It was held that without some system of forced growths, there would be no cultivation at all of those articles required for export, because there were practically no wants of the native which could not be filled with a slight effort at serious cultivation of the land. The institution of slavery in the tropics is largely the result of an effort to find a basis of exchange between the natives and the foreign traders. This is brought about by the introduction of coolies from other countries where the pressure of population is very great. These are indentured and forced to work for a period of years and thus supply not only the labor required in large undertakings, but automatically a market for certain foreign products which the natives do not demand. It is significant that the plentifulness of nature in the tropics causes the native to be improvident and little value is attached to future supplies of goods. For the same reason, perhaps, future labor is held in just as small esteem and promises for future returns in labor are easily obtained in exchange for present enjoyment. Thus by what is termed credit bondage many industrial undertakings have been established and maintained. While this extends trade for a time, it has been held that it checks the growth of true civilization on the part of the native, and leads to no permanent increase in the wealth of the country, but in as much as humanity cannot pass directly from savagery to higher civilization some form of preliminary servitude seems almost essential. The great merit in credit bondage lies in the fact that it leaves all action to individuals, and requires only regulation by the State. Before the coming of the foreigner to the Far Eastern tropics it had a distinct place in the social system and gave the creditor full power over the person, and even the family of the debtor. While not slavery in its inception, there was every probability that the debtor could never pay the debt, and his position would become perpetually that of a subject to the creditor.

Credit Bondage.—The institution of credit bondage as a successor to the culture system in the Dutch East Indies was meant to educate the native both as a consumer as well as a producer. But for some time after its abolition the natives tended to revert to their old hand to mouth system of production and worked only enough to obtain what they had before received, but which they now procured, of course, with much less labor. Political pressure continued for many years to dominate the procuring of labor, and the good will of the headman of a village was all that was necessary to obtain any amount of native contract labor.

Credit Advances as an Inducement to Labor.—In the case of the independent laborers, however, the great productiveness of the land made it difficult for Europeans to induce them to work other than independently. With small wants the scale of living remained low and the natives evinced no ambition to better their mode of living. The practice, therefore, grew up of offering a large part of future wages in advance, and lured on by the bait of immediate enjoyment the native would bind himself to work for a stipulated time. This system of advances to secure the services of laborers has been found effective, and is practiced at the present time all over the Dutch East Indies. The Government, however, does not permit contracts to run for more than five years, and stipulates that full specifications of the services to be rendered, and the pay to be given, should be contained in the contract. Breach of contract became very prevalent, however, and under a law passed in 1872 punishing offenses of this kind there were 9,000 cases tried in three years, but the opinion of theorists in Holland opposed this legislation as reactionary, and it was repealed in 1877. Cases of breach of labor contract are now tried before regular tribunals, where it is necessary to prove that the laborer intended to desert when he made the contract. The difficulty experienced in doing this has had bad economic results, and reform in this respect is demanded.

"Particular" and Other Land Tenure.—The so-called "particular" lands which resulted from the land sales of the Government from 1800 to 1830 have resulted in the ownership of certain lands over which the proprietor exercises certain "particular" rights. On these lands he exacts dues in labor and goods from the natives, appoints a headman to exercise the functions of communal government. These lands are not numerous, and the population thus affected amounts to less than two per cent of the population, but many abuses have crept in through their ownership by absentee landlords, stock companies, and Chinese, and there is agitation for their abolition. Over all other lands the power of the Government is supreme.

Problems of Land Tenure.—The problems of the present Government, so far as the land tenure is concerned, are largely dependent upon an equitable solution of the vexed questions which have arisen out of the preceding centuries of instability and change. Land devoted to rice culture must be guarded closely to insure a steady food supply. This is especially true in view of the fact that such land is particularly well adapted to the growth of export crops like sugar, tobacco, and indigo, and is eagerly sought for by unscrupulous exploiters. The Government has taken the property right in the land and the natives in hereditary possession, interfering as little as possible with the native customs of land tenure. Foreigners can only lease land cultivated by natives for a short time, under many restrictions. These limit the term of the lease to 12 years, while communal lands may be leased in block, for a period of five years, by a two-thirds vote of the village community.

The "Net Profit System."—In 1864 the Dutch India budget had been placed under the Holland Government, and although it limited the power of the Governor General, the "net profit system" remained whereby the Dutch in Holland received the annual surplus from their dependencies. This ranged from 4 to 16 million dollars per year. The injustice of this arrangement was overcome in 1878, when the expenses of carrying on the war with the unsubdued tribes of Sumatra caused this surplus to vanish, and since that time the expenditures of the colony have almost entirely exceeded its income. In 1870 a movement was started to gradually change the culture of sugar, one of the two remaining forced cultures, to free culture and by gradually diminishing the amount of land and labor owned by the natives. This necessitated higher wages to the liberated natives, as well as payment for their land and a tax on the sugar produced, but in spite of these gains to the natives and the slight loss in Government revenues, the planters' profits increased, and production rose 300 per cent in fifteen years. The period after 1884, however, was followed by a severe depression in the sugar industry, due to increased sugar beet production by the bounty system in Europe. This depression, which would have entirely crushed the industry under the culture system, has been met successfully by the freed culture system and the energy and economy of the individual planter, since the final abolishment of the sugar culture system in 1898, following its practical suspension since 1870, has resulted in considerably reduced costs of production.

The Retention of the Coffee "Culture."—The other culture reserved to the Government, on the abolishment of the culture system in 1870, was the coffee culture, which is still maintained and, this alone, under the old system, returned four-fifths of the total revenue from sale of government products. This has led to its survival as a culture after all others have been abolished. The whole coffee culture can be carried on by the natives, and requires no elaborate machinery. This culture, however, is rapidly passing away, and the change to complete freedom in all culture in the colony is only a question of time.

The Philippines

Modern Government and Policies of the Philippines.— It is the universal rule in the history of every nation, that, upon reaching a certain stage in economic development, it has embarked upon enterprises of territorial expansion. This rule is common to all races, in all climates, under every form of government, and America's adventure in the Philippines is more attributable to this natural tendency in human evolution than to any abnormal development in our national life. On the other hand, the American occupation of the Philippines has been characterized by independent and original experiments in colonial government, induced either by blindness to local conditions or contempt for universal experience, and carried out in a spirit of detached disinterestedness which is largely accountable for their success.

The Continued Activities of Aguinaldo.—Aguinaldo and his followers had left the Philippines in 1897, after the Treaty with Spain, but suspecting that Spain did not intend to carry out the terms of the Treaty and institute the reforms, they had begun to plot another revolution, with the avowed motive of achieving the political independence of the Philippines. Of this the American authorities at Singapore and Hongkong were aware, and the proclamation that Aguinaldo issued, on his arrival at Cavite, was actually drafted by an American official at Hongkong. Aguinaldo was taken to Manila in an American transport, was permitted to seize Spanish arms in Cavite, and encouraged to start the insurrection of 1898; and this encouragement was given after he had declared his intention of establishing an independent Philippine Government. While it is true that neither Admiral Dewey, nor any other agent of the American Government, gave Aguinaldo any assurance that the United States would recognize Philippine independence, he was conveyed to the Islands under circumstances implying a recognition of his purposes, but without any knowledge on the part of Admiral Dewey as to what the United States' policy would be in case the Philippines were taken from Spain. On June 16, 1898, Secretary Hay wrote to the Consul at Singapore to the effect that the United States looked upon the Philippine insurgents as discontented and rebellious subjects of Spain, and *was not acquainted with their purposes.* Any other impression which the Consul had given General Aguinaldo was unauthorized. There is no evidence that this pronouncement was ever given publicity at the time, or communicated either to Aguinaldo or the military and naval commanders in the Philippines. Indeed the correspondence between Generals Anderson and Otis with Aguinaldo after that date prove that such a policy was unknown to them.

In January, 1899, after the proclamation of the assumption of governing power by the United States, it was evident that the American forces and those of the insurgent leader could remain in their undefined positions no longer and after vainly endeavoring to force American action, on February 4, 1899, hostilities were begun which were to result in the downfall and capture of the insurgents under Aguinaldo.

The Arrival of the Philippine Commission.—The Philippine Commission which arrived the next month was not invested with any authority to intervene in the military situation. After a month's survey of the situation it issued a proclamation which declared that American supremacy must be upheld at whatever cost, and that "the object of the American government was the well being, the prosperity, and happiness of the Philippine people, and their elevation to a position among the most civilized peoples of the world." These reforms were to be effected briefly through the reformation of all branches of the public service, and the corporations and associations affecting the lives of the people; through the establishment of schools; through the encouragement of trade, agriculture, and industry; through the construction of roads, railroads, and public works; and through the introduction of a sound system of taxation. These reforms were to be accompanied by granting to the people "ample liberty of self-government reconcilable with the maintenance of a wise, just, stable, effective, and economical administration of public affairs, and with sovereign and international rights and obligations of the United States."

On September 1, 1900, the legislative power was transferred from the military governor to the Philippine Commission, under William H. Taft, and on the same day a year following the civil executive power was also transferred to the Commission, which was enlarged to include three Filipino members.

The First American Government.—The lowest rungs of the ladder of the first American Government set up in the Philippines were the municipal councils, which corresponded to the New England township and numbered 623, with 3,600 presidents, secretaries, treasurers, clerks, and 8,000 councilors. These were all elected by the people and any male of 23 or over having six months' residence in a municipality could vote, provided he had held certain offices under the Spaniards, or owned $250 worth of real estate, or paid $15 or more in taxes, or spoke, read, and wrote English or Spanish.

These councils raised and disbursed money for local purposes such as schools, police, etc., but their early operations were not satisfactory because of the anxiety of higher officials to assure their own salaries from the public coffers first, at the expense of all other needs.

The provincial governments were controlled by provincial boards consisting of a provincial Governor elected by the municipal councilors of the Province for a two-year term, and the provincial supervisor and treasurer, who were appointed by the Philippine Commission. The duties of these boards were to levy and collect taxes, to direct provincial public works, and supervise the administration of the municipalities.

The First Commission and Present Powers of the Governor General.—Perhaps the weakest link in the commission form of government in the Philippines was the Commission itself. Possessed of little discretionary power, and influenced largely by politics at home, and entirely relying upon Congress for the direction of its policies, the Commission was little respected by the provincial or municipal officials, who realized that Congress had the final authority.

The changes which have taken place in the form of the Philippine Government since 1903 have gradually evolved a Government very nearly independent in its local functions, and only held to the home Government by a single tie, the authority of the Governor General. The policy of the Wilson administration has been consistently one of granting the fullest measure of self-government to the Filipino people, and in his report for 1918 the Governor General went so far as to express his belief that the people had established the stable government demanded by Congress, as a prerequisite for the granting of their independence. This Government now consists of a Governor General and Vice-Governor General appointed by the President. Under the Governor General are the six Departments of the Interior, Public Instruction, Justice, Finance, Agriculture and Natural Resources, and Commerce and Communications, the heads of which form a Cabinet corresponding in its functions very much to the Cabinet of the United States. Besides these Departments several official organizations have been formed under the direction of the Governor General. Thus during the war the Council of Defense, and the Council of State performed certain duties in connection with the preservation of order, while the Philippine National Guard has been of great service in maintaining order during the withdrawal of the regular American Army during 1918 for service in Siberia. Three Government corporations, the Philippine National Bank, the Manila Railroad Company, and the National Coal Company, are under the direct control of the Governor General.

Legislative and Judicial Functions of the Government.—The legislative functions of the Philippine Government are performed by a House and Senate, constituted along the lines of legislative bodies in this country. Legislation passed by this body must be approved by the Governor General and, in certain specified cases, proposed laws must receive the approval of the President of the United States.

The judiciary consists of a Supreme Court, courts of first instance and justice of the peace courts, who are all under the supervision of the Department of Justice.

The Department of Mindanao and Sulu is under a separate Governor, and maintains a special position in the Philippine Government because of the large proportion of non-Christian and uncivilized tribes. Comprising one-third of the area of the archipelago, and seven per cent of the population, this Department is organized in such a way as to meet the peculiar problems which the large proportion of Mohammedan and pagan peoples, representing almost ninety per cent of the whole, present.

The American Policy of Education.—The policy of the American Government has been based upon education. While this question has been approached from the point of view of the political development of the people, it has been felt that with the establishment of a complete system of education, many other problems would also be solved. The chief difference between the policy of the American Government in the Philippines and the Dutch and English Governments in India is that while we are seeking to prepare the Filipinos for popular self-government, through primary and secondary education offered freely to all, up until very recently the Dutch and English have sought to maintain their suzerainty by opposite means. Not that education of the natives is not being carried on in the Dutch and English colonies, but the education is designed to strengthen the natives' ideas of dependence and solidarity with the home government, rather than to fit them to ultimately govern themselves. The desire for independence has existed in the Filipinos for many years, but it could not in justice to them be granted until they had been properly fitted to undertake self-government.

The English language has been adopted as the common language in the schools and has been taught for 20 years—first, because a single language was necessary in order to develop an effective public opinion, and, secondly, because English is the language of Anglo-Saxon freedom. One-fifth of the total revenue of the Islands, or about $3,000,000, is expended on public education. The average daily attendance at public schools in the Philippines in 1918 was 521,377, in a total of 4,747 schools.

Other Developments under American Rule.—But aside from education, great attention has been given to public health and modern sanitary methods, and the use of preventative measures, such as vaccination, have greatly reduced disease and prevented epidemics. Scientific assistance in crop growing has been established under the Department of Agriculture and Natural Resources, and the total value of the six leading crops, rice, abaca, sugar, coconuts, corn, and tobacco, totaled in 1918 $175,000,000, an increase of $54,000,000 over 1917, and of $91,000,000 over 1913. The Department of Commerce and Communications was increased in its importance in January, 1918, by the creation of a Bureau of Commerce and Industry, which is to pay especial attention to port development, establishment of radio stations, proper distribution of labor between the Islands, and the development of foreign trade by the establishment of agencies abroad. Under the same Department, the Bureau of Public Works has built first-class roads in all Provinces, and the road systems of each province have been consolidated. New bridges and new piers at Manila, Cebu, Toeloban, Iloilo, and elsewhere have been begun.

The industrial and commercial development of the Islands has received a great impetus by the war, when demands for coconut oil have far exceeded the supply. The result has been an influx of capital into the Islands which is being employed to develop coal, and mineral and agricultural enterprises, on a scale never before attempted. The capacity of the Filipinos to carry out these projects proves that the policy of the United States in furnishing a groundwork of education has not been without results.

Questions

1. Describe the functions of the three branches of the Dutch East Indies Government, and discuss disadvantages of the system.
2. Why is it difficult to control labor in the tropics?
3. What are the contributory causes of credit bondage?
4. How is land now held by foreigners in the Dutch East Indies?
5. What was the "net profit system" in the sugar culture?
6. What led Aguinaldo to assume that an independent government in the Philippines would be recognized by the United States?

7. What were the avowed objects of the American Government as set forth in the proclamation of the Philippine Commission?
8. Describe the organization of government under the Philippine Commission in the Philippines.
9. Describe the present Government.
10. Outline American policy in the Philippines.

CHAPTER XI

THE TOPOGRAPHY, AGRICULTURE, AND INDUSTRIES OF THE PHILIPPINES

Seven-eighths of the 10,000,000 people in the Philippines are known as Filipinos. The balance are primitive and semi-civilized tribes among whom are the Negritos, the Subanuns, the Igorots, Bontoks, and Ifugaos. The wants of these tribes are as primitive as their civilization, and their place in the economic structure of the Islands is a comparatively insignificant one.

Rice.—Rice and fish or corn and fish furnish the principal food for the inhabitants of every part of the Islands, although vegetables form a large part of the diet of those people living far from the coast. Rice is the chief foodstuff and consequently the main crop. As a dry crop, rice is grown in the mountain regions, but the greatest part of the crop is raised in the lowlands in paddy fields and on terraced slopes leading down to the valleys. In some parts, particularly the eastern and northeastern slopes of some islands, there is a continuous rainfall and the season is indefinite. In other central and western sections of these islands there is a dry season requiring irrigation for rice culture, and, as such regions comprise the chief rice regions and irrigation is not much practiced because of the scarcity of storable water, there is generally but one crop of rice a year. This is planted and cultivated in the rainy season from June to December and harvested from then until February. The domestic production of rice is about 530,000 metric tons, while 150,000 long tons are imported. Since 1877 the Philippines have been dependent upon imported rice in an ever increasing ratio. Various reasons are assigned for the lack of rice production. In the Philippines the use of the carabao, or water buffalo, is considered essential to the cultivation of rice, and when many of these were killed off by the rinderpest the production of rice fell off correspondingly. With the increased demand for the money crops for export, the tendency has also been to dispense with the disagreeable and unprofitable task of rice raising and importations have increased. The growing dependence of the Philippines upon outside food, however, is a state of affairs which is liable to become very disastrous in the event of crop failures in those countries which form the basis of supply. Numerous remedies for this situation have been suggested, including an increase in the number of work animals, reduction of production costs in order to yield a greater profit, the abolition of the share system of harvesting in favor of a wage system, thereby giving greater profit to the grower, and better methods of cultivation, including the use of modern agricultural machinery. Other considerations might be enumerated as better seed selection, better irrigation, and the bringing of more virgin soil under cultivation.

Corn.—The status of corn as a food crop in the Philippines is a low one, as it is known as "poor man's rice," and the value of the crop is one-eighth that of the rice crop. Many localities are admirably adapted to the cultivation of corn, and as one-fifth of the population resides in these districts it has become the principal food of a large portion of the population. Corn cultivation and storage are both in a crude state. The soil preparation is poor, there is no seed selection, the distance between the stalks is too small, and fertilizers are not sufficiently used. The methods of storing employed are either by fastening the whole ear to a framework, tying the ears together and drying on the roof of the house or by shelling and storing for a short time. The efforts to increase production have been largely along the lines of remedying the defects in cultivation outlined above and in the introduction of modern steel corn mills to replace the crude stone mills.

Other Food Crops.—There are several other crops which serve to supplement the rice and maize crops of the Islands as food crops. The sweet potato is cultivated in certain sections where the soil is not suitable for rice and the high winds do not permit maize to grow. Generally the sweet potato is the food of the very poor classes. Numerous species of yams also grow wild and are cultivated. Sweet potatoes also figure as an important catch crop before and after rice planting. The taro root is a starch food of secondary value which is grown principally along streams and in other localities where the necessary water is obtainable during the dry season. Cassava root, from which we make tapioca, is the chief food crop in the Sulu Archipelago. Among the fruits produced mangos and mandarins are the most generally used. The demand for bananas is greater than the supply, and while they are a main article of diet in the rural districts, being grown in many gardens, the best species are also in great demand by the better classes and bring high prices in the cities. Intelligent work has been done in introducing a large variety of pulse and vegetables into the Philippine dietary. Cowpeas, lima beans, and green gram furnish the necessary protein to the Filipino, and other varieties, including soya beans are being introduced. Efforts are being made to educate the people to use more vegetables.

Hemp.—The principal export crop is *abaca*, or hemp, which was grown in the Islands before the coming of the white man. In 1919 132,000 long tons were exported, 70,000 tons to the United States, 47,000 tons to Great Britain, 9,000 tons to Japan, and the rest to other countries. Hemp is free from attack by pests and fungous diseases, resists drought, and may be cultivated without much labor at all times of the year. Early in the nineteenth century the cultivation of the wild plant was begun, and to-day the production consists principally of the cultivated plant, although some uncultivated varieties are still produced. In the older districts the holdings are very small due to the scarcity and immobility of labor. Hemp buyers, through advances on the crop, usually gain control of the crop, although in the newer districts larger plantations are growing up which are largely independent. As most of the fiber must be stripped by hand, the necessary labor for this operation is difficult to obtain and often demands, as wages, a share in the product. The hemp stripper is usually not a farmer, but when the price of hemp falls, there is generally an exodus of strippers from the hemp fields to the rice fields where they engage in harvesting the rice. The question of transportation of the hemp from the hill fields to the coast is a serious one, and the market price of the product usually determines whether much of the hemp shall not be left to waste on the stalk rather than be transported to the coast by the costly labor of man and beast. Carelessness in drying and delay in drying and stripping are the principal causes of low quality hemp production, which has shown a steady tendency to increase in recent years. This tendency has been heightened by the fact that the local hemp buyers maintain a discrepancy in prices in favor of lower grades, twice as much of which can be produced in an hour as of the high grade, at only something like a 25 per cent reduction in price. This is due, of course, to the high cost of labor in the stripping process which absorbs half the value of the product. Most of the high-grade fiber is produced by growers who are independent of the local buyers and who sell directly to Manila. The local buyers are seldom expert judges of quality and prefer to buy low-grade hemp, not being such good judges of the quality of the high-grade product. Moreover, such buyers make their commission at so much per *picul* (133 pounds) and their gains are greater if they buy more piculs of low-grade hemp than less piculs of high-grade hemp.

There are three distinct problems facing the hemp industry in the Philippines: (1) to raise the quality of the product; (2) to increase the size of the holdings and to decrease the number of middlemen handling the fiber; and (3) the greater use of machinery in stripping.

In a sense the two last problems are contributory to the first, for until the high cost of hand stripping is eliminated the tendency to produce low-grade hemp will continue to exist, and with many small holdings, whose product is controlled by local buyers, the possibility of relief from price discrepancy in favor of the low-grade product is remote.

Like all export crops, the state of the hemp market is determined by factors entirely removed from domestic considerations, and the fall and rise of the price due to foreign demand, influences directly the production and the attraction of labor to hemp raising and stripping. Good crops in the United States, causing a brisk demand for binder twine, react immediately upon the price of hemp and its production in the Philippines.

Copra.—The Philippines produce about one quarter of the world's coconuts, and while the export of the dried coconut meat, or copra, practically all of which went to the United States, dropped from 103,000 long tons in 1918 to 14,000 long tons in 1919, the export of coconut oil increased in the same years from 71,000 long tons to 128,000 long tons, 120,000 of which went to the United States. Coconut trees are grown in two ways, in large groves owned by landholders and in small patches around the homes of small farmers. Pests, including insects, mammals, birds, and diseases which infect the trees, destroy a great deal of the product annually, and the most harmful of these is the rhinoceros beetle which attacks the bud in the palm, although the red weevil, which bores into the trunk, destroys a great deal. These insects breed in rubbish consisting of old leaves and husks which accumulate around the bases of the trees, and, for this reason, the best results are obtained from groves that are kept free from this rubbish. The wild pig roots up the seedlings in many places and can be kept away only by strong fences. But larger losses in production are suffered from poor harvesting and drying. The fear of thieves stealing the ripened fruit, the need of ready money, and the tendency to gather all the nuts in a cluster, whether they are ripe or not, cause green nuts to be harvested at a consequent loss in quality. Copra is cured either by sun drying or smoking. The product of the drying process is suitable for food, but the product of the smoking process contains creosote, which limits its use only to the manufacture of soaps, candles, etc. Due to crude drying methods, 10 to 15 per cent of water is left in the copra when shipped, which often causes it to mold and deteriorate. In order to avoid this, the introduction of mechanical driers which evaporate the moisture by hot air is being urged.

For the reasons outlined above the low quality of the Philippine copra causes it to command the lowest price in the market. Local buyers, by advancing money on crops, also thwart any incentive to produce better copra.

Sugar.—The Philippines became prominent as a sugar producing country about 1869 when the opening of the Suez Canal and the great demand and high price of sugar during the Crimean war made it an important source of supply. A British central was established in 1877, but closed in 1880 as unprofitable. In 1893 the production was 300,000 tons, of which 261,000 tons were exported. The Island of Negros was the leading producer. After peace was restored in 1899 the Philippine sugar production was reduced to almost nothing. Since then failure to adopt modern methods has held the production below the 1893 figures, which have only been equalled during the past few years. The exports for 1918 were 225,000 long tons and in 1919, 236,000 long tons. The principal markets are the United States, which take 91,000 long tons; Hongkong, 66,000 long tons; China, 40,000 long tons; Japan, 35,000 long tons; and other countries, 4,000 long tons. A very recent move has been made to replace the antiquated methods employed in sugar milling by modern centrals at a consequently lower cost of production, and it is hoped that Philippine sugar will gain a preëminent place in the world's market.

Tobacco.—In 1919 the Philippines exported 397,000,000 cigars, 276,000,000 of which went to the United States, 34,000,000 to China, 8,000,000 to Australia, 8,000,000 to Hongkong, and 71,000,000 to other countries. In the same year 48,000,000 pounds of unmanufactured tobacco were exported, 22,000,000 pounds of which went to Spain, 9,000,000 pounds to France, 3,000,000 pounds to the United States, and 14,000,000 pounds to other countries. In addition to these exports there is a large domestic consumption of locally grown leaf and Manila made cigarettes. The aim of tobacco growers is to produce a sufficient quantity of higher grade leaf for the increasing demand for Philippine cigars in the United States. This requires the training of more cigar makers at Manila. The chief causes of low grade tobacco production is the lack of supervision over the small growers who produce the bulk of the tobacco and are ignorant of the proper culture and curing methods. These small growers sell to the factory agents through local buyers. Just as in the hemp trade, these buyers are ignorant of quality and offer the same price for all grades of tobacco with the result that there is no incentive for the small growers to cultivate the high-grade leaf. Moreover, the small growers are often at the mercy of the buyers who lend them money on their crops and compel them to turn over their product at a very low price. The Government is now attempting to improve these conditions by instruction and example through experimental stations.

Fibers.—Maguey fiber, obtained from the *agave cantala*, was introduced into the Philippines from Mexico where *henequin* and *sisal* had long been grown. This plant thrives on poor soils, and is consequently raised in Ilocos, Norte, Cebu, and Bohol, where other crops could not be made to pay. The production is still small and only 9,000 tons were exported in 1919.

Kapok trees grow in some abundance, but the gathering of the fiber has not reached the importance it has in Java. One or two plantations exist, but most of the trees grow along the roads and their fiber is lost. Only 100 tons are exported.

Other Possible Crops.—Among other minor and possible crops are fruits, and rubber, the cultivation of which is handicapped by the 2,500 acre limitation in the land laws; silk, for which a plentiful supply of labor is lacking; essential oils, particularly for perfumery and coffee, which has never recovered from the 1889 pest, and does not yield the certain returns of copra and other crops.

Animal Industry.—The Philippines furnish an excellent grazing country in over 40 per cent of the area. The carabao is indigenous to the Philippines, while cattle, horses, and goats were introduced by the Spaniards from Mexico, China, and Spain. Since 1888 the rinderpest, *surra,* and internal strife have reduced the number of animals until they no longer nearly fulfill the agricultural needs of the community. The carabao does 90 per cent of the agricultural work and transportation in the Philippines, and, being by nature fitted to work in the muddy rice fields, it is preferred to other animals by the natives. The cattle of the Philippines have been greatly reduced in number by disease, and due to the lack of cross breeding for many years their type has deteriorated. Recently an Indian breed has been introduced which is peculiarly immune from rinderpest and tick. Many domestic cattle are killed for meat. There are few milch cows, as little milk is used by the natives. The Philippine horse, by a process of natural selection, has developed from a cross of the Sulu horse and those from Mexico and China into a type best suited for the climate and the riding and light hauling for which it is almost exclusively used. Due to careless breeding the stock has deteriorated, and in order to provide the necessary work animals scientific breeding and improvement is proposed. Swine raising is carried on to some extent in all parts of the Islands, but the total number of swine is not large. The swine are permitted to run loose and are only penned up shortly before killing in order to fatten them. Much of the meat supply is pork, which is found in practically all local markets. Poultry is almost as plentiful as pork, but the laying qualities are affected by the tendency to breed for cockfighting, which results in a high mortality among the males, and a small, tough type of chicken. About 4,000,000 eggs are imported annually from China.

Fisheries.—The catch from in-shore fishing, conducted mainly at night, is the principal source of food for a large proportion of the inhabitants, fish being prolific in the shallow waters of many of the Islands. In some sections 80 per cent of the population derive their livelihood from fishing. Many people move to the good fishing grounds during the seasons when fish are plentiful, drying the catch and shipping it inland. The dragnet is the most widely used method of fishing, and the work is often carried on by the share system. Usually the owner of the boat, nets, and traps receives one-half of the catch and the rest is divided among the fishermen. Fish culture is carried on near Manila and Iloilo.

Forestry.—About half the total area of the Islands is covered with forests and about one-third of the total area are virgin forests. The principal forest production consists of the lumber of the *lauan, apitong,* and *yacals* trees, which is used for construction rather than the finer furniture woods which are only found at occasional places in the forests. Strict Government regulations to prevent deforestation have been made, although the difficulty of enforcing regulations which conflict with the Kaingin system of clearings for agricultural purposes is very great.

Three improvements are necessary in the actual preparation of the lumber for market: (1) the reduction of the number of licenses, the putting the logging operations on a large scale basis, and the avoidance of the waste now caused by crude methods and equipment; (2) the reduction of high milling costs by better equipment more scientifically arranged and the elimination of waste; (3) a decrease in transportation costs through better shipping facilities.

There is still a good demand for Philippine lumber in the domestic market, and, after that is supplied, in China and the United States.

Manufacturing Industries.—As a rule manufacturing may be said to be in the household stage of development. Hats, mats, bamboo and rattan chairs, baskets, pottery, rope, embroidery, and knotted *abaca* are all made in the households and sold to commission men for export. In addition to these articles many articles for domestic use are manufactured in the households. The Islands have not yet reached the stage of development where large-scale, or factory, industry can be successfully undertaken, and as long as the agricultural industries remain undeveloped for lack of population there will be no incentive for the agriculturist to abandon the independent life of the farm for the circumscribed existence of the factory.

Questions

1. Discuss the rice crop of the Philippines and enumerate remedies for low production.
2. What part does maize play in the agricultural economy of the Islands?
3. Discuss three other food crops.
4. What factors tend to keep the quality of the hemp produced low?
5. What are some suggested improvements in copra harvesting and drying?
6. Discuss the sugar production of the Philippines.
7. What is the aim of Philippine tobacco growers and how may it be carried out?
8. What are the principal animals of the Philippines and how is each used?
9. In what three ways may the lumber industry be improved?
10. Discuss manufacturing industries.

CHAPTER XII

TOPOGRAPHY, AGRICULTURE, MINES, AND INDUSTRIES OF THE DUTCH EAST INDIES

The area of the Dutch East Indies is about 736,400 square miles, which includes the Islands of Java, Sumatra, part of Borneo, Celebes, Dutch or Western New Guinea, and a great many smaller islands, the Archipelago extending over 3,000 miles east and west and 1,100 north and south. The population is 47,000,000, 33,000,000 of which are concentrated on the Island of Java. Included in this figure are 138,000 Europeans, 832,000 Asiatics, including 91 per cent Chinese, 5 per cent Arabs, and 4 per cent other Asiatics. The density of population is 64 to the square mile for the Archipelago, although 675 people inhabit a square mile in Java and only seven in Borneo. The large number of Chinese in the Dutch East Indies are employed as laborers, small farmers, and merchants. The Chinese merchant is the most important factor in the retail business of the Islands. With few exceptions, the European or Dutch residents are mostly officials and large importers.

Trade Areas of the Dutch East Indies, Java and Madoera.—For administrative purposes the islands are divided into an area embracing the Islands of Java and Madoera, and another area embracing the Outer Possessions, or all other islands. There are four trade regions in the first area; that of East Java, based on the port of Soerabaya, includes the eastern portion of Java, the Islands of Bali, Lombok adjacent, and the southern part of southeast Borneo; that of East Central Java, based on the port of Samarang, includes the area that its name indicates; that of West Central Java, based on the port of Cheribon; and that of West Java based on the port of Batavia (also known as Tandjoeng Priok) includes west Java, southern Sumatra, and the Islands of Banka and Billiton.

The Outer Possessions.—There are likewise four trade regions in the Outer Possessions; the Eastern Archipelago, based on the port of Macassar, includes the Celebes, Menado, the eastern part of southeast Borneo, Ambonia, the northern Moluccas, Dutch New Guinea, and Timon; the Padang region includes Sumatra West Coast, and Bankoelen; the Medan region includes Sumatra East Coast; while Singapore region includes northern Sumatra, and western Borneo.

Java's total export trade averages normally about $140,000,000, although during 1915, 1916, and 1917, due to the abnormally high prices obtained for products abroad and the increased productions incidental to the war, the export trade of the Java and Madoera area averaged $176,000,000 for 1915, $207,000,000 for 1916, and $180,000,000 for 1917. By 1918 the normal pre-war figure of $140,000,000 had been reached, although due to high prices and the dislocation of shipping this value represented about half the tonnage shipped out in 1914. The principal items are sugar, rubber, tin, petroleum, tea, coffee, tobacco, copra and coconut oil, fibers, cinchona, pepper, and tapioca. The export trade of the Outer Possessions may be divided in the following way. For the Eastern Archipelago: $3,000,000 for Celebes, nearly half of which is for copra, although damar, coconut oil, birds' skins, and rattan are important; and $2,500,000 for Menado, of which 90 per cent is for copra. For the Sumatra West Coast the direct exports are negligible, most of the goods going out by way of Batavia. The Sumatra East Coast exports $40,000,000 worth of products annually, the principal ones being petroleum, valued at $14,000,000; rubber, $13,000,000; tobacco, $10,-

000,000; tea, $400,000; gambier, $400,000; and others $2,200,000.

It is estimated that $93,000,000 are invested in Sumatra East Coast estates, of which $36,000,000 is Dutch; $29,000,000, British; $10,000,000, American; $7,000,000, Belgian; and all others, $10,000,000.

The exports from the Singapore trade region total $30,000,000 annually, consisting principally of mineral oils, rubber, copra, gambier, rattan, sago, guttas, hardwoods, fish, damar, and hides.

Agriculture.—In 1830 the Dutch Government introduced the culture system, which, as has been stated, was based on the claim of the Dutch to the ownership of the land, the natives being compelled either to part with a certain portion of their crops or pay a certain sum as ground rent. An attempt was made to induce the natives to plant a fifth of their land with products for European consumption, which would not enter into the native scheme of life, such as sugar, coffee, tea, rubber, tobacco, fibers, etc. The products then became the property of the Government, and when the ground rent was deducted from their value the difference was returned to the natives. The system had its merits, but was found to weigh heavily on the natives as the European population increased, and proved a growing obstacle to individual enterprise. Since the abolition of this system in 1870, the production of the Islands has increased many fold, and though the machinery through which the products are marketed is still in the hands of the Dutch, the natives are constantly raising their standard of living. Reformed land laws, which do not permit the alienation of native owned land to foreign holders, but merely provide for their lease for certain stipulated periods, have also tended to emphasize this development.

Sugar.—One million five hundred thousand tons of sugar are produced every year in the Dutch East Indies, and due to the incessant scientific research of the Dutch Government improved methods of cultivation are constantly increasing the yield per acre. This is also being increased by the use of artificial fertilizers, and improved facilities for manufacturing the sugar cane. The total value of the sugar export amounts to $75,000,000.

The distribution of sugar centrals and exports for the various trade regions is East Java, 102 centrals, 666,000 metric tons; East Central Java, 85 centrals, 356,000 metric tons; West Central Java, 85 centrals, 146,000 metric tons. These three regions control the sugar production of the Dutch East Indies.

Rubber.—There are to-day about 700 estates in the Dutch East Indies producing rubber. The rubber plant has been artificially grown for 30 years, the species thus produced being known as Para rubber, and was introduced from Brazil, although the culture of the native Java rubber is also gaining headway. The total value of the rubber exports amount to $12,000,000 dollars from Java, and $13,000,000 from the Sumatra East Coast. The principal rubber region is West Java, and the port is Batavia. The rubber is produced in the lowlands of this region, and tea is grown on the higher lands.

Tea.—The mountainous districts of Sumatra are also particularly well suited to the cultivation of tea, although the largest production is still on the Island of Java. Systematic effort to increase the foreign market for Java tea has resulted in a very large sale, particularly in this country. The yearly value of tea exports from the Dutch East Indies amounts to about $6,600,000. Tea is grown on estates as in India, and not in small garden patches as in China, and because of the improved methods used the price and quality led to an increased sale abroad.

Coffee.—Java coffee is probably the best known product of the Dutch East Indies in this country. The culture suffered severely some years ago from a disease and pest, but this was overcome by the introduction of Robusta and Liberian coffees, which are found to thrive best in this climate. Annually 20,000 tons of coffee are produced, and the exports total $10,000,000, which are largely sent to the Netherlands, France, and the United States.

Tobacco.—Tobacco was introduced under the culture system with disappointing results, but after the abolition of the culture system the natives were taught the proper method of cultivation, and the production is now increasing rapidly. Sumatra is the center of the tobacco growing district of the Dutch East Indies, and the Government is giving every attention to teaching and advising the natives as to the best methods. There are a number of tobacco estates under European management, although planting is also carried on largely by the natives, who are supported by public land credit banks. The export totals $10,000,000 in value, and is sent chiefly to Holland, although the domestic consumption is increasing with the introduction of Western civilization.

Copra and Coconut Oil.—Copra was one of the few export crops which was not introduced by the culture system, the coconut palm being indigenous throughout the Islands, and from early times having played an important part in the native economy. With the increased demand for coconut oil for use in the manufacture of glycerine, oleomargarine, soaps, and candles, the planting of coconut trees has been encouraged and large plantations are now devoted to this culture; 20 large, modern copra pressing oil mills, with modern machinery, furnish a profitable outlet for the products of this industry, the value of which is indicated by the exports, which total $7,000,000 per year for copra and $7,000,000 for oil. The principal shipments of copra were: from Menado, about $2,000,000 worth; from the Celebes, about $1,200,000 worth; from Borneo, about

$1,200,000 worth; and from all other islands about $2,000,000 worth. The principal copra-crushing mills are in the Soerabaya district, from which port much of the coconut oil is exported.

Fibers.—The principal fiber is kapok, the cotton-like fiber which surrounds the seed of the cotton tree, and which is in great demand in the West for stuffing pillows and in the manufacture of life preservers. Sisal and hemp are other fibers now being raised in West Java on an experimental scale. The total value of fiber exports is $5,000,000 annually.

Quinine and Cinchona.—Cinchona, or Peruvian bark, from which quinine is made, is grown in the high plains and hills of western Java where tea is grown and it is shipped from Batavia. The annual export of quinine amounts to about $5,000,000, and of cinchona $1,000,000.

Pepper.—One of the earliest exports from the Dutch East Indies was pepper, which, with other spices, was used extensively in Mediæval Europe for the preservation of meats and other foods before the use of ice and of canning. The present annual export of pepper is valued at $4,000,000.

Tapioca.—The root of the cassava plant, which is extensively grown in Java, is manufactured into tapioca products for the Western market. The exports are valued at $2,000,000 annually.

Rice.—Rice is the staple food of the natives, although the best quality is exported, and the total production of the lower grades is not sufficient to feed the whole population, large quantities being imported from Indo-China, India, and Siam. Rice is produced by dry and wet farming, depending largely upon the character of the land. Terraced paddy fields are in vogue, such as are used in the Philippines and Japan. The annual production is about 7,000,000 tons, and the better qualities are exported to the value of $2,000,000 annually. Other agricultural products in the order of their export value are indigo, peanuts, cocoa, damar, spices, essential oils, gambier, etc.

Tin Mining.—The Government tin mines on the Island of Banka are the most important mines in the Dutch East Indies, producing annually 15,000 tons of tin, and exporting to the value of $16,000,000. The mines employ 21,000 workmen. The ore is mined exclusively from open pits, which are in the alluvial deposits of many rivers, and in the alluvial strata on the slopes of the smaller hills. There are no underground galleries, the work being carried on entirely near the surface. The laborers are chiefly Chinese coolies, and the work is supervised by qualified Dutch mining engineers. Other tin mines are the Billiton Company's mines on the Island of Billiton, which have an anual production of 5,000 tons.

Coal Mining.—The method of steam navigation in the tropical waters of the Dutch East Indies has been a large factor in opening up the coal fields. The Ombilin mines on the west coast of the Island of Sumatra have been worked since 1892, and produce about 5,000,000 tons annually. The laborers in these mines are chiefly recruited from the convict station, and one-half of the 7,000 laborers employed are of this character. The government takes great care to supervise the conditions under which the laborers work, and their efforts along these lines have proven worthy of emulation.

Gold Mining.—Although the Dutch East Indies have had the reputation of being rich in gold, the total value of gold produced amounts only to about $2,000,000 annually. Gold is found in Sumatra, Borneo, and the Celebes in beach deposits, alluvial deposits, and gravel beds.

Petroleum.—The development of the petroleum industry is of comparatively recent date, the chief centers of production being Borneo, northern Sumatra, eastern Sumatra, and Java. The growth in the use of kerosene by-products has contributed very greatly toward the development of the industry. About 1,500,000 tons of crude oil are produced annually in the Dutch East Indies, being marketed in China by three large companies known as the Royal Dutch, the Rochelle, and the Asiatic Petroleum companies.

Estate Products and General Trade.—There are two quite distinct kinds of trade in Dutch East Indian products. The trade in the estate products of the Island of Java and Sumatra is pretty generally controlled by large Dutch interests, while the trade in the many miscellaneous gums, and other tropical products of the Outer Possessions, is nearly all centered in the hands of the Chinese, whose *entrepot* is Singapore. It is this trade in Dutch East Indian products, carried on by Chinese, that has built up Singapore into one of the greatest primary markets of the world. The importance of shipping her products directly to the United States and other markets, rather than through Holland, has become more and more apparent to the Colony during the war when direct trade with the United States was made imperative. Since that time a very strong movement has been on foot among a large section of the Dutch colonials to build up their own markets direct, rather than through Holland. The importance of this movement to our export trade in the Dutch East Indies cannot be overestimated. By controlling large stocks of Dutch East Indian products the Germans and British, before the war, were able to divide the trade in manufactured goods between them. Commerce is an exchange of commodities, and no successful trade can be established unless our ships come back as well filled as they go out. It is necessary, therefore, to purchase direct those products which we formerly bought through the European trading countries, and in turn to sell our goods directly to the Colony.

Questions

1. How are the Dutch East Indies divided for administrative purposes? Name the four trade regions of the second division with ports.
2. Discuss the development of agriculture in general.
3. How has the sugar industry been developed? In what trade areas is it principally grown?
4. In what region is rubber grown? Discuss the tea production.
5. Where is tobacco chiefly raised and under what methods is it cultivated? Discuss coffee production.
6. What are the present and future prospects of copra production and the coconut oil industry?
7. What is kapok? Discuss cinchona, pepper and tapioca production.
8. Describe the tin-mining industry and its location.
9. Discuss coal and gold mining.
10. Where is petroleum found and where marketed?

CHAPTER XIII

COMMERCIAL METHODS AND MARKET ANALYSIS OF THE PHILIPPINES AND DUTCH EAST INDIES

THE PHILIPPINE ISLANDS

The import trade of the Philippines for the twelve months ending June, 1919, totaled $107,000,000, of which $64,000,000 was with the United States, $13,000,000 with Japan, $6,000,000 with China, $6,000,000 with French Indo-China, and most of the balance with Great Britain and her colonies. This trade represented a substantial increase over the total imports during 1918, when only $83,000,000 worth of goods were brought in, the proportion in which they were supplied by the various countries remaining the same.

Cotton Cloths.—The greatest single item of import was cotton cloths, of which 80,000,000 yards, valued at $16,000,000, were bought in 1919, $13,000,000 worth being supplied by the United States. The Philippines are one of the few Oriental markets where American cloths are predominant, and this position is only held, it is feared, because of the preferential treatment accorded the American product by the Philippine tariff, which is so constructed as to give American goods a market, where it is possible to do so without unnecessarily, or too seriously, increasing the cost of living of the Filipinos. Another factor which, even without a tariff, would place American cotton goods in a favorable position is the efficient marketing methods of America's premier merchandising company in the Philippines, the Pacific Commercial Company, whose organization is well established throughout the Islands and is in a position to distribute American goods with comparatively very little overhead expense. This fact looms large in the cotton goods industry, in which business is generally done on so slight a margin that every cent added to the cost price means so much more difficulty in competing with others.

Iron, Steel and Machinery.—The second largest item of the import trade of the Philippines comprises iron and steel and machinery. Iron and steel and machinery which totaled $7,000,000 each are supplied almost wholly from the United States. In 1919 machinery almost doubled in value and this was accounted for by the number of trucks and tractors which were brought in from America. In the spring of 1919 a tractor demonstration was held under Government auspices, in which a number of American machines were entrants, and the results, though not given wide publicity, furnished the Government with a clue to the most satisfactory types for its own use, and its selections have been widely followed. The labor scarcity in the Philippines is accountable, more than anything else, for the demand for tractors, and, with no policy which would seem to alleviate conditions in sight, the demand seems bound to increase.

The Future of the Agricultural Implement Trade.—With vast quantities of undeveloped land simply awaiting the plow, and only a very limited population, the future development of the Philippines must depend either upon the more extended use of labor saving agricultural implements or a change in the immigration laws which would permit indentured Chinese to work the estates. As the latter alternative seems remote in its adoption, attention has been turned for the present to the use of agricultural implements. The present land laws, which restrict holdings to 2,500 acres, are also a great handicap to any large-scale development of the Islands. Many companies who would like to invest money in the development of rubber, coconut, and other estates cannot do so under the present law. If the United States is to grant the Philippines their independence, they should not be turned loose with large tracts of rich, tropical, undeveloped land, practically beckoning to neighboring powers to come in and exploit. In preserving this land for the future generations of the Filipinos, whose numbers do not increase, the United States may be working against the best interests of present generations, who should enjoy at the present time the prosperity and development incident to a wise and fair investment of American capital on a sufficiently large scale to make it both profitable and safe.

Rice.—Although the Islands are underpopulated they do not produce enough food for the population they have, because the high prices which the principal exports command abroad make it more profitable to raise hemp, coconuts, sugar, and tobacco and to import rice than to devote the Islands' lands and labor to rice culture. As a result about 150,000 tons of rice are imported every year, valued at $8,000,000, principally from French Indo-China and Siam. The dependence upon foreign sources of food supply caused the Filipinos much concern during the shipping shortage in 1917 and an attempt was made to convert a certain acreage to rice growing, but the return of shipping to normal soon made this program unpopular.

Wearing Apparel.—Cotton wearing apparel valued at $3,000,000 is the next largest item on the list of imports, and this trade is divided almost equally between the United States and Japan, where low grade goods can be produced much more cheaply.

Coal.—The import of coal reached a total value of $3,000,000 in 1919, which was almost double the value of the 1918 import, although the tonnage remained the same at about 395,000 tons. About 80 per cent of this coal came from Japan, and a small percentage from China. The Islands are practically dependent upon outside sources for coal, and what deposits there are in the Philippines are of lignite or brown coal, which are too highly combustible for storage or transportation. The development of the coconut oil crushing industry has made this deficit in the Philippine fuel resources doubly apparent, and plans to develop hydro-electric power and to exploit new coal fields are under way. There is little likelihood of the Islands becoming an industrial center, however, and outside of the coconut oil industry the only added demands for coal in the future are likely to be for bunkering in case Manila develops as an *entrepot* for the Oriental shipping trade.

Wheat Flour.—The next most valuable import is wheat flour, $2,500,000 worth of which was brought in during 1919, over 90 per cent coming from Australia. The Filipinos in the cities and other more civilized centers are acquiring a taste for wheat, rather than rice, and although this taste in many cases has been acquired through necessity, because of the high price of rice, it seems to have become a permanent one and may change the source of the Philippines' food supply from French Indo-China to Australia. The possibility of the United States gaining a share of this wheat trade is rather remote, owing to the longer rail and water haul from America's wheat belt.

Illuminating Oil.—Illuminating oil imports valued at $2,400,000, practically all of which came from the United States, were imported during the 1919 fiscal year. The preferential duty has also worked in favor of American trade in this commodity, because if all things were equal, there is every possibility that American oil would have to divide the market with Dutch East Indian oil, as is the case in China.

Cotton Yarns.—Cotton yarns valued at $1,800,000 and other yarns valued at $2,300,000, the cotton yarns coming largely from Japan and the other yarns from the United States, were imported during 1919. Comparatively little home woven cloth is made in the Philippines, the standard of living being high enough to afford the purchase of the machine woven cloth.

Paper Goods.—Paper and manufactures valued at $2,250,000 is the next most valuable import, practically all coming from the United States. There are plans on foot to manufacture paper in the Philippines from hemp refuse, but so far the project has not advanced beyond the experimental stage. Unless some such development takes place there is every likelihood that the paper imports will increase gradually along with the rising standards of the people.

Other Imports.—Other imported articles in the order of their value are leather and manufactures, $1,500,000; "other meat and dairy products," $1,700,000; condensed milk, $1,300,000; and fresh beef, $700,000. Most of these items come from the United States, except the last, which China and Australia supply.

The Future of American Trade.—Future American trade in the Philippines depends largely upon what policy is adopted toward the Islands in the next decade. With a strong commercial policy, and the investment in harbor facilities to make Manila a shipping center of the Orient, our trade should not only increase, but our commercial future should be assured. If independence is to be granted the Islands, it seems desirable that a strong commercial hold should be maintained in order that our influence may remain supreme. There is room for considerable development in Philippine-American trade, and the sooner a policy looking toward the development of the Islands' natural resources is adopted, the sooner may we look forward to a higher purchasing power of the people and a greater market for our goods.

The Dutch East Indies

The war discovered the Dutch East Indies as a market for American goods. The close commercial control which Dutch policy had maintained up to that time and which had played largely into the hands of Germany, whose investments through Holland in the Dutch East Indies were large, was broken down by the closing of Mediterranean shipping lanes. It was not until then that American business discovered that many of the raw products, and partly manufactured materials which had been imported from Holland and Germany originated in the Dutch East Indies. At the same time, a large portion of the colonial population began to realize that by selling their products through Europe, they were not only deprived of the best prices, but were actually paying a tribute in high freight and discount rates. This mutual recognition of interdependence awakened a keen interest in this country in Dutch East Indian products and in the Islands themselves as a potential market for our goods to replace those formerly supplied by Germany. Direct steamship lines were inaugurated, and direct banking connections opened up in New York, and the result was a tremendous increase in Netherlands Indian-American trade. With the return of peace there has been a strong tendency on the part of the "Little Hollander" element, whose affiliations with the home country are so close, to place business back in the normal channels, and to a certain extent this has been done, but the direct contact with America has awakened an interest in trade with this country among those known as the "Dutch Colonials" which will not be soon allayed.

Total Imports—Java and Madoera.—For statistical purposes the import figures for the Dutch East Indies are divided into the same general classes as the export figures, namely those for Java and Madoera in one class, and those for the Outer Possession in the other. The total import trade of Java and Madoera for 1918 was valued at $145,000,000 for private transactions, and $1,000,000 for Government account. For analytical purposes it will not be necessary to consider the Government imports separately, because they constitute the same general items as the private transactions. This total in value represents a considerable increase over the 1913 import value, which was only $113,000,000, and which was the normal value of imports for the first three years of war, increasing in 1917, because of inordinately high prices, to $132,000,000. If the statistics showing volume were available, they would probably show a considerable decrease under 1914 in the actual tonnage of imports. It was the gradually rising prices that tended to equalize the value with the imports of preceding years.

The Possibilities for American Cotton Goods.—After deducting such items as rice, coal, tobacco, and tea, articles which the United States could not supply the Dutch East Indies at all, or only at a great disadvantage, there remains $75,000,000 worth of goods in which it is possible for the United States to compete. Of this remainder 26 per cent was in cotton textile imports of all kinds, representing a total value of $35,000,000. This trade in cotton textiles is a trade in which Japan is now greatly interested, although before the war it was monopolized by Germany and Great Britain. The competition was very keen and the margin of profit so small that American manufacturers, who specialized in the low-grade prints required, preferred to spend their efforts on some other markets which were less effectively exploited. The hold which Germany, through Holland, had on this trade and other trade in low-grade necessities is explained by the fact that most of the plantations and estates are owned by Hollanders, and no small part of the profit from these estates has been derived from the estate stores, which carry a complete line of all goods required by the native. When the natives employed on the estate are paid off, it is estimated that the transfer of the actual money is only temporary, and those who are not already indebted to the company for their supplies soon turn their wages back into the company's coffers in exchange for such articles as they need. The Dutch Government is in need of American capital at the present moment to develop the vast resources of Sumatra, and the opportunity for introducing American goods into the Dutch East Indies would seem to depend largely upon how much money we care to invest in the undeveloped resources of the Islands.

Iron, Steel and Machinery.—The second largest item of importance comprises machinery and iron and steel, representing 12 per cent of the total imports, or about $15,000,000, and in the further extension of the copra-crushing industry, the development of the sugar estates, and railroad and hydro-electric development in the outlying possessions, there would seem to be a large opportunity for American machinery. The German and British, however, maintain on the ground engineers familiar with the language. Some of the German engineers who were detained in the Islands at the outbreak of the war devoted all of their available time in perfecting their acquaintance with the Islands, and unless American firms are prepared to go after the business in the same manner, only a small portion of it may be hoped for.

Fertilizers.—Fertilizers, representing seven per cent of the total imports, or $9,000,000, are next in importance. It would seem that this item was inordinately large for such a tropical country, but under intensive cultivation in Java, the soil rapidly deteriorates, especially as it is now only possible to lease it for a limited period after which it must be turned back to the native owners. As a result little interest is taken in the preservation of its qualities, and although the Government requires certain rotations of crops from the lessees, there is no incentive to give this more than the perfunctory attention required. As a market for American fertilizers there seems little possibility in the Dutch East Indies, since the Chilean nitrate is equally available, and while shipments of phosphate rock from the South have been made, the high freight is a disadvantageous factor.

Foodstuffs.—The import trade in foodstuffs is very great, representing five per cent of the whole, or $8,000,000. This is largely accounted for by the large Chinese population, who import many of their native delicacies from China, although the large European population demands more imported food than ever under the prosperous conditions which the war has caused. There is a good demand for American canned goods and delicacies, including our specially cured hams, which the Dutch prize very highly. The trade in cigars, cigarettes, clothing, and millinery represents another five per cent of the total import trade, or $8,000,000, and comes within the same category. The European population naturally demands European styles in clothing and millinery, but in all these things there is a certain amount of trade which America may do if the field is properly covered.

Total Imports—Outer Possessions.—The import trade of the Outer Possessions presents a much more varied, but infinitely smaller, opportunity, and in general the percentages in the main items already mentioned remain the same. In the Eastern Archipelago the demand is principally for cotton textiles and textiles of wool and silk mixture, representing 25 per cent of the import trade of that district and amounting to a total of $5,000,000. The demand for cigarettes represents 10 per cent of the total trade; rice about 12 per cent; while kerosene and cotton yarn represent about four per cent each. Macassar in the Celebes is the principal import center for this district.

The Sumatra West Coast.—The Sumatra West Coast import trade totals about $4,000,000, of which 50 per cent was in textiles, six per cent in machinery and tools, five per cent in cigars and cigarettes, and three per cent in sheet tin. Padang is the center for this district, and is an outport of Batavia.

The Sumatra East Coast.—The Sumatra East Coast import trade is the most important outside of Java, representing a total value annually of $26,000,000, of which $7,000,000, or about 26 per cent, is rice to feed the many coolies employed on the rubber and tobacco plantations. The item of second importance is cotton textiles, which totals 10 per cent, iron and steel products, five per cent, machinery, four per cent, sheet tin, three per cent, beverages, three per cent, cement, two per cent, and railway material, two per cent. Many other items including such foodstuffs as canned goods, flour, preserved fruits, etc., as well as chemicals, paper, fertilizers, cigars and cigarettes enter into the import trade, most of the supplies being transhipped from Batavia to Medan and Belawan Deli, the chief ports.

The Singapore Trade Area.—The imports into the trade area which is dominated by Singapore were divided as follows: out of a total import of $16,000,000 for this region one-third was with Palembang District, one-third with the Riow Archipelago, and one-third was divided between West Borneo, Djambi, and Indragiri. The proportions by commodities are about the same in all these districts, being 25 per cent rice, 25 per cent cigars and cigarettes, 15 per cent cotton textiles, and the balance distributed between foodstuffs, sheet tin, matches, and machinery.

Credit Terms.—A thorough study of the Dutch East Indies market should well repay any firm in a position to extend the long 90 and 120-day credits which European practice has made necessary. Since the risks are mostly Chinese whose reputations are usually beyond reproach, good business could be worked up with proper effort. To those manufacturing firms requiring larger quantities of rubber, coconut oil, tapioca, etc., the opportunity is open for investment in undeveloped land and the enjoyment of a correspondingly large share of the import trade.

The Growth of Free Trade in the Dutch East Indies.—In the Dutch East Indies, the abolition of the narrow protectionist system in 1872, which had acted so detrimentally upon the general development of the colony was brought about largely by the example of the development of Singapore under British free trade. A number of ports were opened subject to the same provisions as applied to Dutch ports under Holland's commercial treaties with the powers. The heavy anchorage and pilot dues under the protectionist régime were abolished, and the vessels of all friendly powers were freely admitted to the "open" ports. To the other ports only native vessels and those authorized to take part in the coasting trade under the Dutch flag are admitted. The port of Macassar in the Celebes has been a free port since 1848. The import duties in other open ports are nominal, and for revenue only, ranging from three to seven per cent, there being no reason for a protectionist policy due to the absence of industries and the dominant position of agriculture.

The Dutch East Indies Trade-Mark Law.—In 1893 a law was passed providing for the registration of trademarks in the colony, and this law has been revised twice, once in 1905 and again in 1908. In 1912 the increased demands for trade-mark registration necessitated the organization of a special office for the control of property rights and this was termed the Industrial Property Bureau (Trade-mark Branch) under the Department of Agriculture, Industry, and Commerce. Applications for trade-marks must be accompanied by accurate descriptions and two clear proof impressions, together with specified dimensions. They may be refused on the following grounds:

1. Where a trade-mark resembles another mark, already applied for, either in subject or in its entirety.

2. Trade-marks containing immoral words and contrary to the public interest.

3. Where the trade-mark resembles the seal of a public association or company.

Appeal over decisions of the Bureau may be taken to the Court of Justice in Batavia. Trade-marks may also be cancelled when they are found to resemble marks of prior registry or infringe upon a firm name already in use.

The Dutch Colonial Legal System.—The Dutch colonial system falls under two heads, laws relating to Europeans and foreigners, and laws governing natives, including in criminal procedure Chinese, Arabs, and other Asiatics. Where foreigners are concerned both the law invoked and its administration are made as similar as practicable to the law of the foreigner's native country. This is particularly true of the civil and commercial codes, and the "New Indian Criminal Code," recently adopted, is based upon the Criminal Code of Holland, which follows the same principle. On the other hand, in administering the law where natives are concerned, the old native law, as originally evolved from their religions, customs, and institutions is followed as far as possible, and where it does not conflict with the principles of equity. Dutch civil and mercantile law is used where the native law is inadequate. The great difficulty in a proper administration of uniform native law throughout the colony, is the heterogenous character of the law itself, influenced as it has been by different creeds including Hinduism and Mohammedanism, and the varying economic conditions of the different tribes. It has been possible, therefore, to codify the native law only in certain parts of the colony. The Arabs, Hindus, and other Asiatic settlers, who would ordinarily be subject to native law, have been exempt from this, and enjoy the same rights as Europeans as far as civil and commercial law is concerned. But in matters relating to family life, succession, marriage, divorce, etc., European law is not applied, but rather the laws and customs of their own native countries. In certain cases, as in drawing up a contract, natives and Asiatic aliens may conform to European law if they so desire, but in such cases it is usually stated which of the two prevailing legal systems, native or European, is to be used in interpreting the document.

The Character of the Courts.—There is a still further distinction in the administration of the law in the Dutch East Indies. The courts which administer law in the name of the Crown are thus distinguished from those which do not. In the former category there are three groups of courts.

1. The Magisterial, or Residential Courts, are held by officials in the legal branch of the civil service, and deal with minor civil and criminal cases.

2. The Superior Courts of Justice, of which there are three in Java, one in Sumatra, and one in Celebes, try similar cases of a major character.

3. The High Court of Justice at Batavia is the Court of Appeal or Cassation.

The "Landraads."—In addition to these courts are the "Landraads," which are the most important administrative and judicial bodies in the colony, as far as the native is concerned. They are presided over by Dutch judges and their membership is composed of the native nobility, some being nominated for the position by the Governor General, and some sitting by reason of another official position. They take cognizance of both criminal and civil actions.

Appeal from these courts may be taken to the courts of justice outlined above. A native adviser attached to each "Landraad" is consulted by the court as to the tribe and religion of the accused in order that the proper native law may be applied.

Native Courts in Independent Principalities.—Among the courts which do not administer the law in the name of the Crown are the native courts in the independent principalities and those in certain parts of the colony which, for political reasons, have been left in the enjoyment of their own jurisdiction. The transactions of these courts are under the direct supervision of the Dutch East Indian Government, which sees that justice is done and barbarous punishments are forbidden. A Dutch civil service official attends these courts as an adviser.

As a whole the administration of the commercial law in the Dutch East Indies is simple and not costly and the procedure is much the same as in Holland. The High Court exercises supervision over the entire legal administration of the colony, and in this way abuses and corruption are very much more easily prevented.

Questions

1. What factors contribute to the American control of the textile trade of the Philippines?
2. What has accounted for the large increase in machinery imports in the Philippines?
3. Why are the Philippines dependent upon outside supplies of rice?
4. What is the significance and reason for coal imports in the Philippines?
5. What are some of the considerations upon which future American trade depend?
6. Discuss the triangular trade of the Dutch East Indies with America before the war.
7. How does ownership of estates in the Dutch East Indies control the import trade?

8. How does Germany dominate the machinery trade of the Dutch East Indies?
9. What led to the revision of the Dutch colonial tariff policy?
10. Describe the Dutch colonial judicial system.

BIBLIOGRAPHY TO PART II

The Dutch East Indies and the Philippines

General History

Dutch East Indies

Crawford, John:
History of the Indian Archipelago. Edinburgh, 1820.
Day, Clive:
The Dutch in Java. New York, 1904.
De Witt, Augusta:
Java, Facts and Fancies. Philadelphia, 1906.
Sheltema, J. F.:
Monumental Java. New York, 1912.

Philippine Islands

Arnold, J. R.:
The Philippines, the Land of Palm and Pine, an official guide and handbook. Manila.
Atkinson, F. W.:
The Philippine Islands. Boston, 1905.
Barrows, D. P.:
History of the Philippines. Indianapolis, 1908.
Blair, E. H., and Robertson, J. A.:
The Philippine Islands, fifty-five volumes. Cleveland, 1909.
Chamberlin, F.:
The Philippine Problem, 1898-1913. Boston, 1913.
Crow, Carl:
America and the Philippines. New York, 1914.
Foreman, J.:
The Philippine Islands. London.
Ireland, Alleyne:
The Far Eastern Tropics. Boston, 1905.
Jernegan, P. P. F.:
A Short History of the Philippines. New York.

LEROY, James A.:
The Americans in the Philippines. Boston, 1914.
LINDSAY, C. N. Forbes:
America's Insular Possessions. Philadelphia, 1906.
MILLER, Hugo H. and STORMS, Charles H.:
Economic Conditions in the Philippines. Boston, 1913.
Philippine Government:
Report of the Philippine Commission to the Secretary of War (1914). Washington.
Report of the Governor General of the Philippine Islands to the Secretary of War (1916). Washington.
Report of the Governor General of the Philippine Islands to the Secretary of War (1917). Washington.
Philippine Government:
The Code of Civil Procedure of the Philippine Islands. Manila.
WILLIAMS, D. R.:
The Odyssey of the Philippine Commission. Chicago, 1913.
WORCESTER, Dean C.:
The Philippines Past and Present. New York, 1914.
The Philippine Islands and Their People. New York, 1909.
WRIGHT, H. M.:
A Handbook of the Philippines. Chicago.

GEOGRAPHY—COMMERCIAL, POLITICAL AND PHYSICAL, AND MARKET ANALYSIS

Dutch East Indies

BOYS, H. S.:
Some Notes on Java and Its Administration. Allahabed, 1892.
Bureau of Foreign and Domestic Commerce:
Commerce Reports Supplements (Dutch East Indian Ports). Washington, D. C.
Miscellaneous Series, No. 10, "Advertising Mediums." Washington, D. C., 1913.
Special Agent Series, No. 92, "Canned Goods." Washington, D. C., 1915; No. 120, "Cotton Goods." Washington, D. C., 1916.
Special Consular Reports, No. 53, "Automobiles." Washington, D. C., 1912; No. 56, "Paints and Varnishes." Washington, D. C., 1912.

CABATON, A.:
Java, Sumatra and the Dutch East Indies. London, 1914.
Department of Agriculture, Industry and Commerce:
Exporters' Directory of the Dutch East Indies (1918). Buitenzorg.
Yearbook of the Netherlands East Indies (1916). Buitenzorg.
JENKS, J. W.:
Report on Certain Economic Problems in the English and Dutch Colonies of the Orient. Washington, 1902.
MOREY, J. W. B.:
Java, or How to Manage a Colony. London, 1861.

AGRICULTURE, INDUSTRY AND MARKET ANALYSIS

Philippines

Bureau of Foreign and Domestic Commerce:
Annual Series, No. 80a, supplement to Commerce Reports, "Analysis of Exports and Imports." Washington, D. C.
Miscellaneous Series, No. 106, "Trade of the United States with the World, 1918 and 1919," Part I, "Imports"; Part II, "Exports." Washington, D. C.
Special Agent Series, No. 67, "Resources and Industries." Washington, D. C., 1913; No. 161, "Shoe and Leather Trade in the Philippine Islands." Washington, D. C., 1917; No. 88, "Lumbering Industry of the Philippines." Washington, D. C., 1914; No. 95, "Rattan Supply of the Philippines." Washington, D. C., 1915; No. 91, "Pineapple-Canning Industry of the World." Washington, D. C., 1915; No. 13, "Cotton Fabrics in the Philippines." Washington, D. C., 1907; No. 92, "Canned Goods in the Far East." Washington, D. C., 1915.
Annual Series, No. 80b, "Industrial and Agricultural Conditions." Washington, D. C.
MILLER, Hugo H. and STORMS, Charles H.:
Economic Conditions in the Philippines. Boston, 1913.
IRELAND, Alleyne:
The Far Eastern Tropics. Boston, 1905.
Philippine Government:
Report of the Philippine Commission to the Secretary of War (1914). Washington, D. C.

Report of the Governor General of the Philippine Islands to the Secretary of War (1916). Washington, D. C.

Report of the Governor General of the Philippine Islands to the Secretary of War (1917). Washington, D. C.

Philippine Commerce, Shipping and Immigration. Annual Report of the Bureau of Customs of the Philippines for the Year Ending December 31, 1917. Manila.

PART III

BRITISH INDIA, BURMA AND CEYLON

CHAPTER XIV

HISTORY AND GOVERNMENT OF BRITISH INDIA

When Vasco de Gama, as a representative of King Manuel of Portugal, arrived at Calicut on the west coast of India in 1498, he was acting in accordance with an agreement between the Spanish and Portuguese sovereigns, sanctioned by Pope Julius II, which partitioned the world from a meridian in the Atlantic into an eastern and a western hemisphere allotted respectively to Portuguese and Spanish exploration. The history of Indian contact with the West is nearly as ancient as Western history itself, and while such early intercourse had always been actuated by commercial motives, this visit of the Portuguese may be said to mark the beginning of direct, modern intercourse between India and Europe. The Moors, who had conducted a lucrative trade with the Indian princes, attacked the Portuguese and prevented the full consummation of de Gama's plans, and although his returning ships brought home no cargo, his accounts of the riches of India soon stirred the Portuguese to ambitious and far reaching plans for commercial conquest. A fleet of 13 ships and 1,500 men under Cabral arrived in Calicut after a stormy voyage which drove them upon the coast of South America as the discoverers of Brazil. After waiting in vain for a cargo they were again attacked by the jealous Moors. In this encounter the Portuguese were the victors and after killing 600 Moors and enslaving the rest, they appropriated the Moorish ships and cargo and set sail for Cochin farther down the coast. Here the accounts of their prowess had preceded the Portuguese who were welcomed with much pomp and received by ambassadors from all the neighboring principalities. Before returning to Portugal in 1501 Cabral had opened "factories" at Cochin and Cananore and left in charge Portuguese factors.

The Conquests of Albuquerque.—The opening of direct intercourse with India now incited the envy of the Sultan of Egypt, through whose domain Indian wares had formerly reached Europe, and with the aid of Venetian carpenters he built a fleet in the Red Sea. This fleet, manned with Turkish sailors, was finally defeated by the Portuguese in the Indian Ocean in 1508. In 1506 Alfonso Albuquerque with 460 men sailed for India, met and defeated a large force under the King of Ormus, and established a Portuguese fort. He also finally subdued the King of Calicut and captured and fortified the island of Goa, which he chose as the capital of the new Portuguese empire in Asia. By a system of forts, custom houses, and law courts he succeeded not only in supporting his army from Indian resources but established a commercial and political supremacy over the neighboring princes which was the real beginning of Western domination. Malacca was chosen from the standpoint of its strategic position as secondary only in importance to Goa, and a settlement in Ceylon was made the *entrepot* for the spice island trade of the Indian Ocean.

The Portuguese in India.—On his death in 1515 the dominions which Albuquerque had established were turned over to a succession of cruel and rapacious Portuguese Governors who well nigh destroyed the prestige of the Portuguese in India. In 1524 Vasco de Gama was selected for a third voyage to India in an effort to bring order out of chaos, but his attempts to suppress the Moors, once more the thorn in the Portuguese side, were cut short by his death the next year. Nunio de Cunha, who now assumed the governorship at Goa, was a wise and just administrator and the colony which he turned over to his successors had undergone a remarkable period of progress. During all this time, however, the Turks were conspiring with disaffected Hindu princes in an attempt to overthrow Portuguese power. While not entirely successful, this confederacy was able to effect the expulsion of the Portuguese from the Molucco Islands, Malacca, and Ceylon, and when in 1580 King Philip II of Spain became master of Portugal, the amount of goods shipped from India to Lisbon was found to be insufficient to defray even the expenses of the Indian Government. In 1587 King Phillip, in consideration of an annual payment, turned over the exclusive privilege of trading with India to the Portuguese East India Company, still retaining the sovereignty and territorial revenue of India.

A period of private exploitation now set in, during which not only was all attempt at just administration abandoned, but officials and merchants alike combined to plunder all those too weak to resist them. To add to the general distress an order from the Pope in 1594 regarding conversion of the natives was used as an excuse for destroying the pagodas and temples and confiscating the wealth in the sacred depositories.

The Decline of Portuguese Influence.—Meanwhile, the Dutch, deprived of the supply of Indian goods through Lisbon, arrived in Java in 1595 and in 1602 the first ships belonging to the English East India Company arrived in India, both in quest of direct trade. This aroused the hostility of the Portuguese who practiced on the newcomers all the arts of warfare, which a century before had been used upon them by the Moors. The Portuguese of India were by this time mostly natives of the country, of a mixed race, with Indian blood predominating. The Viceroys gave their whole attention to the accumulation of wealth. Every commander of a fort and every captain of a vessel was an independent sovereign, and the Spanish court, which paid little attention to Portuguese affairs, was still less interested in the government of India. By 1606 the Portuguese had lost many of their settlements and ships and their commerce was continually harassed by the Dutch from without and the Moguls and native princes from within, while despairing of receiving any revenue from his Indian possessions, now a burden on his treasury, the King of Spain ordered every colonial office sold to the highest bidder. In 1656 Ceylon was captured by the Dutch, while the ecclesiastical viceroys in power at Gao made no exertions to recover their sinking empire.

Portuguese Conciliation with England.—With the restoration of a Portuguese King in 1640 an era of conciliation with the English set in, largely as a result of the friendly relations between the new Portuguese Government and England. Furthermore, many Portuguese captains and vessels were employed by the English East India Company in the Indian coasting trade. In 1687 the King of Portugal rescinded the privileges granted the Portuguese East India Company and prohibited private trade between India and Lisbon. In 1773 the title of Viceroy was abolished and a Captain-General was appointed at Goa, while the garrison was paid in money instead of food and necessaries, as heretofore, thus ending a long standing abuse. By 1812 the Portuguese possessions in India had diminished until they consisted only of those at the Island of Diu and several posts on the Gulf of Cambay.

Early Adventures of the London Merchants.—After many attempts to reach India by some other route than by way of the Cape of Good Hope, notably the northwest passage of the Cabots, the London merchants finally succeeded in 1606 in sending a representative to Agra, where he obtained an ample grant of commercial privileges from the Great Mogul. Because of the prior rights of the Portuguese to the Good Hope route, English merchants had been forced to trade through Venetian "factories" in Turkey and Arabia, at the same time depending upon Lisbon for the greater part of the supply of Indian products. But the war with Spain in 1587 and the success of the Dutch in Java spurred the London merchants to form an East India Company in 1599 with an original capital of £30,000. This company, which received a royal charter from Queen Elizabeth the next year, was granted the privilege of trading "during fifteen years to all parts of Asia, Africa, and America, beyond the Cape of Good Hope, eastward to the Straits of Magellan, except such countries or ports as may be in the actual possession of any Christian Prince in amity with the Queen." The Company was granted (1) the right to make by-laws regulating its business and the people in its employ consistent with the laws of the realm; (2) exemption from export duties for the first four voyages, and the right of re-exportation of Indian goods within a year free of import duty; (3) the right to export silver coin to the amount of £6,000, provided a like amount was imported within six months; (4) all other subjects of the Queen were forbidden to trade in the territory assigned to the Company. At the expiration of fifteen years if the trade was found to be beneficial to the realm the letters patent were to be renewed for another fifteen years.

Early Activities of the East India Company.—In 1602 four of the East India Company's ships under Admiral Lancaster arrived at Acheen on the Island of Sumatra and a treaty of amity was concluded with the King. Failing to obtain a cargo because of the failure of the pepper crop, Lancaster decided to join the Dutch in driving the Portuguese from Malacca, and on the journey a richly laden Portuguese ship was captured. The cargo was sent home in one of the English ships and the others proceeded to Bantam in Java. After a favorable reception, they sailed for London arriving there in 1603 with full cargos. After a second voyage in 1604 many of the members of the East India Company, overstocked with pepper for which there was no ready market, were inclined to drop the Indian trade altogether. They were disheartened moreover by a license which had been granted to Sir Edward Michelbourne by King James to conduct a voyage to China, Japan, and Korea which, though unfruitful, was properly regarded as an infringement upon their charter. More courageous counsels prevailed and in 1607, on the third voyage, an attempt was made to open trade with the Mogul at Agra by establishing a "factory" at Surat. This was thwarted by the machinations of the Portuguese. It was not until the fifth voyage, made by Captain Meddleton in 1609 to the Moluccas, that a really profitable cargo was returned netting the members 211 per cent. Encouraged by this the Company asked for an extension of their charter from 1615 and the King was so well disposed toward the venture that a charter in perpetuity was granted the Company in the same year.

The "Separate Traders."—The varying fortunes of the East India Company during the next century, during which period the trade steadily increased, finally culminated in a contest for the supremacy in the Indian trade with a rival company in 1698. The Government, being in need of a loan, was able to obtain it on more advantageous terms from a new group known as the "separate traders" and they were "empowered forever to trade personally or by their agents in all parts of Asia, Africa, and America beyond the Cape of Good Hope eastward as far as the Straits of Magellan, *each on his own separate account* and to an amount not exceeding in any one year the total stock held by him." Any number of members, however, could unite their capital and trade together under a royal charter. It is believed that these "separate traders" were supported by the Dutch who hoped to destroy the English East India Company and certainly the option left to each of the subscribers to trade upon his own account was aimed in this direction. "The English Company Trading with the East Indies," with a capital of £2,000,000 was formed in the same year with many privileges. The flood of Indian goods, including muslins, silks, etc., now resulting from this unrestricted trade soon began to work hardship upon the English textile workers of London, Norwich, and Coventry and in 1700 Parliament passed an act providing "that after the 29th of September, 1701, no wrought silks, bengals, no stuffs mixed with silk and herba shall be worn or used in England except such as are made into apparel or furniture before that day and that all goods imported after that day must be warehoused and exported." This law had a disastrous effect upon the stock of the Old Company, as the original East India Company was called, and merely incited both groups to keener hostility and competition for the Indian trade. This ruinous course was finally brought to an end by a combination of the rival interests, effected in 1702 when the "United Company of Merchants of England Trading to the East Indies" was formed. The Old Company conveyed to the New Company the forts and islands of Bombay; the factories of Surat, Swally, Broach, Amadavod, Agra, and Lucknow; the forts of Carwar, Tellichery, Anjergo, and Calicut; Fort St. David at Pondichery, Fort St. George at Madras, Fort William at Calcutta and numerous other forts, posts, and factories in India, Persia, Cochin-China, Sumatra, and Java.

Clive and the French.—With the Persian invasion in 1739 the power of the Great Mogul was weakened and the political importance of the English and French in India was greatly increased. The history of the wars, intrigues, and counter-intrigues between the Europeans and the native princes is only important in its results. It was about this time that Colonel Clive of the East India Company vied with the French in extending the influence and commercial supremacy of the English. In the course of the war between Great Britain and France which was ended in 1763, the French destroyed the English factory at Bender Abassi in Persia, took Fort Marlborough near Bencoolen in Sumatra, and Fort St. David, while the English deprived the French of all their minor settlements on the coast of India and in 1761 took Pondichery, where all the French settlers from the smaller posts had gathered. With the loss of their Indian capital, French influence waned and by the treaty of peace they were restricted from building any fortifications or maintaining any garrisons in any of the returned "factories" at Goromandel, Malabar, Orissa, or Bengal.

The Reorganization of the East India Company.—With the destruction of French competition the Company raised its dividend in 1766 from six to ten per cent and an immense increase in the value of its stock took place. The great prosperity of the company now brought it under the surveillance of Parliament and in 1773 an act "regulating the affairs of the East India Company" provided that (1) no stockholder of less than one thousand pounds of the Company's stock, held for at least twelve months, was henceforth permitted to vote; (2) the Government of Bengal, Bihar, and Orissa was vested in a Governor-General (Warren Hastings), appointed by the Crown; (3) the Presidencies of Madras, Bombay, and Bencoolen were rendered subordinate to Bengal; (4) a Supreme Court was established at Calcutta consisting of a Chief Justice and three other Judges all appointed by the Crown; (5) no person in the King's or Company's service was permitted to accept any presents and the Governor-General, Counselors, and Judges were prohibited from having any concern whatsoever in trade; and (6) no person residing in the Company's settlements was allowed to take more than twelve per cent for a year's interest on money. By another act Parliament advanced the sum of £1,400,000 in Exchequer bills to the Company at four per cent and agreed to forego a previous claim of £400,000 a year from the territorial revenue until the debt should be discharged, at the same time restricting the Company's dividend to six per cent until the bonded debt should be reduced to £1,500,000. They were required to present a statement of their accounts every half year to the Lords of the Treasury and were restricted from accepting Indian bills to the amount of more than £300,000 in a year. They were, moreover, required to export a quantity of British merchandise. As an interesting sidelight, the licensing act passed by this same Parliament permitting the Company to export its surplus stock of tea to America, and the fact that tea was the one article on which Parliament had retained a duty as a mark of supremacy when all other duties on American imports had been repealed, furnished the basis for the "Boston Tea Party" finally culminating in the Declaration of Independence.

The Weakening of the Company's Monopoly.—In 1793 the exclusive charter of the Company was renewed by Parliament for a period of twenty years which further provided that the Government of India was to be vested in a Governor and three Counselors in each of the Presidencies of Bengal, Madras, and Bombay, the two latter being subordinate to the former. These officials were to be appointed by the Directors of the Company to which position no person was eligible until he had resided twelve years in India in the Company's service. In case the Company's exclusive privilege was terminated they were still empowered to carry on free trade in their corporate capacity in common with other British subjects. The number of British subjects in India now increased notably and, due to the enormous amount of wealth accumulated in India which they desired to bring to England, an act was passed in 1793 providing for a legitimate channel of conveyance outside the facilities afforded by the Company. The Company's civil servants in India and also the free merchants were enabled to act as agents of the Company and employ its ships for conveying their goods to India and returning Indian merchandise. In this way the Company's monopoly was weakened by law in favor of British residents in India and British manufacturers at home. Indeed, the purpose of the law was misunderstood by the British India residents who built a number of ships in India in order to compete with the Company, but aside from their use for transporting Indian rice in a food shortage in 1795, they were not permitted to engage in the regular trade. The agitation for permission to use these ships continued until, in 1803, the Company consented to extend its own fleet and permit individuals to ship their merchandise to such an extent as not to interfere with the Company's exports.

The Mahratta Wars.—In 1802 the Company's governments in India became engaged in war with the Mahratta princes which terminated in a considerable addition of territory to the Company's domain. The expense of this and previous conflicts was very great, necessitating the borrowing of vast sums in India on very disadvantageous terms, and the withdrawal of much bullion from trade. In 1808 the Company's finances had come to such an embarrassing pass that they petitioned Parliament and obtained the payment of £1,500,000 claimed as expenses connected with political wars in India. With this assistance the Company regained its financial equilibrium and remained the one example of successful monopolistic enterprise in the East.

The End of the Company's Monopoly.—By 1808, however, conditions had changed considerably in the Eastern trade. Indian textile imports had fallen from £3,000,000 to £400,000 and the Company's trade in general was pretty well disorganized. Moreover, the insistence of the Governor-General (Lord Minto) on the sovereign rights of the Company in its relations with Persia brought up the question of whether a sovereign ought to trade. As the result of the investigation of a select committee of Parliament extending over four years, the Company was notified that on April 10, 1814, its commercial monopolistic privileges would cease. Extended debate on other prerogatives of the Company brought about the acceptance of the principle that the same fair field should be left to the faith of the ruling nation as was open to the creeds of the Muslims, Hindus, and others and provision for extending the work of education and the organization of the field work of the Church of England was begun. As for the patronage formerly enjoyed by the Company, a system of civil appointments by competitive examination was put in its place.

The Sepoy Mutiny.—The long series of uprisings which now followed culminated in the Sepoy Revolt of 1857. These difficulties were largely the result of too hasty reform legislation on the part of the British administration. The law regarding the marriage of Hindu widows, the curtailing of polygamy among certain classes of Brahmins, the law requiring native recruits to engage in overseas campaigns, and a number of other acts viewed lightly by the British, made an indelible effect upon the native mind. The rumor that cow's fat had been used to grease cartridges, which the sepoys (or native troops) were required to bite off in the course of their military duties, was enough to cause two regiments of Hindu sepoys in Bengal to revolt. The massacre at Cawnpore, the uprising in Oudh, and the siege of Delhi are all stirring chapters in the Great Indian Mutiny.

Reforms of 1859.—The reform in the British administration of India which took place in 1859 had the effect of abolishing the last political prerogatives of the Company and the new Government which was organized resembled in almost every respect the system now in force. Together with this reorganization, tax reform and financial reform, as well as the revision of the Indian Penal Code and the opening of the East Indian railway marked the opening of a distinct era in Indian progress.

Political Divisions of India under British Rule.—At the present time India may be divided politically into two great territories, the fifteen provinces under British rule and the 900, more or less, native states under the titular rule of native princes. Of the provinces, Madras with 1,142,-330 square miles and 41,405,404 population is the largest in point of area and the third largest in population, followed by Burma with 230,839 square miles and 12,115,217 inhabitants; Bombay with 123,059 square miles and 19,672,642 population; the United Provinces of Agra and Oudh with 107,267 square miles and 47,182,044 people, the most thickly populated of all provinces; the central provinces and Berar with 99,823 square miles and 13,916,308 people; Punjab with 99,779 square miles and 19,974,956 population; Bihar and Orissa with 83,181 square miles and 34,-490,084 inhabitants; Bengal with only 78,699 square miles but 45,483,077, or the second largest population; Baluchistan with 54,228 square miles but only 414,412 people; Assam with 53,015 square miles and 6,713,635 people; the Northwest Province with 13,418 square miles and 7,196,933 people; Andamans and Nicobais with 3,143 square miles and 26,459 people; Ajmer-Merwara with 2,711 square miles and 501,395 people; and Coorg with 1,582 square miles and 174,976 inhabitants. This shows a total area of 1,093,074 square miles and a total population of 244,267,542 in India directly under British rule.

The British Indian Government.—The Secretary of State for India in the British Cabinet is at the head of a council in London in general charge of Indian affairs. In India the authority of the Emperor, as the King of England is called, is delegated to a Viceroy, or Governor-General, assisted by a Council, who has supreme control over the Indian Government. Under him are Departments of Finance, Commerce, Home and Foreign Affairs, Revenue and Agriculture, Army Regulation, Education and Public Works, and the headquarters of the Government are at Delhi in winter and Simla, in the Himalaya foothills, in summer. The Department of Commercial Intelligence which is maintained at Calcutta, furnishes useful information on business matters. The Government has control of the customs, post offices, telegraphs, and the financial system of the Empire, owns some of the principal railroads, and regulates others. The administrative details, such as the assessment and collection of revenue, local public works, etc., are left to the provincial governments, which are divided into districts governed by Collectors and Chief Magistrates with administrative and judicial powers. Aden, in Arabia, is under the administration of the Bombay Presidency.

Political Divisions of Native States.—The native states consist of the groups forming the Rajputana agency, with 128,987 square miles and 10,530,432 population; Kashmir State, 84,432 square miles and 3,158,126 population; Hyderahad State, 82,698 square miles and 13,374,676 population; Baluchistan States, 80,410 square miles and 396,432 population; the Central India Agency, 77,367 square miles and 9,356,980 population; Bombay States, 63,864 square miles and 7,411,675 population; Punjab States, 36,551 square miles and 4,212,794 population; the Central Provinces States, 31,174 square miles and 2,117,002 population; Mysore State, 29,475 square miles and 5,806,193 population; Bihar and Orissa States, 28,648 square miles and 3,945,209 population; the Northwest Province Agencies, 25,500 square miles and 1,622,094 population; Madras States, 10,084 square miles and 4,811,841 population; Assam State (Manipur), 8,456 square miles and 346,222 population; Baroda State, 8,182 square miles and 2,032,798 population; Bengal States, 5,393 square miles and 822,565 population; the United Provinces States, 5,079 square miles and 832,036 population; and Sikkim, 2,818 square miles and 87,920 population. This shows a total of 709,118 square miles and 70,864,995 population in the native states. These states are autonomous in their government, the British Government exercising a supervisory control through political officers, or "Residents," who reside at the seat of government of each. The native states are not allowed diplomatic relations with foreign countries except through the British Government, although many of them have their own customs houses and collect duties on imported goods in addition to those collected by the Government of India at the seaports. Some have post office systems for internal mail service only, although the Government of India post office must be used for correspondence with other parts of India and abroad. Currency for local circulation is also made in some of the native mints but the Indian rupees circulating throughout India are used even in these States. The rulers of all the larger states except the Nizam of Hyderabad are known as Maharajas, and in the smaller Hindu states as rajas, while in the smaller Mohammedan states they are known as nabobs.

Ceylon is a crown colony, with an entirely separate administration from India, with a distinct system of customs, posts, and telegraphs.

The French colony of Pondichery on the southeast coast and several small French settlements farther up the coast constitute all that remains in India of French power and influence. The Portuguese still retain the colony of Goa on the southwest coast.

Questions

1. Describe the first attempts at Indian trade by the Portuguese.
2. What were the causes of the decline of Portuguese commercial power?
3. (*a*) What led the English to seek direct trade with India?
   (*b*) What privileges were granted the first East India Company?
4. Who were the "separate traders" and how did their charter differ from that of the East India Company?
5. (*a*) What caused the coalition of the Old Company and the "separate traders"?
   (*b*) Name four of the posts transferred to the New Company.
6. What led to the regulation of the Company by Parliament?
7. Discuss five important regulations imposed upon the Company.
8. Why did the Company agree to engage in trade on behalf of individuals?
9. Name five important provinces of modern India and describe their government.
10. Name five native states and discuss the limitations placed upon their government.

CHAPTER XV

AGRICULTURE AND INDUSTRIES OF BRITISH INDIA

The economic structure of Indian village life explains India's reputation among financiers as a "sink for silver." Mutual exchange of services, rather than the use of money as a medium of exchange, has been the rule, and the villagers, with no practical use for gold and silver coins when acquired, have hoarded them or melted them into ornaments. This, however, is only one of the many characteristic customs of Indian life which have so vitally affected their industrial progress in the past. The utter lack of desire for better living conditions both among agriculturists and artisans led them to no competitive enterprise and no improvement in method. But the village is being transformed from a self-contained economic unit by the introduction of cheaper imported goods, which not only have changed the nature of the industries, but the whole character of the village itself. The gravitation of the laborer formerly employed in the rural industries or fields toward the large industrial centers and more profitable plantation work at home and abroad have developed a landless class of transient rural labor, which is an economic danger, especially in those provinces liable to periodic famines. The increased demand for more and better food, which the higher returns from this transient employment afford, has exceeded the production, curtailed by shortage of rural labor, and a rise in food prices has resulted. The present problems in India, therefore, almost exactly parallel the problems in the United States, with the exception that in India the population is triple ours and the area one-half, thus greatly aggravating the dangerous phases of these problems.

Basic Considerations in Indian Economics.—While this condition shows a tendency to spread, it is by no means universal. Eighty-five per cent of the 303,041,179 population is still rural and 72 per cent is agricultural, and although the railroad has tended to destroy the self-sufficiency of the village, long established custom has kept many artisans at home. Some of the large industries and plantations find labor difficult to get, because the factory hand is still primarily an agriculturist and his temporary migration to the city or town does not always mean his permanent settlement there. Moreover, while coming more and more into use, money is by no means as universally used as a medium of exchange as is grain, the medium through which the landlord and laborer are still paid in many villages. As a result, prices in villages on a commodity basis remain steady while town and city prices on a money basis fluctuate.

India is a self-supporting, agricultural country except when adverse weather conditions cause crop failures. The rainfall necessary to sustain the crops is brought each year by the monsoon, or moisture laden wind from the Indian Ocean, and if this is late or of short duration crop failure is almost sure to result. In past years such crop failure meant famine and starvation for millions of the population, but now the Government, through the encouragement of thrift and conservation in good years, and the prohibition of foodstuff exports in poor years, is able to prevent famine.

The pre-war percentages of exports were raw materials, 50 per cent; foodstuffs, 27 per cent; and manufactures, 23 per cent.

Area and Topography.—The area of India is 1,802,192 square miles, or a little more than half that of the United States. Of this area 709,118 square miles comprises native states which are autonomous as regards their government except that the British Government exercises a certain supervision through British resident officials. The Empire is divided into four well marked regions. The first comprises the peninsula of India, embracing the country that lies south of a line drawn from Kerachi to Calcutta, with a population of 132,000,000. The Ganges plain, lying between this line and the Himalayas, contains a population of 162,000,000. The Himalayan country contains the very small population of 9,000,000, while Burma has a population of 12,000,000, making the total population of India with Burma about 315,000,000. The peninsula region may be described as an elevated plateau bounded on the north by a line of low hills and on the south by coastal ranges which overlook the sea from a height varying from a few hundred to many thousand feet. This forms a gigantic and continuous sea wall pierced by no valleys of any size except for a gap of 200 miles at the extreme southern point. The surface of the peninsula is uneven and rocky and not more than one-third is under cultivation. The Ganges plain is the most extensive area under level cultivation in the world. Throughout this last area the land is composed entirely of river sand and silt. Across this plain five rivers flow to the west, forming what is known as the Punjab, or Five River Delta, while seven flow to the east and form the Ganges Delta. At the present time three-fourths of the area is under cultivation and the population is extraordinarily dense, reaching in some places one person to the acre, and there are no large towns, only 10 per cent of the population being classed as urban. This region supports the largest population per square mile in the world. There is little about the Himalayan country of commercial importance as nothing can be grown without irrigation. At the eastern end of the Himalayas the lower slopes are characterized by dense forests but, as a whole, the country is a desert of gloomy rocks and barren valleys swept by piercing winds. The province of Burma consists of the valleys of three rivers, the principal of which is the Irrawady. Some 200 miles above the river mouth the valley opens to a broad cultivated plain which gradually extends into a delta of remarkable fertility.

Religion and Caste.—Religion plays an extremely important part in the lives of the Indian people and has a very important bearing on trade and industry. The Hindus regard the cow as a sacred animal and abhor the use of grease. It is sacreligious to kill a cow and a good Hindu will never touch any article of commerce which has its origin in this manner. In some castes it is not permitted to touch an object which is touched by a foreigner or by one of a lower caste. This refusal of the natives to work together is largely responsible for the great industrial inefficiency of the country. Happily these religious prejudices are gradually disappearing, although they will exercise a potential influence for a long time. There are several hundred dialects spoken in India but the Hindustani is the language most useful and the most widely spoken by the educated class.

Principal Cities.—The principal city of India is Calcutta, with a population of 1,200,000, which is the eastern port of the Ganges delta region. The port extends 10 miles along the river and has a fine system of docks. The principal products exported through Calcutta are jute and tea. It is also a distributing center for foreign imports.

Bombay on the west coast, with a population of 1,000,000, is known as the gateway of India. It is built on a small island shaped much like Manhattan Island, New York. The export trade of Bombay is principally in raw cotton, grain, oil seeds, cotton yarn, spices, goat skins, and manganese ore.

Madras, with a population of 500,000, is the leading commercial center of south India and is located on a sandy shore without a natural harbor. The chief trade is in exports of cotton, tobacco, skins, drugs, and spices and the import consists largely of manufactured goods and machinery from Great Britain. Delhi, the capital of the British India Empire, has a population of 250,000. It is the chief distributing center for the district between Calcutta and Bombay and a manufacturing center of jewelry, lace work, silver, brass and copper work, ivory carving, and pottery. Cotton spinning under modern conditions is carried on both in Delhi and Bombay, which latter is the center of the industry.

Agriculture and Pastoral Industry

Wheat.—India, the world's second largest wheat grower, produces annually about 10,000,000 long tons of wheat, which is one-tenth of the world's production. About 1,300,000 tons are exported in normal years, making India the fourth largest exporter, although lack of shipping during the war and crop failure (in 1919) kept the exports down to 650,000 tons in 1916 (years noted are the fiscal years ending March 31st); 750,000 tons in 1917; and 475,000 tons in 1919. In 1918, 1,450,000 tons were exported. Nine-tenths of the wheat exported is shipped from Karachi, the port of the great Punjab wheat district, and the same proportion goes to the British Empire, France and Italy being the other buyers. Flour for domestic use is prepared almost universally by the *janta,* or hand mill, by which three grades of flour are made. The first is made by the regrinding of rich gluten wheats and is used in confections, and the other two are made from the flour separated in the preparation of the first and consists of a fine and a coarse flour, the former used by the rich and the latter by the poorer classes. The coarser grade is sometimes mixed with barley and other grains. In addition to the hand mills, water power mills are used in the hill districts, while about 50 modern flour mills are in existence, half of them in the Punjab, the others in Bengal, Bombay, and the United Provinces.

Rice.—India produces about 30,000,000 tons of rice every year, of which only 400,000 tons are exported. The crude methods still employed in threshing rice paddy by means of bullock treading and by beating the grain thus separated on blocks of wood or stone and the crude process of husking by means of a beam balanced on a peg, produces a grade of rice not suitable for export, at a cost much higher than if machinery were used. Cheap labor in the agricultural districts, however, still prevents the introduction of mechanical husking, which in Burma has entirely superseded the indigenous method to the great improvement of the product. One of the great problems of Indian agriculture may be said to be that of diverting the preparation of rice from the crude methods of the village to the more advanced methods of mechanical husking. This transformation, once begun, would open up an immense market for rice husking machinery.

Millet, Barley, Maize, and Pulse.—Of the minor foodstuffs, millet is most important, supplying food for the poorer classes and feed for cattle. The average export is 100,000 tons annually, largely to countries with Indian populations accustomed to reliance upon India for food. Barley is of minor importance as a domestic crop but its export averages 225,000 tons per year. Maize is exported to the extent of about 25,000 tons annually. Barley and maize are shipped chiefly to the United Kingdom and Europe. The average pre-war export of gram was 132,000 tons, although in 1919 282,000 tons were sent abroad. On the other hand an average pre-war export of lentils of 159,000 tons, which had reached 230,000 tons in 1918, fell off to 30,000 tons in 1919 because of the unfavorable crop conditions.

Sugar.—The most striking phenomena in the sugar production of India is the continued increasing demand for refined sugar imported from the Dutch East Indies, and the steady decline in domestic production. The decline in sugar production in the past ten years has reached 400,000 tons, while the imports during that period have averaged 500,000 tons annually. Notwithstanding this change, India remains the second largest producer of sugar cane in the world, her total production reaching 3,000,000 tons annually, or 34 per cent of the world's production. The declining use of domestic sugar is said to be due primarily to the small scattered cane plantations preventing concentration around a central factory, coupled with the peculiar demand for low-grade sugar known as *gur,* which is produced by wasteful methods but commands a price out of all proportion to its refinery value. Thus, while the price of *gur* had risen 26 per cent in the sixteen years before the war, the price of Java sugar cultivated and refined under modern methods had actually declined 25 per cent.

It is doubtful whether the central factory system will ever develop in India, due to the scattered holdings of individual farmers and the lack of economy of cane production on large estates. The manufacture of refined sugar from *gur* has been advanced as a possible solution of the sugar problem in India, but the sugar loss in *gur* manufacture and the relatively high price of *gur* in proportion to its sugar content renders this project unsound. It is possible, however, that a combination factory refining cane for several months and *gur* for the rest of the year could be successfully established in many districts.

Sugar from the date palm is produced to the extent of 300,000 tons annually in the United Provinces. The palm is cultivated on ground too high for rice growing and requires seven years to ripen into a juice producer. The palm is then tapped every three days during the winter season and from the juice *gur* and a fermented drink known as *toddy* are produced. Sugar is also refined from date palm *gur* and is used chiefly in the manufacture of confectionery.

Tea, Coffee, and Spices.—India exports more tea than any other country in the world, the shrub being grown on large plantations in Assam, Bengal, and in Southern India. The 1918 production was estimated at 190,000 tons, of which 162,000 tons were exported, seventy-seven per cent to the United Kingdom. Only five per cent of the total exports are shipped directly to the United States, although large quantities of the Indian teas shipped to England eventually find their way to this country. Modern methods of cultivation on a large scale have so lowered the cost of production of Indian tea that it has superseded Chinese teas on the English market. It is also claimed that the strong flavor of Indian black tea has destroyed the Western taste for the more delicately flavored Chinese product.

The production of Indian coffee is centered in the Madras district and the export reaches only 14,000 tons annually, the value in 1919 being $3,800,000.

India annually exports about $3,500,000 worth of spices, the most important being black pepper, of which 6,900 tons are produced annually. Madras is the chief producing district, shipping 5,800 tons of black pepper, 4,800 tons of red pepper, and 650 tons of ginger.

Jute.—Jute and jute manufactures, of which India is practically the world's only producer, represented 27 per cent of the total Indian exports in 1919, as against 19 per cent in the five years before the war. Of this proportion jute manufactures accounted for 22 per cent as against nine per cent of the five pre-war years, indicating a remarkable advance in the manufacture of jute bags and cloth. The production of raw jute in 1918 was 1,253,000 tons, practically all of which was grown in Bengal Province. Raw jute exports in 1919 amounted to 398,000 tons, or 2,230,000 bales of 400 pounds each. The United Kingdom took 56 per cent of the total exports, or 224,000 tons, as against 40 per cent in the five pre-war years. The direct export to the United States fell off one-third to 61,000 tons, while Japan, Spain, France, Italy, and Brazil accounted for the rest of the raw jute exports.

Burlap bags and cloth were exported in 1919 to the extent of 682,000 tons, an increase of eight per cent over the pre-war tonnage, while the value was $170,000,000, an increase of 158 per cent over the pre-war value. The 1919 proportion of burlap bags was 57 per cent of burlap cloth, 42 per cent, and other jute manufactures, one per cent. Of the burlap bag exports 23 per cent went to United Kingdom, 14 per cent to Egypt, 12 per cent to Australia, eight per cent to the United States, seven per cent to Chile, and 36 per cent to other countries including France, Cuba, Java, and the Argentine. The burlap cloth exports including 58 per cent to the United States, 12 per cent to Argentine, 11 per cent to United Kingdom, seven per cent to France, and the balance of 12 per cent to Australia, Egypt, Chile, and other countries. Several factories with American capital have been established in Calcutta for the manufacture of much of the burlap shipped to the United States. Seventy-six mills with 40,000 looms and 824,000 spindles operated by 50 companies, four of which are private concerns, manufacture the jute for export.

Cotton and Cotton Goods.—India normally produces 4,000,000 bales of 400 pounds each of raw cotton annually and is the world's second largest producer. The 1919 yield was slightly below normal, about 3,670,000 bales being produced, of which 1,030,000 bales were exported at a total value of $100,575,000. This was just 50 per cent of the exports of 1918 and 57 per cent of the five pre-war years, the decrease being due to shipping difficulties and industrial growth at home. Of these exports Japan took 76 per cent, Italy 11 per cent, the British Empire nine per cent, and all others four per cent.

The production of cotton yarn was 615,000,000 pounds in 1919, a seven per cent decrease compared with the preceding year, and five per cent under the five-year pre-war average. Of this amount the exports were 64,000,000 pounds, valued at $23,500,000, 47 per cent below the quantity of the year before, and 67 per cent below the pre-war average. Nearly all of these exports consisted of one to 20 counts and China took 80 per cent, or less than half the amount taken in 1918. The decrease in exports to China was due largely to competition with cheap Japanese yarns. Egypt, Straits Settlements, Persia, Siam, the United Kingdom, Aden, and Mesopotamia were the other buyers.

The exports of piece goods in 1919 amounted to 149,000,000 yards valued at $21,000,000, 62 per cent of which were colored, 35 per cent gray, and three per cent white. The exports were only 17 per cent of the imports of piece goods, but were 65 per cent above the pre-war average exports.

The cotton which India produces is of the short-staple variety and can consequently only be utilized in the production of very low-grade yarn and piece goods. For this reason the greater portion of it is utilized in Japan. It is doubtful whether the soil and climate of India will ever permit the successful production of such grades as American upland cotton, which is being grown so widely in China.

Silk.—A general decline in silk rearing throughout India has taken place within recent years due primarily to the *tukra* disease in the bush mulberries and *pebrine, muscardine, Flacherie,* and *grasserie* diseases among the worms.

While the eradication of these diseases is comparatively simple, it requires scientific and painstaking attention which the middle-class silk breeder is unwilling to give. The discouragement to worm breeding has in turn reacted upon mulberry growing and other crops have been found more profitable than mulberry raising. Microscopic selection of seed by the Pasteur method has been found most successful in eradicating *pebrine,* which is by far the most serious and prevalent disease, and this has been put into practice on a large scale in the nurseries of the Bengal Government Silk Committee. An adequate supply of pure seed cocoons and properly constructed rearing houses for protection against the silk-worm fly known as *muscardine, grasserie,* and *Flacherie,* are suggested reforms which the provincial governments are being urged to adopt.

The apathetic attitude of the Government toward these reforms is probably due to the declining exports which have been brought about by severe competition of Italian, Chinese, and Japanese silks. Crude methods of reeling which cannot compete with the more advanced Japanese methods, a backward system of crossing affecting the quality of the product, unscientific boiling of the cocoon, and failure to re-reel exported silks, have, perhaps, more seriously curtailed Indian silk exports than any other factors. On the other hand the indigenous methods are cheaper and if the native product were rewound it would probably find a ready market in Europe. The present production of raw silk is about 500,000 pounds and of silk cloth about 360,000 yards. In 1919 France took $1,000,000 worth of raw silk, or twice the value of her 1918 purchases, while the United Kingdom bought about $950,000 worth, a slight decline from her 1918 purchases. Most of the silk cloth is made in Benares, Nagpur, Mirzapur, and Agra from silk produced in the Maldah district of Bengal, and sold locally.

Silk from the *tassar* worm, or wild silk worm, from which

eri cloth is produced, furnishes livelihood for some 45,000 persons in Bengal and the Central Provinces. The worm feeds upon the castor-bean plant which grows almost like a weed in many districts. The worm has been domesticated so that it closes regularly in May and June. There is little foreign demand for the product and the relatively low price has led to the decline of the industry. The climate of Assam is admirably adapted to the growth of this silk and as the worm is prolific, the labor required in its rearing slight, and skilful reeling unnecessary because the pierced shell may be readily sold abroad, an effort is being made to encourage the industry. The cocoons are simply combed and carded like wool and no attempt to unreel the single strands is made.

Oilseeds.—In 1919 India exported 487,700 tons of oilseeds valued at $36,400,000, and this, while an increase of seven per cent in quantity and 36 per cent in value over the preceding year, was only one-third the pre-war average. The United Kingdom took 73 per cent of this trade, France, 10 per cent, Italy, five per cent, the United States, two per cent, and all others, 10 per cent. Before the war a third of the export had gone each to England and France and a sixth to Belgium and Germany. Of the seeds exported, 46 per cent originated in Bombay, 30 per cent in Bengal, 10 per cent in Sind, and five per cent in Madras.

Linseed, produced from flax grown exclusively for the seed, showed a total yield of about 450,000 tons in 1918, of which 158,000 tons were exported. In 1919 this had increased to 292,000 tons. Bengal and the Central Provinces are the principal centers of cultivation. This crop is the most important export oilseed crop, very little being used domestically. About 80 per cent of the 1919 linseed exports went to the United Kingdom, Australia took seven per cent, and Italy and the United States most of the remainder. The United Kingdom's decreased imports of linseed from the Argentine in 1917 and 1918 were largely responsible for this increased import from India.

Rape and mustard seed are much more universally used domestically, the former to anoint the body. Mustard is grown most extensively in Bengal and Assam while rape is produced chiefly in upper India. Calcutta is the chief oil mill center of these oils, which are crushed from seed brought in from the United Provinces, the oil being shipped to Eastern Bengal and Assam. The 1918 yield of rape and mustard seed was 1,111,000 tons of which only 66,000 was exported. In 1919 these shipments increased to 80,000 tons, the United Kingdom, France, and Italy being the chief purchasers.

Cottonseed is an important by-product of the cotton growing industry and about 300,000 tons are produced annually, only 1,450 tons being exported in 1919. This seed is used largely as a cattle food at home, the exports varying as good or poor monsoons affect the cotton crop.

Castor seeds were exported to the amount of 82,000 tons in 1919, nearly 80 per cent of which went to the United Kingdom. The export of these seeds has steadily decreased in recent years with the growth of the castor oil manufacturing industry in India.

Peanut exports fell from a pre-war average of 212,000 tons and 115,000 tons in 1918 to 17,000 tons in 1919. Forty per cent of these exports went to the Straits Settlements for transhipment to Hongkong and the United States, while France took 15 per cent and the United Kingdom only three per cent. In 1918 the production of peanuts was 940,000 tons, or eight times the export, and the sharp decline in exports in 1919 was due to poor crop conditions which curtailed the exportable surplus.

Copra exports in 1918 amounted to 6,600 tons but fell to 450 tons in 1919, because of unfavorable crop conditions.

The sesame seed crop amounted to only 386,000 tons in

1918, a decrease of 35 per cent from 1917 and 13 per cent from the pre-war average. The 1918 exports of 18,000 tons fell to 2,400 tons in 1919.

Vegetable Oils.—The manufacture of vegetable oil has been a very important village industry in India for centuries. The introduction of cheaper kerosene has reduced the demand for coconut and castor oil, both of which had long been used as illuminants. The former is still used for cooking purposes and for soap making, but the chief demand for the latter is now for export. Til oil is perhaps the most popular oil for cooking purposes. Vegetable oil is made in almost every village by the old native method, consisting of a wooden pestle working in a cavity of a wooden block sunk into the ground and shaped like an inverted cone. The motive power is furnished by bullocks and two pressings do not suffice to abstract the oil efficiently. This native method is much more expensive than modern crushing methods employed in Europe and as a result India reimports much vegetable oil exported in the seed to Europe. The loss of the oil cake to India as a fertilizer as well as the transfer of a lucrative industry to Europe have both been advanced as reasons why the vegetable oil industry should be established on modern lines in India. Popular prejudice against the supposedly discolored oil produced by machinery, however, and the influence of custom have discouraged the erection of modern oil mills, although their number is growing. There would seem to be a market for a modern hand press crushing about a third of a ton of seed a day, which would cost about $250 and be within reach of the small capitalist.

Coconut oil produced largely from Ceylon copra was exported to the extent of 7,000,000 gallons in 1919 as against 3,000,000 gallons in 1918 and 1,750,000 before the war. The United Kingdom took 80 per cent and the balance went to Italy and Egypt.

Linseed oil exports of 1,675,000 gallons in 1919 were three times those of 1918 and went principally to Italy, New Zealand, Australia, and South Africa.

Castor oil exports in 1919 were 1,658,000 gallons, showing a decrease of 20 per cent as against 1918. The United Kingdom and Italy took 92 per cent of the 1919 exports.

Hides and Skins.—Possessing 132,000,000 cattle, most of which are work animals, few being slaughtered for food because of the religious prohibition against meat eating, India has become a large producer of hides and the tanning and leather industry has attained a very important place in Indian industry. The hide and skin trade which had been largely controlled by the Germans before the war was diverted to the United States in 1917, when 36 per cent of the 36,800 ton raw-hide trade was with this country. In 1919 this had fallen to 19,100 tons, 74 per cent of which were cowhides for the United Kingdom and Italy. The tanned hide export which reached 20,600 tons in 1917 was all but 2,000 tons for British Government account, due to restrictions imposed by the Government on tanned hide exports for private account. In 1918, 17,300 tons of tanned hides were exported. Due to the increase of tanning in India during 1918, aided by the Government prohibition on certain classes of raw-hide exports until April, 1919, the tanned hide exports reached 25,500 tons in 1919, an increase of 39 per cent over 1918. The entire quantity of these tanned hides was shipped to the United Kingdom, and 98 per cent were tanned cowhides.

Raw-skin exports reached 25,000 tons in 1919, a 12 per cent increase over 1918, and a decrease of 3,200 tons as against 1917 shipments. Three-fourths of the 1919 shipments went to the United States and 85 per cent of the total shipments were raw goat skins. Tanned skins were exported to the amount of 3,000 tons, an increase of 75 per cent over 1918, and a decline of 3,300 tons from 1917 exports. Seventy-five per cent of the exports were to the United Kingdom, and the remainder went to the United States and Japan.

The modern tanneries of India are located in Madras and Bombay and there is a heavy rail movement of raw hides into these Presidencies from Northern India each year. The indigenous industry is found all over India and is carried on exclusively by the low-caste *chamars* and *muchis,* who are shunned and avoided by all other castes because of their profession. The defects in the native tanning methods are many and serious, consisting of over liming, antiquated fleshing and hair removing, insufficient bathing, improperly graduated tanning periods, and inadequate currying.

European patterns in shoes are in greatest demand and the shoemaking industry as well as the native tanning industry is controlled by the *muchi,* who often purchases the better tanned leathers from Calcutta, Agra, and Cawnpore for shoemaking. The shop keepers often finance the household manufacture of shoes by the *muchi,* but the exploitation is usually so great that many of the native tanners and shoemakers are now organizing along coöperative lines, whereby credit is more cheaply obtained and better tools can be purchased. The basic caste organization so strong in this and other industries lends itself very readily to the coöperative movement.

Wool and Carpets.—Raw-wool shipments in 1919 amounted to 23,500 tons, against 22,500 tons in 1918, and 22,000 tons in 1917. In addition to these exports a small amount of wool is brought to Indian ports from Afghanistan and Tibet and shipped abroad. The United Kingdom takes all of the Indian wool exported, 74 per cent of the 1919 export being shipped from Bombay and 24 per cent from Karachi.

Woolen carpets and rugs to the value of $485,000 have been shipped abroad annually in the past two years.

Indigo.—The production of indigo dropped from 4,000 tons in 1918 to 2,000 tons in 1919, although the 1919 exports of 1,500 tons, valued at $4,000,000, were five per cent over those of 1918 and 112 per cent above the pre-war average. Japan took about 40 per cent of India's indigo exports, the United States, 20 per cent, and the United Kingdom, 15 per cent. The return of aniline dyes to British markets accounted for much of the slack demand from that source and this in turn affected the area planted in indigo because of the drop in price of the natural dye due to competition with the artificial product.

Other Agricultural Products.—Opium exports in 1919 were $2,300,000 over the $7,800,000 exports of 1918, but considerably under the pre-war average export of $32,300,-000. Of the total exports in 1919, $2,100,000 went to Japan. Bettter shipping facilities account somewhat for the large shipments in 1919, although lax control over smuggling into China accounts in no small degree for the increased foreign demand for Indian opium, large quantities finding their way to China by way of other countries.

Raw-hide exports almost doubled in value in 1919, the total being $4,700,000. Nearly $4,000,000 of these exports were shipped to the United Kingdom.

Mines and Minerals

Coal.—The production of coal in India has steadily risen from an average annual output of 16,600,000 tons from 1913 to 1916 to 18,200,000 tons in 1917 and 20,700,000 tons in 1918. The quality is poor, running from 14 per cent to 20 per cent ash and, because of transportation difficulties, Welsh coal has been found cheaper in Karachi and Bombay than the home product. The need of a higher quality coal is also a factor in the coal import trade which averages

34,000 tons annually. The exports of coal dropped to 143,600 tons in 1919 from 255,900 tons during the previous year and a pre-war average export of 823,800 tons. In addition to these exports, 1,490,000 tons of bunker coal left India in 1919 and a considerable tonnage on Government account.

Manganese Ore.—India is the largest producer of manganese in the world despite the fall in production from 828,000 tons in 1913 to 641,000 tons in 1917. Magnesite production has likewise fallen from 17,500 tons in 1916 to 7,400 tons in 1917. The 1919 exports of 385,400 tons of manganese ore valued at $2,500,000 was a decrease of 11 per cent from 1918. The United Kingdom took 77 per cent of the exports, the balance going to France, Japan, the United States, Belgium, and Italy. Ferro-manganese amounting to 10,900 tons was exported in 1919, chiefly from Bengal.

Mica.—With an annual average production of 2,200 tons India is the chief source of sheet mica in the world. The 1919 exports of 2,800 tons, valued at $3,000,000, were restricted to the United Kingdom and these showed a decline of 15 per cent compared with 1918 exports, but an increase of 14 per cent over the pre-war average.

Iron and Steel.—Iron-ore production in 1916 was 142,600 tons, while in 1918 the output of the two principal iron works, the Tata Iron and Steel Works and the Bengal Iron and Steel Works, was 731,200 tons and in 1919, 781,100 tons; the production of the latter year consisting of 262,600 tons of pig iron, 182,800 tons of steel, and 160,500 tons of iron blooms and billets, the balance of 175,200 tons being miscellaneous products. Most of this production was used domestically.

The 100,000 tons of chromite produced in 1916 was almost four times the 1915 output. In 1919 39,400 tons of chrome ore were shipped abroad.

Other Minerals.—With an annual production of 18,000 tons of saltpeter India possesses a practical world monopoly of this mineral. The 1919 exports were chiefly to the United Kingdom, $2,000,000 worth, and to the United States, $600,000 worth.

Of the 4,870 tons of wolfram ore, valued at $3,600,000, shipped entirely to the United Kingdom in 1919, all but 71 tons were produced in Burma but shipped abroad through Indian ports.

Mysore is the principal location of Indian gold placers which produce about 600,000 ounces of gold annually.

Other minerals produced in lesser quantities are antimony, cobalt, graphite, corondum, bauxite, pitchblende, magnesia, copper, lead, and monazite.

Forests and Forest Products

Shellac.—*Lac,* a secretion from wounded branches of the *kusumb, phalsa,* and *baer* trees forming an incrustation about certain insects, is now sought more for its resinous qualities, which develop after the larvae have swarmed, than for the red dye properties, which it possesses before the larvae swarm. After incrustation this excretion is known as the shell-lac. The larvae first produce on the twigs the red dye lac, and on swarming crawl to new wood and remain on it, sucking the juice until they are entirely enveloped in the stick lac. For this purpose, sticks inoculated by tying them with a bundle of grass to different parts of the tree, are placed conveniently so that the swarming may take place on them, the resinous lac so produced being known as stick lac. As the stick lac is now sought in preference to the dye or shell-lac, the collection is very generally delayed until the swarming has taken place, so as to obviate the necessity of removing the dye and thus injuring the resinous qualities of the shell-lac.

Lac serves a multitude of useful purposes in India where it takes the place of putty in carpentry and woodwork, and serves the same as varnish and paint. Colored ornamentations of lac are made on copper, glass, and ivory wares, and it is used as a cement and a glue in many trades. In Europe and America lac is the basis of many varnishes and is the chief ingredient of sealing wax. It is used as a stiffening material for hats, in the preparation of lithographic ink, and in the manufacture of phonograph records, and electrical insulating material.

India enjoys a virtual monopoly of the world's lac production, but the export has steadily declined from 3,400 tons in 1917, to 2,800 tons in 1918 and 2,200 tons in 1919, the value of the latter year's exports reaching $9,000,000. The United States took 44 per cent of the 1919 exports, the United Kingdom, 29 per cent, Japan, eight per cent, the Philippines, five per cent, and other countries, 14 per cent.

Other Forest Products.—Teak, *sal*, and *deodar* timber are the three principal timber products of India. About 2,400 tons of rosin were produced in 1917, over twice the production of 1913. Turpentine production increased from 59,000 gallons in 1913 to 125,000 gallons in 1917. Rubber produced chiefly in Assam and Madras reached an export value of $8,000,000 in 1919, the average pre-war export value being only $1,300,000. Due to shipping difficulties during the war large stocks had accumulated, resulting in a very low price. The 1919 shipments, therefore, represent considerably more than the average production for export.

Fisheries.—It is estimated that 90 per cent of the population of western India is dependent upon fish for sustenance, but lacking modern methods of catching, curing, and preserving the fish which abound in the inlets and rivers, much of this food remains unavailable and little is exported. Artificial hatching, such as is practiced in Europe and Japan, for restocking the streams which have become exhausted, is being undertaken by the Bengal Government. The fish supply is decreasing yearly due to the passing of the supplementary occupation of boatmen for the fishermen, caused by the increasing number of river steamers and railways. The exorbitant profits demanded by the middlemen are also discouraging to the fishermen.

Questions

1. How has Indian village life affected the demand for silver?
2. (*a*) What is India's position as a wheat exporter?
   (*b*) Describe the native manufacture of flour.
3. Why does Indian rice fail to find a market abroad?
4. Discuss India's sugar production and import trade and give suggested remedies for present situation.
5. Describe India's position in jute production.
6. Why does India's cotton go to Japan?
7. Give the reasons for the decline in Indian silk culture.
8. Name three kinds of oilseeds shipped from India and the principal destination of each.
9. How does India suffer by shipping oilseeds to Europe?
10. Describe the production of lac.

CHAPTER XVI

MARKET ANALYSIS OF BRITISH INDIA

India's Trade Balance.—India's normal excess of exports, in the five years before the war, was 50 per cent of her imports, but in 1915 this dropped to 27 per cent, increasing in 1916 to 46 per cent and in 1917 to 84 per cent. This marked the peak of Indian production for war needs, and in 1918 excess of exports was only 55 per cent of the imports, while in 1919 the $776,400,000 export trade was just 41 per cent in excess of the $548,400,000 import trade. The value of the 1919 export trade was $64,000,000 more than the pre-war average and $76,000,000 more than the average for the war period, while the import values for 1919 were $75,000,000 over the pre-war average and $69,-000,000 in excess of the average imports during the war. These figures denote a general rise in prices and indicate little, if any, increased tonnage in the goods brought in or shipped during 1919. This constantly cumulating credit in favor of India has had to be met by corresponding shipments of gold and silver to India, and when the amount to India's credit reached $384,000,000 in a single year, as it did in 1917, the demand for silver from this source, from China, and by soldiers in the field, together with the decreasing supply from war-torn Mexico, caused an inordinate rise in the price of that metal. This rise in the virtual medium of Indian exchange automatically checked exports in 1918 and stimulated imports, cutting the excess to $269,-000,000, and this was further reduced to $228,000,000 in 1919. Were the standard of living raised in India and the wants of the people increased, the resulting increase in imports would establish a more equitable balance of trade, which would not only prevent a heavy drain on metal reserves of the West, but prove an ultimate stimulus to trade as a whole by furnishing outbound cargo from those countries whose purchases of Indian produce are now limited by high freight rates due to an excessive carriage of exports from India with little return cargo. Moreover, with a lighter demand for silver, resulting from a more balanced trade, India would receive implements and goods for her products instead of a comparatively useless metal which ultimately disappears from circulation in the form of ornaments and jewelry and is of no real economic benefit to the country. The fallacy of the supposed benefits of a favorable balance of trade is nowhere better illustrated than by India's constant struggle to produce by antiquated methods food and raw materials for western consumption, receiving in return only two-thirds as much in goods of economic value and tangible benefit.[1]

The Chief Suppliers of Indian Markets.—The fifteen principal items of India's import trade are, with one or two exceptions, all such articles as are manufactured on a large scale in the United States, but less than 10 per cent of India's purchases in 1919 were made in this country, as against eight per cent in 1918. The United Kingdom sold India 45 per cent of her imports in 1919 and other parts of the British Empire furnished 13 per cent additional, in all an increase of six per cent over the British Empire's share in the Indian import trade in 1918. The most phenomenal increase was Japan's shipments to India; they rose from 12 per cent of India's import trade in 1918 to 20 per cent of the 1919 trade. Java's exports to India, consisting al-

[1] The recent depression has witnessed a decided falling off of Indian exports and the establishment of an unfavorable balance of trade, together with a depression in the value of the rupee. This violent fluctuation has been more serious than the normal condition outlined above.

most entirely of sugar, constituted seven per cent of the latter's 1919 import trade, while the remaining five per cent was divided between China, France, Persia, Italy, Norway, Sweden, and other countries.

Cotton Piece Goods.—Notwithstanding India's increasing importance as a cotton goods manufacturer, cotton piece goods still account for 30 per cent of her total imports, and the 1919 value of $167,700,000, while slightly under 1918 figures, shows an excess of $14,000,000 over the pre-war average. In quantity, however, piece goods have suffered a serious decline since 1918 in all grades, amounting to 43 per cent in both white and colored goods, which also declined eight per cent and 27 per cent, respectively, in value to $42,000,000 and $38,000,000. Gray goods, which showed only a seven per cent decrease in quantity, owing to heavy Japanese sales, increased 28 per cent in value to $76,000,000. Tents and hosiery both declined about 30 per cent in value to $2,800,000 each, while the imports of thread fell off 10 per cent to $1,900,000, and handkerchiefs and shawls increased 30 per cent to $670,000. Sixty-two per cent of the gray goods, 95 per cent of the white goods, and 87 per cent of the colored goods were supplied by the United Kingdom, while the balance of the imports in these classes of goods, as well as 80 per cent of the hosiery, came from Japan. The trade of all other countries in piece goods amounted to a little over one per cent of the total imports. The share of the United States amounted to a trifle over $1,000,000, but exceeded that of Italy, France, and Holland.

Cotton Yarn.—The value of cotton twist and yarn imports in 1919, $28,700,000, was more than double that of 1918. This fact taken in conjunction with the decline in the imports of piece goods denotes an increasing use of foreign yarns in Indian looms. Sixty per cent of the yarn imports came from Japan and 39 per cent from the United

Kingdom, leaving one per cent, or less than half a million dollars worth, to be supplied by all other countries. There is every indication that much more of the better class of cotton piece goods may be supplied to the Indian market in the future through native looms operating on imported yarns.

Sugar.—India's imports of sugar amounted to 506,700 tons in 1919, or 36,000 tons more than the 1918 imports, and 33,400 tons over the pre-war average. Of this total tonnage Java supplied 363,100 tons, or 72 per cent, Mauritius, 77,200 tons, or 13 per cent, and the Straits Settlements 62,100 tons, or 12 per cent, while the balance of three per cent was supplied by China, Egypt, and Japan. The 1919 imports of sugar, though considerably larger in amount than 1918, show only a $1,000,000 increase in value, indicating a considerable drop in prices.

Iron and Steel.—The tonnage of iron and steel imports has declined continuously since the 1909 to 1914 period when a yearly average of 735,300 tons was imported. The 608,600 tons brought in during 1915 dropped to 424,000 tons in 1916, to 257,200 tons in 1917, and to 152,000 tons in 1918. In 1919 the difficulty of obtaining supplies was not as great, although resulting high prices and the use of substitutes still held the imports to 181,400 tons, while the value rose 60 per cent from $25,000,000 in 1918 to $40,000,000 in 1919, or only $4,000,000 more in value than the pre-war import average, but representing only one-fourth the amount of actual goods.

The imports from the United Kingdom, which had amounted to 60 per cent of the whole before the war, and 70 per cent in 1915, 1916, and 1917, dropped to 51 per cent in 1918 and 42 per cent in 1919. The imports from the United States, which amounted to only three per cent before the war and five per cent in 1915, jumped to 27 per cent in 1916 and 1917, 41 per cent in 1918, and 42 per cent, or the same as United Kingdom's share, in 1919. The imports from Japan were nil before the war and only reached one per cent in 1917, three per cent in 1918, and eight per cent in 1919. The remaining eight per cent of the iron and steel imports were supplied by other countries.

The principal classes of goods imported in 1919 were steel bars and channels, 21,600 tons from the United States, and only 3,500 tons from the United Kingdom, showing an increase of 20,000 tons in all. There were increased imports of nails, rivets, washers, screws, hoops, strips, bolts, nuts, steel angles, and springs. Due to competition from home, manufacturers' corrugated sheets, which had represented 175,500 tons of the pre-war tonnage, declined to 5,500 tons in 1918, and 2,500 tons in 1919. Tin plates amounting to 32,000 tons showed little change over 1918 and were three per cent above the pre-war average. Ungalvanized sheets and plates amounted to 18,000 tons, and were four per cent below 1918 and only one-fifth the pre-war average, the United States and United Kingdom being the principal suppliers.

Machinery.—The 1919 imports of machinery were valued at $19,000,000, compared with $17,000,000 for 1918, and, while quantity statistics are not available, it is probable that price advance accounted for only a part of the increase in import values. Cotton-mill machinery, valued at $5,350,000, showed an increase of $1,600,000 over 1918, and fully 83 per cent came from the United Kingdom, only nine per cent from the United States, and eight per cent from Japan. Ninety-one per cent of this machinery was for the Bombay district. Jute-mill machinery was the second largest item, amounting to $1,850,000, a decline of nearly $400,000 from 1918 figures. Ninety-five per cent of these imports came from the United Kingdom, Japan being the other supplier. Electrical machinery, valued at $1,260,000, over a third more than the 1918 imports, was divided equally between the United Kingdom with $650,000, and the United States with $520,000, the balance of $90,000 being supplied from all other countries. Before the war the share of these two countries had been $1,000,000 for the United Kingdom and $65,000 for the United States, and the gratifying growth of America's share in this line of the Indian import trade indicates greater possibilities in the future. Boiler imports amounted to only $750,000 in 1919, against $325,000 in 1918, while sewing and knitting machines declined $30,000 from $57,000 in 1918, 97 per cent of the supplies coming from the United States. Other important items in the machinery imports were tea-garden machinery, $485,000, and mining machinery, $350,000.

Of the total imports of $19,000,000, the United Kingdom led with $10,500,000, half a million more than in 1918, while the United States with $4,500,000 showed nearly a 50 per cent increase over their 1918 share. Japan with nearly $800,000 was the next largest supplier of this item, leaving $3,200,000 to come from all other countries.

Silk.—Raw and manufactured silk imports amounted to $15,400,000 in 1919, about $2,600,000 more than the prewar average. This value, however, indicates an actual decrease in quantities because of high prices. Forty-five per cent of the total was supplied by Japan, practically all being silk manufactures, including yarn, while five per cent were French products, two per cent British, and two per cent Italian. The balance of this trade was with China, Hongkong, the Straits Settlements and other Eastern countries, and included mostly raw silk and yarn.

Chemicals and Drugs.—A decline of $300,000 in the chemical and drug trade from the 1918 figures marked the 1919 period when imports only reached $13,700,000. This value, however, was almost double the pre-war import figures of $6,900,000. Of the total 1919 imports of this class over $8,000,000 were chemicals, including calcium carbide, soda bicarbonate, and acids in large quantities, while decreasing quantities of sulphur, alum, ammonia, caustic soda, and sodium carbonate marked the cessation of many war industries. Sixty-three per cent of the chemical imports were from the United Kingdom, 24 per cent from Japan, and six per cent from the United States. Drug imports in 1919 amounted to $4,700,000, while patent medicines valued at $850,000 accounted for the remaining imports.

Mineral Oils.—During 1919 60,441,000 gallons of mineral oil valued at $11,700,000 were brought into India, showing a decrease of more than 30,000,000 gallons from the pre-war average, although the pre-war value was over $12,000,000. Fuel oil imports of 27,000,000 gallons were over three times the pre-war imports of 8,000,000 gallons, and lubricating oil imports of 19,000,000 gallons also showed a considerable gain over the 13,500,000 gallons of this commodity brought in the average pre-war year. Kerosene in bulk, however, fell from 50,000,000 gallons before the war to 7,000,000 gallons in 1919, and kerosene in tins dropped from 16,000,000 gallons before the war to 5,000,000 gallons in 1919. This change in the character of India's oil trade is almost entirely explained by shipping difficulties which have encouraged production nearer home. Nearby, Persian fuel oils have supplied the increasing Indian demand, and lubricating oils from Borneo have taken the place of those previously brought from the West. Burma supplied India with 117,000,000 gallons of kerosene in 1919, supplanting much of the quantity formerly imported from the United States.

Liquors.—India's liquor imports amounted to $10,700,000 in 1919, about 60 per cent coming from the United Kindom, 16 per cent from France, and 24 per cent from other countries. This is a substantial increase over pre-war imports of $6,500,000 in value, though actual quantities have remained about the same.

Hardware.—The value of hardware imports was $10,400,000 in 1919 and this showed only a slight increase of about $100,000 over the pre-war average. The United Kingdom, which had supplied 59 per cent before the war, furnished only 36 per cent of the 1919 imports, while the United States' pre-war share of seven per cent increased to 31 per cent, and Japan's one per cent to 29 per cent. Other countries had supplied 33 per cent of the pre-war imports, but this fell to four per cent in 1919. The change in character of hardware imports not only accounts for much of this diverted trade, but also indicates changes in India's economic life. Agricultural implements increased threefold over 1918 to $600,000 in 1919, and builder's hardware soared from $30,000 to $600,000. Other implements reached $1,950,000 in value in 1919, an increase over the preceding year of 50 per cent, a fifth being shipped from Japan. Enameled ironware showed decreased imports of 40 per cent to $350,000, the domestic product supplanting Japanese ware. Imports of metal lamps fell from 4,662,000 in number before the war to 800,000 in 1919, 85 per cent coming from the United States and nine per cent from Japan. Cutlery imports of $600,000 were supplied, 43 per cent from the United Kingdom, 32 per cent from the United States, and 23 per cent from Japan. The United Kingdom supplied most of the $130,000 worth of electroplated ware.

Paper and Pasteboard.—Imports of paper products doubled from the period before the war reaching $8,800,000 in 1919. Japan supplied 26 per cent against practically nothing before the war, while the United States and Norway, each with 22 per cent, the United Kingdom with 20 per cent, Sweden with five per cent, and other countries with five per cent, all combined to supplant the 58 per cent supplied by the United Kingdom, the 17 per cent by Germany, the nine per cent by Austria-Hungary, and the 10 per cent furnished by all other countries before the war. In 1919 the 9,700 tons of printing paper that were purchased abroad comprised 47 per cent from Norway and 27 per cent from the United States, while the United Kingdom, Japan, and Sweden furnished the balance of 26 per cent. Writing paper and envelopes valued at $1,600,000 came largely from the United States. Indian paper mill production, increasing from 26,450 tons before the war to 31,360 tons in 1919, supplied some of the growing demand which would otherwise have been imported, although the shortage of *sabai*, from which the domestic product is made, has held the industry in check. The difficulty experienced in obtaining foreign pulp, which reduced the imports from 3,000 tons in 1918 to 2,100 tons in 1919, has led to definite steps to develop the bamboo pulp industry in India and Burma.

Salt.—India's demand for salt is supplied almost entirely from the Orient, only about $790,000 worth of the $7,500,000 worth imported coming from the United Kingdom, and $290,000 worth from Spain.

Provisions.—The total value of provisions imported in 1919 was $6,300,000, of which 32 per cent were canned and bottled provisions, 26 per cent farinaceous and patent foods, 15 per cent condensed and preserved milk, and 27 per cent other provisions, including bacon, hams, cocoa, chocolate, biscuits, and cakes. Larger quantities of sago and sago flour are being imported from the Straits Settlements annually, accounting for the increased proportion of farinaceous food, while biscuits purchased in 1919 were only one-twelfth the pre-war supply, 48 per cent coming from Japan, 37 per cent from Australia, and 15 per cent from other countries. About 41,000 tons of canned and bottled provisions are brought in every year, while 820 tons of jams and jellies were imported in 1919, a third more than the preceding year; 83 per cent of which originated in Australia, whose pre-war share of the trade had been only two per cent. Cocoa and chocolate came principally from the United States, while that country supplied 40 per cent of the 2,100 tons of condensed milk, Australia provided 23 per cent, and other countries 37 per cent. The United Kingdom, which had shipped 680 tons of condensed milk to India in 1918, showed only 10 tons among the 1919 receipts.

Railway Materials.—One of the most striking effects of the war on India's import trade was the falling off in the purchases of railway equipment and rolling stock abroad. The 1919 imports were only $3,300,000, which was double the 1918 figures, but considering advanced prices, negligible in quantity as compared with the $19,800,000 average imports in the five years before the war. Practically all new construction, except for war needs, has been held in abeyance, and the 1919 imports practically represent only much needed repairs. With the return to normal conditions, Indian railway construction, in common with that of all the world, will experience renewed activity.

Motor Cars, Cycles, and Accessories.—The value of the imports of automobiles and motor cycles was $1,200,000 in 1919, just half the 1918 figure, and a little more than one-third the pre-war average. This was accounted for by the embargo on motor car imports, which extended throughout eight months of the 1919 fiscal year. The pre-war, or 1914, number of motor cars imported was 2,880, while the war years showed 2,005 in 1915, 3,121 in 1916, and 4,778 in 1917. In the 1918 fiscal year the embargo first became effective, and the number brought in dropped to 1,262, including 76 trucks, while the 1919 total came to only 400, including eight trucks. The increasing share of the United States in this trade is indicated by the fact that while only 30 per cent of the motor cars imported in the pre-war year came from the United States, our share had grown to 70 per cent during the 1915 to 1919 period.

In March, 1919, there were 19,385 motor cars and 8,058 motorcycles registered in India.

During 1919 only 94,658 motor car and cycle tires were imported against 92,428 in 1918, while only 76,000 tubes were imported compared with 89,000 in the preceding year. The value of these imports decreased from $475,000 to $350,000, and the United Kingdom increased its share of the trade from 46 per cent to 51 per cent.

Conclusions of Indian Market Analysis.—India's import trade, consisting principally of manufactured goods, is being supplied largely by three countries, the United Kingdom, Japan, and the United States. The trade which the United Kingdom was forced by the war to relinquish has been appropriated to a great extent by Japan, and in certain lines by the United States. The struggle to retain the share that she has will depend upon the ability of British manufacturers to meet the conditions in the Indian market which the new competition has created. These manfacturers are more alive to the situation, probably, than any of their new competitors, and few steps will be overlooked which may lead to the restoration of British predominance in Indian commerce.

Questions

1. How is India's favorable balance of trade detrimental to the country?
2. Describe the trade in cotton piece goods and cotton yarn.
3. (*a*) To what extent has the United States entered the iron and steel trade of India?
   (*b*) The machinery trade?
4. Discuss the import trade in mineral oils and the reasons for changes.
5. Discuss the growth of automobile and motor cycle imports.

CHAPTER XVII

AGRICULTURE, INDUSTRIES, AND MARKET ANALYSIS OF BURMA

Burma, with a population of 12,115,217 in 1911, is economically, though not administratively, distinct from British India. An unusually mountainous hinterland feeds the Irawaddy River, in whose delta region the principal crop, rice, is extensively grown. This product, together with petroleum products, constituted 80 per cent of Burma's export trade in 1919. Ethnologically Burma may be grouped with Siam and French Indo-China, although commercially its interests lie with British India, with which $81,000,000 worth, or 57 per cent, of its $141,000,000 export trade was carried on in 1919. The balance of its exports went principally to the United Kingdom, Japan, the Straits Settlements, Ceylon, the Dutch East Indies, and European countries.

Agriculture and Industries

Rice.—About two-thirds of Burma's rice crop comes from Lower Burma, or the Irawaddy delta, where it represents 90 per cent of the cultivated area. The paddy is usually taken over from the cultivator towards the end of November on the threshing floor, either by middlemen from the mills or speculators, and carted in bags and baskets to railhead or river, whence it is transported in bulk to the mills. The mills own their own boats which make three or four trips a month to the up-river districts. The crop is handled by coolies without mechanical aid and storage is now provided up country for half the normal crop. As the paddy deteriorates in color by heating it is usually milled as soon as possible and is on the market commercially from January 15 until April 15. The milling consists of several successive processes according to the grade of rice desired. Rice which has simply been husked and winnowed, consisting of about 80 per cent *loonzain* and 20 per cent paddy, is known as cargo rice. To produce white rice this is milled by cones to remove the outer cuticle, and then graded into broken and unbroken rice by sieving. High-grade rice for Europe is further polished in wool and wire gauze cylinders with revolving sheep-skin rollers. The mills run on paddy husk for fuel and are operated night and day for about three months. There are 300 mills in Burma employing 20 hands or more and many smaller ones. The total capacity of Burma's rice mills is about 6,000,000 tons per annum, which is considerably in excess of the 2,400,000 long tons valued at $78,000,000 exported from Burma in 1919. Burma's ratio of acreage under rice to population is so high that her exportable surplus is able to supply any deficit in India and still leave a large quantity for export. In 1919 the exports to India were 797,000 tons, to the Straits Settlements, 334,000 tons, to the United Kingdom, 261,000 tons, to Japan, 205,000 tons, to Ceylon, 185,000 tons, to France, 132,000 tons, to Italy, 129,000 tons, to the Dutch East Indies, 112,000 tons, and to all other countries, 245,000 tons. Sixty-eight per cent of this trade went through the port of Rangoon, 13 per cent through Bassein, 10 per cent through Moulmein, and the balance, or nine per cent, through Akyab.

Petroleum Products.—All of Burma's 117,444,000 gallons of exported kerosene in 1919 went to India where its use has largely superseded vegetable oil as an illuminant and which offers a market for more kerosene than Burma can supply. The chief producing field in Burma is Yenangyuang which supplied 200,000,000 gallons of the 277,500,000 gallons produced in all India in 1913. Of the

23,600,000 gallons of motor spirits exported from Burma in 1919 all but 1,000,000 gallons, shipped to India, went to foreign countries. India took 15,700,000 gallons of other mineral oils, however, leaving only 2,000,000 gallons for export abroad. In all Burma shipped 158,700,000 gallons of mineral oils, 134,000,000 gallons of which went to India; 490,000 hundredweight of paraffin, 463,000 hundredweight of which went to India; and 138,000 hundredweight of candles, 65,000 hundredweight going to India. The total value of these products was $24,000,000.

Cotton.—Cotton exports in 1919 showed a notable increase with a total of 273,000 tons valued at $7,500,000 against 204,000 tons in the preceding year. The United Kingdom took 117,000 tons, India 82,000, and Japan 74,000 tons. Burma has had an average of 254,000 acres under cotton during the war, seven-eighths of the product being a three-fourths-inch short staple raised principally in the dry zone. In the Shan Hills a one-inch staple is produced. The average production is 54,000 bales of 400 pounds each. Of this quantity 53,700 bales or eight per cent of the total exports were sent abroad in 1919.

Beans.—Burma white beans, formerly used as a cattle feed, have lately developed as an important export for human consumption in Europe. The total exportable surplus in 1919 of 105,000 tons was purchased by the Royal Commission for Wheat Supplies and shipped to England. With the return to normal conditions in Europe the demand for this product, which supplanted the haricot bean of the Danube region, is expected to fall off. The value of gram and bean exports in 1919 was $7,200,000.

Teak and Timber.—The production of teak is about 366,000 cubic tons per year, of which 116,000 tons were exported in 1919, 89,000 tons to India and 27,000 to other countries. This was the smallest amount shipped abroad in many years, largely because of unsettled conditions following the close of the war and lack of shipping space. Other timber exports consisted of deodar, sal, rosewood, etc., amounting to 4,300 tons, all of which went to India. The total value of Burma's timber exports in 1919 was $5,100,000.

Tungsten.—The export of tungsten in 1919 was 4,800 tons valued at $3,600,000 or several hundred tons more than the 1917 and 1918 exports, notwithstanding a fall in prices since the war. The demand for this product, which is used in high-speed steel manufacture, has ceased. Before the war Burma's wolfram was shipped to Germany for metallurgical treatment, but the entire output is now controlled by the Government. The Tavoy district alone furnished three-fourths of the output, while Yemethin, Manchi, and Mergui contributed the balance. Scientific methods, including hydraulic mining, modern concentrating mills, the use of hydro-electric power, air compressors, and machine drills are replacing the crude methods formerly employed.

Raw Hides and Skins.—In 1919 150,000 hundredweight of raw hides were shipped from Burma, one-half of which went to the United Kingdom and Italy and one-half to India. This was an eight per cent increase over the 1918 shipments, but a 10 per cent decrease compared with 1917 exports. The value of raw hide and skin exports was $2,600,000.

Silver.—The Bawdwin mine in the Northern Shan States produced 1,970,000 ounces of silver in 1918, which was 400,000 ounces more than the 1917 production and nearly three times that of 1916. The exports in 1919 were valued at $1,930,000, all of which went to the British Indian Government for minting purposes.

Rubber.—The Burma Government plantation at Mergui had demonstrated by 1910 that Para rubber could be grown in Burma and the product grown there was sold to a limited company while other plantations were started near Rangoon. In 1916 new rules governing rubber plantations were promulgated to encourage the industry, many suitable areas being still unexploited. In 1918, 63,500 acres were under rubber in Burma and in 1919, 4,149,000 pounds valued at $1,500,000 were shipped abroad, largely to the United Kingdom. A two per cent royalty is levied on Burma rubber exports calculated on the net value each month on the London market, less Government allowances towards cost of production, freight, and sale charges.

Pig Lead.—Exports of pig lead in 1919 amounted to 17,900 tons, practically the entire production of the Bawdwin mine for 1918. The value of the export was $1,400,000. Eight thousand seven hundred tons went to India and half the balance to Ceylon for tea chests.

Tobacco.—In 1919 14,500,000 pounds of unmanufactured tobacco, or 46 per cent of the combined export of India and Burma, were shipped abroad, principally to France, Aden, the Straits Settlements, and the United Kingdom. In addition to these exports, 8,000,000 pounds of manufactured tobacco, mainly "Burma cheroots," made in Rangoon from Burmese tobacco and from that grown in Bengal and Madras, were shipped principally to Malaya, Siam, and the United Kingdom. The total value of these tobacco shipments was $1,200,000.

Cutch.—Cutch exports, mainly to the United Kingdom for tanning and dyeing vary with the licenses for boiling issued by the Forestry Department. It is derived from the *acacia catechu* found in the western Himalayas and northeastern Burma. A ton of wood cut in chips from the heart of this tree and boiled to the consistency of syrup yields from 250 to 300 pounds of cutch. The total exports of 79,000 hundredweight in 1919 were valued at $500,000, going mainly to the United Kingdom, France, Germany, and Holland. The Rangoon unit of sale is the hundredweight and shipment is made in cases weighing from 50 to 124 pounds net.

Tin.—Block tin, entirely from Mergui, amounting to 2,000 hundredweight and tin ore weighing 15,600 hundredweight, over half from the Southern Shan States and one-quarter from Tavoy, was produced in 1918. The exports in 1919 were 460 tons valued at $425,000, four-fifths of which went abroad, mainly to England for separation, the remainder to India. The ore is recovered by washing alluvial gravels and formerly mixed tin and tungsten concentrates were shipped to the Straits Settlements for separation, but a plant for this purpose has now been erected at Tavoy.

Jade and Rubies.—In 1919 jade exports, of certain kinds of which Burma is the chief source of supply, amounted to 2,700 hundredweight, valued at $400,000. Hongkong was the chief purchaser and about one-fifth went to China across the frontier.

No record is kept of ruby, sapphire, and spinel exports as most of these jewels go out as personal effects. Mogok in Upper Burma, where the Burma Ruby Mines are located, produced 198,200 carats, principally of pigeon blood rubies, in 1917, valued at about $200,000, the inferior stones being sold locally and the larger ones going to London.

Lac.—In 1919 19,000 hundredweight of lac valued at $350,000, 18,700 hundredweight of which was stick lac for shipment to India, were exported. The remaining 200 hundredweight of shell lac went to the United Kingdom. Three-fifths of these exports came from the Shan States and two-fifths were imported from western China.

Analysis of Imports

In Burma's $82,000,000 import trade in 1919 the principal sharers were India, the United Kingdom, Japan, and the United States, our portion being less than $3,000,000.

The actual quantities of goods brought in showed little if any increase over 1917 and 1918, although high prices caused an increase of $20,000,000 over the 1918 total values and $13,000,000 over the 1917 values.

Cotton Goods.—Cotton piece goods imports valued at $17,000,000 consisted of 16,800,000 yards of unbleached gray goods, three-fourths from India and nearly one-fourth from other countries, principally Japan, only 800,000 yards coming from the United Kingdom, as against 9,000,000 yards supplied by that country in 1917, out of a total import for that year of 24,000,000 yards. As India's supply has remained steady this means that in 1919 the United Kingdom had been supplanted in this trade, consisting of long cloth and skirting, by Japan.

In bleached white goods the trade had dropped from 41,000,000 yards in 1917 to 23,000,000 yards in 1919 and the United Kingdom's share decreased from 31,000,000 yards to 12,000,000 yards. India, the other supplier, had increased her sales from 9,000,000 yards to 10,000,000 yards, while the remaining 1,000,000 yards was steadily supplied by other countries.

Printed and dyed colored goods showed a drop of 20,000,000 yards in 1919 from the 83,000,000 yard imports of 1917. The 39,000,000 yards supplied by the United Kingdom in 1917 were transferred to India in 1919 and the United Kingdom's share fell to 13,000,000 yards. The Netherlands' trade in these goods fell from 9,000,000 yards in 1917 to 900,000 yards in 1919, while other countries, largely Japan, increased their share from 7,000,000 yards in 1917 to 9,000,000 yards in 1919.

Cotton twist and yarn imports amounting to 14,000,000 pounds and valued at $6,400,000, 13,400,000 pounds from India and the rest from the United Kingdom, formed an additional part of the cotton goods trade, while the trade in this commodity across Burma from India into Yunnan

Province of China increased 50 per cent in quantity in that year.

Other cotton manufactures consisting chiefly of sewing thread, hosiery, blankets, canvas, etc., showed a decided drop in value from $1,900,000 in 1917 to $1,400,000 in 1919.

Jute Manufacturers.—Jute gunny bags for rice increased in value from $4,000,000 in 1917 and 1918 to $9,700,000 in 1919. These goods, which are brought entirely from Calcutta, vary in quantity with the size of the paddy crop and the amount of rice stored, milled, and exported.

Silk Goods.—Imports of raw silk and silk manufactures by land and sea increased from $2,000,000 in 1917 to $3,700,000 in 1919, although the quantity of raw silk decreased from 910,000 pounds in 1917 to 369,000 pounds in 1919, China being the principal seller across the land frontier. Pure silk piece goods also dropped from 4,000,000 yards in 1917 to 3,800,000 yards in 1919, with Japan almost sole supplier. Likewise, mixed silk piece goods, mainly from the United Kingdom, fell from 380,000 yards in 1917 to 80,000 yards in 1919.

Metals.—The increase in value of imported metals, from $4,700,000 in 1917 to $5,800,000 in 1919, was accounted for largely by iron and steel imports, although the actual tonnage in these goods decreased from 28,000 tons in 1917 to 20,000 tons in 1919. The principal fall was in pipes, tubes, and fittings from 10,000 tons to 3,000 tons, although sheets and plates showed a rise from 8,000 tons to 10,000 tons. Zinc imports remained steady at 5,000 hundredweight, but tin jumped from 242 to 3,000 hundredweight and lead fell from 1,600 to 600 hundredweight. The United Kingdom furnished 59 per cent and the United States 16 per cent of Burma's 1919 metal imports.

Hardware and Machinery.—The trade in hardware and cutlery showed a falling off from $1,900,000 in 1917 to

$1,600,000 in 1919, of which the United Kingdom furnished $400,000 worth in 1919, Japan $300,000 and the United States $200,000. Implements and tools, enameled ironware, agricultural implements, metal lamps, and builders' hardware formed the chief classes of imports.

Machinery imports remained about $1,200,000 during 1917, 1918, and 1919, metal working machinery showing a slight increase. The United Kingdom and the United States took most of this trade.

Provisions and Foodstuffs.—The decline in imports of provisions from $3,500,000 in 1917 to $2,600,000 in 1919 was due to shipping restrictions of the United Kingdom and the United States. Canned milk dropped from 3,000,000 pounds in 1917 to half that amount in 1919, and biscuits and cakes from 1,300,000 to 40,000 pounds.

Sugar from the Dutch East Indies increased one-third in quantity from 300,000 hundredweight in 1917, but only $500,000 in value of imports over the $1,300,000 of 1917. Fish imports remained steady at $1,300,000.

Other Imports.—Spices, chiefly *areca,* or betel, nuts, chillies, pepper, and cardamons from India, increased from $2,100,000 to $2,400,000.

Coal imports remained at $2,200,000 throughout the three years.

Tobacco, mainly manufactured, from India for the making of cheroots, rose from $1,900,000 to $2,200,000.

Gram and beans showed an increase of from $1,800,000 to $2,200,000, while oils, mainly vegetable oils, dropped from $1,900,000 to $1,600,000.

Questions

1. Describe the handling and milling of rice in Burma.
2. Discuss the production and export of petroleum products.
3. What is the nature of Burma's cotton and where is it sold?
4. (*a*) Discuss Burma's bean trade.
   (*b*) Why did teak shipments drop during the war?

5. Discuss tungsten, silver, tin, and lead.
6. (*a*) How has rubber production grown?
   (*b*) How is cutch made and for what used?
7. What were the principal changes in Burma's cotton goods imports from 1917 to 1919?
8. What was the principal metal import in 1919 and the chief suppliers?
9. Discuss the hardware and machinery trade of Burma.
10. (*a*) What caused provision imports to decline in 1919?
    (*b*) Name three other imports into Burma.

CHAPTER XVIII

AGRICULTURE, INDUSTRIES, AND MARKET ANALYSIS OF CEYLON

The Island of Ceylon with a population in 1916 of 4,547,200, made up of 2,892,900 Cinhalese, 1,314,000 Tamils, 332,300 other Orientals, and 8,000 Europeans, is largely an agricultural colony, about 64 per cent of the population being engaged in agriculture. The total export trade in 1918 of $68,500,000 showed a decided drop from the export figures of 1917 of about $30,000,000, due mainly to trade restrictions in the United States and the United Kingdom. Of the 1918 exports, the United Kingdom took 42 per cent, the United States, 17 per cent, British India, 12 per cent, Australasia, nine per cent, Canada, five per cent, British Africa four per cent, France two per cent, and all other countries, nine per cent.

Agriculture and Industries

Tea.—Tea shipments dropped from 195,000,000 pounds in 1917 to 180,000,000 pounds in 1918 and the value from $31,000,000 to $27,000,000. This was the smallest amount of tea shipped from Ceylon since 1908, the record year being 1915 when 215,000,000 pounds were shipped abroad. Fifty per cent of the entire 1918 output was requisitioned by the British Food Controller through the Ceylon Tea Commissioner. Shipments to the United States fell from 25,000,000 pounds in 1917 to 11,000,000 pounds in 1918, while Russian exports dropped from 14,000,000 pounds in 1917 to nothing in 1918. Approximately 200,000,000 pounds of tea are raised in Ceylon each year on 400,000 acres. The estates, ranging from 100 to 2,500 acres, are worked under European supervision with Tamil labor from southern India, and are located on elevations ranging from sea level to 7,000 feet. Large quantities of artificial fertilizers are used but the making of the crop depends primarily upon the monsoon which brings the rains. The planting of permanent green manure trees has been found a satisfactory method of fertilizing. There are 1,040 tea firing and rubber drying establishments in Ceylon.

Rubber.—Restrictions placed on rubber shipments by the United States in 1918 caused a drop in exports of from 75,000,000 pounds valued at $44,000,000 in 1917 to 50,000,000 pounds valued at $22,000,000 in 1918, indicating a drop in price of serious proportions. Notwithstanding this temporary reaction the area in Ceylon rubber continues to expand and 255,000 acres were under cultivation in 1919. There is a tendency among small owners to plant rubber on lands formerly used for growing food products and this is only accentuating the problem of feeding the population of Ceylon, which is already dependent upon India and Burma for foodstuffs.

Coconut Products.—The export of coconut products which had reached $16,000,000 in 1913 had fallen in 1918 to $11,500,000, which was a slight increase over the 1917 exports.

Copra shipments increased from 1,000,000 hundredweight, valued at $4,300,000, in 1917 to 1,200,000 hundredweight, valued at $4,100,000, in 1918. The shipments were mainly to India.

Coconut oil increased from 430,000 hundredweight, valued at $3,200,000, in 1917 to 520,000 hundredweight, valued at $5,000,000, in 1918. Much of this product was shipped to Europe by the Imperial Government.

Desiccated coconut, largely for the United States, dropped from 270,000 hundredweight, valued at $3,000,000, in 1917 to 200,000 hundredweight, valued at $1,700,000, in

1918, while shipments of coir fiber, rope, and yarn showed a 50 per cent increase in quantity and a 100 per cent increase in value. These products were manufactured in 119 factories throughout the island. As a whole the Ceylon coconut production is bound to be low for some time, as low prices have discouraged new plantings and proper fertilizing and cultivated areas have actually decreased.

Cacao.—Cacao exports increased from 72,000 hundredweight, valued at $585,000, in 1917 to 73,000 hundredweight, valued at $760,000, in 1918. The United Kingdom, Australia, the Philippines, and Japan were the largest buyers. The area under cultivation remains stationary at 22,000 acres, although there is a tendency to sacrifice cacao acreage for rubber. There are five chocolate factories in Ceylon and indications point to their expansion.

Cinnamon.—Cinnamon exports rose from 29,000 hundred-weight, valued at $310,000 in 1917 to 37,000 hundredweight, valued at $430,000, in 1918, going largely to the United Kingdom and the United States. Cinnamon quills represented 70 per cent of the exports, the balance being in chips. There has been little change in the acreage. Cinnamon oil exports in 1918 doubled to 320,000 ounces, valued at $49,000.

Citronella (Lemon-Grass) Oil.—There was a decrease in exports of citronella oil of 100,000 hundredweight to 1,030,000 hundredweight in 1918 and of $100,000 to $280,000. The largest purchasers were the United Kingdom and the United States.

Tobacco.—Exports of tobacco in the form of cigars and chewing tobacco increased in 1918 from the 3,400,000 pounds of 1917, valued at $216,000, to 4,700,000 pounds valued at $290,000. The Joffra District, with 6,600 acres under cultivation, is the chief producing district. At present the principal market for cigars outside of Ceylon itself is India and for chewing tobacco, Cochin China and the Malay States. An attempt is being made to cultivate a tobacco suitable for the European market.

Other Products.—Areca nut exports increased from 154,000 hundredweight, valued at $95,000, in 1917 to 214,000 hundredweight, valued at $1,230,000, in 1918. They are shipped to nearby points exclusively.

Cardamon exports increased in quantity from 3,300 hundredweight to 3,500 hundredweight but declined in value from $120,000 in 1917 to $98,000 in 1918. This product is grown in marshy ground and on hillsides below 6,000 feet altitude, both in Sinhalese villages and on estates.

The cultivation of castor seed for oil has been begun in Ceylon owing to the restrictions placed upon its exportation from India to Ceylon. About 135 acres were planted in 1918 and a yield of 700 pounds of seed per acre was expected.

The high price of imported rice from India has encouraged rice cultivators to take up lands which had not been cultivated for some time. Rice mills have been established in several districts. Larger areas have been planted in food products in every district. Manioc, sweet potatoes, and plantains, together with maize, beans, and dry grains are all being grown in increasing quantities to meet the food shortage.

Plumbago.—The exports of plumbago showed a notable drop from 26,000 tons valued at $7,000,000, in 1917 to 15,000 tons, valued at $1,570,000, in 1918. Fifty-five per cent, mostly better grades, went to the United States, the remainder to the United Kingdom. Many of the mines are worked in a primitive fashion, but some employ modern machinery. The product is subject to fluctuating demand from Europe and America because of competition with Madagascar plumbago and Korean graphite. Ceylon can produce 30,000 tons of plumbago a year, but the actual production in 1918 was slightly over 12,000 from 263 mines employing 6,400 men.

Market Analysis

The import trade of Ceylon suffered a slight decline from $60,000,000 in 1917 to $57,000,000 in 1918. Of this total 40 per cent was with India, 20 per cent with Burma, 16 per cent with the United Kingdom, five per cent with Japan, five per cent with British Africa, four per cent with the Straits Settlements, three per cent with the United States, two per cent with Sumatra, and five per cent with other countries.

Rice.—Ceylon's imports of rice in 1918 of 6,400,000 hundredweight, valued at $17,000,000, amounted to 30 per cent of the total import trade. These figures were 1,300,000 hundredweight under the 1917 imports, whose value was $19,000,000, and were considerable below the average imports of rice in recent years. This was due to the prohibition of rice exports from southern India owing to crop failures. As a result Ceylon imports in 1918 were placed under a licensing system, which with high freight rates raised the price considerably. This situation has shown that Ceylon must become less dependent upon imported rice and with this in view the Government undertook a campaign of education in 1918, distributed seeds, and took steps to utilize irrigable crown lands now allowed to lie fallow. At the same time an effort will be made to increase the yield of rice per acre which is now very low.

Cotton Piece Goods.—From a total of $4,530,000 in 1917 piece goods imports in Ceylon increased in 1918 to $5,060,000. Over 90 per cent of this total was supplied by the United Kingdom and British possessions.

Dyed goods imports increased from 15,000,000 yards in 1917 to 19,000,000 yards in 1918, while bleached goods imports fell from 12,000,000 yards in 1917 to 9,000,000 yards in 1918. Printed goods also experienced a drop of from 6,000,000 yards in 1917 to 3,000,000 yards in 1918, while gray goods jumped from 2,200,000 yards in 1917 to 3,000,000 yards in 1918.

Metals and Metal Ware.—The imports of metal and metal ware were $2,600,000 in 1918, being the same as the 1917 imports. Thirty-two per cent of these imports came from the United States, chiefly hoop iron, nails and rivets, cast steel, hardware, and galvanized barb wire; 31 per cent came from Burma, mostly pig lead and lead for tea chests; 24 per cent came from the United Kingdom; six per cent came from Japan; and seven per cent came from all other countries.

Sugar.—Sugar imports in 1918 were 415,000 hundredweight, 10,000 more than 1917, with a value of $2,300,000 or $100,000 over the 1917 values. Java and Sumatra were the chief suppliers.

Fertilizers.—Fertilizer imports increased from 900.000 hundredweight, valued at $16,000,000, in 1917 to 1,300.000 hundredweight, valued at $2,100,000, in 1918. They consisted of nitrate of soda, whale bone, guano, fish, and peanut cake, and practically all came from British India.

Coal.—Colombo being a bunkering station, imports of coal reach considerable proportions. The 1918 imports of 218,000 tons were much less than the 1917 figure of 311,000 tons, although the value rose from $3,300,000 to $4,000,000. India supplies most of the coal imported.

Rubber.—Trade in rubber amounted to $2,000,000 in both 1917 and 1918 although the quantity brought in rose from 3,500,000 pounds to 5,500,000 pounds. Though Ceylon is a large exporter of rubber, this import trade is the result of the Colombo market being the assembling place for shipments originating in India.

Petroleum Products.—Imports of petroleum products rose from $2,050,000 in 1917 to $2,150,000 in 1918. Liquid fuel imports showed the most notable gains, rising from 6,600,000 gallons to 11,800,000 gallons, while kerosene dropped from 4,200,000 gallons to 3,900,000 gallons and gasoline from 800,000 gallons to 600,000 gallons. Lubricating oils also showed a decline of from 300,000 to 200,000 gallons. Dutch Borneo, Persia, and Sumatra supplied the bulk of the imports and the decline in kerosene imports which were the lowest of any year since the war represented decreased case oil shipments from the United States.

Motor Cars.—Motor cars, of which 590 had been brought in in 1916, fell to 126 in 1917 and 15 in 1918, because of the imposition of a 100 per cent import duty in February, 1917. This duty was removed early in 1919 and a renewed trade in automobiles and trucks, largely from the United States, should result.

Other Imports.—Among other manufactured articles imported in 1918, many of which could be supplied by the United States, were haberdashery worth $800,000, ream paper worth $500,000, acids worth $300,000, chemicals worth $300,000, machinery worth $350,000, and cigarettes worth $430,000.

Questions

1. Name Ceylon's best tea customers and describe the methods used in growing.
2. How does the popularity of rubber planting affect Ceylon economically?
3. Name three other products of Ceylon, giving the buyers of each.
4. How is the Government of Ceylon encouraging rice growing?
5. Name three imports of Ceylon in which America's sales could be increased.

BIBLIOGRAPHY TO PART III

British India, Burma and Ceylon

Allen, J. G.:
A Narrative of Indian History. London and New York, 1900.

Archer, William:
India and the Future. New York, 1918.

Boggess, A. C.:
First Days in India. New York, 1912.

Bruce, Richard K.:
The Forward Policy and Its Results. London and New York, 1900.

Bryce, J. R.:
The Making of British India. London and New York, 1915.

Campbell, Rev. William:
British India. London, 1839.

Coates, W. H.:
The Old "Country Trade" of the East Indies. London, 1911.

Crane, Walter:
India Impressions. New York, 1907.

Curzon, George M., First Baron:
Lord Curzon in India. London and New York.

Elphinstone, M.:
The History of India (Hindu and Mahetan period). London, 1911.

Elwin, E. F.:
India and the Indians. London, 1913.

Fisher, Fred:
India's Silent Revolution. New York, 1918.

Fuller, Sir B.:
The Empire of India. London, 1913.

Gilliat, Edward:
Heroes of Modern India. London, 1910.

GRIFFIN, Rev. Z. F.:
India and Daily Life in Bengal. Philadelphia and Boston, 1912.
HARDEE, J. Kier:
India—Impressions and Suggestions. New York, 1900.
HAVELL, Ernest B.:
History of Aryan Rule in India. New York, 1918.
HOLDICH, Sir Thomas:
The Gates of India. London, 1910.
HUNTER, Sir W. W.:
India. New York, 1916.
KEENE, H. G.:
History of India. Edinburgh, 1906.
LAJPAT, Raya:
Political Future of India. New York, 1918.
LAJPAT, Raya:
England's Debt to India. New York, 1917.
MCPHERSON, David:
History of European Commerce with India. London, 1912.
MORISON, Theodore:
The Economic Transition in India. New York, 1911.
MUKERJEE, H.:
Foundation of India Economics. London, 1918.
MUNSON, Arley:
Kipling's India. New York, 1915.
MURRAY, John:
Handbook for Travelers in India, Burma, and Ceylon. London, 1913.
NEWCOMBE, A. G.:
Village, Town and Jungle Life in India. Edinburgh and London, 1905.
RAM, R. B.:
India Problems. London, 1911.
RAPSON, R. J.:
Ancient India. Cambridge, 1914.
RAWLINSON, H. G.:
Indian Historical Studies. London and New York, 1913.
REES, J. D.:
The Real India. Boston and Tokyo, 1910.
SHOEMAKER, M. M.:
Indian Pages and Pictures. London, 1912.
STRECHEY, Sir John:
India—Its Administration and Progress. New York, 1911.

SURRIDGE, Victor:
India. London and Edinburgh, 1909.
THOMPSON, Lt. Col. S. J.:
The Silent India. Edinburgh and London, 1913.
TIBLY, A. W.:
British India, 1600-1826. London, 1911.
TOZER, H. J.:
British India and Its Trade. London and New York, 1902.
VAMBERRY, A.:
The Coming Struggle for India. London, 1885.
WARE, Mary S.:
The Old World Thru Old Eyes. New York and London, 1917.
YOUNGHUSBAND, Sir G. J.:
The Story of the Guides. New York, 1911.

PART IV

MALAYSIA, FRENCH INDO-CHINA, AND SIAM

CHAPTER XIX

HISTORY AND GOVERNMENT OF MALAYSIA

The history of the growth of British power in Malaysia is bound up with the extension of British influence and control in India. The council at Madras decided upon Priaman, on the West Sumatran Coast, rather than Bencoolen, as the first settlement, because of the large pepper shipments received by the East India Company from that vicinity and in 1685 established a "factory" there. The fact that the Dutch had already arrived at Priaman probably influenced the first British ships to sail by, attributing their action to adverse winds. But the Company, not foreseeing such disobedience to their orders, had despatched the supplies and stores from home to Priaman and this, together with the unhealthy location, caused much suffering, sickness, and death in the new post at Bencoolen. But despite all discomforts the small band of traders held out and thus saved from Dutch domination and influence a large portion of Malaysia and established nearer the source of production the Company's outposts for the control of the pepper trade. The attempts to control pepper production through agreement with local chiefs to purchase all produced at a fixed rate required disciplinary measures, with the result that fortifications and garrisons added greatly to the overhead expense of the "factory." But with all this effort at control, the Company could not combat the inherent love of ease of the native, and the greater leisure which gambier cultivation promised, with equally lucrative return, had in a hundred years practically ruined the pepper trade with this region.

The Founding of Penang.—Realizing that if British commercial influence in India were to be retained, a source of supply in Malaya must be maintained, the Supreme Government in India, after restoring British authority in 1761 as a result of the successful French attack on Bencoolen of the preceding year, decided to make it a first class station. But because of its unhealthy location and the resulting scarcity of population the proposition was abandoned in 1785 and the colony disappeared completely. A search for a new settlement had already been begun, and due to the farsighted and courageous wisdom of Francis Light, a representative of a large number of Madras merchants, whose relations with the King of Kedah were most cordial, the Company accepted from the King the grant of the Island of Penang and Light was sent in 1786 as superintendent of the new colony. In return for the use of the Island the Company granted the King $30,000 and agreed to advance necessary ammunition and men to defend the King against any enemies that might threaten the destruction of his kingdom. After four years Light had built a large town and considerably beautified the Island, and when, in 1790, the King of Kedah had prepared an expedition on the mainland for the purpose of recovering the Island, Light attacked and scattered it and forced the King to cede the Island in perpetuity, in consideration of a subsidy of $6,000. Ten years later, in return for an additional subsidy of $4,000, territorial rights over Province Wellesley on the mainland were given to the Company. Thus the importance of Penang, which the death of Light in 1794 and the capture of the new port of Malacca, on the Straits, from the Dutch in 1795 had temporarily overshadowed, obtained a new significance and in 1805 it was made a Presidency.

The Establishment of Singapore.—The original intention of the British conquerors of Malacca was to destroy this Dutch post and with it all Dutch commercial influence in the Straits, but a young official, Thomas Stanford Raffles, who was destined to play a leading rôle in the later occupation of the Dutch East Indies, saw the strategic advantage of retaining a British trading post at that place. He based his plea on the faith of the 20,000 natives in the protection of the British, adroitly adding that Malacca had always proven a profitable station. The post was retained and later, when the British policy of permanent trade centres in Malaya was decided upon, the importance of a post farther to the south, as the means of keeping open the trade with China, was recognized and Raffles was delegated to carry out these plans.

The Island of Singapore was chosen after much reconnoitering and many vicissitudes, including the difficulty of obtaining assistance and supplies from Penang, and in February, 1819, a treaty with the elder brother of the reigning Sultan of Johore transferred the Island to British sovereignty in return for British support of the claims of the aspirant to the throne, who claimed to have been wrongfully excluded from succession. Considerable opposition to this move now arose at home and necessitated many eloquently penned appeals on the part of Raffles to resist the prior claims to the island by the Dutch. Finally, in 1824 the controversy was settled by agreement between the British and Dutch Governments in Europe and British rights in Singapore were recognized. Realizing the necessity of reviving the trade of Singapore, Raffles made it a free port, with the object to drawing to it the trade of a wide area, and a free port it has since remained, its magnificent growth as a transshipping point bearing tribute to the wisdom and far-sightedness of its founder.

The Creation of the Post of "British Resident."—The early policy of the British was one of non-interference with the native rulers and of confining their activities to the possessions of the Company. But the continual quarrels between rival princes, the growth of lawlessness in general, and particularly the interference with commerce by uncontrolled native pirates, led to the appointment of a British commission, in 1873, under Major General Sir Andrew Clarke, to ascertain the condition of affairs in each of the native states, with the view to appointing British officers to reside in the various states, with the consent of the native rulers, and at British expense. The result of the visit of this mission was the Treaty of Pangkor in June, 1874, which provided:

1. That the Sultan receive and provide a suitable residence for a British officer, to be called Resident, who shall be accredited to his court and whose advice must be asked and acted upon in all questions other than those touching Malay religion and customs.
2. That the collection and control of all revenues and the general administration of the country be regulated under the advice of these Residents.

The chiefs of the native states accepted the arrangement without enthusiasm, but the Sultan of Perak resisted the new decree and threatened to kill any Resident sent to his village. When the British Resident, Mr. Birch, appeared, the Sultan's men, true to their word, attacked and killed him. An expedition of 2,000 British troops succeeded in enforcing the British protectorate after experiencing much resistance. The Sultan was exiled and those who had ordered the attack were executed. The lesson this taught was an important factor in strengthening British prestige in the peninsula. In 1888 Pahang came into the system and in 1895 nine other states coalesced under Negri Sembilan and accepted British control. The States, Perak, Selangor, Negri Sembilan, and Pahang, were formally federated in 1896 and the present Federated Malay States formed with a combined area of 27,000 square miles and a population of 1,000,000 with Kuala Lumpur in Selangor as capital. Those not federated are Kedah, Kelantan, Trangganu, and Johore, but the British claim a sphere of influence over these Non-Federated States as well.

The Governor and the Councils.—The supreme authority in the Crown colony of the Straits Settlements, including Singapore, Penang, Province Wellesley, Malacca, and Dindangs, is in the hands of the Governor, who is assisted by an Executive Council composed entirely of officials. A Legislative Council on which non-officials have representation, but which is dominated by the official element, supplements the Executive Council. Due to the diversity of the population anything resembling a representative government of the colony would not be found practicable, but with the growth of the European element in the population in recent years, a less rigid system of Government will probably be devised.

The Governor of the Straits Settlements is also High Commissioner of the Federated and Non-Federated Malay States, as well as Governor of Cocos Island, Christmas Island, Labuan Island, and High Commissioner of Brunei in North Borneo. The Chief Secretary is the principal British official in the Federated Malay States, and a Federal Council of native rulers and their British advisers corresponds to the Legislative Council of the Straits Settlements. The Non-Federated States are under an advisory system whereby the British official acts more as an adviser than a legislator, with duties that are semi-diplomatic.

The Judicial System.—The judicial system in the Straits Settlements was established in 1760 when a charter was granted the inhabitants of Bencoolen granting them the authority to establish a Court consisting of a mayor and nine aldermen, who were to be British and appointed for life, for the purpose of dealing with criminal and civil cases. In 1807 a Court of Judicature was established by charter at Prince of Wales Island and from this date the character of the judiciary in the Straits took on a more settled character. When Malacca was captured the Recorder of the Judicature held court there and by letters patent his duties were extended to Singapore and Penang in 1826. Later a Supreme Court was established in Singapore and now consists of a Chief Justice and four puisne judges and these five constitute a court of appeal from whose decision appeal lies in the Privy Council. In the Federated Malay States the administration of the law is in the hands of the Chief Judicial Commissioner and two Commissioners, who together form a Supreme Court at Kuala Lumpur. The penal law is based on the Indian Code, while the civil procedure code is based on the English Judicature Acts.

Local Self-Government.—The local government in the colony is left largely in the hands of the local residents. In 1827 a Committee of Assessors was appointed to Penang to superintend the cleansing, watching, and repairing of the streets of the Settlement. In 1829 a similar authority, set up in Singapore, was charged with "making, repairing, and cleansing the roads, streets, bridges, and ferries and the removal of public nuisances," and to fulfill for police functions. A rate of five per cent was assessed on all houses in Singapore for this purpose. In the Federated States local ordinances are put into effect with the consent of the Resident or his representative, and in the Non-Federated States local matters are left to the native government.

The British genius for retaining actual governmental control while relinquishing the petty non-essentials of routine administration has, perhaps, displayed itself more clearly in the government of the Malay States than in any other part of the world. Out of a group of constantly warring states has been constructed a well knit and stable government, under whose protection, what is probably the most diverse population in the world lives in peace and prosperity.

QUESTIONS

1. What commercial motive actuated the British East India Company in establishing trading posts in Malaya?
2. Describe the acquisition of Singapore?
3. What led to the assumption of Protectorates over the native Malay states and what is the nature of this protectorate?
4. Outline the form of government of the Federated Malay States?
5. Describe (*a*) the judicial system.
   (*b*) The local government.

CHAPTER XX

PRODUCTS AND MARKET ANALYSIS OF MALAYSIA

The great agricultural development of Malaysia has been the one distinct contribution of the foreign occupation of the peninsula. While, of a total population of 1,036,999 for the Federated States in 1911 only 3,284 were Europeans, the 433,444 Chinese outnumber the 420,840 Malays. Energetic Scotch colonists have spared neither pains nor capital in proving that, despite many handicaps, the country could be made to produce profitably such crops as were needed at home and could only be grown in a tropical land. Chinese adventurers were also responsible in no small degree for the success of many agricultural ventures. Between these two groups of Chinese and Europeans the natives were coaxed and urged to engage in regular work. As for the handicaps, the ravages of wild hogs, deer, and monkeys upon the young crops of coconuts, betel nuts, gambier, and pepper, were only equalled in their disastrous effects by the utter indifference of the officials to the great projects which these pioneers had visioned. "Instead of placing the whole cultivating population on a fair equal footing," says one writer, "by permitting the holders of grants and leases to commute their rents, the commutations were fixed at unequal and, in most cases, excessive rates." Coffee was the first product cultivated but the price ultimately fell and the estates were not able to pay expenses. Such products as tea and cinchona could not be raised because of the peculiar topographical and climatic conditions. In a final attempt to make agriculture pay the planters turned to Para rubber.

Rubber.—For many years after the introduction of the Para rubber tree into Europe by the Spaniards, there was no serious effort to cultivate plantation rubber. The early British settlers at Penang had reported on the existence of wild rubber there, but little attention was paid to it. With the discovery of the vulcanization process the new uses of rubber began to be realized. In 1876 the first shipment of rubber seeds was received from British agents in Brazil from which 2,800 seedlings were set out not only in Malaya, but in Ceylon and other tropical British colonies of the East. The fact that four or five years were required to bring the plant to the producing stage, which meant the sinking of capital in land and labor without any return during that period, at first reacted upon the development of the industry, and it was not until 1895 that the rubber industry had passed beyond the experimental stage. With the promising development of the automobile the demand for rubber was foreseen and many estates were planted which came into bearing about 1904. The fall in coffee prices also had some effect in releasing plantations for rubber at this time. Virgin ground was taken up in interior regions of the peninsula where no white man had ever penetrated, forests were cleared, roads constructed and permanent buildings erected. The seedlings in the Singapore nurseries were now called for not only by Malay planters but by planters from all over the world and some 9,000,000 rubber seeds soon were distributed. In 1911, 11,118 tons of rubber were produced. By 1915 the exports from Malaya were 44,523 tons; in 1916, 62,764 tons; in 1917, 79,831 tons; in 1918, 78,283 tons; and in 1919, 106,452 tons valued at a little over $107,000,000 were exported. The superiority of Malay rubber over African rubber lies in the greater purity, there being only a one per cent loss through purification of the Malay product as against a 20 to 40 per cent loss in the African product, and while the latter has remained stationary in output, the Malay production has increased beyond the greatest expectations. The evils of close planting are beginning to be understood, and experience has shown that the best results are obtained by allowing fullest development of the tree, in which cases the later supply is well maintained and increases steadily from year to year. While definite figures are not known it is estimated that tapping may continue for 40 years under proper conditions.

The British Indian Tamils and the Chinese constitute the real nucleus of the labor employed on the plantations. The Government has adopted a liberal labor policy and free influx from India has been encouraged. Many of the laborers have been recruited in Madras and their passage to Malaya is defrayed by an Immigration Fund raised by all rubber planters who employ Tamil labor, on the basis of average employment of Tamil labor. The laborers are not obliged to repay their passage and many leave an estate on a month's notice. The greater majority of them have stayed in their new homes and the Government has seen that proper housing, water supply, and sanitation were provided, and it maintains a staff of inspectors for the purpose. The recent commercial use of rubberseed oil, which has many of the qualities of cottonseed oil, and also provides a cake for cattle feeding, forms an important outgrowth of the rubber industry.

Coconuts.—The planting of coconuts has become one of the leading industries of Malaya. While it has not attained anything like the position of rubber in the colony's agriculture, the steady and growing demand for coconut oil abroad, as well as the increasing number of uses made of copra cake; the coir fibre, the rough hair like substance of the outer husk; the leaves, for basket making; and the juice of the blossoms, for sugar or fermented drinks, have all increased the value of the product. In 1911 there were

142,774 acres under coconuts, one-half of which were in the Federated State of Perak. The exports of copra in 1915 amounted to 15,610 tons valued at $1,043,000. In 1919 this amount had risen to 29,847 tons and the value to $2,-918,000.

Aside from these two there are few agricultural products which contribute materially to the prosperity of Malaya. About a hundred thousand acres are devoted to rice and *padi,* but most of this is consumed locally, only 2,000 tons being exported in 1919. Some coffee and sugar are grown but the exports are negligible. About 1,300 tons of areca nuts and the same quantity of tapioca are shipped abroad annually.

Tin.—The tin and gold mines of the peninsula have been worked for many centuries, first by Chinese and later by Portuguese, who record the unbounded riches of Pahang in gold deposits. It was not until 1903 that the Government of the Federated Malay States appointed a geologist to conduct a scientific survey of the country. The tin ore exported within recent years has been taken almost entirely from alluvial deposits. The Machi tin field of Pahang is perhaps the most characteristic of these. At Chin-Chin in Malacca and Serandah in Selangor the ore is deposited in small lodes under the soil. In 1911 only 1,200 tons of tin ore were produced by lode mining. Until the Federated Malay States were formed the favorite method of working the tin mines employed by the Chinese was that of digging holes in the surface and after exhausting the supply moving on to another area. The Kinta Valley in Perak and the valley of the Klang River near Kuala Lumpur are the chief tin producing centres. Here most of the tin mined in Malaya, which is half the world's production, is taken from deposits near the granite foothills. Open cast mining is used almost exclusively. This is simply an extension of the older methods employed by the Chinese, and with the use of modern hauling machinery the mines are worked to a depth of 100 feet or more. The tin-bearing gravel is conveyed by hand to wash boxes where the tin stone is separated by raking it in the running water. Other methods employed are the hydraulic or sluicing method, the underground workings, and dredging. The first depends upon the water supply and the location of the deposit in a narrow valley in the hills where the water may be trained upon it. After the gravel is washed down suction dredges lift it to wooden flumes where the tin ore is extracted. Bucket dredges have been used in parts of Kelantan and Perak. The underground method is least popular because of the heavy charges for timbering and the process is not an exhaustive one. Many underground workings abandoned as exhausted have been later worked on the open cast principle with great profit. Large smelters of the Straits Trading Company at Singapore and Prai now smelt the ore which was formerly refined at the mines. The Eastern Smelting Company at Penang also is equipped with modern devices, but notwithstanding the economical and effective services these large smelters render, some of the Chinese miners still resort to the primitive blast furnace. All but a small fraction of the labor employed in the mines is Chinese. Where the miner owns the land he usually employs the labor and takes all the profits and risk. In some cases land is let to the actual laborers who pay a fixed return. The "truck" system, formerly employed, whereby the laborer was advanced his food, cash, and necessaries and in return was under obligations to work until a certain delivery had been made, has now been abolished. Under the present, or "tribute," system a local capitalist advances the necessary money for food and stores and assumes the risk of the project failing. As the ore is mined it is turned over to him and when its sale is effected he adjusts the accounts by deducting his tribute agreed upon, and placing the balance to the credit of the laborers. This system has just enough element of chance in it to attract the Chinese entrepreneur. The exports of tin have increased from 4,893 tons in 1915, valued at $3,255,000, to 5,753 tons in 1919, valued at $5,892,000. The exports of tin ore have decreased from 67,835 tons, valued at $31,565,-000 in 1915 to 49,465 tons with an increase in valuation to $36,569,000. The difficulties in obtaining the necessary shipping have played the leading part in reducing the output. Due to the monopolistic character of Malaya's position in the tin market, the Straits Government has successfully collected an export duty on tin for many years which annually yields it many millions in revenue.

Other Minerals.—About 250 tons of scheelite and 235 tons of wolfram were exported in 1919. The mining of gold has attracted many adventurers from Europe and the peninsula is dotted with abandoned workings, but so far only the Raub Company, an Australian concern, has had any degree of success, due more to skill in application of modern mining methods, than the discovery of any exceptional deposits.

Market Analysis.—The export trade of the Federated Malay States has increased from $91,000,000 in 1915 to $155,000,000 in 1919. Seventy per cent of this latter figure represented rubber and 28 per cent tin and tin ore, leaving only two per cent for all other exports.

The import trade increased from $34,200,000 in 1915 to $67,830,000 in 1919. Of the 1919 imports, 27 per cent was rice valued at $18,800,000, which is a considerable increase in value over the $8,550,000 imports of 1915, although the actual tonnage brought in dropped from 208,000 tons to 187,000 tons during that period. Cigarettes increased in value from $800,000 in 1915 to $2,000,000 in 1919. Sugar is the next largest import, amounting to $1,880,000 in 1919 while petroleum was imported to the value of $1,770,000 during the same year. Both of these commodities show 100 per cent increases in import value, with about a 10 per cent decrease in quantity as evidence of high prices.

Wheat flour valued at $1,710,000, prepared opium worth $1,590,000, tobacco worth $1,480,000, condensed milk worth $1,330,000, swine worth $1,140,000, Kachang oil worth $1,100,000, bran valued at $970,000, and benzine worth $912,000 are among the other leading imports. The import trade of 1919 may be divided into five large groups of materials. Of these the first group, consisting of live animals, food, drink, and narcotics, shows a total value of $41,000,000, or 61 per cent of the total; the second group, including all metals and metal manufactures, totals $7,240,000 in value, or 11 per cent of the total import trade; the third group, consisting of miscellaneous manufactured articles, shows a valuation of $6,840,000, or 10 per cent of the import trade; the fourth group, composed of textiles, amounts to $6,100,000, or nine per cent; the fifth group, containing miscellaneous raw materials, is valued at $6,050,000, or nine per cent.

The import trade of the Federated Malay States offers an attractive field for American exporters. With over half the import trade consisting of foodstuffs, such as cakes, crackers, hams, lard, preserved vegetables, beans and peas, preserved fruits, etc., there is no reason why, with the ever increasing prosperity of the colony, our manufacturers of these commodities could not share in the trade. The metal and metal manufactures group contains such items as ironware, tramway and railway materials, engines, boilers and parts, motor cars, tools, instruments and implements, steel, hardware and cutlery, and other items which play a large part in our export trade. Under miscellaneous manufactured articles chemicals, rubber tires, stationery, and paper and paper goods are among the items which we could supply to advantage. In textiles, the fourth group, cotton prints, dyed goods, plain goods, sarongs, slendangs and kains, foreign apparel, hosiery and millinery, might all be supplied by the United States, while under raw materials, besides petroleum, benzine, and Kachang oil, which are largely supplied from the Dutch East Indies, lubricating oils are indicated as being a potential item of import from this country. Proper methods of distribution and an understanding of the peculiar desires of the natives, both of which ends can only be brought about by establishing American import and export houses, are necessary in order to obtain and hold this trade.

Questions

1. (*a*) What policy discouraged the early planters in Malaya?
   (*b*) Describe the introduction of rubber planting and the growth of the industry. What labor policy is pursued? With what success?
2. What are the uses of coconuts and the extent of the coconut industry in Malaya?
3. Review the development of the tin industry in Malaya.
4. Give the percentages of the total export trade of Malaya in rubber and tin.
5. What are the principal imports of Malaya and indicate their relative importance?

CHAPTER XXI

HISTORY AND GOVERNMENT OF FRENCH INDO-CHINA

In 1861 the French acquired the colony of Cochin China by conquest, but it was not until 1896 that the colony was finally pacified and placed under an effective colonial government. In 1884 Tonkin was made a French Protectorate, but the administration of the French was so weak and Frenchmen showed such reluctance in emigrating to the colony and in developing its industries, that the history of the French in Indo-China until 1896 was one in which military and administrative problems overshadowed all commercial considerations. From 1887 to 1895 the French Indo-China Government cost the French Government 40,000,000 francs and the colonial venture had cost France a total of 750,000,000 francs from the time of the first conquest in 1861 to 1895. In 1896 a colonial loan of 80,000,000 francs was raised to discharge pressing obligations and to construct needed public works. The failure of French administration was not hard to explain. The officials were transferred direct from the Home Service, rather than trained in the colony and military and naval officers were often appointed to executive posts who possessed no knowledge of colonial government and were ignorant of the language of the country. Political influence in Paris rather than efficient service in the colony was the basis of promotion. In 1893 France was exercising a merely nominal protectorate over Annam and Cambodia, and no French administration had been introduced into these two States. Laos had just been acquired, but Tonkin was still under military protection, although a civil government had been instituted seven years before. Moreover, the foreign trade of the colony was nearly all under the control of foreigners.

The Success of Doumer.—In December, 1896, M. Paul Doumer, leader of a radical wing in the Chamber of Deputies, was appointed Governor General of French Indo-China in an effort to get him out of French politics at home. The reforms which he proposed were as follows:

1. The creation of a suitable financial policy.
2. The pacification of Tonkin.
3. The organization of a Government General.
4. The completion of reforms of the Protectorate.
5. The extension of French influence in China and Siam.

The success of his administration is shown by the remarkable commercial growth of the colony by 1902. During the ten years from 1893 to 1902 the foreign trade of the colony increased from 162,000,000 francs to 400,000,000 francs, of which France's share increased from less than one-fifth to more than one-third. The exports doubled in value and the value of exports to France in 1902 was nearly four times as large as in 1893.

The Reorganization of the Government.—This remarkable growth was brought about largely by reforms in administration. The Government General was reorganized on the principle of governing the whole of Indo-China, but leaving the administration to the Resident Superiors in the Protectorates. The Superior Council of Indo-China was re-created and endowed with legislative powers. It consists of the Governor General, the military and naval commanders in French Indo-China, the Secretary General of Indo-China, the Lieutenant Governor of Cochin China, and the Resident Superiors of the four Protectorates. In addition to these officials the heads of departments in the Government General, the President of the Colonial Council of Cochin China, the Presidents of various Chambers of

Commerce, four natives, and the Chief-of-Cabinet of the Governor General. This body has charge of the general and local budgets and advises the Governor General on local legislation. It is divided into four committees; one on military and naval affairs, public works, railways, commerce, and agriculture; a second on legislation and administrative organization; a third on budgets; and a fourth on finance.

The Executive Administration.—The executive branch of the Government General consists of the following services: military and naval; civil affairs; finances; excise and customs; public works; agriculture and commerce; and posts, telegraphs and telephones. The Cabinet of the Governor General consists of four bureaus, one covering political, one administrative, one military, and one secretarial matters. The French Government General is more elaborate than the Government of the Federated Malay States and its one distinctive feature is the legislative body.

The Budget System.—A budget system was devised in 1898 on the principle that money from indirect taxes should go to the general government of French Indo-China while direct taxes should be levied to carry on the local governments. This assignment of revenue resulted in 1904 in 65,000,000 francs being turned over to the Government General and only 32,000,000 being assigned to the local Governments.

The Judicial System.—In 1898 a Supreme Court of Appeal was established for the whole of French Indo-China, which consists of three Chambers, one Chamber under a Vice-President and two Counsellors sitting at Hanoi. The criminal court is composed of magistrates of another Chamber who sit with four assessors selected from 50 of the leading residents. Another Chamber of the Court of Appeal composed of three counsellors and two mandarins reviews the cases from the native courts, where the Annamite code is administered by local mandarins and then decisions submitted to the Resident Superior for approval. Mixed courts of commerce are held at Hanoi and Haiphong and are composed of a presiding judge and two judges elected by the Chambers of Commerce.

Railroad Development.—The railroad from Haiphong across the Chinese border into Yunnan is a remarkable tribute to the energy and foresight of Governor General Doumer, but this actual achievement is only one of a number of projects in French Indo-China involving an expenditure of 400,000,000 francs and contemplating the construction of about 2,000 miles of railroad. The program contemplated, will connect Saigon with Hanoi, Savanakek on the Mekong River with Kwantai on the coast, Ouinhone with Kontoum, and will open up Southern Annam, and connect Saigon with Bankok. Only 700 miles of road were actually needed, but Doumer insisted upon a larger program and 200,000,000 francs were finally appropriated for the following lines:

1. From Haiphong to Hanoi and on to Chinese border.
2. From the Chinese border to Yunnan.
3. From Hanoi to Vinh on the coast.
4. From Tourane to Hue and Kwangtu.
5. From Saigon to Khan-hoa on the coast and to Liangbian on the interior plateau.
6. From Mytho to Vinhlong on the Mekong River.

The Present Government.—In the five years ending 1904 France actually received 40,000,000 francs in military contribution from the colony; the administration of justice had been immeasurably improved; the Protectorates were effectively governed; and the general prestige of the colony had been raised. The present government, though far from being a model colonial government and possessing many faults, is still a great achievement in the face of changing political conditions at home. The French have gone to great expense to beautify the cities of Hanoi, Haiphong, and Saigon with public buildings and good roads have been constructed throughout the colony. The investment of private French capital in Indo-China has been a difficult matter to bring about. What private capital is there, has been induced to come through guarantees of State support. But notwithstanding this backwardness of the French toward colonizing their Far Eastern possessions, the Government General seems unwilling to adjust the customs and other regulations so as to permit other nations to undertake the development which only private initiative can give.

Questions

1. Why was the French Government of Indo-China unsuccessful until 1896?
2. What reforms did M. Doumer institute and what were the results?
3. Outline the legal system of French Indo-China.
4. What is the extent of railroad development?
5. Enumerate some of the achievements and shortcomings of present French colonial administration in Indo-China.

CHAPTER XXII

PRODUCTS AND MARKET ANALYSIS OF FRENCH INDO-CHINA

With a population of 16,000,000, 25,000 of which are Europeans, mostly French, the Delta people of French Indo-China, or Annamites, constitute 79 per cent of the population. The principal industry is agriculture, although mining has been developed within recent years. The total area is 256,000 square miles, but lack of transportation has retarded the development of the mountain regions, such as those of Laos. The delta regions of Cochin-China and Tonkin are the principal agricultural districts, containing respectively 4,000,000 and 250,000 acres. Forests cover 28,000,000 acres and furnish great opportunities for development.

Rice.—As in Siam, the predominant product of French Indo-China is rice. The normal production is 2,200,000 tons, of which 1,000,000 tons is consumed at home, leaving 1,200,000 tons for export. Practically all of this exportable surplus, about 1,000,000 tons, is raised in Cochin-China; the balance, about 200,000 tons comes from Tonking. Of this tonnage about 50 per cent is normally shipped to Hongkong where it is transshipped to Japan, Europe, and elsewhere; Japan alone takes 400,000 tons of Indo-China rice through Hongkong. Of this 20 per cent is shipped direct to France, 10 per cent to Singapore, 10 per cent to the Philippines, eight per cent to the Dutch East Indies, and the balance of two per cent is shipped direct to Europe. Japan, with its constantly increasing population and its growing importance as a manufacturing nation, is coming to depend more and more upon French Indo-China and

Siam to make up the ever increasing deficit in her rice production, and crop failures in French Indo-China which reduce the exportable surplus 20 or 30 per cent, as in 1919, are of serious consequence to Japan.

Rubber.—The cultivation of rubber has been started on an extensive scale during the war. Nearly 3,000,000 trees exist in the colony and while their production is still insignificant, a production of only 389 tons being officially recorded, planting is proceeding at a good pace and the 1917 trees will soon begin to bear. At Saigon an official rubber laboratory has been planted as a branch of the local Pasteur Institute and rubber culture is being encouraged by the recently established Scientific Institute of Indo-China. The development of the colony as a source of rubber supply is probably one of the most significant agricultural undertakings in the Orient.

Coconut and Vegetable Oils.—Another agricultural development of the colony of commercial importance is the encouragement of the growth of the coconut palm. The normal export of copra before the war was 7,000 metric tons, most of which was shipped to France and was produced in the provinces of Mytho and Bentre along the Mekong River. About 40,000 acres were devoted to coconuts before the war and by 1917 new plantations had been set out not only in the coastal regions, but throughout the interior of Cochin-China. Because of shipping difficulties during the war the planters have had to market their product mainly in the Orient, and this has had a decided effect upon production, the exports falling to 2,000 tons in 1917. Much of this went to Japan. In 1917 an oil mill for crushing the copra and producing coconut oil was established near Saigon with a capacity of 2,000 tons. It is estimated that if planting proceeds at the present rate, the colony will be producing France's total copra requirements in 20 years. About 40,000 acres of areca nuts are now bearing.

Many other oil bearing plants and seeds are capable of increased production in the colony. Oil from cotton seed, *kajok* seed, hemp seed, sesame seed, oil palm nuts, castor beans, and rubber seed are all looked to as of great future importance. Manufacturers of oil crushing machinery should find an opportunity here in the future for the sale of their machinery.

Other Agricultural Products.—Peas, maize, tobacco, sugar cane, bananas, cotton, and silk have all been cultivated on a small scale but to an ever increasing degree. Peas and maize form staple food crops for the natives of the interior. Tobacco cultivation has increased steadily as evidenced by the tax receipts which increased 50 per cent from 1911 to 1916. From the 12,000 acres planted in sugar cane, 4,200 tons of sugar were produced in 1917, 60 per cent in Giadinh Province, and 30 per cent in Bienhoa Province. By more intensive methods it is thought that at least 15,000 tons may be produced in this area, since in the older colonies from two to four tons are produced per acre. Of the 678 native sugar mills which exist in the colony, 544 are in Bienhoa Province. Silk culture centres in Culao-gieng and Cho-moi Provinces and has made satisfactory progress. The establishment of a silk reeling industry at Tanchan has offered the needed encouragement to growers.

Mining.—In 1918 there were 218 different mining concessions granted in Indo-China, 91 per cent of which were for zinc, 63 for coal, 30 for tin and tungsten, 12 for gold and the balance for copper, antimony, lead and silver, iron and mercury.

The coal production was 643,000 tons in 1917 and 636,000 tons in 1918, about half of which was exported.

Zinc, which is mined only in Tonking, was mined to the extent of 39,000 tons in 1917 and 28,000 tons in 1918. The ores are exported, chiefly to Japan, for refining.

Tin and tungsten increased in production from 519 tons

in 1917 to 604 tons in 1918, the latter production consisting of 218 tons of 70 per cent wolfram, 263 tons of tungsten and tin ore and 119 tons of 60 per cent tin ore.

Industries.—Native rice hulling mills increased in number from 1,691 in 1915 to 2,056 in 1916. These establishments vary in their activity with the size of the rice crop but with increasing acreage their number is growing. Two electrically driven hullers of American make, with a capacity of three tons per day, have been installed at Saigon. Two important distilleries exist at Cholon, one of which produced 1,100,000 litres of alcohol in 1916 and the other 60,000 litres. An interesting result of the shortage of aniline dyes is the reversion to the native indigo and other vegetable dyes. Several new establishments of this kind were set up during the war.

Market Analysis.—The best index to the normal foreign trade of French Indo-China is furnished by the 1914 statistics. These show a total export trade of $66,000,000 and a total import trade of $53,000,000. Of the export trade 66 per cent originated in Cochin-China and 33 per cent in Tonking, leaving only one per cent from Annam, Cambodia, and Laos. Of the import trade 60 per cent was destined for Cochin-China and 36 per cent for Tonking, leaving only four per cent for other dependencies. In the same year the imports from France and French Colonies amounted to 40 per cent of the import trade, while imports from Hongkong and Singapore, representing transshipments from other European countries, amounted to 40 per cent. The imports from the United Kingdom amounted to two per cent and those of the United States to one per cent. During the war, however, the lack of shipping cut down France's share of the imports to 20 per cent while Hongkong with 30 per cent and Singapore with 15 per cent made up the bulk of the foreign supply. The share of the United Kingdom and the United States has not increased perceptibly. In the export trade, mostly rice, 50 per cent is with Hongkong, 20 per cent is with France, 10 per cent with Singapore, 10 per cent with the Philippines, eight per cent with the Dutch East Indies, and two per cent direct with Europe. Deducting the products of Oriental origin for native consumption, France in normal years supplies the colony with 90 per cent of the imported manufactured goods, such as cotton piece goods, clothing, hosiery, canned goods, etc. This is insured by a preferential tariff system. During the war France has not been able to supply all the goods desired and these have been brought in from other sources, but the preferential arrangement still exists. Even with this handicap, American firms should be able to get a large share of the business in such goods as France must import from America and re-ship to French Indo-China. This is also true of many lines which France does not normally produce.

The best method of merchandising in French Indo-China and the one which has proven most successful is the use of the general store. Such an establishment should engage in both import and export trade, own rice mills to supply their own rice for export, and retail such articles above enumerated that find a ready sale. Several European firms, including before the war many German firms, followed this method of selling with great success, many of them purchasing their supplies in France. In this manner intimate relations with all the established industries of the country may be created and the sale of American products, while small in the aggregate, would increase as the industrial and agricultural development of the country proceeds.

Questions

1. In what states of Indo-China is the population and agricultural development centred?

2. What is the production and export of rice and the chief countries of destination?
3. (*a*) How has rubber cultivation been encouraged?
   (*b*) Outline the effects of the war on coconut production.
4. (*a*) Name the principal mineral products.
   (*b*) The leading industries.
5. (*a*) How has the war affected France's share of the import trade?
   (*b*) Who are the principal buyers of Indo-China products?

CHAPTER XXIII

HISTORY AND GOVERNMENT OF SIAM

Siam's shadowy claim to suzerainty over the Kingdom of Malacca brought her in first contact with the Portuguese. These adventurers of the West had subsequently penetrated to Ayuthia and had been found fighting on both sides during the Burmese-Siamese wars, while in 1548 three Portuguese ships were destroyed in the defense of that ancient capital. Early in the seventeenth century Portuguese missionaries were given land for churches in Ayuthia and otherwise favored. At the same time the vanguards of English and Dutch commerce reached Siam and a struggle for the King's favor and resulting trade began. In 1619 English and Dutch trading vessels fought a battle in Patani roads. In 1634 the Dutch had established a fortified "factory" at Ayuthia and in 1641 when the Dutch took Malacca from Portugal, the downfall of Portuguese influence in Siam was completely accomplished.

Influence of the Dutch.—Pursuing their usual policy, the Dutch devoted themselves entirely to trade and took no part in Siamese politics. In 1664 the first treaty between any foreign power and Siam was signed with representatives of the Dutch East India Company. The temperament of the Dutch was too phlegmatic and their aims too grasping, however, and in 1706, as a result of a rupture with the Government, they withdrew their factory.

The Rise of Faulkon.—Under the guidance of Constantine Faulkon, a French sailor, who rose to be a trusted advisor of the King, Siam now granted many privileges to the English and French East India Companies and the

King himself embarked upon a mercantile career which proved very profitable. Meanwhile the Dutch were assuming a threatening attitude in Malacca and the King, to protect himself from this new menace, garrisoned the ports of Bangkok and Mergui with French troops and kept a bodyguard of French troops about his person. This aroused the Siamese, who fearing the ever increasing influence of France, rose in rebellion, deposed the King, and killed Faulkon.

The War with Burma.—In 1765 the city of Ayuthia, after a six-year war with Burma, was captured and destroyed and the Burmese were prevented from pushing their conquest farther by a threatened Chinese invasion. In the meantime the Siamese were given an opportunity to collect their scattered forces and not only regained the territory lost, but were strengthened enough to push on and invade Cambodia to the east. After another unsuccessful attempt to conquer Siam, Burma was finally repulsed and the wars between the two states, which had continued intermittently for many centuries, came to an end in 1792. As a result of her conquest, Siam had come to regard Cambodia as her territory, but in 1809 this was disputed by the King of Annam and after a brief campaign an agreement between Siam and Annam was reached, ceding that part of Cambodia containing the ruins of the ancient capital of Angkor to Siam.

The First Treaty.—In 1821 the British East India Company sent an envoy to the Siamese Court for the purpose of making a treaty but without results. In 1826, however, Captain Burney concluded a treaty between Great Britain and Siam providing for the settlement of petty disputes, the mutual surrender of criminals, a definition of spheres of influence on the Malay Peninsula, and the freedom of trade. In 1833 the United States signed a treaty providing for the treatment of American citizens coming to

Siam, but the King refused both the British and the Americans the right to send consuls.

The Accession of King Mongkut.—In 1851 Prince Mongkut, who had been deprived of his rightful inheritance of the throne, was invited to rule. The Prince had spent his time to the age of forty-seven in seclusion, studying, among other things, the English language, mechanics and other sciences, practically unknown in Siam, and Western systems of government. The new King did much to encourage intercourse with the West as well as to further the welfare of his people. In 1855 Sir John Bowing negotiated a new treaty between Great Britain and Siam, introducing the extraterritorial system and providing for the appointment of a British Consul and the exercise by that official of civil and criminal jurisdiction over all British subjects in Siam. These subjects were given the right to buy or rent land within a belt of territory extending from four to 40 miles from the capital in all directions. The rates of taxation were fixed, as well as import and export duties and the rights of British subjects to travel and trade throughout the Kingdom were secured. Similar arrangements were made with France and the United States[1] the following year and with other European powers in succeeding years.

[1] On December 16, 1920, a new treaty of commerce and navigation was signed between the United States and Siam. The treaty follows in large part the usual lines of treaties of commerce and navigation between the United States and other countries. Full fiscal autonomy is granted Siam and a protocol is annexed to the treaty under which the United States surrenders extraterritorial jurisdiction over American citizens in Siam, reserving the right of evocation for a period of five years from the date on which the treaty comes into force. This action follows proposals made some years ago that extraterritorial jurisdiction be surrendered by the United States, Great Britain, and other leading powers. Great Britain, by its treaty with Siam signed in or about 1910, surrendered her extraterritorial rights. Negotiations were renewed with the United States, but the breaking out of the war in 1914 and other causes brought about a temporary suspension of the negotiations which were not again taken up until 1919. An exchange of notes was also effected by which the titles to American missionary property owned in Siam are quieted.

The French in Cambodia.—In 1863 the King of Cambodia made treaties with both France, now in control of Annam, and Siam, in which they both pledged themselves to protect Cambodia. In return both expected to conduct the foreign policy of Cambodia, neither knowing until later of the existence of the other treaty. After four years of negotiations Siam abandoned her rights in Cambodia in favor of France.

Progress under King Chulalonkorn.—The King now devoted himself to encouragement of canal digging, road construction, and ship building, while the introduction of printing opened the way to better education. On his death in 1868 he was succeeded by the father of the present monarch, King Chulalonkorn, who abolished slavery, established law courts, and reformed the fiscal administration and the military service. Communications were improved and trained officials replaced the former chieftains with the result that the various races and clans were welded together into a firmly established and homogenous nation. These reforms were not accomplished, however, without great opposition on the part of the upper classes who reluctantly gave up their ancient privileges only after much opposition.

Siam as a "Buffer" State.—As a result of a border dispute France and Siam once more encountered difficulties resulting in the occupation of the approaches of the River Menam by French gunboats and the dictation of a humiliating treaty by France, to insure the enforcement of which France established a military occupation of Chantaburi. The position of Siam now became desperate and England, anxious to maintain a "buffer" state between her own and French possessions, intervened and after negotiations with France concluded an agreement in 1896 guaranteeing the autonomy of Siam. In 1909 a treaty was concluded between Great Britain and Siam whereby, in abolishing her extraterritorial rights, Great Britain obtained suzerainty over 15,000 miles of former Siamese territory on the Malay Peninsula with a population of nearly one million, as well as the right to make a loan for railroad construction on the Peninsula.

The Executive Government.—The present executive Government of Siam consists of the King, under whom are ten chief Departments. These are the Departments of Foreign Affairs, War, Interior, Finance, Royal Household, Justice, Public Works, Public Instruction, Agriculture, and the Ministry of the Capital. The Sovereign presides at the meetings of these officials, known as the Executive Council, acting as his own Prime Minister and exercising the veto power. A Legislative Council composed of the most influential men in the state considers all laws before they become effective.

The Judicial System.—With the establishment of the Ministry of Justice in 1892 the following courts were organized: two magistrates' courts, a central criminal court, a civil court, a court of foreign causes, for dealing with foreign subjects, a court of appeal, and a Supreme Court of Appeal. Each of the provinces is provided with a Court, from which appeal lies with a Special Court of Appeal of the Provinces at Bangkok, whence final appeal can be made to the Supreme Court. Efforts are being made to raise the standard of personnel of the judiciary and every year a dozen or so young graduates from the Law School go out to take the minor judicial positions, relieving the older officials. An effort is already being made to codify the law, bringing it more into harmony with Western law, so that extraterritoriality may be abolished by the other nations as it has been by the British. This work is under the supervision of a French Legislative Adviser who is engaged in the general codification to include the Penal Code, the Criminal Procedure Code, the Civil Code, the Code of

Civil Procedure, the Commercial Code, and a Law of Judicial Organization.

The Encouragement of Education.—The Ministry of Education is divided into two Departments, the Educational Department and the Ecclesiastical Department. Under the supervision of the former are three classes of schools:

1. Government schools maintained at Government expense.
2. Local schools maintained partly or wholly by local subscriptions.
3. Private schools.

In addition to maintaining its own schools, the Educational Department has set up model primary and secondary schools in the Provinces and established local normal schools to provide teachers. Courses of instruction have also been drawn up which, while giving considerable latitude to the local authorities, dictate the minimum requirements that a scholar shall be able to read, write, make simple calculations, and have some knowledge of his own country, and some vocational training. The number of Government schools has increased from 247 in 1913 to 451 in 1917 and the scholars from 20,712 to 34,525 in the same period. The local schools have increased from 3,144 to 3,299 during this period and the scholars from 88,936 to 144,693. In addition to the primary and secondary schools the Government maintains six colleges: the Civil Service College, with a total enrollment of 273 in 1917; the Law College, with 1,281; the Military College, with 767; the Naval College, with 128; the Police School, with 84; and the Post and Telegraph School with 24.

The Railroads.—The state railways of Siam are divided into a Northern Line from Bangkok to Pre and a Southern Line from Bangkok down the Peninsula to the Malaya border where connection is made with Singapore. The Northern Line, with a total capital outlay of 59,262,432 ticals in 1917, has shown a consistent increase in annual earnings of from 54,564 ticals in 1897 when first operated to 2,963,606 ticals in 1917. The total goods tonnage during the latter years was 367,461, of which rice accounted for 112,835 tons, stone 50,140 tons, timber 28,767 tons, packages 24,729 tons, merchandise 12,552 tons, and charcoal 13,265 tons, all other commodities totaling 125,173 tons. The livestock tonnage on the Northern Line included 118,204 pigs, 13,097 head of horned cattle, and a total of 133,475 head of livestock. There were 2,568,926 passengers carried in 1917, practically all of which were third class. The Southern Line with a total capital outlay of 46,578,025 ticals in 1917 has shown a much smaller increase in net earnings of from 245,246 ticals in 1904 to 703,725 ticals in 1917. The goods tonnage was smaller, amounting to 145,692 tons of which 20,032 tons were packages, 13,221 tons rice, 7,746 tons timber, and the other classifications in much smaller amounts. Out of a total of 38,137 head of livestock carried, 21,241 were pigs and 9,033 horned cattle. The passenger traffic was 1,661,111 for 1917. The through connection with Malaya will probably show greater tonnage and earnings on this line for 1918 and succeeding years.

Questions

1. Describe the early influence of the Dutch and French in Siam.
2. What was the significance of Prince Mongkut's early training?
3. What was the reason for British interference in the border dispute between Siam and France?
4. Outline the present executive Government and the judicial.
5. Describe the growth of public education and railway development.

CHAPTER XXIV

PRODUCTS AND MARKET ANALYSIS OF SIAM

Practically the whole of Siam's 8,149,487 population is dependent upon agriculture and fishing for livelihood. During the hot season when the ground is baked and untillable and during the wet season when storms prevent sea fishing, other occupations engage some of the people, but these are of a minor character and include boat building, pottery, brick making, silk growing, etc. The immigrant Chinese have developed such small-scale industries as rice milling, distilling, sugar refining, mining, and forestry and they also dominate the retail trades and minor occupations of shoemaker, tailor, carpenter, tinsmith, carriage builder, bricklayer, shopkeeper, and pawnbroker. The native Siamese is by custom of long standing either a farmer or a fisher, and the more lucrative trades are thus easily taken over by others.

Rice.—In 1918 of Siam's total acreage of 5,552,240 acres, 5,492,600 acres were planted in rice. The only other crops of which there are official records are tobacco, 22,012 acres; maize, 14,320 acres; cotton, 7,940 acres; pepper, 7,418 acres; peas, 5,460 acres; and sesame, 1,442 acres. Rice, therefore, is the predominant product of Siam and dominates her social, political, and commercial life. It constitutes not only the principal, but the sole, staple food of the entire population. Until the introduction of European banking methods, the only means of investing money was in rice fields and nobles were graded according to the grants of rice land from the King. Rice is the principal subject of litigation in the courts and the prospects of the next harvest the absorbing topic of conversation. It is the cargo of the river boats on the Menam River and of the ocean liners which load at Bangkok and from it the Government derives almost all of its revenue. The ancient invasions of Siam from Burma and Cambodia were actuated by the desires of one ruler to obtain the rice lands of the other. Rice, therefore, is now and always has been the great staple crop of Siam. There are four species: the common rice of lower Siam; glutinous rice, grown in large quantities in the north; "red" rice, so named because of its dark appearance when boiled; and hill rice, grown by the mountain peoples. These species are divided into as many as a hundred different varieties, the chief distinguishing characteristics being color, size, and flavor. The common rice is very popular in districts liable to irregular rainfall because of its peculiar ability to stop growing after reaching a certain size in the nursery and remain perfectly healthy until the heavy rains come to soften the earth. One variety of this species has been adapted to grow at an accelerated pace to keep above the rising waters when heavy floods occur. The straw acts as a float and keeps the head of the plant above the water, which throws out lateral shoots and draws added nourishment from the water. A crop is thus assured no matter how severe the flood or drought.

The rice crop is harvested with sickles and reaping knives and the sheaves brought to the winnowing ground on light bamboo sledges drawn by the plough cattle, which are also used to tread out grain on the winnow floor. Winnowing is performed by blowing the husks and chaff away, pouring the grain from a raised platform in the wind. The common farm implements used consist of a heavy knife with a handle at right angles for cleaning long grass off the land; a plough made of two pieces of wood bound together with cane and having a small iron share; a cattle drawn harrow resembling a large hay rake, upon the back of which the driver stands; a planting stick used where the water is too deep for planting to be done by hand; an ordinary hoe; a sledge consisting of a light platform mounted on runners, all of bamboo and used in the lower plain where the water still renders the soil too soft for the wheels of a cart; and the reaping knife which varies in different localities. Many attempts have been made to introduce modern implements for the cultivation of rice and some iron ploughs and threshing machines have been imported, but they have not been favorably received by the conservative native. Lately, however, the Government has been experimenting with a tractor which would work satisfactorily on hard, baked soil, and enable the farmer to plow his land earlier than is now the case. The exports of rice from Siam have averaged about 1,272,000 short tons for the last five years, valued at about $25,382,000, although the quantity fell in 1919 to 946,700 short tons while the value rose to $43,560,000. The principal classes exported are white rice, white broken rice, and white rice meal.

Tobacco.—While not entering into the export trade, a comparatively large acreage has been devoted to tobacco for home consumption. Some tobacco is cultivated in the rice fields during dry weather but the best crops are raised in the rich alluvial soil in the upper Menam River. The production does not equal the demand and considerable tobacco is imported. Since few precautions are taken to protect the crops from insects, it is often lost and the methods used in cultivation are so crude that good results are not obtained. The leaves are cut into coarse shreds and exposed to the sun on mats or racks. It is then manufactured into cigarettes wrapped in lotus flower petals for local consumption.

Maize.—This crop is grown in small garden patches throughout Siam and some fields are devoted to its growth. It is consumed locally and often dried and stored for feed.

Cotton.—The cotton plant was probably brought from India about 2,500 years ago. Several varieties of the species *gossypium herbaceum* are grown in the north, but with cheaper cotton goods obtainable from abroad its cultivation is declining. The plant is often allowed to remain in the ground two or three years, growing six or eight feet high and bearing a smaller crop each year. This indifference on the part of the farmer leads to deep rooting of the plant and necessitates much digging to clear the ground of roots. About $30,000 worth is exported overland to China and Burma.

Pepper.—Although it formed a leading article of commerce in Siam in the seventeenth century, which had a production at that time of some 3,000 tons, pepper has declined in importance in recent years, due to uncertain markets and better methods employed in other producing countries. Its cultivation is now confined to the littoral provinces of southern Siam and is largely in the hands of Chinese. Its cultivation requires much care and it is an expensive undertaking. The export in 1918 amounted to $368,610.

Sesamum.—This plant is grown in the rice fields before planting is begun and on the high lands, but is not extensively grown on the lower plains. The oil is extracted from the seed by rough wooden presses worked by hand or bullock and is used for cooking. The seed cake is fed to cattle and is used as a fertilizer. None is exported.

Other crops include coconuts, which grow well in the sandy soil of southern Siam and are little affected by beetles as in central Siam where the coconut trees have almost disappeared. In 1918 $31,000 worth of copra was exported. Rubber planting has only recently taken place in Siam due to the early introduction of a very slow growing species which led to the erroneous conclusion that rubber could not be grown. One large rubber plantation has been started in southern Siam which has been fully as successful as the Malay plantations. Rubber exports totaled $13,228 in 1918. Sugar cane, which was once a leading export crop of Siam, is now only grown for local consumption and many ruins of sugar mills testify to the victory of beet sugar over the product of Siam.

Fisheries.—The Buddhist religion, deprecating the destruction of animal life, and the proximity of Siam to the sea have perhaps played the greatest part in developing the fisheries of Siam. Fishing is now thoroughly regulated by law and the methods, time, and places for fishing are strictly set down. Licences are granted in accordance with the kinds of nets or traps used. The fish when caught are dried, cured, and pickled and also made into a sort of fish paste. About 40,000 tons of fish are dried and cured annually and in 1919 11,600 tons of this amount were exported, mainly to Singapore. The 1918 value was $426,343.

Forestry.—Teak wood is the principal forest product entering into the export trade and $2,036,356 worth of this product was exported in 1918. The teak trade was begun in 1882 by Britishers who were working teak in Burma, and when the Siamese Government took over the teak forests of northern Siam in 1895, a State Forest Department was created and British forest officers were brought from Burma to develop scientific forestry. The teak tree is girdled near its base two years before it is actually cut down and allowed to stand and season. Four British firms and one Danish firm have invested about $10,000,000 in the teak logging industry of Siam, taking leases from the Government. Elephants haul the logs to the nearest stream and they are floated down to the saw mills at Bangkok. Agila and other woods were exported in 1918 to the value of $490,973.

Mines and Mining.—Ten thousand tons of tin are now mined annually, partly from hillside deposits and partly from the alluvial deposits of southern Siam. The Chinese have long dominated the industry, but up to 20 years ago had received little aid from the Government and the methods which they pursued remained comparatively primitive. Active prospecting was then undertaken by the Government and large ore deposits were revealed. New mines with modern machinery were opened up and the 3,600 tons production at that time has now increased threefold. The ore taken from the shallow pits of the alluvial deposits is washed from the hillsides by a series of sluices. These are supported by mazes of bamboo, and led to the proper point from a distant stream through gullies and ravines. The action of the water is assisted by laborers with picks. The dressed ore is smelted at the mine or in nearby villages in earthen blast furnaces and run off into pigs of 90 pounds. Charcoal is used as a fuel and its preparation for this purpose has denuded the forests surrounding the tin mines. The Government revenue is derived from a royalty fixed according to a sliding scale based on market prices, and amounts to about 10 per cent of the gross value.

Gold.—Many attempts to find gold in paying quantities have been made by foreign enterprise in Siam but with no success. A few Chinese still wash gold in the hills but no large gold mining undertakings exist.

Gems.—Sapphires have been found in the Chantaburi district for many years, the mines being formerly worked by speculators who leased the mines from the Government. In 1895 the Government granted a concession to a British company which took from the speculative miners many privileges previously enjoyed and since that time the profit and interest in the indiviual mines has disappeared, while the operations of the company and its successors have not been particularly profitable.

Market Analysis.—While 87 per cent of Siam's export trade of $45,804,168 in 1918 was with Singapore and Hongkong, indicating the position of Bangkok as a secondary market, the tendency toward direct imports has been growing more and more noticeable. Of the $35,918,730 import trade for 1918, 18 per cent was from the United Kingdom direct, 18 per cent from Singapore, and 18 per cent from Hongkong, while 16 per cent was from India, nine per cent from China, eight per cent from Japan, five per cent from the United States, five per cent from Dutch possessions, and the balance of three per cent from all other countries.

Cotton Goods.—Of the $9,000,000 cotton goods trade of 1918 and 1919, which constituted 25 per cent of the total imports, white shirtings head the list, with grey shirtings a close second. Other items in order of their importance were *papoons, sarongs* (a skirt-like wrapper), *pakamas,* prints, and cotton blankets. A large share of this business is with the United Kingdom, practically all of the *papoons, sarongs,* and prints originating there and half of the white shirting. Japan furnished half of the grey shirting, an eighth of the white shirting and a quarter of the cotton goods designated as all others. The United States share in the trade was negligible.

Gunny bags for rice shipment form the second largest item of import, amounting to $2,300,000 in 1918. These come almost solely from India.

Opium.—Opium imports of $2,000,000 in 1918 also came from India. Since 1909 the Government has controlled the sale of opium, which is imported raw, prepared by the Government and sold in marked, sealed tubes, through contractors, the wholesale prices being fixed annually by the Government. In 1916 it was decided that from that time onward the amount of opium to be offered for sale should be annually decreased. All opium smokers are to be registered and every precaution taken to prevent others from acquiring the habit.

Kerosene.—Mineral oil, mostly kerosene, but including benzine and liquid fuel, to the value of $1,500,000, mainly from the Dutch East Indies, constitutes the next largest item of import. The ratio by countries is Dutch East Indies, 80 per cent and the United States, 19 per cent.

Gold leaf valued at $1,260,000 is imported for use in guilding pagodas and the interiors of temples. All of this comes from Hongkong.

Silk Piece Goods.—Silk piece goods valued at $1,000,000, 90 per cent of which came from Hongkong, were imported in 1918, other suppliers being Japan and China. Other items in order of their importance were tobacco and manufactures, $861,655, half from the United States and a quarter each from the United Kingdom and China; chemicals and medicines, $654,179, one-third from Japan and one-sixth each from the United Kingdom and Hongkong; white cotton yarn, $604,409, half from India; and matches, $501,124, 80 per cent from Hongkong. The balance of Siam's imports constitute a long list of articles such as dyestuffs, brass manufactures, machinery, matting and rattan goods, paper and paper goods, tea, dried vegetables, colored yarn, electrical goods and apparatus, no one of which amounts to more than $300,000 or less than $100,000 but which depend for increased import in the steadily rising standards and purchasing power of the people.

Questions

1. (*a*) What is the importance of rice culture in the agricultural economy of Siam?
   (*b*) Describe the methods of growing and harvesting rice.
2. (*a*) Describe the cultivation of three other crops.
   (*b*) How are fish used and what is their importance?
3. (*a*) How is teak forestry carried on?
   (*b*) Describe tin mining in Siam.
4. What change has been noted in the destination of Siam's exports?
5. Mention three leading imports giving chief suppliers of each.

BIBLIOGRAPHY TO PART IV

Malaysia, French Indo-China, and Siam

British Malaysia

Angier, A. Gorton:
The Far East Revisited. London, 1908.
Arnold, Wright, and Reid, T. H.:
The Malay Peninsula. New York, 1912.
Curtis, William Eleroy:
British Malaysia. Chicago and New York, 1905.
Clifford, Sir H. C.:
In Court and Kampong. London, 1903.
Harrison, C. W.:
The Magic of Malaya. London and New York, 1916.
Rathborne, A. B.:
Camping and Tramping in Malaya. London, 1898.
Swethenham, Sir F. A.:
British Malaya. London, 1907.
Swethenham, Sir F. A.:
Real Malay Pen Pictures. London, 1900.

Indo-China

Clifford, Sir A. C.:
Further India. New York, 1904.
De Montpensier, Duc:
La Ville au Bois Dormant. Paris, 1910.
Madrelle, M. Claudius:
De Marseille & Canton. Paris, 1902.
Vincent, Frank:
Land of the White Elephant. New York, 1874.

Siam

Campbell, J.:
Siam in the Twentieth Century. London, 1902.
Carter, A. Cecil:
The Kingdom of Siam. New York and London, 1904.

GRAHAM, A. W.:
Siam—A Handbook of Practical, Commercial and Political Information. London, 1913.
LOTI, Pierre:
Siam, translated from the French by W. P. Baines. 1898.
SMYTH, H. W.:
Five Years in Siam. London, 1898.
THOMPSON, P. A.:
Siam—An Account of the Country and People. Boston and Tokyo, 1910.
WHITNEY, Caspar:
Jungle Trails and Jungle People. New York, 1905.
YOUNG, Ernest:
Kingdom of the Yellow Robe. New York, 1900.

CHAPTER XXV

COMMERCIAL POSSIBILITIES IN THE FAR EAST

In presenting the history, laws, and commerce of the Far Eastern peoples an attempt has been made to rob of its mystery a subject of vital importance to the business men of the United States. Much has been said in recent months about Far Eastern trade but it has been approached as though it were a new subject and in many respects the discussions resemble those which took place in England in 1814 when India's great possibilities were beginning to dawn on party leaders.

Strictly speaking the possibilities for commercial activity in the Far East by the American people were limited before the war to three countries—China, Siberia, and the Philippines. In all other territories artificial handicaps are given the manufacturers of the mother country and the field is open to American goods only when they are not of a competitive nature. Since the armistice the industrial paralysis in Europe has greatly increased the numbers of articles demanded by the Far East which cannot be manufactured in the respective home countries of the different colonies. As a result the United States has been called upon to furnish increasingly larger supplies of iron and steel, machinery, hardware, chemicals, dyes, and a number of other commodities. This sudden demand from the Orient has opened the eyes of our traders to a tremendous market whose real proportions were never before realized. The business that has literally fallen into their laps forced many of them to open up selling organizations in Far

Eastern countries and this in turn has broken enough traditions in some of the long established firms to make their sally into the Oriental field permanent.

This need for permanence, this building for future profits, and a realization that a proper foundation means much in practical returns, is the one lesson that is hardest for many of our business men to learn. Firms who have "nursed" a domestic customer for years until they have built up a growing business for him and themselves will often violate every rule of good business practice when they enter the foreign field. To "switch" agents in the Orient, where stability has attained the significance of a cult, is tantamount to commercial suicide, yet it is difficult to convince many business men of the error of such a course. In a country where the past is living and the future never comes, the precedents of yesterday and not the possibilities of tomorrow are the ruling passion. In such a country and with such a people decisions made slowly but with a view to permanency are ultimately the most profitable.

But curiously enough the spirit of the new and strange is all pervading and human pyschology is pretty much the same everywhere. The West, in its mad progress, has been forced to invent new machines and new articles of a utilitarian value which the East in its slower advance has found attractive. The fact that these symbols of a new order precede rather than succeed the coming of the new order in the East is of little practical consequence. The spirit which accepts them is the same as that in the West and they are accepted first for their novelty and later for their utility. In no other way may the acceptance of Western invention by the East be accounted for, especially by those peoples who as a rule have steadily refused to accept any other symbol of Western civilization, either moral or material.

This widespread use of the symbols of Western civilization in the Far East is having a slow but certain effect. The Oriental who has ridden in an automobile can never be the same Oriental again. This experience has awakened first a lively interest in what Western civilization really means and finally a respect for what this civilization has accomplished. If this respect, once instilled, is followed by a proper presentation of what Western, and particularly American, business ideals mean, the net result must inevitably be a general strengthening of good understanding between the East and West. Unfortunately, however, such a result has not always been attained.

The most successful accomplishments have been achieved in China and American business methods and American business morals have had a more pronounced effect there than in any other country in the Orient. There are many other reasons for this feeling, however, besides the one suggested; the pyschological similarity between the continental peoples of China and the United States; the position as protector of a disintegrating Empire which was early assumed by the United States in promulgating the Hay Doctrine; the return of the Boxer Indemnity; and the fact that China and the United States are trade cognates, each furnishing and demanding commodities not produced by the other; all of these and other reasons of a political character have brought the two people closer together during the past decade.

In Japan, unfortunately, most of these basic considerations which tend toward closer relations are lacking. The insularity of the Japanese has the same reaction upon Americans as the insularity of the British has upon the French. Some American author might have written *l'Isle Inconnue* about Japan, and the same whimsical allusions, evincing a total lack of mutual appreciation, would hold true. In the case of America and Japan, however, the absence of geographical propinquity makes an otherwise humorous situation somewhat tragic. The net result has been a widening, rather than a narrowing, of the ocean of illusion which separates the two people. The two slender threads of traditional friendship, and a rather over-worked gratitude for Perry's daring diplomacy, are only reinforced by the same supplementary trade relations that exist with China. To say that American steel and cotton and Japanese silk bind America to Japan with ties of unbreakable friendship is to place too much dependence upon mere material ties, which recent experience has proven are not entirely immune from the effects of strain. Besides, these economic ties, unless reinforced by mutual moral understanding, tend to force themselves apart and we can see this development under way now in the efforts of Japan to become economically independent of American steel and cotton and of America to protect the silk industry of China and other Far Eastern countries from gradual decay. America's best interests require a seeking out of a more lasting basis for friendship and understanding with Japan than exists to-day.

It is difficult to approach the problems underlying American trade expansion in the European colonies of the Far Eastern tropics with anything like an engaging frankness. Our idea of what a tropical colony should be, as typified by the Philippines, may not be acceptable to the rulers of other Oriental tropical peoples. However, the very example of our work in the Philippines cannot be without its effects. The whole question of whether we should not make the Philippines the *entrepot* for American business, as well as the Oriental base for American ideals in all fields of endeavor, is one which should receive the recognition which its importance deserves. The impulse which our generous treatment of the Filipinos in matters of self-government has aroused in the natives of other colonies should not be permitted to die, because in that impulse rests all that is hopeful in a future Oriental civilization which should bring some distinct contribution to the world.

The duty of the Western trader is, therefore, a very important one. Through the medium of commerce, which after all is the one great clearing house of human understanding, he is permitted to make that impression upon the mind of the East which sometimes has been denied in full to both his religious and scholarly predecessors. "By their deeds ye shall know them" would seem to be the one criterion by which a full fledged acceptance or rejection of Western civilization by the East is to be accomplished. It is incumbent upon us, therefore, to realize the double mission which American foreign traders are performing in the East. Every sale is either a strengthening or a loosening of the bonds of human friendship between peoples long remote in their mutual understanding and sympathies. As one historian remarked of the hasty and ill advised British reforms in India, which brought on the Sepoy revolt, "there is a common sympathy in the human heart which should have guided the British administration." When laws which relieved the people of cruel and unjust practices were passed they received the popular support of all castes, but those which dealt with the academic questions of administration incited nothing more than apathetic indifference. This common understanding is no more surprising or gratifying than when discovered in a people whose whole tradition and civilization is so diametrically opposite to our own. Yet it is the one safe chord which successful intercourse both in business and in politics can strike.

A formula is at hand then for overcoming the artificial handicaps which may be raised against American trade in the Orient. The language of the "square deal" is the Esperanto of commercial success. The possibilities of the field are great but they must always be subordinated to American ideals and the high purpose of the American tradition. If we stand for anything in commerce or politics, we stand for freedom, and we cannot afford to deviate from this ideal in our Far Eastern commercial policy. Every American salesman in the Orient either stands for this ideal or falls by it, and the measure of his Americanism is the measure of his purpose to represent the generous impulses of a free people.

APPENDICES

APPENDIX I

THE FAR EASTERN SILVER SITUATION [1]

In 1893 the free coinage of silver in India was discontinued and in 1898 an exchange rate of 15 rupees per pound sterling (or 1 shilling 4 pence per rupee) was adopted, making the par 32.44 cents per rupee. A gold standard reserve was established to be used for the purpose of purchasing exchange at the fixed rate whenever the market price should show a tendency to rise above that rate. This fixed rate of exchange has remained in effect until the recent rise in the price of silver. In 1914 a commission reported favorably on the continuance of this scheme, recommending that it consist largely of gold in London and that it be used exclusively for maintaining the fixed rate of exchange and not loaned for other purposes.

Methods Used in Indian Exchange.—The transfer of funds from India to London for the use of the Secretary of State for India is carried on as follows:

Tenders are invited weekly for bills of exchange and telegraphic transfers on the Indian Government authorities at Calcutta, Madras, and Bombay. A limit is designated which the aggregate amount will not exceed, but the authorities do not bind themselves to allot the whole amount mentioned and, as a matter of policy, prior to 1914 they would not accept any applications at prices lower than 1 shilling 3 and 29/32 pence per rupee for bills. The price charged for telegraphic transfers was ordinarily 1/32 pence per rupee higher than that charged for bills. The rate at which these drafts were sold to the public varied in normal times from the fixed rate of 1 shilling 4 pence, within the narrow limits of the cost of shipping gold from India to England. Owing to England's normally large excess of exports over imports, this system of drafts offered a convenient and profitable way to settle balances due from England to India and was adopted, therefore, as the machinery through which the Government regulated the

[1] An article by F R. Eldridge, Jr., reprinted from *Commerce Reports*, 1920.

rate of exchange. The customary procedure in recent years before the war was to sell council drafts free as long as there was a demand which could be met from the resources of the Government in India.

Effect of War on Silver Exchange.—The immediate effect of the war was a falling off in both imports and exports, due to the shortage of cargo space. Germany had always been a large importer of Indian cotton, jute, rice, and coconut products, and the war had a depressing effect upon these industries. In a very short time, however, the great demand for Indian products by the Allies and by the Orient, to whom the belligerent nations were no longer able to supply goods, resulted in increased activity throughout India. Japan was in the market for all the cotton she could buy and there was a corresponding demand for jute, tea, hides and skins, raw wool, and indigo. This increase is reflected in the trade of the United States with India during a period of from 1912-1919.

TRADE OF THE UNITED STATES WITH INDIA

June 30	Imports	Exports	Excess of Imports over Exports
1912	50,948,901	15,628,059	35,320,842
1913	67,949,259	11,040,039	56,909,220
1914	73,630,680	10,854,591	65,776,209
1915	51,982,703	11,696,094	40,286,609
1916	71,745,626	19,297,016	52,448,610
1917	102,106,632	28,396,043	73,710,639
1918	105,277,743	42,395,622	62,682,121
1919	125,471,468	50,501,740	74,969,728

The gold standard reserve which had gone to India as a result of Government support of the exchange rate in 1914, was transferred back to London in 1915. Indian industries were prosperous, prices high, and securities were being bought back from Indian creditors and large investments made in British war loans and other securities. The ratio between the London price of silver per ounce and the gold value of silver in the rupee is shown in the table on the following page.

This great increase in the price of silver has already been explained and, coupled with the increased trade balance in favor of India and the prohibition of the export of gold from England, the rate of exchange for council drafts underwent the following changes:

Normal.—1 shilling 4 pence per rupee.
September 1, 1917.—1 shilling 5 pence per rupee.
April 11, 1918.—1 shilling 6 pence per rupee.
August 12, 1919.—1 shilling 10 pence per rupee.
September 10, 1919.—2 shillings per rupee.

At the same time the Indian Government regulations provided that all silver imports were to be turned over to the Government and enacted drastic legislation against the breaking up or melting of rupees. During 1919 council drafts were sold in New York through the New York branch of the Bank of Montreal and have

SILVER VALUE RATIO TABLE

Date	London Price of Silver per Ounce, 1,000 Fine	Gold Value of Silver in Rupee
1910	$.58462	$.20096
1911	.58300	.20041
1912	.66454	.22644
1913	.65360	.22468
1914	.59797	.20555
1915	.56099	.19204
1916	.74213	.25511
1917	.94627	.32520
1918	1.12602	.38707

met with great success. The scarcity of silver in India menaced the convertibility of the Indian currency and would have entailed most serious consequences had not the Pittman Act of 1918 authorized the Secretary of the Treasury to melt American silver dollars to the maximum of $350,000,000. Under this Act 200,000,000 ounces of silver were sold to the British Government at $1.00 per ounce plus transportation, melting, and recoinage costs. In one year, from May 1, 1918, to May, 1919, $248,580,000 worth of silver was shipped on British Government account.

THE CHINESE SITUATION

The question has arisen as to how this Government may encourage commercial interests to take advantage of the adverse exchange situation in China to export our commodities to that market. It would probably be of interest first to point out that the excess of commodity imports from China has not had nearly as much effect upon the Chinese exchange market as has the rise in the price of silver as a commodity and the correspondingly low exchange value in gold which Chinese exporters receive for their commodities. Had China been on a gold basis the opportunity for exporting our commodities to China in order to balance exchange would have been easily encouraged, but China is so immediately dependent upon her exports for the funds with which to purchase goods from abroad that, although the high price of silver is technically favorable to the import of commodities, practically it is so unfavorable to the necessary prerequisite of exporting Chinese products as to have seriously interrupted these exports and consequently impaired the purchasing of foreign imports.

SILVER PRODUCTION OF THE WORLD [1]

	Ounces	Dollars	Average Price per Ounce	Average Value Haikwan Tael U. S. Gold	Silver Production of Mexico Ounces
1910	221,708,000	119,723,000	$ .54077	$ .66	71,372,000
1911	225,338,000	121,682,000	.53928	.55	79,032,000
1912	224,311,000	137,884,000	.61470	.74	74,640,000
1913	225,908,000	135,246,000	.60458	.73	70,640,000
1914	211,105,000	116,719,000	.55512	.67	70,704,000
1915	178,851,000	92,809,000	.51892	.62	39,570,000
1916	156,627,000	107,519,000	.68647	.76	22,838,000
1917	163,995,000	146,814,000	.99525	1.08	31,214,000
1918	179,900,000[2]	179,900,000[2]	1.00000	1.19	51,000,000

[1] Estimates of the Director of the Mint, as given in the *Federal Reserve Bulletin* for February 1, 1919, page 141.
[2] Preliminary estimate of the Federal Reserve Board.

Causes of High Silver in China.—The rise in the price of silver has been due primarily to an inordinate demand from India, whose domestic production of commodities has been enormously increased during the war by Government measures as a war necessity in order to obviate excessive shipments of raw materials to England for manufacture and re-export to India. As a result India is now industrially self-sufficient in many lines, and as the production of raw materials has at the same time been rapidly increasing, the enormous trade balance in her favor has had to be met by increasingly large shipments of silver. This demand for silver as a medium of exchange, coupled with a world shortage of silver as a commodity, due primarily to the conditions in late years in the Mexican mining districts, the diversion of labor in other mining districts to war industries, the increased use of silver money by soldiers in the field, and the general rise in all commodities in terms of gold, has brought about the present high price of silver, with the resulting effects upon our Far Eastern trade which are noted above.

Silver Demand Independent of Commodity Exchange.—With the bulk of the world's supply of bullion, both gold and silver, in this country, we have naturally been called upon during recent months to supply considerably more bullion to the Far East than

China's Trade Balance with the United States

June 30	Imports	Exports	Excess of Imports over Exports
1912	29,573,732	24,361,199	5,212,533
1913	39,010,000	21,326,834	17,683,966
1914	39,302,780	24,698,734	14,604,244
1915	40,156,139	16,402,475	23,753,664
1916	71,655,045	25,131,459	46,523,536
1917	105,905,531	37,195,608	68,709,925
1918	116,644,981	43,476,623	73,169,358
1919	105,762,859	82,992,495	22,770,364

the excess of commodity imports has warranted. With this demand for silver bullion largely independent of any exchange of commodities, but due in a very great degree to the rise in the value of silver itself as a commodity, the Far Eastern exchange situation is greatly complicated, and as long as silver retains this high commodity value, its value as a medium of exchange will remain correspondingly high. The adverse rate of exchange between Chinese silver currency and American gold will continue, therefore, to be determined more by this factor than by the movement of commodities, and conversely, the attempt to rectify the exchange rate by shipments of commodities would have little effect. In this connection the cumulative effect of China's excess of exports to this country since 1912 is of considerable interest.

There is one way in which the situation may be taken immediate advantage of, however, and that is by supplying the Chinese markets in the interior with needed manufactured goods, and

FLUCTUATIONS IN SILVER RATES, 1920

Week Ending		Value in U. S. Gold	
		Calcutta Rupee Par .3244	Shanghai Tael Par 1.20
January	3	.4475	1.54
	10	.4430	1.56
	17	.4330	1.60
	24	.4265	1.56
	31	.4125	1.575
February	7	.4475	1.60
	14	.47	1.58
	21	.46	1.58
	28	.455	1.58
March	6	.465	1.58
	13	.455	1.36
	20	.445	1.45
	27	.46	1.46
April	3	.46	1.45
	10	.465	1.39
	17	.465	1.28
	24	.46	1.36
May	1	.4475	1.31
	8	.4425	1.24
	15	.405	1.15
	22	.4175	1.18
	29	.415	1.19
June	5	.415	1.14
	12	.405	1.04
	19	.39	.96
	26	.39	1.03
July	3	.375	1.03
	10	.38	1.03
		Par .39 [1]	*Par 1.1436* [2]
	17	.365	1.02
	24	.3625	1.03
	31	.37	1.06
August	7	.355	1.05
	14	.35	1.07
	21	.3375	1.13
	28	.34	1.13
September	4	.335	1.09
	11	.3275	1.06

[1] On basis of 1/10 average value of £ sterling quarter ending June 30, 1920.

[2] On basis average value of silver, quarter ending June 30, 1920.

effecting a practical barter of these goods for Chinese raw materials. This may be accomplished by large organizations such as the Standard Oil Company, or the British American Tobacco Company, but for those firms who wish to sell only or to buy only in the large ports the present difficulties seem insuperable. It would be well for such firms to seriously contemplate broader organizations through which "wash" sales may be effected, thus eliminating as far as possible the entrance of silver into their transactions.

Present Situation More Hopeful.—Aside from various fluctuations a glance at the gold values of Indian rupees and Shanghai taels for the 34 weeks from January 3rd to September 4th, 1920, shows a constant downward trend.

Effect of the American Peg.—The heavy Chinese buying of silver to restock a denuded market, when the embargo was lifted in May, 1919, which was followed by the heavy exports from China during the same year, tended to bull the silver market. Satiation resulted, and the decline in silver set in because exports from Far Eastern countries dwindled. The break in the market which occurred in June, 1919, was not expected to be as severe as it was, because of a misunderstanding of the provisions of the Pittman Act, making it applicable to American produced silver only. The net result has been to establish two silver rates: the New York rate which is held near $1.00 per ounce by repurchases of American mined silver at that price to replace the $260,000,000 melted down and shipped to India in 1918; and the London rate which, though affected by the New York peg, is somewhat lower, being 94½ cents per ounce on September 15th, 1920. The effect has been stimulating to American silver production. A new mine operating in California has increased the production in that state for the first half of 1920 to 503,794 ounces, as compared with 376,310 ounces for the same period in 1919. The Texas mines, if operated at the same rate of production for the whole year as for the first half, will produce 500,000 ounces. In 1920 Idaho production will considerably surpass the 1919 figures, while the Utah mines are making large shipments, although their smelters were affected recently by labor troubles. In Arizona, Montana and Oregon the production will decrease varying from 60 per cent of normal in Montana and 81 per cent in Oregon. This increased production, on the whole, however, will not affect the world's market unless the London price of silver exceeds $1.00 per ounce. Mexican production, however, has increased in 1920 over the record figures of 1919, as evidenced by the $68,881,053 worth imported into the United States in the year ending June 30, 1920, as compared with $56,218,587 imported during the previous year, while Peru contributes an increase of $4,000,000 over the $7,574,526 imports from that country in 1919. It is estimated that Mexico's 1920 production will reach 75,000,000 ounces, or 12,500,000 ounces more than 1919, because hundreds of abandoned mines are being worked. In all, our silver imports for the year designated were $102,899,506, as compared with $78,825,266 in 1919. Our exports of silver, on the other hand, have declined almost 50 per cent from the $301,174,550 exported in the year ending June 30, 1919, $214,481,099 of which went to India, to only $179,037,260 exported in the same fiscal year 1920. China took $117,570,415 of these total United States silver exports in 1920.

With India's proverbial appetite for silver somewhat diverted by the fixing of the rupee at the higher exchange rate, with the United Sates silver market kept steady by artificial means, resulting in increased production, and with conditions tending to increased silver production all over the world, especially in Mexico and Peru, on the one hand, and on the other hand a tendency to lower commodity values, necessitating a lesser use of the circulating medium in all countries, and slackened use of silver coin by soldiers in the field, a period of normal prices in the silver market, approximating production costs, may be looked forward to with considerably more assurance than at any time during the past six years.

As can be clearly perceived, the net result of the high price of silver in China has been stagnating to foreign trade with that country. The actual need of our commodities is great, and our need for Chinese raw materials is equally urgent, but the American merchant cannot offer enough gold, in terms of silver, to induce the Chinese merchant to part with his goods, and as long as the Chinese merchant holds his materials, the world shortage continues and the prices rise. The paper profit is of no benefit to the Chinese producer of these materials who is unable to exchange his surplus raw materials for foreign manufactures. The result has been a tremendous stimulus to Chinese domestic manufactures which has been greatly encouraged by the boycott of Japanese imports. It will be interesting to note the effect this development has upon the future foreign trade of China, but it is felt that it will be many years before the Chinese will become an economically self-sufficient people, and until this is brought about the opportunity for large-scale commodity exchange transactions in the interior will remain. The good will which the Chinese people feel toward America is a factor of inestimable importance in such development.

APPENDIX II

THE INCORPORATION OF AMERICAN COMPANIES IN CHINA

For some time there has been more or less of a lively interest in Chinese trade with this country. Congress has been liberal in providing funds for the promotion of commerce with China and the Far East. The Shipping Board is ready to allocate tonnage wherever the volume of trade warrants. The Navy Department has recently been authorized to relieve the cable situation by accepting commercial messages for transmission by naval radio to the Far East and elsewhere. The American consuls in China are working indefatigably in the interest of American trade. The Bureau of Foreign and Domestic Commerce has special trade commissioners in China to push the sale of our goods and learn new ways of facilitating commercial transactions, and a whole army of salesmen and representatives of American firms are flooding the hotels in Chinese ports taking initial orders and looking over the ground. But there are certain weak links in this chain of endeavor, which if not strengthened may cause the whole effort to be of little avail. America must have strong selling organizations in China permanently.

Permanency Essential for Success.—Permanency usually means profits and Great Britain realized this when the British Companies Act was framed to permit British companies to incorporate abroad, and operate free of all income or excess profits tax by the home government. The British Government very wisely believed that the indirect benefits to the country from increased overseas trade created by those foreign established British companies would more than offset any direct income to the Government in the form of taxation, tending to discourage these foreign-trade operations. Moreover, as soon as the company's profits created in this foreign trade are distributed to the individual stockholders at home, or to those abroad and subsequently remitted to England, they are taxed just the same as any home earned individual income. Moreover, severe fluctuations in silver in China require larger reserves to assure safe trading, and these cannot be encouraged if they are taxed. The tendency, therefore, is to encourage just what England wishes to encourage, the re-investment abroad of the profits of British companies, profits earned in foreign ventures.

The Hongkong Companies.—This law is administered in China, where due to extraterritorial rights, British companies operate under British law, through ordinances of the Crown Colony of Hongkong. The only tax on Hongkong Companies, as they are called, is, therefore, only a nominal stock fee payable when the articles of incorporation are filed. Companies operating under such a law are naturally at a great advantage over companies not so favored, so that many large undertakings in China, financed by Americans, Germans, Japanese, and nationals of other countries have incorporated under the Hongkong Ordinances and are to all intents and purposes British companies. During the war, however, certain Orders in Council were issued by the British Government, requiring that a majority of the board of directors of such companies should be British subjects, and they were followed by subsequent orders which went into effect March 15, 1920, requiring in addition that the managing directors of these companies should be British subjects. These orders, while aimed at the Germans endeavors to "comeback" in the China trade, hit a number of corporations which were majority American owned. These corporations were faced with the alternatives of either continuing under entire British control or withdrawing from Hongkong incorporation and incorporating under some other law.

The Methods of Incorporation.—A survey of the situation revealed the fact that there were only a limited number of courses to pursue. They could incorporate under the laws of some state in the United States in which case they would be subject to heavy state and Federal income tax; they could dissolve as corporations and register as partnerships at the American Consulate, in which event they would be subject to Federal income tax on the partnership profits; or they could, under a ruling of the judge of the American Court at Shanghai, register as corporations under the territorial laws of Alaska, but unless these laws were amended they would still be subject to Federal income tax. Few of them adopted the first method, and only those companies in which the individual stockholders were very few, could adopt the second, but a number have accepted the rather doubtful status of the third method in the hope that Congress would adopt the necessary amendment. The great majority, however, have appointed British managing directors and continued as full fledged British companies.

American Incorporation Needed.—For years the Bureau of Foreign and Domestic Commerce has pointed out to American manufacturers who desire to extend their business to China two things: First, they should choose as far as possible American agents for their lines in China. The reason is as old as our foreign trade experience. Foreign agents usually have interest in building up a line only so long as they cannot obtain a substitute line in their own countries, but as soon as they do, the American line is dropped, or worse still, held inert in order to cripple possible competition. Second, as soon as the business warrants, branches should be established in China by the manufacturer and operations directed from there rather than from the United States. In both instances the manufacturer who attempts to follow this policy is checkmated by the present situation. The establishment of American import and export houses in China under American management is impossible because the profit on many staples is too low to permit competition with non-taxed British houses, and in many lines the income tax would represent all the difference between encouragement and discouragement for such ventures. Moreover, such companies where organized for operation in China usually invite local Chinese capital as a matter of policy in facilitating the marketing of goods, and if they are taxed they cannot compete with the British non-taxed companies in attractiveness of their stock offerings. The establishment of branch houses of manufacturers is discouraged in the same way.

Coöperative Selling Requires American Incorporation.—But the way in which the present conditions work against American export trade to China are more far reaching still. For years the favorite method of selling machinery has been on the coöperative plan, whereby the Chinese capitalists who desire to set up an ice plant, for example, form a company with fifty-one per cent German capital furnished by the German ice plant manufacturer who thereby pays himself for his machinery and the remaining stock is subscribed by Chinese who furnish the working capital. The German machinery company's stock is gradually taken up out of the profits of the undertaking and the whole plant soon remains the sole property of the Chinese stockholders. Such a plan cannot work under forms of incorporation now available to Americans and a very facile method of placing large consignments of American machinery, therefore, is relegated to the scrap heap.

The Dyer Bill.—There is one method of meeting this situation constructively and without makeshift and the Bureau of Foreign and Domestic Commerce was instrumental in drafting a law for the "Incorporation of certain Companies Operating in China" which has been before Congress for several years. In its latest form (the Dyer Bill, H. R. 16043, 66th Congress, 3rd session) it was passed by the House on February 21, 1921 and referred to the Senate Committee on Judiciary. The bill provides among other things that the majority stock in companies created under it shall be held by American citizens and that companies so incorporated for carrying on business in China alone, shall not be subject to any other or higher taxation by this Government than corporations organized under the laws of other nations for the purpose of operating in China are taxed, as ascertained by the Secretary of the Treasury. This is all that is required to place American business on an equality with other business in China, but until we have this opportunity of equal expansion, our efforts to promote trade on any large scale in China are greatly handicapped.

The text of the Dyer Bill, as amended, is as follows:

A Bill to authorize the incorporation of companies to promote trade in China.

Be it enacted by the Senate and House of Representatives of the United States of America in Congress assembled, That this Act may be cited as the "China Trade Act, 1921."

Sec. 2. When used in this Act, unless the context otherwise indicates,—

The term "person" includes individual, partnership, corporation, and association;

The term "China" means (1) China including Manchuria, Tibet, Mongolia, and any territory leased by China to any foreign government (2) the Crown Colony of Hongkong and (3) the Province of Macao;

The term "Secretary" means the Secretary of Commerce;

The term "corporation" means a corporation chartered under the provisions of this Act;

The term "federal district court" means any federal district court, the United States Court for China, and the Supreme Court of the District of Columbia;

The term "this Act" includes all lawful regulations issued thereunder by the Secretary.

Sec. 3. The Secretary shall exercise all power and perform all duties conferred on him by this Act only through such officers or agents in China as he shall by regulation designate and authorize so to act, and for this purpose the Secretary may utilize such existing or create such new offices or agencies, as he deems necessary. For the purposes of this Act, the action of any officer or agent so designated and authorized shall be made in the name and held to be the act of the Secretary: *Provided,* That upon appeal to the Secretary any such action may be affirmed, modified, or set aside by the Secretary, as he deems advisable.

SEC. 4. (*a*) Three or more individuals (hereinafter in this Act referred to as the "incorporators"), a majority of whom are citizens of the United States, may, in accordance with the provisions of this Act, form a corporation.

(*b*) Such corporation may engage in any business or enterprise conducted wholly within China and carried on with persons in China; except that the corporation—

(1) Shall not engage in any business or enterprise unlawful in the territory in which it is carried on; and

(2) Shall not engage in the business of discounting bills, notes, or other evidences of debt, of receiving deposits, of buying and selling bills of exchange, or of issuing bills, notes, or other evidences of debt, for circulation as money; nor engage in any form of banking business.

(*c*) The corporation shall not engage in any business or enterprise other than that authorized by subdivision (*b*), except that it—

(1) May purchase in the United States for transportation to China, goods, wares, or merchandise necessary to the establishment and conduct of a business or enterprise in which it is authorized to engage;

(2) May do in the United States and elsewhere any act which is incidental to the organization of the corporation or to the issue, sale, transfer, or redemption of its stocks, bonds, or other evidences of indebtedness; and

(3) May do in the United States and elsewhere any act which is approved by the Secretary and necessary to the establishment and conduct of any business or enterprise in which it is authorized to engage.

SEC. 5. The incorporators shall make application for a charter and file it with the Secretary in such manner and in such form as the Secretary shall by regulation prescribe. The application shall state—

(*a*) The name of the proposed corporation, which shall end with the legend, "Federal Inc. U. S. A.";

(*b*) The location of its principal office, which shall be in China;

(*c*) The purpose for which it is formed and the character of the business in which it is to engage;

(*d*) The amount of capital stock, the designation of each class of stock and the terms upon which it is to be issued, and the number and par value of the shares of each class of stock;

(*e*) The duration of the corporation, which may be permanent or for a limited time;

(*f*) The names, addresses, and designations of directors and officers, who shall be citizens of the United States, and who are hereby authorized to manage the affairs of the corporation until their successors are elected by the stockholders in accordance with the by-laws of the corporation;

(*g*) The fact that an amount equal to 25 per centum of the amount of capital stock has been in good faith subscribed and actually paid in cash, personal property, tangible or intangible, or real property, and is in the custody of the individuals specified in subdivision (*f*); and the name and address of each such subscriber. If any part of such payment is made in property other than cash, no charter shall be issued unless the Secretary finds that the property is described and its value stated in the same manner as provided in section 9, and that such value is the fair market value, and is at least equal to the difference between 25 per centum of the capital stock and the amount of cash, if any, so paid in; and

(*h*) The time and place of the first stockholders' meeting, which shall be not later than one year after the issuance of the charter.

SEC. 6. No corporation shall have or use a corporate name which, in the opinion of the Secretary, is likely to mislead the public. No corporation shall maintain any office, including its principal, and home and branch offices, if any, at any place other than in China.

SEC. 7. The application for a charter shall be filed with the Secretary. If the Secretary finds that the application and statements therein conform to the requirements of, and that the incorporation is authorized by, this Act, he shall, upon the payment of such fee as he shall by regulation prescribe, issue a charter authorizing the incorporators to act as a body corporate. The application shall thereupon constitute the articles of incorporation, and a copy of such articles shall be made a part of the charter and printed in full thereon. The Secretary shall, upon the payment of such fee as he shall by regulation prescribe, issue as many certified copies of the articles of incorporation or of the charter, as amended, as may be desired by any interested party. The corporation shall keep a copy of the charter, as amended, at the principal office specified in its articles of incorporation. Any failure, previous to the issuance of the charter, by the incorporators, or in respect to the application for the charter, to conform to any requirement of law which is a condition precedent to such issuance, may not subsequent thereto be held to invalidate the charter or alter the legal status of any act of the corporation thereunder, except in proceedings instituted by the Secretary to revoke the charter.

SEC. 8. (*a*) The corporation shall be a citizen of the United States invested with the powers and subject to the conditions and restrictions of this Act. A majority of the voting shares issued by the corporation shall at all times be owned by citizens of the United States.

(*b*) The corporation—

(1) Shall have the right of succession;

(2) May use a corporate seal and alter it at pleasure;

(3) May sue and be sued;

(4) May make contracts and incur liabilities;

(5) May acquire and hold personal property, tangible and intangible, and real estate, necessary to effect the purposes for which it is formed, and dispose of the same when no longer needed for such purposes; and

(6) May borrow money and issue its notes, coupon or registered bonds, or other evidences of debt therefor, and secure their payment by a mortgage of its property.

SEC. 9. All shares of stock shall, when issued, be paid for in cash, personal property, tangible or intangible, or real property, at not less than their par value, and when so issued shall be held to be full-paid and nonassessable; but no stock shall be issued for personal property, tangible or intangible, or real property, unless (*a*) a description of the property for which the stock is to be issued and a statement of the value at which the property is to be received has been filed with the Secretary in such a manner and upon the payment of such fee as he shall by regulation prescribe, and (*b*) the Secretary finds and has certified to the corporation that such value is not more than the fair market value of the property and is at least equal to the par value of the stock issued therefor.

SEC. 10. (*a*) The by-laws may provide—

(1) The time, place, manner of calling, giving notice, and conduct of, and determination of a quorum for, the meetings, annual or special, of the stockholders or directors;

(2) The number, qualifications, designations, and manner of choosing and fixing the tenure of office and compensation, of all directors, officers, and employees: *Provided,* That the number of directors shall be not less than 5, and the president, treasurer, and secretary, or corresponding officers, and a majority of the directors, shall be citizens of the United States resident in China;

(3) The designation of each class of stock and the terms upon which it is issued, the number and par value of the shares of each class of stock, the manner of calling for and collecting payments upon stock subscribed for, the penalties and forfeitures for nonpayment, the preparation of certificates of stock, and the manner of recording the sale or transfer of stock and its representation at stockholders' meeting.

(*b*) The by-laws of the corporation may be amended by the stockholders at a stockholders' meeting. No by-law or amendment thereto shall be in effect until (1) the corporation files a copy thereof in such manner and form and pays such fees in respect thereto as the Secretary shall by regulation prescribe, and (2) such by-law or amendment is found and certified by the Secretary to conform to the requirements of this Act.

SEC. 11. The following questions shall be determined only by the stockholders at a stockholders' meeting: (*a*) amendments to the articles of incorporation or by-laws; (*b*) authorization of the sale of the entire business of the corporation or of an independent branch of such business; (*c*) authorization of the voluntary dissolution of the corporation. The adoption of any such amendment or authorization shall require a vote cast by at least a majority of the voting shares and the approval of at least three-fourths of such votes cast. No such amendment or authorization shall take effect until (1) the corporation files a statement of the action in such manner and form and pays such fees in respect thereto as the Secretary shall by regulation prescribe, and (2) such amendment or authorization is found and certified by the Secretary to conform to the requirements of this Act.

SEC. 12. For the purposes of this Act the fiscal year of the corporation shall correspond with the calendar year ending December 31. The corporation shall make and file with the Secretary, in such manner and form and at such time, as the Secretary shall by regulation prescribe, a report of its business for each such fiscal year and of its financial condition at the close of the year. The corporation shall furnish a true copy of the report to each of its stockholders.

SEC. 13. Every dividend declared by the corporation shall be derived wholly from the surplus profits of its business, to be determined in such manner as the Secretary shall by regulation prescribe.

SEC. 14. It is hereby declared to be the purposes of this Act (1) to promote trade and commerce with China and create and develop markets in China for articles of commerce exported from the United States; (2) to provide a means whereby citizens of the United States may form corporations therefor; (3) so to regulate such corporations as to keep them at all times in control of individuals who are citizens of the United States, and (4) to provide for the proper conduct of such corporations. The Secretary of Commerce is authorized to prescribe and promulgate such regulations and issue such orders, not in conflict with the provisions of this Act, as he deems necessary to carry into effect the provisions and purposes of the Act, including the manner and form in which the corporation shall keep its records and accounts, and the amounts of any fees authorized to be prescribed by the Secretary. All fees paid to the Secretary shall be covered into the Treasury of the United States as miscellaneous receipts.

SEC. 15. The Secretary may examine the business and affairs of the corporation whenever he has reason to believe that such business and affairs are being conducted in a manner (1) contrary to the provisions of this Act or any other law or treaty of the United States, or of the articles of incorporation or by-laws of the corporation, or (2) detrimental to the business interests and good will of the United States. The cost of the examination shall be paid by the corporation upon the demand of the Secretary. If the corporation fails to pay such costs upon such demand, the Secretary may collect the amount of the costs in a civil suit against the corporation brought in the name of the United States.

SEC. 16. The Secretary may suspend the charter of a corporation whenever, with or without examination as provided in section 15, he becomes satisfied that the business and affairs of the corporation are conducted or have been conducted within the year last preceding in a manner (1) contrary to the provisions of this Act or any other law or treaty of the United States, or of the articles of incorporation or by-laws of the corporation, or (2) detrimental to the business interests and good will of the United States. Such suspension shall not take effect until 10 days after the Secretary files suit in the United States Court for China for revocation of the charter of the corporation. Upon the petition of the corporation to the court at any time within 10 days after such suit is filed the court may in its discretion stay the suspension for such time up to its final decision in the suit as it deems advisable. The court shall revoke the charter of the corporation if it finds that the affairs and business of the corporation have been conducted in such a manner.

SEC. 17. In case of the voluntary dissolution of the corporation or the suspension or revocation of its charter, the directors of the corporation shall be the trustees of the creditors and stockholders of the corporation; except that upon application to the United States Court for China by any interested party, or upon the court's own motion in any proceeding pending before it, the court may in its discretion appoint as the trustees such individuals other than the directors, as it may determine. In case of the voluntary dissolution or revocation of the charter of the corporation, the trustees are invested with the powers, and shall do all acts, necessary to wind up the affairs of the corporation and divide among the stockholders according to their respective interests the property of the corporation remaining after all obligations against it have been settled. In case of the suspension of the charter of the corporation, the trustees shall conduct the corporate affairs and are invested with the powers and subject to the liabilities and duties provided in this Act for the corporation, its directors, officers, and stockholders. For the purposes of this section the trustees may sue and be sued in the name of the corporation and shall be jointly and severally liable to the stockholders and creditors of the corporation to the extent of the property coming into their hands as trustees.

SEC. 18. For the efficient administration of the functions vested in the Secretary by this Act, he may require, (*a*) by subpœna issued by him or under his direction, the attendance of any witness and the production of any book, paper, document, or other evidence from any place at any designated place of hearing in China, or if the witness is actually resident or temporarily sojourning outside of China, at any designated place of hearing within fifty miles of the actual residence or place of sojourn of such witness, and (*b*) the taking of a deposition before any designated person having power to administer oaths. In the case of a deposition the testimony shall be reduced to writing by the person taking the deposition or under his direction, and shall then be subscribed to by the deponent. The Secretary may administer oaths and examine any witness. Any witnesses summoned before the Secretary and any witness whose deposition is taken shall be paid the same fees and mileage as are paid witnesses in the courts of the United States.

(*b*) In the case of failure to comply with any subpœna or in the case of the contumacy of any witness appearing before the Secretary, he may invoke the aid of any federal district court. Such court may thereupon order the witness to comply with the requirements of such subpœna, and to give evidence touching the matter in question. Any failure to obey such order may be punished by such court as a contempt thereof.

(*c*) No person shall be excused from so attending and testifying or deposing, nor from so producing any book, paper, document, or other evidence on the ground that the testimony or evidence, documentary or otherwise, required of him may tend to incriminate him or subject him to a penalty or forfeiture; but no natural person shall be prosecuted or subject to any penalty or forfeiture for or on account of any transaction, matter, or thing, as to which in obedience to a subpœna and under oath, he may so testify or produce in evidence, documentary or otherwise. But no person shall be exempt from prosecution and punishment for perjury committed in so testifying.

(*d*) For the efficient administration of the functions vested in the Secretary by this Act, he, or any officer, employee, or agent thereof, duly authorized in writing by the Secretary, shall at all reasonable times for the purpose of examination have access to and the right to copy any book, account, record, paper, or correspondence relating to the business or affairs of a corporation. Any person who upon demand refuses any duly authorized officer, employee, or agent such right of access or copying, or hinders, obstructs, or resists him in the exercise of such right, shall be liable to a penalty of $500 for each such offense. Each day during any part of which such offense continues shall constitute a separate offense. Such penalty shall be recoverable in a civil suit brought in the name of the United States, and shall be covered into the Treasury of the United States as miscellaneous receipts.

SEC. 19. The federal district courts shall have exclusive original jurisdiction of all suits (except as provided by the Act entitled "An Act creating a United States Court for China and prescribing the jurisdicton thereof," approved June 30, 1906, as amended) against a corporation, or a stockholder, director, or officer thereof in his capacity as such. Suit against the corporation may be brought in the United States Court for China, or in the district in which the cause of action arose or in which the corporation has an agent and is engaged in doing business. A federal district court having jurisdiction of such suit is authorized to direct service of process by registered mail upon the corporation. Any judgment, order, or decree rendered by the court in any such suit shall, upon the presentation of a certified copy thereof to any other federal district court, be enforced by such other court, as the judgment, order, or decree may require.

SEC. 20. No (*a*) individual, partnership, or association, (*b*) corporation not incorporated under this Act or under a law of the United States, or (*c*) corporation of the District of Columbia, shall engage in commerce among the several States or with foreign nations under a name in connection with which the legend "Federal Inc. U. S. A." is used. Any person violating this section shall upon conviction thereof be fined not more than $100 for each violation. Each day or fraction thereof during which the violation continues shall be deemed a separate offense.

SEC. 21. No stockholder, director, officer, employee, or agent, of a corporation shall make, issue, or publish any statement, written or oral, or advertisement, in any form, as to the value or as to facts affecting the value of stocks, bonds, or other evidences of debt, or as to the financial condition or transactions, or facts affecting such condition or transactions, of any corporation which has issued or is to issue stocks, bonds, or other evidences of debt, if he knows or has reason to believe that any material representation in such statement or advertisement is false. No stockholder, director, officer, employee, or agent of a corporation shall, if all the authorized capital stock thereof has not been paid in, make, issue, or publish any written statement or advertisement, in any form, stating the amount of the authorized capital stock, without also stating as the amount actually paid in a sum not greater than such amount paid in. Any person violating any provision of this section shall, upon conviction thereof, be fined not more than $5,000, or imprisioned not more than ten years, or both.

SEC. 22. The following Acts, including administrative and penal provisions thereof, shall extend to the acts, failures, and omissions of a corporation or the stockholders, directors, officers, employees, and agents thereof, in their capacity as such, even though such acts, failures, or omissions occur without the territorial jurisdiction of the United States:

(*a*) The Act entitled "An Act to create a Federal Trade Commission, to define its powers and duties, and for other purposes," approved September 26, 1914;

(*b*) The National Prohibition Act of October 28, 1919; and

(*c*) The Act entitled "An Act to provide for the registration of, with collectors of internal revenue, and to impose a special tax upon all persons who produce, import, manufacture, compound, deal in, dispense, sell, distribute, or give away opium or coca leaves, their salts, derivatives or preparations, and for other purposes," approved December 17, 1914, as amended.

SEC. 23. (*a*) Section 231 of the Revenue Act of 1918 is amended by striking out the period at the end thereof, inserting in lieu thereof a semicolon, and adding a new subdivision to read as follows:

"(15) A corporation organized under the China Trade Act, 1921, but only if and with respect to any taxable year for which (*a*) it files a return at the time and place provided in section 241, made in the manner provided in section 239, and containing such information as the Commissioner of Internal Revenue, with the approval of the Secretary of the Treasury, may by regulation prescribe; (*b*) it declares dividends during the taxable year in an amount equal to one-third of its net income the payment of which not later than 60 days after the close of such taxable year is assured in such manner as the Commissioner of Internal Revenue, with the approval of the Secretary of the Treasury, may require; (*c*) it derives less than 5 per centum of its gross income from sources within the United States; and (*d*) the Secretary of Commerce certifies to the Commissioner of Internal Revenue that during the taxable year the corporation in all respects has complied with the provisions of the China Trade Act, 1921, and regulations made thereunder. The Commisssioner of Internal Revenue with the approval of the Secretary of the Treasury shall make all regulations necessary for the determination of such exemption and of the liability of shareholders or members to taxation in respect to dividends paid by such corporation."

(*b*) Section 1 of the Revenue Act of 1918 is amended by adding at the end thereof a new paragraph to read as follows:

"A corporation organized under the China Trade Act, 1921, shall for the purposes of this Act be considered a domestic corporation."

(*c*) Sections 232, 233, and 234 of the Revenue Act of 1918 are amended by inserting in each of such sections after the words "corporation subject to the tax imposed by section 230," the words "or organized under the China Trade Act, 1921."

(*d*) Section 240 of the Revenue Act of 1918 is amended by adding at the end thereof a new subdivision to read as follows:

"(*d*) A corporation organized under the China Trade Act, 1921, shall not be deemed to be affiliated with any other corporation within the meaning of this section."

(*e*) Section 254 of the Revenue Act of 1918 is amended to read as follows:

"SEC. 254. That every corporation subject to the tax imposed by this title, every personal service corporation, and every corporation organized under the China Trade Act, 1921, shall, when required by the Commissioner, render a correct return duly verified under oath, of its payments of dividends, stating the name and address of each stockholder, the number of shares owned by him, and the amount of dividends paid to him."

SEC. 24. The Congress of the United States reserves the right to alter, amend, or repeal the provisions of this Act.

APPENDIX III

EXTRACT FROM HONGKONG ORDINANCES RELATING TO COMPANIES ESTABLISHED OUTSIDE THE COLONY

Requirements as to companies established outside the Colony. 252. 1. Every company incorporated outside the Colony which shall establish a place of business within the Colony, shall within one month from the establishment of the place of business file with the Registrar of Companies: (*a*) A certified copy of the charter, statutes, or memorandum and articles of the company, or other instrument constituting or defining the constitution of the company, and, if the instrument is not written in the English language, a certified translation in the English language thereof; (*b*) A list of the directors of the company; (*c*) The names and addresses of some one or more persons resident in the Colony authorised to accept on behalf of the company service of process and any notices required to be served on the company; and, in the event of any alteration being made in any such instrument or in the directors or in the names or addresses of any such persons as aforesaid, the company shall within the prescribed time file with the Registrar a notice of the alteration. 2. Any process or notice required to be served on the company shall be sufficiently served if addressed to any person whose name has been so filed as aforesaid and left at or sent by post to the address which has been so filed. 3. Every company to which this section applies shall in every year file with the Registrar such a statement in the form of a balance sheet as would, if it were a company formed and registered under this Ordinance and having a share capital, be required under this Ordinance to be included in the annual summary. 4. Every company to which this section applies, and which uses the word "Limited" or the equivalent Chinese characters, as part of its name, shall: (*a*) In every prospectus inviting subscriptions for its shares or debentures in the Colony state the country in which the company is incorporated; and (*b*) Conspicuously exhibit on every place where it carries on business in the Colony the name of the company and the country in which the company is incorporated; and (*c*) Have the name of the company and of the country in which the company is incorporated mentioned in legible characters in all bill-heads and letter paper, and in all notices, advertisements, and other official publications of the company. 5. If any company to which this section applies fails to comply with any of the requirements of this section the company, and every officer or agent of the company, shall be liable to a fine not exceeding five hundred dollars, or in the case of a continuing offence, fifty dollars for every day during which the failure continues. 6. For the purposes of this section: The expression "certified" means certified in the prescribed manner to be a true copy or a correct translation; The expression "place of business" includes a share transfer or share registration office; The expression "director" includes any person occupying the position of director, by whatever name called; and The expression "prospectus" means any prospectus, notice, circular, advertisement, or other invitation, offering to the public for subscription or purchase any shares or debentures of the company. 7. There shall be paid to the Registrar for registering any document required by this section to be filed with him a fee of three dollars or such smaller fee as may be prescribed.

Imp. § 274.

Power of companies incorporated outside the Colony to hold lands. 253. 1. No company incorporated outside the Colony may hereafter acquire immoveable property unless: (*a*) It is empowered by its constitution to acquire immovable property; and (*b*) It shall have filed with the Registrar of Companies the documents and particulars specified in paragraphs *a, b* and *c* of subsection 1 of section 252; and (*c*) It shall have obtained the special consent of the Governor-in-Council. 2. Subject to the provisions of this section any company incorporated outside the Colony shall have power to acquire, hold and dispose of lands in the Colony as if it were a company incorporated under this Ordinance.

Imp. § 275.

APPENDIX IV

THE CHINESE TARIFF OF 1918

Cotton and Cotton Goods

Name of Article	Agreed Value		Proposed Duty Rate
	Per	Hk. Tls.	Hk. Tls.
Cotton Piece Goods, Grey:			
Grey Shirtings and Sheetings, not over 40-in. by 41 yards:			
(a) Weight 7-lb. and under	piece	1.817	0.091
(b) Weight over 7-lb. and not over 9-lb.	"	2.681	0.13
(c) Weight over 9-lb. and not over 11-lb.	"	3.530	0.18
Grey Shirtings and Sheetings, not over 40-in. by 41 yards and with more than 110 threads per square inch:			
(a) Weight over 11-lb. and not over 12½-lb.	piece	3.933	0.20
(b) Weight over 12½-lb. and not over 15½-lb.	"	4.668	0.23
(c) Weight over 15½-lb.	"	5.400	0.27
Grey Shirtings and Sheetings, not over 40-in. by 41 yards and with 110 threads or less per square inch:			
(a) Weight over 11-lb. and not over 15½-lb.	piece	3.293	0.16
(b) Weight over 15½-lb.	"	4.000	0.20
Drills and Jeans, Grey, not over 31-in. by 31 yards	"	2.960	0.15
Drills and Jeans, Grey, not over 31-in. by 41 yards:			
(a) Weight 12½-lb. and under	piece	3.900	0.20
(b) Weight over 12½-lb.	"	3.215	0.16
T-Cloths, Grey, not over 34-in. by 25 yds.:			
(a) Weight 7-lb. and under	piece	1.722	0.086
(b) Weight over 7-lb.	"	2.312	0.12
T-Cloths, Grey, over 34-in. but not over 37-in. by 25 yards	"	2.900	0.15
Imitation Native Cotton Cloth (including Machine-made), Grey, not over 24-in. wide and with not more than 110 threads per square inch	picul	32.400	1.60

Name of Article	Agreed Value		Proposed Duty Rate Hk. Tls.
	Per	Hk. Tls	
Cotton Flannel or Flannelette of Plain or Twill Weave, Grey:			
(*a*) Not over 32-in. by 31 yards	piece	3.484	0.17
(*b*) Over 32-in. but not over 40-in. by 31 yards	"	4.800	0.24
Cotton Piece Goods, White or Dyed (irrespective of finish):			
Plain White Shirtings and Sheetings, not over 37-in. by 42 yards	piece	4.183	0.21
White Irishes, not over 37-in. by 42 yards	"	5.096	0.25
Drill and Jeans, White, not over 31-in. by 32 yards	"	3.296	0.16
Drills and Jeans, White, not over 31-in. by 42 yards	"	4.348	0.22
T-Cloths, White, and Mexicans, not over 32-in. by 41 yards	"	3.614	0.18
Dimities, Piqués, Vestings, Quiltings, and Bedford Cords, White, not over 30-in. by 30 yards	"	4.749	0.24
Cambrics, Lawns, and Muslins, White, Plain, not over 46-in. by 12 yards ...	"	0.810	0.041
Cambrics, Lawns, and Muslins, White, Figured, not over 46-in. by 12 yards .	value	5 %	....
Cambrics, Lawns, and Muslins, Dyed, Plain or Figured, not over 46-in. by 12 yards	"	5 %	....
White or Dyed Plain or Figured Muslins, Lawns, Cambrics, Limbrics, Pongees, Brocades, and Striped, Spotted, Corded, and Figured Shirtings:			
(*a*) Not over 30-in. by 31 yards	piece	4.443	0.22
(*b*) Over 30-in. but not over 37-in. by 42 yards	"	5.000	0.25
Lenos, White or Dyed, not over 31-in. by 30 yards	"	2.161	0.11
Leno Brocades, White or Dyed	value	5 %	....
Dyed Shirtings and Sheetings, Plain:			
(*a*) Not over 30-in. by 33 yards	piece	2.7555	0.14
(*b*) Not over 30-in. and over 33 yards but not over 43 yards	"	3.5905	0.18
(*c*) Not over 36-in. by 21 yards	"	2.1048	0.11
(*d*) Not over 36-in. and over 21 yards but not over 33 yards	"	3.30759	0.17
(*e*) Not over 36-in. and over 33 yards but not over 43 yards............	"	4.30989	0.22
Dyed Drills and Jeans, Plain:			
(*a*) Not over 31-in. by 33 yards	"	3.600	0.18

Name of Article	Agreed Value		Proposed Duty Rate
	Per	Hk. Tls.	Hk. Tls.
(b) Not over 31-in. and over 33 yards but not over 43 yards	piece	4.676	0.23
Dyed T-Cloths, Embossed Cantons, Alapacianos, Real and Imitation Turkey Reds, not over 32-in. by 32 yards:			
(a) Weight 3¼-lb. and under	piece	1.889	0.094
(b) Weight over 3¼-lb. but not over 5¼-lb.	"	2.400	0.12
(c) Weight over 5¼-lb.	"	3.320	0.17
Mercerised Crimps, White, Dyed, or Printed, Plain or Figured, not over 32-in. by 32 yards	"	5.478	0.27
Oatmeal Crapes, White or Dyed, Plain or Figured, not over 33-in. by 33 yards .	"	5.265	0.26
Cotton Crape (excluding Oatmeal Crapes), Grey, Bleached, Dyed, Printed, or Dyed in the Yarn:			
(a) Not over 15-in. wide	value	5 per cent	
(b) Over 15-in. but not over 30-in. wide	yard	0.106	0.0053
Lastings, Italians, Satteens, Ribs, Cords, Moreens, Beatrice Twills, Tientsin Twills, Satteen Drills, Satteen Stripes, Repps, and Imitation (Weft-faced) Venetians, White or Dyed, Plain or Figured, not over 33-in. by 33 yards	piece	4.540	0.23
Poplins and Venetians, White or Dyed, Plain, not over 33-in. by 33 yards ...	"	8.0946	0.40
Poplins and Venetians, White or Dyed, Figured, not over 33-in. by 33 yards..	"	10.000	0.50
Cotton Flannel or Flannelette of Plain or Twill Weave:			
(1) White, Dyed, or Printed, or Dyed in the Yarn, exclusive of Duplex or Reversible Prints:			
(a) Not over 25-in. by 15 yards ...	piece	1.400	0.07
(b) Over 25-in. but not over 30-in. by 15 yards	"	1.700	0.085
(c) Over 25-in. but not over 30-in. by 31 yards	"	3.600	0.18
(d) Over 30-in. but not over 36-in. by 15 yards	"	2.000	0.10
(e) Over 30-in. but not over 36-in. by 31 yards	"	4.300	0.22
(2) Duplex or Reversible Prints	value	5 per cent	
Dyed Cotton Spanish Stripes:			

Name of Article	Agreed Value		Proposed Duty Rate
	Per	Hk. Tls.	Hk. Tls.
(*a*) Not over 32-in. by 20 yards	piece	2.241	0.11
(*b*) Over 32-in. but not over 64-in. by 20 yards	"	4.482	0.22
Dyed Cotton Velvets and Velveteens, Plain, not over 26-in. wide	yard	0.2884	0.014
Cotton Velvets, and Velveteens, Printed, Figured, or Embossed, Velvet and Velveteen Cords, Corduroys, Fustians, Moleskins, and Plushes	value	5 per cent	....
Canvas, Cotton (including Cotton Duck), for Sails, etc.	yard	$0.30\overline{0}$	0.015
Stockinet or Knitted Tissue:			
(*a*) Raised	picul	44.000	2.20
(*b*) Not Raised	value	5 per cent	....
Cotton Piece Goods, Printed:			
Printed Cambrics, Printed Lawns, Printed Muslins, Printed Shirtings, Printed Sheetings, Printed T-Cloths (including those known as Blue and White Printed T-Cloths), Printed Drills, Printed Jeans, Printed Diagonal Twills, Twill Cretonnes, Printed Silesias, Printed Repps (excluding Repp Cretonnes):			
(*a*) Not over 20-in wide	value	5 per cent	....
(*b*) Over 20-in. but not over 46-in. by 12 yards	piece	$1.0\overline{20}$	.1.051
(*c*) Over 20-in. but not over 32-in. by 30 yards	"	$2.\overline{302}$	0.12
(*d*) Over 32-in. but not over 42-in. by 30 yards	"	3.094	0.15
Printed Mercerised Crimps.			
Printed Oatmeal Crapes and Oatmeal Crape Cretonnes not over 32-in. by 30 yards	piece	$2.\overline{705}$	0.14
Printed Cotton Crape.			
Printed Turkey Reds, Real and Imitation, not over 31-in. by 25 yards	piece	2.068	0.10
Printed Lenos, not over 31-in. by 30 yds.	"	2.350	0.12
Printed Satteens and Satinets, Printed Brocades (including Printed Fancy Woven Stripes or Checks), Printed Italians, Printed Damasks, Printed Venetians, Printed Lastings, Printed Beatrice Twills, Printed Cords, Printed Poplins, Printed Moreens, not over 32-in. by 30 yards	"	5.000	0.25
Printed Flannelette.			

Name of Article	Agreed Value		Proposed Duty Rate Hk. Tls.
	Per	Hk. Tls.	
Duplex or Reversible Prints of Shirting Weave and one colour only, not over 32-in by 30 yards	piece	3.000	0.15
Printed Velvets and Velveteens.			
Printed Domestic Cretonnes, Printed Satteen Cretonnes, Printed Repp Cretonnes, Printed Embossed Figures, Printed Art Muslins and Casement Cloth, Printed Cotton Coatings, Trouserings, and Gabardines, and all other Duplex or Reversible Prints except those enumerated	value	5 per cent	....
Printed Blankets.			
Printed Handkerchiefs.			
The term "Printed" in this Tariff includes Pigment Style, Direct Printing Style, Steam Style, Discharge Style, Madder or Dyed Style, Resist Style, Resist Par Style, Metal Style, and so forth, irrespective of finish.			
The term "Duplex or Reversible Print in this Tariff includes all Printed Cotton having (*a*) a different pattern printed on each side of the cloth; (*b*) the same design on both sides of the cloth, whether printed with one or more rollers.			
Cotton Piece Goods, Yarn-dyed:			
Cotton Crape.			
Cotton Flannel, or Flannelette.			
Stockinet.			
Not otherwise enumerated	value	5 per cent	....
Cotton, not otherwise enumerated	"	"	....
Cotton, Raw; Cotton Thread, Cotton Yarn, and Goods made of Cotton:			
Ankle Bands, Plain or Decorated	picul	80.000	4.00
Bags, New			
Blankets, Plain, Printed, or Jacquard (including those with a taped or whipped edge of Silk or other material), and Blanket Cloth	picul	40.000	2.00
Canvas.			
Crape.			
Counterpanes, Honeycomb or Alhambra:			
(*a*) Not over 2½ yards long	"	45.000	2.95
(*b*) Over 2½ yards long	value	5 per cent	....
Embroidered Edging or Insertion, Machine-made	value	5 per cent	....

Name of Article	Agreed Value		Proposed Duty Rate
	Per	Hk. Tls.	Hk. Tls.
Flannelette.			
Handkerchiefs, neither Embroidered nor Initialled:			
(1) White, Dyed, or Printed, Hemmed (but not with a drawn-thread hem):			
(*a*) Not over 13-in. square	dozen	0.220	0.011
(*b*) Over 13-in. square but not over 18-in. square	"	0.360	0.018
(*c*) Over 18-in. square but not over 30-in. square	"	0.530	0.027
(2) White, Dyed, or Printed, with drawn-thread hem:			
(*a*) Not over 13-in. square	"	0.360	0.018
(*b*) Over 13-in. square but not over 18-in. square	"	0.750	0.038
(*c*) Over 18-in. square but not over 30-in. square	"	0.920	0.046
(3) Printed Handkerchiefs, Unhemmed:			
(*a*) Not over 18-in. square	"	0.190	0.01
(*b*) Over 18-in. square but not over 25-in. square	"	0.640	0.032
(*c*) Over 25-in. square but not over 29-in. square	"	0.800	0.04
(*d*) Over 29-in. square but not over 34-in. square	"	1.030	0.052
Knitted Clothing, Raised (including that stitched with Silk Thread and with facings of Silk or other material) ..	picul	74.000	3.70
Raw Cotton	"	16.000	0.80
Singlets or Drawers, not Raised (including those stitched with Silk Thread and with facings of Silk or other material)	dozen	2.800	0.14
Socks and Stockings:			
(*a*) Not Raised on either side:			
(1) Made of Ungassed or Unmercerised Thread	picul	70.000	3.50
(2) Made of Gassed or Mercerised Thread or stitched or embroidered with Silk	"	150.000	7.50
(*b*) Raised	value	5 per cent	....
(*c*) Others	value	5 per cent	....
Stockinet.			
Towels:			
(*a*) Turkish	picul	50.000	2.50
(*b*) Honeycomb or Huckaback	"	44.000	2.20

Name of Article	Agreed Value		Proposed Duty Rate Hk. Tls.
	Per	Hk. Tls.	
Thread, Dyed or Undyed (irrespective of finish):			
(1) Sewing Cotton:			
(*a*) In balls or skeins:			
3-cord	picul	100.000	5.00
6-cord	"	190.000	9.50
(*b*) On spools or cops:			
2-cord, 50 yards or less	gross	0.586	0.029
3-cord, 50 yards or less	"	0.786	0.039
6-cord, 50 yards or less	"	1.458	0.073
Other lengths in proportion.			
(2) Crochet or Embroidery Cotton, in skeins or balls	picul	82.449	4.10
Waste Cotton	"	9.600	0.48
Yarn:			
(1) Grey (irrespective of fold):			
(*a*) Counts up to and including 17	picul	25.500	1.28
(*b*) Counts above 17 and up to and including 23	"	27.668	1.38
(*c*) Counts above 23 and up to and including 35	"	38.000	1.90
(*d*) Counts above 35 and up to and including 45	"	43.600	2.18
(*e*) Counts above 45	value	5 per cent	....
(2) Dyed, Bleached, Mercerised, etc.	"	5 per cent	....

WOOL, SILK, LINEN AND HEMP GOODS

Name of Article	Per	Hk. Tls.	Proposed Duty Rate Hk. Tls.
Flax, Hemp and Jute Goods:			
Gunny Bags, New	picul	8.480	0.42
Gunny Bags, Old	value	5 per cent	....
Hemp	picul	14.000	0.70
Hemp or Hessian Bags, New	"	18.900	0.95
Hemp or Hessian Bags, Old	value	5 per cent	....
Hessian Cloth	picul	18.000	0.90
Canvas of Hemp and Jute for Sails, etc.	yard	0.38165	0.019
Canvas Linen (elastic), for Tailoring	value	5 per cent	....
Tarpaulin of Hemp or Jute	yard	0.229	0.011
Silk Goods and Silk Mixtures:			
Silk Piece Goods (all Silk), Plain, Figured, or Brocaded	value	5 per cent	....
Silk Plushes and Silk Velvets, Pure	catty	10.984	0.55
Silk Seal, with Cotton back	"	2.9418	0.15
Silk Socks and Stockings, Knitted (including those made of Artificial Silk)[1]	"	7.000	0.35

[1] The French Delegation stated that it could not agree to the duty treatment proposed for these goods until it had referred the question to its Government.

Name of Article	Agreed Value		Proposed Duty Rate
	Per	Hk. Tls.	Hk. Tls.
Silk Mixture Plushes and Velvets (i. e., made of Silk mixed with other fibrous material, with Cotton back)	catty	2.6537	0.13
Silk and Cotton Satins, White or Dyed in the Piece:[1]			
(*a*) Plain	"	2.533	0.13
(*b*) Figured	"	3.233	0.16
Silk and Cotton Satins, Dyed in the Yarn.[1]	"	4.000	0.20
Silk and Cotton Mixtures not otherwise enumerated	value	5 per cent	....
Silk Ribbons, all Silk and Mixtures	value	5 per cent	....
Wool and Cotton Unions:			
Union Shirtings, not over 33-in. wide ...	yard	0.4853	0.024
Cloth made of remanufactured Wool and Cotton, such as Meltons, Vicunas, Beavers, Army Cloths, Union Cloths, Leather Cloths, Presidents (including Cloth containing a small quantity or new Wool for facing purposes), not over 56-in. wide	"	0.800	0.04
Italian Cloth, Plain or Figured, Alpacas, Lustres, Orleans, and Sicilians	value	5 per cent	....
Wool and Woollen Goods:			
Wool, Sheep's	picul	17.000	0.85
Blankets and Rugs	pound	0.560	0.028
Bunting, not over 24-in. by 40 yards	piece	0.560	0.33
Camlets, not over 31-in. by 62 yards	"	15,600	0.78
Flannel, not over 33-in. wide	yard	0.480	0.024
Lastings, Plain, Figured, or Crêped, not over 31-in. by 32 yards	piece	14.620	0.73
Llama Braid	picul	150.000	7.50
Long Ells, not over 31-in. by 25 yards ...	piece	6.657	0.33
Russian, Broad, Superfine, Medium, and Habit Cloth, not over 76-in. wide ...	yard	1.520	0.076
Spanish Stripes, not over 64-in. wide ...	"	0.636	0.032
All Woollen and Worsted Yarn and Cord, including Berlin Wool	picul	126.000	6.00

METALS

Name of Article	Per	Hk. Tls.	Hk. Tls.
Aluminum	value	5 per cent	....
Aluminum Sheets	value	5 per cent	....
Antifriction Metal	value	5 per cent	....
Antimony Regulus and Refined	picul	14.000	0.70
Antimony Ore	value	5 per cent	....
Brass and Yellow Metal:			
Bars and Rods	picul	30.183	1.50

[1] See footnote, page 374

Name of Article	Agreed Value		Proposed Duty Rate
	Per	Hk. Tls.	Hk. Tls.
Bolts, Nuts, Rivets, Washers, and Accessories	value	5 per cent	....
Ingots	picul	30.183	1.50
Nails	"	36.765	1.80
Old (fit only for remanufacture)	value	5 per cent	....
Screws	value	5 per cent	....
Sheets and Plates	picul	30.183	1.50
Tubes	"	47.809	2.40
Wire	"	30.183	1.50
Copper:			
Bars and Rods	picul	33.950	1.70
Bolts, Nuts, Rivets, and Washers	value	5 per cent	....
Ingots and Slabs	picul	28.000	1.40
Nails	"	47.385	2.40
Old (fit only for remanufacture)	value	5 per cent	....
Sheets and Plates	picul	33.950	1.70
Tacks	value	5 per cent	....
Tubes	value	5 per cent	....
Wire	picul	33.950	1.70
Wire Cable	value	5 per cent	....
Wire Rope	value	5 per cent	....
Iron and Steel, Ungalvanized (not including Bamboo, Spring, and Tool Steel):			
Anvils, Swage-blocks, Anchors, and Parts of, and Forgings (each weighing in every case 25-lb. or over)	picul	11.484	0.57
Bolts, Nuts, and Washers	value	5 per cent	....
Castings, Rough	picul	5.132	0.26
Chains, and Parts of	"	7.667	0.38
Cobbles, Wire Shorts, Defective Wire, Bar Croppings, and Bar Ends, Galvanized or Ungalvanized	"	2.658	0.13
Crossings for Railways	value	5 per cent	....
Fish-plates and Spikes	value	5 per cent	....
Hoops	picul	5.451	0.27
Old (fit only for remanufacture)	"	1.946	0.10
Nail-rod, Bars, Twisted or Deformed Bars, Tess, Channels, Angles, Joists, Girders, and other Structural Shapes	"	4.080	0.20
Nails, Wire and Cut	"	5.946	0.30
Pig and Kentledge	"	2.000	0.10
Pipes, Tubes, and Pipe and Tube Fittings	value	5 per cent	....
Plate Cuttings	picul	2.311	0.12
Rails	"	3.120	0.16
Rivets	"	6.287	0.31
Screws	value	5 per cent	....
Sheets and Plates ⅛ of an inch thick or more	picul	4.000	0.20

Name of Article	Agreed Value		Proposed Duty Rate
	Per	Hk. Tls.	Hk. Tls.
Sheets and Plates under ⅛ of an inch thick	picul	5.000	0.20
Tacks	"	9.047	0.45
Wire	"	5.241	0.26
Wire Rope, Galvanized or Ungalvanized	"	14.924	0.75
Wire with or without fibre core	"	....	....
Steel, Tool and Spring:			
Bamboo Steel	"	5.486	0.27
Spring Steel	"	6.420	0.32
Tool Steel (including High-speed) Steel	value	5 per cent	....
Iron and Steel, Galvanized:			
Bolts, Nuts, Rivets, and Washers	value	5 per cent	....
Pipes, Tubes, and Tube Fittings	"	"	....
Screws	"	"	....
Sheets, Corrugated and Plain	picul	7.400	0.37
Wire	"	6.072	0.30
Wire Rope. See Ungalvanized.			
Wire Shorts. See Ungalvanized.			
Iron and Tin Dross	picul	6.000	0.30
Lead:			
Old (fit only for remanufacture)	value	5 per cent	....
Pigs or Bars	picul	9.000	0.45
Pipe	"	9.961	0.50
Sheet	"	11.834	0.59
Wire	value	5 per cent	....
Manganese	"	"	....
Manganese Ferro	"	"	....
Nickel	picul	70.000	3.50
Quicksilver	"	126.654	6.30
Tin:			
Compound	value	5 per cent	....
Dross and Refuse	picul	10.885	0.54
Ingots and Slabs	"	45.462	2.30
Pipe	value	5 per cent	
Sheet	picul	41.208	2.10
Tinned Tacks	"	9.047	0.45
Tinned Plates, Decorated	"	10.176	0.51
Tinned Plates, Plain	"	7.800	0.39
Tinned Plates, Old	value	5 per cent	....
Type Metal	"	"	....
White Metal or German Silver:			
Bars, Ingots, and Sheets	picul	54.531	2.70
Wire	"	43.444	2.20
Zinc:			
Powder and Spelter	picul	12.946	0.65
Sheets (including Perforated), Plates, and Boiler Plates	"	16.849	0.84

FOOD, DRINK AND MEDICINE

Name of Article	Agreed Value		Proposed Duty Rate
	Per	Hk. Tls.	Hk. Tls.
Fishery and Sea Products:			
Agar-agar	picul	6.000	0.30
Awabi, in bulk	"	52.500	2.60
Bicho de Mar, Black, Spiked	"	53.300	2.70
Bicho de Mar, Black, not Spiked	"	40.000	2.00
Bicho de Mar, White	"	20.000	1.00
Cockles, Dried	"	13.822	0.69
Cockles, Fresh	"	1.200	0.06
Compoy	"	43.000	2.15
Crabs' Flesh, Dried	"	16.518	0.83
Fish Bones	value	5 per cent	....
Fish Cod, Dried	picul	5.800	0.29
Fish, Cuttle	"	13.600	0.68
Fish, Dried and Smoked (not including Dried Codfish and Cuttle-fish)	"	9.739	0.49
Fish, Fresh	"	6.410	0.32
Fish, Maws, 1st Quality (i. e., weighing 1 catty or over per piece)	catty	5.000	0.25
Fish, Maws, 2nd Quality (i. e., weighing under 1 catty per piece)	picul	56.500	2.80
Fish, Salmon Bellies	value	5 per cent	....
Fish, Salt	picul	3.600	0.18
Fish, Skin	"	12.711	0.64
Mussels, Oysters, and Clams, Dried	"	16.000	0.80
Prawns and Shrimps, Dried, in bulk	"	22.000	1.10
Seaweed, Cut	"	3.334	0.17
Seaweed, Long	"	2.500	0.13
Seaweed, Prepared	"	26.000	1.30
Seaweed, Red	value	5 per cent	....
Sharks' Fins, Dorsal and Tail	picul	88.660	4.40
Sharks' Fins, Breast Fins	"	37.173	1.90
Sharks' Fins, Prepared	"	128.562	6.40
Seaweed Skins	value	5 per cent	....
Animal Products, Canned Goods, and Groceries:			
Bacon and Hams, in bulk	picul	35.300	1.80
Baking Powder	value	5 per cent	....
Beef, Corned or Pickled, in Barrels	"	"	....
Birds' Nests, Black (including Clarified Refuse)	catty	3.000	0.15
Birds' Nests, White	"	18.000	0.90
Butter	picul	53.270	2.70
Canned Goods:			
Asparagus	picul	17.500	0.88

Name of Article	Agreed Value Per (Incl. weight of immediate packing.)	Agreed Value Hk. Tls.	Preposed Duty Rate Hk. Tls.
Awabi	picul	24.000	1.20
Cream and Milk, Evaporated or Sterilized	"	13.000	0.65
Fruits, Table and Pie	"	14.500	0.73
Milk, Condensed	"	19.200	0.96
Canned Goods, Unenumerated	value	5 per cent	
Chocolate	"	"	....
Cocoa	"	"	....
Coffee	"	"	....
Currants and Raisins, in bulk	picul	12.577	0.63
Fruits, Preserved, in Glass, etc.	value	5 per cent	
Honey	"	"	....
Jams and Jellies	"	"	....
Lard, in bulk	"	"	....
Macaroni and Vermicelli, in bulk	picul	9.125	0.46
Margarine	value	5 per cent	
Meats, Dried and Salted	"	"	....
Pork Rind	"	"	....
Sausages, Dry	"	"	....
Soy	picul	5.000	0.25
Tea	value	5 per cent	
Cereals, Fruits, Medicinal Substances, Seeds, Spices, and Vegetables:			
Aniseed, Star:			
(*a*) 1st Quality (value Hk. Tls. 15 and over per picul)	picul	20.000	1.00
(*b*) 2nd Quality (value under Hk. Tls. 15 per picul)	"	9.000	0.45
Apples, Fresh	"	5.000	0.25
Asafœtida	value	5 per cent	
Barley, Pearl	"	"	....
Beans and Peas	"	"	....
Betelnuts, Dried	picul	4.700	0.24
Betelnut Husk, Dried	"	2.300	0.12
Bran	"	1.600	0.08
Cereals and Flour (including Barley, Maize, Millet, Oats, Paddy, Rice, Wheat, and Flour made therefrom; also Buckwheat and Buckwheat Flour, Cornflour and Yellow Corn Meal, Rye Flour, and Hovis Flour; but not including Arrowroot and Arrowroot Flour, Cracked Wheat, Germea, Hominy, Pearl Barley, Potato Flour, Quaker Oats, Rolled Oats, Sago and			

Name of Article	Agreed Value		Proposed Duty Rate
	Per	Hk. Tls.	Hk. Tls.
Sago Flour, Shredded Wheat, Tapioca and Tapioca Flour, and Yam Flour)	.....	free	....
Camphor, Crude and Refined	picul	66.000	3.30
Camphor, Baroos, Clean	catty	62.000	3.10
Camphor, Baroos, Refuse	value	5 per cent	....
Capoor Cutchery	"	"	....
Cardamon Husk	picul	5.000	0.25
Cardamons, Inferior	"	20.000	1.00
Cardamons, Superior	"	200.000	10.00
Cassia Lignea and Buds	"	18.000	0.90
Cassia Twigs	"	3.600	0.18
Chestnuts	value	5 per cent	....
China-root	picul	14.000	0.70
Cinnamon, in bulk	"	100.000	5.00
Cloves, in bulk	"	18.000	0.90
Cloves, Mother	"	8.000	0.40
Cocaine	value	5 per cent	....
Galangal	picul	3.700	0.19
Ginseng, Clarified or Cleaned:			
1st Quality (value over Hk. Tls. 25 per catty)	catty	56.000	2.80
2nd Quality (value over Hk. Tls. 11 and not over Hk. Tls. 25 per catty)	"	22.000	1.10
3rd Quality (value over Hk. Tls. 3 and not over Hk. Tls. 11 per catty)	"	7.200	0.36
4th Quality (value not over Hk. Tls. 3 per catty)	"	1.800	0.09
Ginseng, Crude, Beard, Roots, and Cuttings:			
1st Quality (value over Hk. Tls. 3 per catty)	"	4.400	0.22
2nd Quality (value not over Hk. Tls. 3 per catty)	"	1.700	0.085
Ginseng, Wild	value	5 per cent	....
Groundnuts, in Shell	picul	3.000	0.15
Groundnuts, Shelled	"	4.600	0.23
Hops	value	5 per cent	....
Isinglass, Vegetable	picul	53.000	2.70
Lemons, Fresh	thous	29.000	1.50
Lichees, Dried	picul	10.600	0.53
Lily Flowers, Dried	"	9.400	0.47
Lungngan Pulp	"	13.000	0.65
Lungngans, Dried	"	7.600	0.38
Malt	"	8.102	0.41
Morphia in all forms	value	5 per cent	....
Mushrooms	picul	47.000	2.40
Nutmegs	"	30.000	1.50

Name of Article	Agreed Value		Proposed Duty Rate Hk. Tls.
	Per	Hk. Tls.	
Olives	value	5 per cent	....
Opium, Tincture of	value	5 per cent	....
Oranges, Fresh	picul	3.600	0.18
Peel, Orange, in bulk	"	13.000	0.65
Pepper, Black	"	19.400	0.97
Pepper, White	"	32.000	1.60
Potatoes, Fresh	value	5 per cent	....
Putchuck	picul	38.000	1.90
Seed, Apricot	"	26.800	1.30
Seed, Lily Flower (i. e., Lotus-nuts without Husks)	picul	20.000	1.00
Seed, Lucraban	"	7.000	0.35
Seed, Melon	"	11.000	0.55
Seed, Pine (i. e., Fir-nuts)	"	4.800	0.24
Seed, Sesamum	"	4.800	0.24
Vegetables, Dried, Prepared, and Salted	value	5 per cent	....
Sugar:			
Sugar, Brown, under No. 11 Dutch Standard, and "Green Sugar"	picul	4.400	0.22
Sugar, White, over No. 10 Dutch Standard (including Refined Sugar)	"	6.200	0.31
Sugar, White, Cube and Loaf	"	10.000	0.50
Sugar, Candy		7.400	0.37
Sugar, Cane		1.000	0.05
Wines, Beer, Spirits, Table Waters, etc.:			
Champagne and any other Wine sold under the label Champagne"	Case of 12 bottles or 24 ½ bottles	20.000	1.00
Sparkling Asti	"	10.000	0.50
Other Sparkling Wines	"	12.000	0.60
Still Wines, Red or White. exclusively the produce of the natural fermentation of grapes not including Vins de Liqueur)	half-bottles		
(1) In Bottles	Case of 12 bottles or 24 ½ bottles	6.000	0.30
(2) In bulk	Imperial gallon	0.700	0.035
Port Wine, in Bottles	Case of 12 bottles or 24 ½ bottles	14.000	0.70
Port Wine, in bulk	Imperial gallon	3.500	0.18
Marsala, in Bottles	Case of 12 bottles or 24 ½ bottles	8.000	0.40
Marsala, in bulk	Imperial gallon	2.000	0.10

Name of Article	Agreed Value		Proposed Duty Rate
	Per	Hk. Tls.	Hk. Tls.
Vins de Liqueur other than Port and Marsala (viz., Madeira, Malaga, Sherry, etc.):			
(1) In Bottles	Case of 12 bottles or 24 ½ bottles	10.000	0.50
(2) In bulk	Imperial gallon	3.00	.015
Vermouth, Byrrh, and Quinquina	Case of 12 litres	5.800	0.29
Saké, in Barrels	picul	8.200	0.41
Saké, in Bottles	12 reputed quarts or 24 reputed pints	2.000	0.10
Ale, Beer, Cider, Perry, and similar Liquors made of Fruits and Berries:			
(1) In Bottles	12 reputed quarts or 24 reputed pints	1.580	0.079
(2) In Casks	Imperial gallon	0.540	0.027
Porter and Stout, in Bottles	12 reputed quarts or 24 reputed pints	2.560	0.13
Porter and Stout, in Casks	Imperial gallon	0.550	0.028
Brandy, Cognac, and Whisky, in bulk	"	2.600	0.13
Brandy and Cognac, in Bottles ..	Case of 12 reputed quarts	13.400	0.67
Whisky, in Bottles	"	7.000	0.35
Gin, in Bottles	"	4.600	0.23
Gin, in bulk	Imperial gallon	1.800	0.09
Other Spirits (*i.e.*, Rum, Aquavit, Vodka, Punch, etc.):			
(1) In Bottles	Case of 12 reputed quarts	4.000	0.20
(2) In bulk	Imperial gallon	1.800	0.09
Liqueurs	12 reputed quarts or 24 reputed pints	10.000	0.50
Waters, Table, Aerated and Mineral	12 bottles or 24 ½ bottles	1.400	0.07
Spirits of Wine and Rectified Spirits or Alcohol	Imperial gallon	0.560	0.028

TOBACCO

Name of Article	Agreed Value		Proposed Duty Rate Hk. Tls.
	Per	Hk. Tls.	
Cigarettes, value over Hk. Tls. 4.50 per 1,000 and all Cigarettes not bearing a distinctive brand or name on each thousand		6.600	0.33
Cigarettes, value over Hk. Tls. 3.00 but not over Hk. Tls. 4.50 per 1,000	"	3.800	0.19
Cigarettes, value over Hk. Tls. 1.50 but not over Hk. Tls. 3.00 per 1,000	"	2.200	0.11
Cigarettes, value Hk. Tls. 1.50 or less per 1,000	"	1.200	0.06
Cigars	"	16.000	0.80
Snuff	value	5 per cent	....
Tobacco, Leaf	picul	22.000	1.10
Tobacco, Prepared, in tins or packages under 5-lb. each	value	5 per cent	....
Tobacco, Prepared, in bulk (not packed in tins or tin-lined cases)	picul	22.000	1.10
Tobacco, Stalk	"	5.600	0.28

CHEMICALS AND DYES

Name of Article	Per	Hk. Tls.	Proposed Duty Rate Hk. Tls.
Acid, Acetic	picul	30.639	1.50
Acid, Boracic	"	21.448	1.10
Acid, Carbolic	value	5 per cent	....
Acid, Hydrochloric (i.e., Muriatic)	value	5 per cent	....
Acid, Nitric	picul	14.282	0.71
Acid, Sulphuric	"	3.317	0.17
Ammonia, in bulk	"	26.513	1.30
Ammonia, Chloride of (Sal Ammoniac.	"	17.823	0.89
Opium, Tincture of	value	5 per cent	....
Ammonia, Sulphate of	"	7.438	0.37
Bleaching Powder (Chloride of Lime)..	"	5.469	0.27
Borax, Crude or Refined	"	11.521	0.58
Calcium, Carbide of	"	7.451	0.37
Copper, Sulphate of	"	11.912	0.60
Glycerine	"	43.930	2.20
Hide Specific	value	5 per cent	....
Manure, Animal, Chemical, or Artificial, not otherwise enumerated	picul	2.951	0.15
Naphthalene	"	12.653	0.63
Saltpetre	"	9.324	0.47
Soda Ash	"	2.499	0.12
Soda, Bicarbonate of, in bulk	"	2.899	0.14
Soda, Caustic	"	6.200	0.31
Soda, Crystal	"	2.659	0.13
Soda, Crystal Concentrated	"	3.178	0.16

Name of Article	Agreed Value		Proposed Duty Rate
	Per	Hk. Tls.	Hk. Tls.
Dyes and Pigments:			
Soda, Nitrate of (Chile Saltpetre)	picul	5.342	0.27
Soda, Silicate of	"	3.603	0.18
Aniline Dyes not otherwise enumerated .	value	5 per cent	....
Bark, Mangrove	picul	1.682	0.084
Bark, Plum-tree	"	3.187	0.16
Bark, Yellow (for Dyeing)	"	4.948	0.25
Blue, Paris or Prussian	"	34.945	1.70
Bronze Powder	"	52.979	2.60
Carbon Black (i.e., Lampblack)	"	20.000	1.00
Carthamin	value	5 per cent	....
Chrome Yellow	"	"	....
Cinnabar	picul	82.400	4.10
Cobalt, Oxide of	value	5 per cent	....
Cochineal	value	5 per cent	....
Cunao or False Gambier	picul	3.340	0.17
Cutch or Gambier	"	10.000	0.50
Dyes and Colours, Unclassed	value	5 per cent	
Gamboge	picul	56.951	2.80
Green, Emerald, Schweinfurt, or Imitation	"	22.458	1.10
Hartall (Orpiment)	"	9.562	0.48
Indigo, Dried, Artificial	"	125.881	6.30
Indigo, Liquid, Natural	"	6.000	3.00
Indigo, Liquid or Paste, Artificial......	"	40.000	2.00
Indigo, Liquid, Natural	"	6.000	0.30
Indoin	value	5 per cent	....
Laka-wood	picul	3.272	0.16
Lead, Red, White, and Yellow	"	10.294	0.51
Logwood Extract	"	15.492	0.77
Nutgalls	"	.0.863	1.00
Ochre	"	6.545	0.33
Safflower	"	12.908	6.65
Sapanwood	"	2.744	0.14
Smalt	"	40.150	2.00
Turmeric	"	3.938	0.20
Ultramarine	"	13.862	0.69
Vermilion	"	82.400	4.10
Vermilion, Artificial	value	5 per cent	....
White Zinc	value	5 per cent	....

CANDLES, GUMS, OILS, SOAP, VARNISHES, WAX AND MANUFACTURES OF

Candles	picul	14.600	0.63
Candlewick	"	75.200	4.15
Gasolene, Naphtha, and Benzine, Mineral:			
(*a*) In bulk 10	Am. galls.	3.000	0.15

Name of Article	Agreed Value Per	Agreed Value Hk. Tls.	Proposed Duty Rate Hk. Tls.
(*b*) In case	Case of 2 tins, each of 5 Am. galls.	3.500	0.18
Grease, Lubricating, wholly or part mineral	picul	7.000	0.35
Gum Arabic	"	24.000	1.20
Gum Benjamin	"	12.000	0.60
Gum Copal	"	24.000	1.20
Gum Dragon's-blood	"	60.000	3.00
Gum Myrrh	"	9.600	0.48
Gum Olibanum	"	9.600	0.48
Gum Resin	"	6.800	0.34
Gum Shellac	"	40.000	2.00
Gum Sticklac	"	15.000	0.75
Gum Tragacanth	"	18.000	0.90
Oil, Castor, Lubricating	"	12.000	0.60
Oil, Castor, Medicinal	value	5 per cent	....
Oil, Coconut	picul	16.000	0.80
Oil, Kerosene:			
(*a*) In case	Case of 2 tins, each of 5 Am. galls.	2.200	0.11
(*b*) In bulk	10 Am. galls.	1.000	0.06
(*c*) Tins, empty	tin	0.200	0.01
(*d*) Case and two empty tins	each	0.540	0.027
Oil, Linseed	Imperial gallon	1.200	0.06
Oil, Lubricating:			
(*a*) Wholly or partly of Mineral origin	Am. gallon	0.300	0.015
(*b*) Other kinds, not otherwise enumerated	"	0.500	0.025
Oil, Olive, in bulk	Imperial gallon	2.000	0.10
Soap, Household and Laundry (including Blue Mottled), in bulk, Bars, and Doublets: duty to be charged on nominal weights, provided that such weights be not less than true weights and that a bar does not weigh less than 7-oz.	picul	8.800	0.44
Soap, Toilet and Fancy	value	5 per cent	....
Stearine	picul	19.600	0.98
Turpentine:			
(*a*) Mineral	Imperial gallon	0.600	0.03
(*b*) Vegetable	"	0.800	0.04
Wax, Bees, Yellow	picul	32.000	1.60

Name of Article	Agreed Value		Proposed Duty Rate
	Per	Hk. Tls.	Hk. Tls.
Wax, Paraffin	picul	10.00	0.50
Wax, Vegetable	"	15.200	0.76

PAPER, WOOD PULP, BOOKS, AND MAPS

Name of Article	Per	Hk. Tls.	Hk. Tls.
Paper, Cigarette, on bobbins	picul	40.00	2.00
Paper, Common Printing, Calendered and Uncalendered, Sized and Unsized, White and Coloured	"	6.40	0.32
Paper, Marbled, Enamelled, and Glazed Flint	"	12.20	0.61
Paper, M. G. Cap, White and Coloured	"	6.40	0.32
Paper, Packing and Wrapping, Brown or Coloured	"	6.40	0.32
Paper, Printing, Calendered and Uncalendered, Sized and Unsized, White and Coloured (including Simile and M. G. Poster, but not including Printing Paper otherwise enumerated), free of mechanical wood pulp	"	9.20	0.46
Paper, Strawboard	value	5 per cent	....
Paper, Unenumerated	"	"	....
Paper, Unglazed Tissue and M. G. Bleachel Sulphite, free of mechanical wood pulp	picul	10.00	0.50
Paper, Writing, Drawing, Art Printing, Bank-note, Parchment, Pergamyn, and Grease-proof	value	5 per cent	....
Wood Pulp, Chemical	picul	6.00	0.30
Wood Pulp, Mechanical:			
(*a*) Dry	"	3.32	0.17
(*b*) Wet (not containing less than 40 per cent moisture,	"	1.66	0.083
Books	.....	free	....
Charts and Maps	.....	"	....
Newspapers and Periodicals	.....	"	....

ANIMAL SUBSTANCES, RAW AND PREPARED

Name of Article	Per	Hk. Tls.	Hk. Tls.
Hides, Leather, and Skins (Furs):			
Hides, Buffalo and Cow	picul	22.00	1.10
Leather Belting	value	5 per cent	....
Leather, Calf, Kid, Enamelled, Japanned, Patent, and/or Coloured	picul	300.00	15.00
Leather, Cow (including that for Soles and Harness)	"	58.00	2.90

Name of Article	Agreed Value		Proposed Duty Rate
	Per	Hk. Tls.	Hk. Tls.
Leather, Cow, Enamelled, Japanned, and Patent	picul	180.00	9.00
Skins (Furs), Beaver	value	5 per cent	....
Skins (Furs), Dog	"	"	....
Skins (Furs), Fox	"	"	....
Skins (Furs), Fox, Arctic, White	"	"	....
Skins (Furs), Fox Legs	"	"	....
Skins (Furs), Fox, Red	"	"	....
Skins (Furs), Goat, Tanned	"	"	....
Skins (Furs), Goat, Untanned	"	"	....
Skins (Furs), Hare and Rabbit	"	"	....
Skins (Furs), Lamb	"	"	....
Skins (Furs), Lamb, Unborn	"	"	....
Skins (Furs), Land-otter	"	"	....
Skins (Furs), Lynx	"	"	....
Skins (Furs), Marten, Untanned	"	"	....
Skins (Furs), Musquash	"	"	....
Skins (Furs), Raccoon	"	"	....
Skins (Furs), Sable	"	"	....
Skins (Furs), Sheep, Untanned	"	"	....
Skins (Furs), Squirrel	"	"	....
Skins (Furs), Wolf	"	"	....
Bones, Feathers, Hair, Horns, Shells, Sinews, Tusks, etc.:			
Bones, Tiger	picul	56.00	2.80
Cow Bezoar, Indian	value	5 per cent	....
Crocodile and Amadillo Scales	picul	59.00	3.00
Elephants' Tusks, Whole or Parts of	hund	3.60	0.18
Feathers, Kingfisher, Whole Skins	catty	12.00	0.60
Feathers, Kingfisher, Part Skins (i. e., Wings, Tails, or Backs)	"	8.00	0.40
Feathers, Peacock	value	5 per cent	....
Hair, Horse	picul	42.00	2.10
Hair, Horse Tails	"	50.00	2.50
Horns, Buffalo and Cow	"	13.00	0.65
Horns, Deer	"	34.00	1.70
Horns, Deer, Old	"	140.00	7.00
Horns, Deer, Young (Northern)	pair	50.00	2.50
Horns, Deer, Young (Southern)	value	5 per cent	....
Horns, Rhinoceros	catty	80.00	4.00
Musk	"	180.00	9.00
Sea-horse Teeth	value	5 per cent	....
Sinews, Cow and Deer	picul	20.00	1.00

TIMBER, WOOD, BAMBOOS AND RATTANS

Timber:			
Laths .1,000	pieces	4.20	0.21

Name of Article	Agreed Value Per	Agreed Value Hk. Tls.	Proposed Duty Rate Hk. Tls.
Ordinary (not including Teak and other enumerated Woods), Rough Hewn:			
Hardwood	1,000 sup. ft., B.M.	29.00	1.45
Softwood	"	23.00	1.15
Ordinary, Sawn:			
Hardwood	1,000 sup. ft., B.M.	36.00	1.80
Softwood	"	30.00	1.50
Ordinary, Manufactured (including any process further than simple sawing), exclusive of Masts and Spars:			
Hardwood:			
(a) Clear	1,000 sup. ft., net measure B.M.	60.00	3.00
(b) Merchantable	"	42.00	2.10
Softwood:			
(a) Clear	1,000 sup. ft., net measure B.M.	50.00	2.60
(b) Merchantable	"	36.00	1.80
Ordinary, Masts and Spars	value	5 per cent	....
Railway Sleepers	"	"	....
Teak-wood, Beams and Planks	1,000 sup. ft., B.M.	135.00	6.75
Wood, Bamboos, Rattans, etc.:			
Canes, Bamboo	thousand	8.40	0.42
Rattan Skin	value	5 per cent	....
Rattans, Core or Whole	picul	15.00	0.75
Rattans, Split	"	6.41	0.32
Wood, Camagon	"	6.70	0.34
Wood, Camphor	"	3.20	0.16
Wood, Ebony	value	5 per cent	....
Wood, Fragrant	"	"	....
Wood, Garoo	"	"	....
Wood, Kranjee	catty	2.40	0.12
Wood, Laka. See Dyes.			
Wood, Lignum-vitæ	value	5 per cent	....
Wood, Oil	value	5 per cent	....
Wood, Puru	"	"	....
Wood, Red and Rose	catty	1.80	0.09
Wood, Sandal	"	4.10	0.21
Wood, Sandal Dust	picul	8.60	0.43
Wood, Span. See Dyes.			
Wood, Scale Sticks	value	5 per cent	....
Wood, Scented	piece	0.18	0.009

Name of Article	Agreed Value		Proposed Duty Rate
	Per	Hk. Tls.	Hk. Tls.
Wood, Shavings, Hinoki	value	5 per cent	....
Wood, Veneer	"	"	....
In this Tariff, by Softwood is meant the wood of any coniferous tree and of all trees with "needle" or spinous leaves, e.g., Pines, Firs, Spruces, Larches, Cedars, Yews, Junipers, and Cypresses. The wood of all trees with broad leaves is to be classed as Hardwood.			

COAL, FUEL, PITCH AND TAR

Name of Article	Per	Hk. Tls.	Proposed Duty Rate Hk. Tls.
Coal	ton	5.400	0.27
Coal, Briquettes	"	10.000	0.50
Charcoal	picul	1.093	0.05
Coke	ton	10.902	0.55
Liquid Fuel	"	14.572	0.73
Pitch	picul	4.709	0.24
Tar, Coal	"	1.600	0.08

CHINAWARE, ENAMELLED WARE, GLASS, ETC.

Name of Article	Per	Hk. Tls.	Proposed Duty Rate Hk. Tls.
Basins, Tin	gross	6.000	0.30
Chinaware	value	5 per cent	....
Enamelled Ironware:			
Mugs, Cups, Basins, and Bowls, not over 11 centimetres in diameter	dozen	1.000	0.05
Basins and Bowls, over 22 centimetres but not over 35 centimetres in diameter	"	2.000	0.10
Enamelled Ironware, Unenumerated	value	5 per cent	....
Glass and Crystal Ware	"	"	....
Glass Plate, Silvered, Bevelled or Unbevelled, not over 5 square feet each	sq. ft.	0.560	0.028
Glass Plate, Silvered, Bevelled or Unbevelled, over 5 square feet each	"	0.840	0.042
Glass Plate, Unsilvered	value	5 per cent	....
Glass Window, Common, not over 32 oz. in weight per square foot	100 sq. ft.	5.000	0.25
Glass Window, Coloured	"	12.000	0 60
Glass Mirrors	value	5 per cent	....

EARTH, PRECIOUS STONES, STONES AND ARTICLES MADE OF

Name of Article	Per	Hk. Tls.	Proposed Duty Rate Hk. Tls.
Amber	value	5 per cent	....
Cement	picul	0.900	0.045
Coral Beads	catty	16.000	0.80
Cornelian Beads	value	5 per cent	....

Name of Article	Agreed Value		Proposed Duty Rate Hk. Tls.
	Per	Hk. Tls.	
MISCELLANEOUS			
Cornelian Stones, Rough	hund.	6.000	0.30
Corundum Sand	picul	3.800	0.19
Emery and Glass Powder	"	2.400	0.12
Emery-cloth and Sand-paper	.....	....	....
Fire-bricks	value	5 per cent	....
Fireclay	picul	1.220	0.061
Flints (including Flint Pebbles)	"	0.800	0.04
Tiles	value	5 per cent	....
Asbestos:			
Asbestos Boiler Composition	picul	3.600	0.18
Asbestos Fibre and Metallic Packing	"	64.000	3.20
Asbestos Millboard	"	8.000	0.40
Asbestos Sheets and Packing	"	44.000	2.20
Asbestos Yarn	"	40.000	2.00
Bags, Mats, and Matting:			
Bags, Cotton, New	picul	40.000	2.00
Bags, Gunny, New	"	8.480	0.42
Bags, Gunny, Old	value	5 per cent	....
Hemp or Hessian Bags, New	picul	18.900	0.95
Hemp or Hessian Bags, Old	value	5 per cent	....
Bags, Straw and Grass	thousand	30.000	1.50
Mats, Coir (Door)	dozen	8.000	0.40
Mats, Fancy	value	5 per cent	....
Mats, Formosa Grass (Bed)	each	4.700	0.24
Mats, Rattan	value	5 per cent	....
Mats, Rush	hund.	71.000	3.60
Mats, Straw	"	5.100	0.26
Mats, Tatami	each	0.320	0.016
Matting, Coir, 36-in. by 100 yds.	roll of 100 yd.	37.100	1.90
Matting, Straw, 36-in. by 40 yds.	roll of 40 yds.	5.000	0.25
Buttons:			
Buttons, Fancy (Glass, Jewellery, etc.)	value	5 per cent	....
Buttons, Metal (not including those made of Precious Metals or plated with Precious Metals)	gross	0.400	0.02
Buttons, Porcelain	12 gross	0.340	0.017
Buttons, Shell	gross	0.420	0.021
Fans, Umbrellas, and Sunshades:			
Fans, Palm-leaf, Coarse	thousand	7.000	0.35
Fans, Palm-leaf, Fancy	"	20.000	1.00

Name of Article	Agreed Value		Proposed Duty Rate
	Per	Hk. Tls.	Hk. Tls.
Fans, Palm-leaf, Fine	thousand	12.000	0.60
Fans, Paper or Cotton	"	47.000	2.40
Fans, Silk	value	5 per cent	....
Umbrellas and Sunshades:			
With Handles wholly or partly of Precious Metals, Ivory, Mother-of-Pearl, Tortoiseshell, Agate, etc., or Jewelled.	value	5 per cent	....
With all other Handles, all Cotton:			
(a) Length of rib not over 17-in.	value	5 per cent	....
(b) Length of rib over 17-in.	each	0.440	0.022
With all other Handles, Mixtures, not Silk	"	0.730	0.037
With all other Handles, Silk and Silk Mixtures	"	1.300	0.065
Files and Needles:			
Files of all kinds:			
Filing surface only, not over 4-in. long	dozen	1.300	0.065
Filing surface only, over 4-in. but not over 9-in. long	"	2.700	0.14
Filing surface only, over 9-in. but not over 14-in. long	"	5.000	0.25
Filing surface only, over 14-in. long	"	12.000	0.60
Needles, Nos. 7/0 and 6/0	100 mi.	54.000	2.70
Needles, Nos. 3/0 and 2/0	"	50.000	2.00
Needles, Assorted (not including 7/0)	"	40.000	2.00
Matches and Match-making Materials:			
Matches, Wood, Safety or other:			
Small, in boxes not over 2-in. by 1⅜-in. by ⅝-in.	100 gross box	18.400	0.92
Large, in boxes not over 2½-in. by 1⅛-in. by ¾-in.	50 gross box	16.000	0.80
In boxes over above sizes	value	5 per cent	....
Chlorate of Potash	picul	36.000	1.80
Emery and Glass Powder	"	2.400	0.12
Labels	value	5 per cent	....
Phosphorus	picul	70.000	3.50
Wax, Paraffin	"	10.000	0.50
Wood Shavings	"	2.200	0.11
Wood Splints	"	2.000	0.10
Metal Threads and Foil:			
Thread, Gold, Imitation, on Cotton	catty	3.000	0.15
Thread, Silver, Imitation, on Cotton	"	1.800	0.09
Thread, Gold and Silver, Imitation, on Silk	value	5 per cent	....

Name of Article	Agreed Value		Proposed Duty Rate Hk. Tls.
	Per	Hk. Tls.	
Tinfoil	picul	63.000	3.20
Sundry:			
Bamboo Baskets, Bamboo Blinds, and other Bamboo Ware	value	5 per cent	....
Coir Yarn	"	"	....
Cordage and Twine	"	"	....
Emery-cloth and Sand-paper (sheet not over 144 square inches)	ream	5.000	0.25
Furniture and other Woodware	value	5 per cent	....
Glue (not including Fish Glue)	picul	20.000	1.00
Glue, Cow, Refuse	"	20.000	1.00
Glue, Fish	"	75.857	3.80
India-rubber and Gutta-percha, Crude	value	5 per cent	....
Bent-wood Chairs	"	"	....
India-rubber, Old or Waste	"	"	....
Inks of all kinds	"	"	....
Insect Powder	"	"	....
Lampwick	picul	54.600	2.70
Leather Purses	gross	11.200	0.56
Machines, Sewing and Knitting	value	5 per cent	....
Mirrors	"	"	....
Moulding, Picture	"	"	....
Oakum	picul	12.600	0.63
Rope	value	5 per cent	....
Shoes and Boots	"	"	....
Starch	"	"	....
Sulphur	"	"	....
Tinder	picul	9.000	0.45
Worm Tablets, in Bottles, not over 60 pieces	dozen	0.740	0.037

UNENUMERATED GOODS

Unenumerated Goods	value	5 per cent	....

RULES

Rule I

Imports unenumerated in this Tariff will pay Duty at the rate of 5 per cent ad valorem; and the value upon which Duty is to be calculated shall be the wholesale market value of the goods in local currency. This market value when converted into Haikwan Taels shall be considered to be 12 per cent higher than the amount upon which Duty is to be calculated.

If the goods have been sold before presentation to the Customs of the Application to pay Duty, the gross amount of the *bonâ fide* contract will be accepted as evidence of the market value. Should the goods have been sold on c. f. and i. terms, that is to say, without inclusion in the price of Duty and other charges, such c. f. and i. price shall be taken as the value for Duty-paying purposes without the deduction mentioned in the preceding paragraph.

If the goods have not been sold before presentation to the Customs of the Application to pay Duty, and should a dispute arise between Customs and importer regarding the value or classification of goods, the case will be referred to a Board of Arbitration composed as follows:

An official of the Customs;
A merchant selected by the Consul of the importer; and
A merchant, differing in nationality from the importer, selected by the Senior Consul.

Questions regarding procedure, etc., which may arise during the sittings of the Board shall be decided by the majority. The final finding of the majority of the Board, which must be announced within fifteen days of the reference (not including holidays), will be binding upon both parties. Each of the two merchants on the Board will be entitled to a fee of Ten Haikwan Taels. Should the Board sustain the Customs valuation, or, in the event of not sustaining that valuation, should it decide that the goods have been undervalued by the importer to the extent of not less than 7½ per cent, the importer will pay the fees; if otherwise, the fees will be paid by the Customs. Should the Board decide that the correct value of the goods is 20 per cent (or more) higher than that upon which the importer originally claimed to pay Duty, the Customs authorities may retain possession of the goods until full Duty has been paid and may levy an additional Duty equal to four times the Duty sought to be evaded.

In all cases invoices, when available, must be produced if required by the Customs.

Rule II

The following will not be liable to Import Duty: Foreign Rice, Cereals, and Flour; Gold and Silver, both Bullion and Coin; Printed Books, Charts, Maps, Periodicals, and Newspapers.

A freight or part freight of Duty-free commodities (Gold and Silver Bullion and Foreign Coins excepted) will render the vessel carrying them, though no other cargo be on board, liable to Tonnage Dues.

Drawbacks will be issued for Ships' Stores and Bunker Coal when taken on board.

Rule III

Except at the requisition of the Chinese Government, or for sale to Chinese duly authorized to purchase them, Import trade is prohibited in all Arms, Ammunition, and Munitions of War of every description. No Permit to land them will be issued until the Customs have proof that the necessary authority has been given to the importer. Infraction of this rule will be punishable by confiscation of all the goods concerned. The import of Salt is absolutely prohibited.

APPENDIX V

RAILWAY CONCESSIONS IN CHINA HELD BY FOREIGN POWERS

British

1. British section of Hukuang Railways, Canton-Hankow, 250 miles uncompleted. The Hukang Loan under which this concession is held is for £6,000,000 to £10,000,000, bears interest at 5 per cent and was issued at 95. The loan contract is dated May 20, 1911.

2. Shasi-Hsingyi Railway System, about 600 miles in length, no work done. The loan contract embodying this concession was dated July 25, 1914, was for £10,000,000 at 5 per cent, and was signed with Messrs. Pauling & Company.

3. Nanking-Hunan Railway, about 500 miles from Nanking to Pinghsiang in Hunan with an additional 250 miles of branch line from Nanchang to Hangchow. The contract granting this concession was signed on March 31, 1914, calls for a loan of £8,000,000 at 5 per cent, including an advance of £500,000. No construction work on these lines has been done. British-Chinese Corporation Loan.

4. Pukow-Singyang Railway, about 350 miles in length, with an option for further extensions. The loan contract embodying this concession was signed on November 14, 1913, and calls for a loan of £3,000,000 at 5 per cent. British-Chinese Corporation Loan. No work done.

5. Pingyang-Tsinan Extension of the Peking Syndicate Railway. About 150 miles in length, with a western extension of about 100 miles. No work done.

6. Burma-Yunnan Railway, no details available.

7. Nanchang-Canton Railway, with extension to Swatow, probably 600 miles in all. The preferential right to build such a line was granted by the Chinese Foreign Office in a note to the British Legation dated August 25, 1914.

French

1. Yunnanfu-Limchow line, about 700 miles in all, and

2. Yunnan-Szechuan line, probably 600 to 700 miles long. The

loan contract embodying these concessions was signed with the Banque Industrielle de Chine on January 21, 1914, and calls for a loan of francs 600,000,000 at 5 per cent. No work done.

3. Chengtu-Tatung line, about 900 miles long. The contract for this line was signed with the Franco-Belgian Group in July, 1913. No definite figure for the loan was given, but the contractors estimate that it would cost about G. $120,000,000. No construction work done.

4. Lunghai line, about 500 miles to be completed on the western end, and 200 miles on the eastern end. The contract for this railway was signed with the Franco-Belgian Group in September, 1912. The contractors estimate that it will cost about francs 600,000,000 to complete the line. The central section of about 300 miles is complete and has been open to traffic for some years.

5. Kweichow-Chengtu line, about 350 miles in length, the French section of the Hukuang Railways, for details of which see British section above.

GERMAN

1. Hankow-Ichang section of the Hukuang Railways. About 300 miles in length, with a branch line northward which if extended to Honanfu would add 200 miles. For details of the Hukuang loan see British section above. Construction work in progress.

JAPANESE

1. Kirin-Kaiyang line, about 300 miles.
2. Changchun-Taonan line, about 200 miles.
3. Taonan-Jehol line, about 500 miles.
4. Point on above line to sea, about 100 miles.
5. Tsinanfu-Shunteh line (extension of Shantung Railway), about 150 miles.
6. Kaomi-Hsuchow line, about 200 miles.

   All of these are concessions supposed to have been granted under a loan made in September, 1918, providing for a loan of yen 150,000,000, of which yen 20,000,000 was advanced. The details of this loan have not been made public, and it is possible that it may have been for a larger amount and that subsequent advances against it may have been handed to the Chinese Government. No work has been done on any of these lines.

7. Kirin-Hweining line, about 277 miles in length. A contract for the construction of this line has been signed, which provided

for an advance to the Chinese Government of yen 10,000,000. This advance was made and is believed to have been spent for other purposes. It is estimated that the line will cost to construct about yen 10,000,000. There will therefore be a first charge against the line when constructed of approximately double its physical value.

8. Nanchang-Foochow line, about 300 miles. The Japanese have endeavored to secure a concession of this line but have met with a protest by the British who claim that it is in violation of the concession given the Pearsons for the Nanchang-Canton line mentioned above.

9. Kiukiang-Nanchang line, 87 miles in length. This line was built by Chinese with capital borrowed from the Taiwan Bank, amounting to yen 10,000,000, bearing interest at 7 per cent. The Chinese having defaulted on four consecutive interest payments, under the terms of the loan the Japanese are entitled to take possession. In order to prevent this an endeavor has been made to negotiate a loan with the Japanese of yen 60,000,000 for the nationalization of this line and the construction of the line to Foochow mentioned above.

Russian

1. Tsitsihar-Aigun line, about 400 miles, no details available.
2. Mogan-Harbin line, about 300 miles, no details available.
3. Mongolian Railways. The Russians have preferential rights for the construction of railways in Outer Mongolia. It is not believed that any detailed construction contracts exist.

American

1. Chinchow-Aigun line, about 1,000 miles. Concession for this line was granted, but owing to Russian and Japanese protests, no work thereunder has been attempted.
2. Suiyuan-Lanchow line, about 600 miles.
3. Hangchow-Wenchow line, about 150 miles.
4. Chuchow (Hunan) — Pakhoi, about 600 miles.
5. Hainan Island, about 175 miles.
6. Sinyang-Chengtu line, about 650 miles.

   The above lines are routes tentatively selected under the Siems-Carey contract which provides for the construction of 3,000 miles of railway. No construction work has been done.
7. Ichang-Kweichow line, about 200 miles, being the American section of the Hukuang Railways, for details of which see British section above. Construction work is in progress.

APPENDIX VI

PRINCIPAL UNDEVELOPED INDUSTRIAL CONCESSIONS IN CHINA OTHER THAN RAILWAYS HELD BY FOREIGN INTERESTS

British

1. Szechuan Mining Concession, granted to Pritchard Morgan about 1898, in connection with which a certain amount of prospecting work was done in 1900. No field work has been done since 1900, and it is probable that the concession has lapsed, although preferential rights might be claimed under it.

French

1. Pugow Development Loan, of francs 150,000,000, concluded with the Banque Industrielle de Chine, carrying interest at 5 per cent, secured on the public works to be carried out thereunder, on the Peking municipal taxes, and on the wine and tobacco tax north of the Yangtze. The loan was stated to be for the development of the Port of Pukow and for the construction of various public works in Peking. The loan was floated, but only a small portion of the proceeds were turned over to the Chinese Government.

Japanese

1. Hunan Mining Loan, nominal amount yen 5,000,000 of which only about Mex. $100,000 was paid over. This loan was negotiated by the Provincial Governor of Hunan with the Taiwan Bank and was secured on the Shuikoshan antimony mines. Great objection to the loan was displayed by the natives of Hunan, and it is probable that the advance will be repaid and the loan cancelled.

2. Fukien Mining Loan. There are no authentic details known in connection with this loan. It is believed to be for yen 5,000,000 and to have been secured on mining rights in Fukien. The Provincial Assembly protested the loan and unless the Central Government has formally sanctioned it, its validity must be considered doubtful.

3. Fenghuangshan Mining Loan. A concession for the working of the Fonghuangshan iron deposits was granted to a Chinese company prior to 1911. During the revolutionary disturbances of that year the company appears to have sold its rights to a Japanese group for Mex. $1,000,000. On discovery of this the Government cancelled the concession and refused to recognize any foreign interest. It is understood that in December, 1918, an effort was made to form a joint Sino-Japanese Company to repay the advance made and take over the concession. Japan is to have preferential rights in regard to the purchase of ore not required by the company.

4. Arms Loan and Iron Industry Loan. No authentic details are available in respect of either of these loans. It is believed that the former was for a considerable sum which was spent for military purposes and that the loan carried with it preferential rights in regard to the supply of arms and equipments to the Chinese army. The amount of the second is not known but is said to be "staggering." Presumably it carries with it the control of Chinese ore deposits and an agreement to supply to Japan a large percentage of the iron produced. Both of these loans are supposed to have been concluded by military officers acting ostensibly in the interests of national defense. They were negotiated during the autumn of 1918.

5. Communications Bank Loan. Two loans, one of yen 5,000,000 and the other of yen 20,000,000, were negotiated between this bank and the Japanes Industrial-Chosen-Taiwan Bank Group. They carry with them the option of making further loans to this Bank.

6. Bureau of Printing and Engraving Loan of yen 2,000,000 was negotiated in January, 1918, with Mitsui & Company, and carries with it preferential rights for the supply of materials.

7. Kirin Forestry Loan, signed between the Chinese Government and the Japanese Industrial-Chosen-Taiwan Group (acting through the Sino-Japanese Exchange Bank) for yen 30,000,000 at 7½ per cent secured on the forests and gold mines of the provinces of Kirin and Heilungkiang, and carrying with it the right to undertake conjointly with the Chinese Government the exploitation of the securities mentioned.

8. Telephone Loan, of yen 10,000,000, of which yen 3,000,000 was in repayment of an earlier loan. This loan is secured on the national telephone system and carries with it preferential

rights in regard to the appointment of advisers and probably in regard to the supply of materials. The authentic text is not available.

9. Wireless Loan. In November, 1917, a Danish firm (S. Larsen & Co.) concluded a contract with the Ministry of the Navy for the erection of a wireless plant at a cost of about £530,000. This contract was subsequently transferred to Japanese interests. Subsequently, during the autumn of 1918, these Japanese interests were supposed to have concluded a secret wireless loan, the details of which are not known, carrying with it a monopolistic concession for a commercial wireless service to Japan and America, and preferential rights for the supply of wireless materials. So far as the latter condition is concerned, the recent British Marconi contract appears to have rendered it null and void. It is reported that the Japanese holders of this concession have recently endeavored to secure the representation of certain American manufacturers of wireless apparatus.

American

1. Grand Canal Conservancy Loan of G. $6,000,000, of which $3,500,000 was taken up by American interests, and $2,500,000 by Japanese. The loan has not yet received the formal parliamentary ratification provided for in the contract, but an advance of $250,000 has been made to meet the expense of preliminary surveying work.

2. Wine and Tobacco Tax Loan, of G. $5,000,000 was negotiated with the Continental and Commercial Bank in the Spring of 1917, secured on the above tax, and carrying with it the option of further loans against the same security up to G. $25,000,000.

3. Chinese National Iron Industry. In the spring of 1917 certain American interests (Orient Mines Company) undertook the investigation of China's iron resources at the request of the Chinese Government with a view to the submission of a scheme for the development of a Chinese national iron industry financed by American capital. While it does not appear that any contracts have been executed, the whole circumstances of the matter are such as to give the United States a preferential interest in this matter.

German

1. Shantung Mining Rights. The German-Chinese Treaty of 1898 and the supplemental Shantung Railway contract granted to

German interests the right of developing mining properties in Shantung within thirty miles of the railroad. In addition to this, Article IV of the Treaty grants preferential rights for all manner of public works. There has recently come to light a further agreement between China and Germany whereby it was agreed that the exploitation of mines in certain specified areas should be substituted for the general rights mentioned in the treaty.

International

1. The Consortium (now consisting of the British, French and Japanese Groups) holds the option for a currency reform loan and any further reorganization loans. The United States Government, however, claims an individual and national interest in the currency reform loan by virtue of the early history of currency reform in China.

APPENDIX VII

CHINESE NATIONAL DEBT

General Statement, February, 1919

Long-term foreign debts	$1,145,550,000
Short-term foreign debts	67,920,345
Long-term domestic loans	221,523,095
Short-term domestic debts	14,584,514
Total, February, 1919	$1,449,577,954

Additions

Chicago (Continental and Commercial Bank) $	5,500,000
Pacific Company Tobacco Loan	5,500,000
8th Year domestic loan	56,000,000
Yokohama Specie Bank Advance	9,000,000
Total, March, 1920	$1,525,577,954

Total of Foreign Short-term Debts as of February 28, 1919

Kungfs. Taels	739,500.	Francs	22,594,348.75
Sh. Taels	427,316.19	Gold $	280,000.
$	2,639,034.09	Tientsin Taels	2,656,236.46
£	824,967. 2s 2d	Chuan Taels	28,615.15
Yen	41,423,676.24		

FOREIGN LONG-TERM DEBTS AS OF FEBRUARY 28, 1919

Name of Debt	Borrowing Date	Amount	Creditor
1895 4% Gold Loan	Aug. 6, 1895	Fr. 400,000,000	Russo-French Syndicate
1896 5% Gold Loan	March 23, 1896	£ 16,000,000	Anglo-German Syndicate
1898 4½% Gold Loan	March 1, 1898	£ 16,000,000	Anglo-German Syndicate
Crisp Loan	Aug. 30, 1912	£ 10,000,000 (only £5,000,000 paid)	C. Birch Crisp & Co., London
Reorganisation Loan	April 26, 1913	£ 25,000,000	Five Nation Bank Groups
Anglo-Chinese Loan	Feb. 14, 1914	£ 375,000	Anglo-Chinese Corporation
Industrial Loan.	Oct. 9, 1913	Fr. 150,000,000 (only Fr. 100,-000,000 paid)	Banque Industrielle de Chine
Chin-yu Advance.	May 16, 1914	Fr. 100,000,000 (only Fr. 32,-115,500 paid)	Banque Industrielle de Chine
Ko-ah Loan	Sept. 9, 1916	Yen 5,000,000	Ko-ah Co.
Chicago Bank Loan	Nov. 10, 1916	G.$ 5,000,000	Chicago Bank
Supplementary Reorganisation Loan, 1st Advance	Sept. 1, 1917	Yen 10,000,000	Yokohama Specie Bank
Supplementary Reorganisation Loan, 2d Advance	Jan. 6, 1918	Yen 10,000,000	Yokohama Specie Bank
Supplementary Reorganisation Loan, 3d Advance	July 10, 1918	Yen 10,000,000	Yokohama Specie Bank
Gold Mine and Forest Loan	Aug. 1, 1918	Yen 30,000,000	Japanese Bank Group
Participation Loan	Sept. 20, 1918	Yen 20,000,000	Japanese Bank Group
Boxer Indemnity.	Oct. 27, 1900	HK.$355,925,565	11 nations
Total		Fr. 30,958,068.91 G.$ 5,000,000.00 Yen 80,000,000.00 Fr. 317,666,999.00 £ 51,646,622.00 HK.$323,071,052.56	

FOREIGN SHORT-TERM DEBTS AS OF FEBRUARY 28, 1919

Creditor and Name	Country	Amount	Outstanding Principal	Rate of Interest	Security	Borrowing Date	Extinction Date
Tai-hei Co., Ammunitions Bills	Japan	Yen 1,821,760.00	Yen 302,609.19	7% per an.	Tobacco, Wine License Tax & Treasury Bills	1911	Sept., '19
Mitsui Bussan Kaisha, Ammunitions Bills	"	$ 1,935,331.00	$ 1,188,416.75	" " "	"	1912	Nov., '20
Mitsui Bussan Kaisha, Nanking Government Loan	"	Yen 2,000,000.00	Yen 1,505,250.00	" " "	"	Feb., '12	April, '20
Okura Co., Commercial Guarantee Bank Bills	"	T.T. 1,136,398.52	T.T. 1,100,177.40	3% per an.	Promissory Note	Feb., '18	Aug., '19
Yokohama Specie Bank, Students Abroad Loan . . .	"	Yen 100,000.00	Yen 100,000.00	7% per an.	Nil	April, '16	Oct., '19
Yokohama Specie Bank, Students Abroad Loan . . .	"	" 100,000.00	" 100,000.00	" " "	Nil	Nov., '17	Nov., '19
Sino-Japanese Industrial Co. Loan	"	" 2,000,000.00	" 2,000,000.00	" " mo.	Building and Machinery of Hankow Paper Mill	Nov., '16	Nov., '19
Japanese Group Flood Loan	"	" 5,000,000.00	" 5,000,000.00	" " an.	Annual Revenues of Lintsin To-lung-ting & Shia-hu-kow, about $900,000	Nov., '17	Nov., '19
Mitsui Bussan Co. Loan . .	"	" 2,000,000.00	" 2,000,000.00	8% " "	Property of Bureau of Engraving & Ptg.	Jan., '18	Jan., '21
Chosen Bank, Students Abroad Loan	"	" 150,000.00	" 150,000.00	Market Price	Nil	July, '18	July, '19
Chosen Bank, Students Abroad Loan	"	" 150,000.00	" 150,000.00	" "	Nil	Sept., '18	Sept., '19
Chosen Bank, Students Abroad Loan	"	" 200,000.00	" 200,000.00	" "	Nil	Dec., '18	Dec., '19
Tai-hei Co., 1st Ammunition Loan	"	" 17,395,817.05	" 17,395,817.05	Nil	Treasury Bills	Sept., '18	Feb., '20
Tai-hei Co., 2d Ammunition Loan	"	" 12,520,000.00	" 12,520,000.00	Nil	" "	Oct., '18	Jan., '20

FOREIGN SHORT-TERM DEBTS AS OF FEBRUARY 28, 1919—*Continued*

Creditor and Name	Country	Amount	Outstanding Principal	Rate of Interest	Security	Borrowing Date	Extinction Date
Banque Industrielle de Chine, Chin-yu advance P. N.	France	Fr. 7,217,094.75	Fr. 3,093,040.59	7% per an.	Promissory Note	May, '18	April, '19
Banque Industrielle de Chine, Commercial Guarantee Bank Bills	"	T.T. 801,184.06	" 801,184.05	Nil	"	Feb., '18	June, '26
Banque Industrielle de Chine, Ministry of Agricul ture Loan	"	$ 120,000.00	$ 120,000.00	Nil	"	June, '16	Mar., '19
Banque Industrielle de Chine, Students Abroad Advance	"	£ 10,000. 0. 0.	£ 10,000. 0. 0.	9½% per an.	Promissory Note	April, '18	April, '19
Banque Industrielle de Chine, Pukow Loan Interest	"	Fr. 601,308.16	Fr. 601,308.16	7% per an.	" "	Dec., '18	June, '19
Banque Industrielle de Chine, Capital	"	" 3,750,000.00	" 3,750,000.00	" " "	Treasury Bills	Feb., '18	May, '22
Banque Industrielle de Chine Loan	"	" 5,000,000.00	" 5,000,000.00	9% " "	Promissory Note	Jan., '19	Dec., '19
Banque Industrielle de Chine, Supplementary Loan	"	Fr. 5,000,000.00	" 5,000,000.00	9% per an.	"	Jan., '19	Dec., '19
Lunghai Railway Loan Interest	"	" 1,700,000.00	" 1,700,000.00	Nil	Nil	Jan., '19	Mar., '19
Banque de l'Indo-Chine, Tsu-kai-cha Debt, principal and interest	"	Sh.T. 99,735,34	Sh.T. 99,735.34	12% per an.	Salt Surplus	" "	July, '19
Armstrong Co., Ship Cost Bills	England	£ 198,883.19.08.	£ 95,000. 0. 0.	8% " "	Treasury Bills	1910	Aug., '19
Yunnan Syndicate, Treasury Bills	England France	£ 93,791. 8. 3.	" 33,791. 8. 3.	7% " "	" "	1909	Sept., '18
Samuel Co., Advance	England	K.T. 213,000.00	K.T. 213,000.00	8% " "	Nil	Feb., '16	
Hongkong & Shanghai Bank, Commercial Guarantee Bank Bills	"	T.T. 257,750.00	T.T. 257,750.00	Nil	Promissory Note	Feb., '18	Sept., '21
Marconi Wireless Co. Loan	"	£ 600,000. 0. 0.	£ 600,000. 0. 0.	8% per an.	Treasury Bills	Aug., '18	Aug., '28

FOREIGN SHORT-TERM DEBTS AS OF FEBRUARY 28, 1919—*Continued*

Creditor and Name	Country	Amount	Outstanding Principal	Rate of Interest	Security	Borrowing Date	Extinction Date
British Flagship Indemnity Chungking	England	Ch.T. 65,815.15	Ch.T. 26,615.15	Nil	Treasury Bills	Jan., '18	June, '18
Russo-Asiatic Bank, Lunghua Tannery Bills	Russia	$ 1,446,444.60	$ 270,000.00	7% per an.	" "	1912	Nov., '19
Russo-Asiatic Bank, Education Ministry Loan	"	K.T. 300,000.00	K.T. 200,000.00	7½% per mo.	Nil	Dec., '15	Aug., '19
Russo-Asiatic Bank, Commercial Guarantee Bank Bills	"	T.T. 509,542.50	T.T. 499,125.00	8% per an.	Promissory Note	Feb., '18	Sept., '21
Russo-Asiatic Bank, Board of Audit Building Loan	"	K.T. 120,000.00	K.T. 120,000.00	" " "	Nil	May, '16	Nov., '18
Russo-Asiatic Bank, Students Abroad Loan	"	" 113,500.00	" 56,500.00	" " "	Treasury Bills	Mar., '17	July, '19
Russo-Asiatic Bank, Education Ministry Loan	"	" 150,000.00	" 150,000.00	5% per mo.	Dividend of Russo-Asiatic Bank	Sept., '18	Sept., '19
Standard Oil Co., Payment	U. S. A.	$ 543,703.89	$ 60,617.34	6% per an.	Treasury Bills	Mar., '17	Feb., '19
American Intl. Corporation, Conservancy Advance	"	G.$ 250,000.00	G. $ 250,000.00	8% " "	" "	May, '18	May, '19
Intl. Banking Corporation, Students Abroad Advance	"	G.$ 30,000.00	" 30,000.00	" " "	Nil	Dec., '18	Mar., '19
Banque Belge pour l'Etranger, Treasury Bills	Belgium	Sh.T. 677,580.85	Sh.T. 327,580.85	7% " "	Treasury Bills	Jan., '17	Dec., '17
Banque Belge pour l'Etranger. Students Abroad Loan	Belgium	£ 37,097. 1. 3	£ 6,675.13.11.	8% per an.	Nil	June, '16	Mar., '19
Yi-Ping Co., Education Ministry Loan	"	$ 200,000.00	$ 200,000.00	9% " "	Nil	1916	1936
Ansaldo Ship Works, Cost Bills	Italy	£ 86,000. 0. 0.	£ 79,500. 0. 0.			1910	
Kuhara Co., Advance	Japan	$ 300,000.00	$ 300,000.00			Jan., '19	
Banque Industrielle de Chine	France	Fr. 4,300,000.00	Fr. 4,300,000.00	5% " "	Treasury Bills	1919	May, '25
Eight Banks Repatriation Loan	6 nations	$ 500,000.00	$ 500,000.00	8% " "	Salt Surplus	Jan., '19	Dec., '19

SHORT- AND LONG-TERM DOMESTIC DEBTS AS OF FEBRUARY 28, 1919

Name	Actual Amount of Loan Made	Amount Still Due	Rate of interest, per cent	Security	Date Commencing Loan	Date Clearing Loan	Explanation
8% Military Loan	$7,371,150	$3,371,150	8	Land Tax	1912 February, 1st year of the Republic	1918 February, 7th year of the Republic	Redemption of Bonds amounting to $4,000,000 has been made three times. The loan has been extended for two years and supplementary coupons were issued. The fourth payment of principal should have been made in February, 1919, but, owing to the lack of funds in Treasury, it was not carried out. Payment for interest has been made 15 times.
Patriotic Loan	$1,646,790	$656,790	6	National Treasury	1912 1st year of the Republic	1920 November, 9th year of the Republic	Three payments of principal have been made. Payment for interest has been made 15 times.

SHORT-AND-LONG-TERM DOMESTIC DEBTS AS OF FEBRUARY 28, 1919—*Continued.*

Name	Actual amount of loan made	Amount still due	Rate of interest per cent	Security	Date commencing loan	Date clearing loan	Explanation
1st Year 6% Domestic Loan	$81,670,570	$81,670,570	6	Whole Country's Title deeds Tax and Stamp Tax	1914 3d year of the Republic	1943 32d year of the Republic	The first payment of principal should be made by drawing bonds in December, 1919. Payment for interest has been made 11 times.
3d Year Internal Loan	$24,926,110	$19,432,335	6	Surplus of Kin-Han Ry. after it was mortgaged the 4th time	1914 August, 3d year of the Republic	1915 December, 4th year of the Republic	Redemption for this loan has been made twice. Payment for interest has been made 10 times.
4th Year Internal Loan	$25,829,965	$21,946,875	6	Customs dues not mortgaged, Revenue of the Tax Office at Chaipeh of Kalgan, and province of Shansi	1915 April, 4th year of the Republic	1923 February, 12th year of the Republic	Redemption for this loan has been made once. Payment for interest has been made nine times. The second payment of principal amounting to $4,133,000 should have been made on February 15th of the 8th year. The drawing of bonds has not been taking place, due to the fact that the revenue of likin stations has not reached the required amount.

SHORT-AND-LONG-TERM DOMESTIC DEBTS AS OF FEBRUARY 28, 1919—*Continued.*

Name	Actual amount of loan made	Amount still due	Rate of interest per cent	Security	Date commencing loan	Date clearing loan	Explanation
5th Year Internal Loan	$7,770,515	$7,770,515	6	Annual Revenue of the public sale of Tobacco and Wine of the whole country	1916 April, 5th year of the Republic	1922 September, 11th year of the Republic	Payment for interest has been made seven times for this loan. The period for payment of principal has been extended two years and half through request and approval. The first payment will be made in March of 1920 and the last payment in September of the 11th year.
7th Year Short-term Domestic Loan	$48,000,000	$33,600,000	6	Deferred Boxer Indemnity	1918 7th year of the Republic	1922 December, 11th year of the Republic	Redemption for this loan has been made three times. Payment for interest has been made three times.
7th Year 6% Domestic Loan	$45,000,000	$45,000,000	6	2d mortgage of the Revenue of Customs	1918 7th year of the Republic	1937 December, 26th year of the Republic	Payment of interest has been made three times for this loan.

APPENDIX VIII

EXTRACTS FROM THE JAPANESE COMMERCIAL CODE

The Application of Law

1

In case there is no provision in this Code as to a commercial matter, the customary commercial law shall apply, or if there is no such customary law, the Civil Code shall apply.

2

The provisions of this Code apply to commercial transactions of public juridical persons only if not otherwise provided by law or regulation.

3

If a transaction is a commercial one with regard to one party thereto, the provisions of this Code apply to all parties.

Traders

4

A trader in the sense of this Code is a person who in his own name carries on commercial transactions as a business.

5

When a minor or a married woman carries on a commercial business, registration must be made.

6

A minor or a married woman, who has been permitted to become a partner with unlimited liability of a company, is treated as a person of full capacity as to the business of such company.

7

When a guardian carries on a commercial business for his ward, registration must be made.

A restriction on the right of representation of the guardian cannot be set up against third persons acting in good faith.

8

The provisions relating to commercial registration, trade names and trade books do not apply to persons who buy and sell things as pedlars or on the streets or to other petty traders.

Commercial Registration

9

Facts required to be registered according to the provisions of this Code are registered on the application of the person concerned in the Commercial Register kept by the court of his seat of business.

10

Facts required to be registered at the place of a principal office must also be registered at the place of every branch office, except as otherwise provided by this Code.

11

Facts entered in the Commercial Register must without delay be published by the Court.

12

A fact to be registered cannot be set up against third persons acting in good faith, until after it has been registered and published; and not even then against third persons who for a just cause were ignorant of such fact.

13

When a fact to be registered at the place of a branch office has not been registered, the provisions of the preceding article apply only to business transacted at such branch office.

14

A registration may be set up against third persons, even though it differs from the publication.

15

If any alteration takes place in a fact registered, or if such fact ceases to exist, such alteration or cessation must without delay be registered by the persons concerned.

Trade Names

16

A trader may use his family name or his full name or any other denomination as his trade name.

17

In the trade name of a company the word *gōmeikwaisha* or *gōshiwaisha* or *kabushikikwaisha* or *kabushikigōshikwaisha* must be used according to the nature of the company.

18

Where no company exists, no word indicating the existence of a company must be used in the trade name. This applies also when the business of a company is taken over by another person.

A person who acts in contravention of the provisions of the foregoing paragraph is liable to a fine of from five yen to fifty yen.

19

A trade name which is already registered for another person cannot be registered in the same city, town or village for the same business.

20

A person who has his trade name registered may demand against any one using the same or a similar trade name for the purpose of improper competition, that he discontinue such use; but this does not affect any claim for damages.

A person who uses the registered trade name of another in the same city, town or village for the same business is presumed to do so for the purpose of improper competition.

21

The assignment of a trade name can be set up against third persons only if it is registered.

22

When a person has assigned his business together with the trade name, he is, unless the parties concerned have expressed a different intention, not allowed for a period of twenty years to carry on the same business in the same city, town or village.

If the person assigning expressly contracts not to carry on the same business, such contract has effect only for the same *Fu* or *Ken*[1] and only for a period not exceeding thirty years.

The person assigning is irrespective of the provisions of the preceding two paragraphs not allowed to carry on the same business for the purpose of improper competition.

23

The provisions of the preceding article apply correspondingly where the business alone is assigned.

24

When a person for whom a trade name is registered has given

[1] *Ken*, corresponds most nearly to an English "county." *Fu* is a city excluded from the *ken*, in which the city government performs the functions of a *ken* government. There are only three *fu*, namely, Tokyo, Kyoto and Osaka.

up such trade name or has changed it without having registered such fact, any party interested may apply to the court for the cancellation of such registration.

In such case the court must summon the person for whom the registration was made to present his objections within a reasonable time to be fixed by the court. If no objection is made within such time, the registration must be forthwith cancelled by the court.

Trade Books

25

A trader must keep books and record therein accurately and clearly his daily dealings and all circumstances affecting his property. As to household expenses only the total monthly amount need be entered.

As to the dealings of a retail business, only the total amount of each day's sales may be entered, separating cash sales and credit sales.

26

At the time when a trader commences business, or when the formation of a company is registered, and once in each year at a fixed time, a general inventory of movables and immovables, of credits and debts and of other property as well as a balance-sheet must be made and entered in a book specially kept for such purpose.

In the inventory a valuation must be inserted of the movables and immovables and of the credits and other property as at the time of making the inventory.

27

If a company distributes profits twice a year or oftener, it must make an inventory and balance-sheet according to the provisions of the preceding article at the time of each distribution.

28

A trader must preserve his trade books and business correspondence for a period of ten years.

Such period is to be computed for a trade book from the time when it is closed.

Trade Assistants

29

A trader may appoint a procurator to carry on his business either at the principal office or at a branch office.

30

A procurator is authorized to do in the place of the principal all transactions in or out of court relating to the principal's business.

A procurator may appoint and dismiss *banto,*[2] clerks and other assistants.

Any limitation of the power of representation of a procurator cannot be set up against third persons acting in good faith.

31

The principal must register the appointment of a procurator and the termination of his power of representation at the place of the principal office or the branch office for which he is appointed.

32

Without the permission of the principal a procurator is not allowed to do commercial transactions on his own account or on that of a third person, or to become a partner with unlimited liability of a company.

If a procurator in violation of the foregoing provisions undertakes a commercial transaction on his own account, the principal may consider such transaction as done on his account.

This right of the principal ceases, if it is not exercised for two weeks from the time when the principal receives notice of such transaction, or if a year has elapsed since the time of the transaction.

33

A trader may appoint a *banto* or a clerk for particular parts of, or for specially fixed matters relating to his business.

A *banto* or a clerk is authorized to do all acts relating to the matters entrusted to him.

34

Assistants other than procurators, *banto* or clerks are presumed not to be authorized to do juristic acts in the place of the principal.

35

By the provisions of this chapter the application of the provisions of the Civil Code as to the relations arising from the hiring between the principal and trade assistants is not affected.

---

[2] The word *bantō* is generally used in the former treaty ports of Japan, and denotes what in German would be called "*Handlungsbevollmächtigter.*"

Commercial Agents

36

A commercial agent [3] is a person who, without being an assistant, habitually acts on behalf of a particular trader as his representative or intermediary in commercial transactions belonging to the branch of business of such trader.

37

When a commercial agent has acted as representative or intermediary in a commercial transaction, he must without delay give notice thereof to the principal.

38

Without the permission of the principal, a commercial agent is not allowed to do on his own account or on that of a third person commercial transactions falling within the kind of business carried on by the principal, or to become a partner with unlimited liability of a company whose object is the same kind of business.

If a commercial agent acts in contravention of these provisions the provisions of Art. 32, 2 and 3 apply correspondingly.

39

When a commercial agent has been entrusted with the sale of goods, he is entitled to receive any notice relating to a defect in the goods sold or a deficiency in their quantity and to the performance of the sale.

40

When the time of duration of the contract has not been fixed by the parties, it may be terminated by either party on a two months' notice.

Irrespective of whether a time of duration has been fixed or not, the contract may be terminated at any time by either party, if an unavoidable necessity exists for doing so.

41

Unless a different intention has been expressed, a commercial agent has a right of retention against all property whose possession he holds on account of the principal, for all obligations arising in his favour from his acting as representative or as intermediary in commercial transactions.

---

[3] In the English Law the word "agent" has a much wider meaning.

Partnerships

62

Partners who are to represent the partnership are authorized to do all acts in or out of court relating to the business of the partnership.

The provisions of Arts. 44, 1 and 54 of the Civil Code apply correspondingly to ordinary partnerships.

Stock

147

Certificates of shares cannot be issued before registration according to the provisions of Art. 141, 1 has been made at the place of the principal office.

Certificates issued in contravention of this provision are invalid; but this does not affect the right to claim damages against the persons who have issued such certificates.

149

Unless it is otherwise provided by the company contract, a share may be assigned to another person without the assent of the company. Such assignment or a previous promise of assignment, however, cannot be made until registration according to the provisions of Art. 141, 1 is made at the place of the principal office.

150

The assignment of a name-share cannot be set up against the company or any other third person, unless the name and domicile of the assignee is entered in the list of shareholders and his name inserted in the certificate.

155

When the whole amount of the share has been paid up, a shareholder may require his certificate to be made out to bearer.

Debentures

206

The assignment of a name-debenture cannot be set up against the company or against any other third person, unless the name and domicile of the assignee have been entered in the debenture list and his name inserted in the debenture.

207

The provisions of Art. 155 apply correspondingly to debentures.

Capital Issues

217

The company must register the following particulars at the place of the principal office and of each branch office within two weeks from the day of the ending of the general meeting of shareholders convened in accordance with the provisions of Art. 213, namely:—

1. The whole amount of the capital increased;
2. The date of the resolution to increase the capital;
3. The amount paid in upon each new share;
4. If preference shares have been issued, the rights of their holders.

Until registration in accordance with the foregoing provisions has been made at the place of the principal office, no certificate for the new shares may be issued, and no assignment of them nor a previous promise of assignment may be made.

Foreign Companies

255

A foreign company which sets up a branch office in Japan must make the same registrations and public notifications as companies of the same kind or of the kind most resembling it, existing in Japan.

In addition a foreign company which sets up a branch office in Japan must appoint a representative residing in Japan, and must register his name and domicile at the same time with the registration of the branch office.

The provisions of Art. 62 apply correspondingly to a representative of a foreign company.

256

If particulars which are to be registered according to the provisions of Art. 255, 1 and 2 happen in a foreign country, the period for their registration is computed from the time when notice thereof arrives.

257

When a foreign company first sets up a branch office in Japan, other persons may disregard the existence of the company, until it has been registered at the place of such branch office.

258

A company which sets up its principal office in Japan or which makes it its principal object to carry on business in Japan, must, even though it is formed in a foreign country, comply with the same provisions as a company formed in Japan.

259

The provisions of Arts. 147, 149, 150, 155, 1, 206, 207 and 217, 2 apply correspondingly to the issue of shares and to the assignment of shares or debentures of a foreign company in Japan. In that case such branch office as is first set up in Japan is deemed to be the principal office.

260

When a representative of a foreign company which has set up a branch office in Japan commits as to the affairs of such company an act contrary to the public welfare or to good morals, the court may upon application of the public procurator or of its own motion order such branch office to be closed.

Extract from a Legal Opinion by a Foreign Attorney in Japan

A foreign corporation establishing a branch here must pay the same taxes as a Japanese corporation—that is, a business tax and an income tax on the profits. Such taxes are only on the business done in Japan and the profits earned here. There are no taxes on the capital of the corporation and the business done elsewhere. The corporation can, of course, sue and be sued in its own name, and enter into contracts in its own name, and has practically the same powers as a domestic corporation. The registration of a branch is comparatively simple, except in the case of banking and insurance companies, when it is extremely difficult.

As to the advisability of incorporation under the laws of Japan, from what has been said it will be seen that a domestic corporation does have some advantages which a foreign corporation does not, but in respect to the ownership of ships, even a Japanese corporation the majority of shareholders of which are foreigners, cannot own ships registered under Japanese law. In the matter of taxation they stand on an equal footing, except that, of course, a foreign corporation paying the tax in Japan might also find that it had to pay a tax on these profits in the country where it was incorporated, thus being subject to a double taxation. If it was incorporated under the laws of Japan, this might be avoided.

There is one practical disadvantage of the Japanese corporation composed of foreigners, and that is that while it is legally a Japanese juridical person and must look to Japan for the protection of its interests abroad, say, for instance, in Russia, and while this protection will be given, it will not be given with the same enthusiasm as in the case where the shareholders are Japanese. In other words, such a corporation is similar to a half-caste and is regarded in very much the same way.

The necessary documents to be supplied by any corporation desiring to register a branch in Japan are as follows:—(1) Certified copy of the certificate of incorporation; (2) certified copy of the resolution of the board of directors authorising the establishment of a branch and the appointment of a representative; (3) affidavit containing certain information; (4) power of attorney authorizing registration; (5) general power of attorney conferring powers on the representative.

All these papers must bear the certificate of the Japanese Consulate to the effect that the notary or other official before whom the acknowledgment is made is a properly authorised notary.

APPENDIX IX

THE INDIAN MERCHANDISE MARKS MANUAL

Introductory Note

The manual is in the following parts:

I. Extracts from the Indian Merchandise Marks Act, and connected Acts.

II. Notifications under the same.

III. General Instructions.

In the Instructions the following classification of goods is adopted:

A. Goods having applied to them counterfeit trade marks or other indications that they are the manufacture or merchandise of a *person* whose manufacture or merchandise they are not.

B. Goods having applied to them false trade descriptions or other indications in respect of the *country* in which they were made or produced.

C. Goods having applied to them false trade descriptions that are false in other respects.

D. Piece-goods which have not the length properly stamped on each piece.

Class B is further subdivided into:

(a) Goods made or produced in a foreign country, that is, beyond the limits of the United Kingdom and British India, and bearing or purporting to bear *the name or trade mark* of any person who is a manufacturer, dealer or trader in British India or the United Kingdom.

(b) Goods made or produced beyond the limits of the United Kingdom or British India, to which is applied *a false trade description or indication* (other than the name or trade mark of a manufacturer, dealer or trader in the United Kingdom or British India) indicating that they were made or produced in the United Kingdom or British India.

(c) Goods made or produced in one foreign country but bearing a *false trade description* indicating that they were made or produced in another.

PART I.—PRINCIPAL PROVISIONS OF THE INDIAN MERCHANDISE MARKS ACT, 1889, AND CONNECTED ACTS RELATING TO MERCHANDISE MARKS.

Sea Customs Act, 1878, section 18.—No goods specified in the following clauses shall be brought, whether by land or sea, into British India:

(d) Goods having applied thereto a counterfeit trade mark within the meaning of the Indian Penal Code, or a false trade description within the meaning of the Indian Merchandise Marks Act, 1889.

(e) Goods made or produced beyond the limits of the United Kingdom and British India, and having applied thereto any name or trade mark being, or purporting to be, the name or trade mark of any person who is a manufacturer, dealer or trader in the United Kingdom or in British India, unless

(1) the name or trade mark is, as to every application thereof, accompanied by a definite indication of the goods having been made or produced in a place beyond the limits of the United Kingdom and British India, and

(2) the country in which that place is situated is in that indication indicated in letters as large and conspicuous as any letter in the name or trade mark, and in the same language and character as the name or trade mark.

(f) Piece-goods, such as are ordinarily sold by length or by the piece, which

(1) have not conspicuously stamped in English numerals on each piece the length thereof in standard yards, or in standard yards and a fraction of such yard, according to the real length of the piece, and

(2) have been manufactured beyond the limits of India, or

(3) having been manufactured within those limits, have been manufactured beyond the limits of British India in premises which, if they were in British India, would be a factory as defined in the Indian Factories Act, 1881.

Note.—For definition of piece-goods, see Part II.

Indian Merchandise Marks Act, 1889, section 2 (1).—Trade Mark has the meaning assigned to that expression in section 478 of the Indian Penal Code as amended by this Act.

Indian Penal Cole, section 478.—A mark used for denoting that goods are the manufacture or merchandise of a particular person is called a trade mark, and for the purposes of this Code the expression "trade mark" includes any trade mark which is registered in the register of trade marks kept under the Patents, Designs and Trade Marks Act, 1883, and any trade mark which, either with or without registration, is protected by law in any British possession or foreign State to which the provisions of the one hundred and third section of the Patents, Designs and Trade Marks Act, 1883, are, under Order in Council, for the time being applicable.

Indian Penal Code, section 28.—A person is said to "counterfeit" who causes one thing to resemble another thing intending by means of that resemblance to practise deception, or knowing it to be likely that deception will thereby be practised.

Explanation 1.—It is not essential to counterfeiting that the imitation should be exact.

Explanation 2.—When a person causes one thing to resemble another, and the resemblance is such that a person might be deceived thereby, it shall be presumed until the contrary is proved, that the person so causing the one thing to resemble the other thing intended by means of that resemblance to practise deception or knew it to be likely that deception would thereby be practised.

Indian Merchandise Marks Act, 1889, section 2 (2).—"Trade description" means any description, statement or other indication, direct or indirect,—

(a) as to the number, quantity, measure, gauge or weight of any goods, or

(b) as to the place or country in which, or the time at which, any goods were made or produced, or

(c) as to the mode of manufacturing or producing any goods, or

(d) as to the material of which any goods are composed, or

(e) as to any goods being the subject of any existing patent, privilege, or copyright;

and the use of any numeral, word or mark which according to the custom of the trade is commonly taken to be an indication of any of the above matters shall be deemed to be a trade description within the meaning of this Act.

(3) "False trade description" means a trade description which is untrue in a material respect as regards the goods to which it

is applied, and includes every alteration of a trade description, whether by way of addition, effacement or otherwise, where that alteration makes the description untrue in a material respect, and the fact that a trade description is a trade mark or part of a trade mark shall not prevent such trade description being a false trade description within the meaning of this Act.

Indian Merchandise Marks Act, 1889, section 4 (1).—The provisions of this Act respecting the application of a false trade description to goods or respecting goods to which a false trade description is applied, shall extend to the application to goods of any such numerals, words or marks, or arrangement or combination thereof, whether including a trade mark or not, as are or is reasonably calculated to lead persons to believe that the goods are the manufacture or merchandise of some person other than they really are, and to goods having such numerals, words or marks, or arrangement or combination, applied thereto.

(2) The provisions of this Act respecting the application of a false trade description to goods, or respecting goods to which a false trade description is applied, shall extend to the application to goods of any false name or initials of a person, and to goods with the false name or initials of a person applied in like manner as if such name or initials were a trade description, and for the purpose of this enactment the expression false name or initials means, as applied to any goods, any name or initials—

(*a*) not being a trade mark, or part of a trade mark, and

(*b*) being identical with, or a colourable imitation of, the name or initials of a person carrying on business in connection with goods of the same description and not having authorised the use of such name or initials.

(3) A trade description which denotes or implies that there are contained in any goods to which it is applied more yards, feet or inches than there are contained therein standard yards, standard feet or standard inches is a false trade description.

Sea Customs Act, 1878, section 19-A (3).—Where there is on any goods a name which is identical with, or a colourable imitation of, the name of a place in the United Kingdom or British India, that name, unless accompanied in equally large and conspicuous letters and in the same language and character, by the name of the country in which such place is situate, shall be treated for the purpose of section 18 . . . as if it were the name of a place in the United Kingdom or British India.

Indian Merchandise Marks Acts, 1889, section 5 (2).—A trade description shall be deemed to be applied whether it is woven, impressed or otherwise worked into or annexed or affixed to the goods or any covering, label, reel or other thing.

(3) The expression "covering" includes any stopper, cask, bottle, vessel, box, cover, capsule, case, frame or wrapper, and the expression "label" includes any band or ticket.

Indian Merchandise Marks Act, 1889, section 2 (4).—"Goods" means anything which is the subject of trade or manufacture.

(5) "Name" includes any abbreviation of a name.

General Clauses Act, 1897, section 3 (39).—"Person" shall include any company or association or body of individuals, whether incorporated or not.

Indian Merchandise Marks Act, 1889, section 21.—In the case of goods brought into British India by sea, evidence of the port of shipment shall, in a prosecution for an offence against this Act or section 18 of the Sea Customs Act, 1878, as amended by this Act, be *primâ facie* evidence of the place or country in which the goods were made or produced.

Indian Merchandise Marks Act, 1889, section 21.—An officer of the Government whose duty it is to take part in the enforcement of this Act shall not be compelled in any Court to say whence he got any information as to the commission of any offence against this Act.

Sea Customs Act, 1878, section 19-A.—Clauses (2), (4), (5), (6) enable the Governor-General in Council to make regulations respecting the conditions, if any, to be fulfilled before such detention and confiscation, to determine the information, notices and security to be given, the evidence requisite for any of the purposes of the section and the mode of verification of such evidence, as well as the reimbursement of public officers and the State by an informant for expenses and damages incurred in respect of any detention made on his information, and of any proceedings resulting therefrom. Section 19-A (1) authorises the Customs authorities to require regulations so issued to be complied with before taking proceedings.

Indian Merchandise Marks Act, 1889, section 16 (1).—The Governor-General in Council may, by notification in the *Gazette of India* and in local official Gazettes, issue instructions for observance by Criminal Courts in giving effect to any of the provisions of this Act.

(2) Instructions under sub-section (1) may provide, among

other matters, for the limits of variation, as regards number, quantity, measure, gauge or weight, which are to be recognized by Criminal Courts as permissible in the case of any goods.

Note.—Such instructions are also a guide to Customs officers.

Indian Merchandise Marks Act, 1889, section 19.—For the purposes of section 12 of this Act and clause *(f)* of section 18 of the Sea Customs Act, 1878, as amended by this Act, the Governor-General in Council may, by notification in the *Gazette of India,* declare what classes of goods are included in the expression "piece-goods" such as are ordinarily sold by length or by the piece.

Indian Merchandise Marks Act, 1889, section 20.—This section enables the Governor-General in Council to make rules regulating with respect to any goods the first selection and testing of samples, the value of the evidence so obtained, the conditions under which a further selection and testing may be made, and the value of the further evidence so obtained.

For goods not covered by such rules the section enables Customs officers to issue orders having a similar effect, namely:

(2) The . . . officer of Customs . . . having occasion to ascertain the number, quantity, measure, gauge or weight of the goods, shall, by order in writing, determine the number of samples to be selected and tested and the manner in which the samples are to be selected.

(3) The average of the results of the testing in pursuance of . . . an order under sub-section (2) shall be *primâ facie* evidence of the number, quantity, measure, gauge or weight, as the case may be, of the goods.

(4) If a person having any claim to, or in relation to, any goods of which samples have been selected and tested in pursuance of . . . an order under sub-section (2) desires that any further samples of the goods be selected and tested, they shall, on his written application and on the payment in advance by him to the . . . officer of Customs . . . of such sums for defraying the cost of the further selection and testing as the . . . officer may from time to time require, be selected and tested to such an extent as . . . the officer of Customs may determine in the circumstances to be reasonable, the samples being selected in manner prescribed under . . . sub-section (2). . . .

(5) The average of the results of the testing referred to in sub-section (3) and of the further testing under sub-section (4) shall be conclusive proof of the number, quantity, gauge or weight, as the case may be, of the goods.

Part II.—Notifications Under the Indian Merchandise Marks Act, 1889, and Connected Acts.

No. 1430, dated the 6th April, 1891, as subsequently amended.— In exercise of the powers conferred by section 19-A, sub-section (2), of the Sea Customs Act, 1878 (as amended by section 11 of the Indian Merchandise Marks Act, 1889), and sections 19 and 20 of the Indian Merchandise Marks Act, 1889 (as amended by Act IX of 1891), the Governor-General in Council is pleased to make the subjoined rules and orders:

1. Piece-goods, such as are ordinarily sold by length or by the piece, shall be deemed to include woollen goods of all kinds and the undermentioned descriptions of cotton goods, namely:

Book-binding cloth.
Brocades.
Cambrics.
Canvas.
Crimps.
Checks, spots and stripes.
Chudders.
Coatings including tweeds, cashmeres and serges.
Crape.
Denims.
Dhotis, single or in pairs.
Domestics.
Dorias.
Drills.
Flannel and flannelettes.
Gauze.
Grenadines.
Harvards.
Italian cloth.
Jaconets.
Jeans.
Lappets.
Lawns, including allovers.
Lenos.
Long cloth.
Madapollams.
Meltons, dyed and printed.
Mulls.
Muslins.
Nainsooks.
Net.
Oxfords.
Printers.
Prints.
Saris, single or in pairs.
Scarves, including cotton shawls and dupetas.
Sheetings.
Shirtings, including dyed shirtings.
Silecia.
Spanish stripes.
Tanjibs.
Ticks.
Trouserings.
Tussores.
Twills.
T-cloth and Mexicans.
Umbrella cloth.
Velvets and velveteen.
Venetian cloth.
Vestings, including mattings and piques.
Waist coatings.
Zephyr cloth.

2. Other classes of piece-goods shall not be detained if unstamped; and unstamped cotton and woollen piece-goods imported for the personal use of individuals or private associations of individuals and not for trade purposes shall not be detained.

3. Examinations of packages to ascertain whether the goods mentioned in Rule 1 are stamped shall be made at frequent inter-

vals at the discretion of the Customs Collector and either under his personal instructions or under general orders and instructions given by him to an Assistant Collector.

4. The piece-goods contained in the packages so examined need not be examined, when found to be stamped, to test the accuracy of the stamping, except on information received, or when the Customs Collector has reason to suspect that the stamping is false.

5. All measurements of piece-goods shall be made on the table.

6. Yarns need not be examined or measured, except on information received, or when the Collector has reason to suspect that the trade description is false.

7. An examination of yarns to test the accuracy of the description of count or length shall be made, in the first instance, up to the limit of one bundle in every one hundred bales or fraction of one hundred bales in the consignment.

8. If, on such examination, the difference between the average count or length, and the described count or length is in excess of the variations permitted in paragraphs III and IV of the Notification of the Government of India in the Home Department, No. 1474 (Judicial), dated the 13th November, 1891, the importer may require a further examination to be made up to the limit and on the condition stated in Rule 9.

9. The test to determine length of yarns shall be applied as follows:

From every one hundred bales, or fraction of 100 bales, in a consignment one bundle should be selected at random. The hanks in this bundle should then be measured on the wrap-reel, one after the other, in the presence of a representative of the importer, and the lengths noted, the process being continued (within the limits of the bundle) until either the importer is satisfied that the yarn is short, or the average of the lengths noted shows that it is of full length.

When the importer is dissatisfied with this test, he may, on payment of the cost, require the Customs Collector to measure more hanks up to 1 per cent of the total number of hanks in the consignment, such hank being taken at random by an officer of Customs out of any bundles in the consignment.

10. The Customs Collector may require from any informant a security not exceeding five hundred rupees. If the Collector should be satisfied that the information given is wilfully false, the security shall be forfeited.

No. 1474, dated the 13th November, 1891, as subsequently amended.—In exercise of the powers conferred by section 16 of the Indian Merchandise Marks Act, IV of 1889, and in supersession of all existing orders on the subject, the Governor-General in Council directs that Criminal Courts, in giving effect to the provisions of the Act in respect of trade descriptions of quantity, measure, or weight of the goods specified hereunder, shall observe the following instructions:

I.—A trade description of length stamped on *grey, white* or *coloured cotton piece-goods* shall not be deemed to be false in a material respect, unless

(*a*) where a single length is stamped, the description exceeds the actual length by more than

4 inches in pieces stamped as 10 yards long and under;
5 inches in pieces stamped as above 10 yards and up to 23 yards long;
7 inches in pieces stamped as above 23 yards and up to 36 yards long;
9 inches in pieces stamped as above 36 yards and up to 47 yards long;
18 inches in pieces stamped as above 47 yards long:

Provided that the average length of the goods in question shall not be less than the stamped length;

(*b*) where a maximum and a minimum length are stamped, the described maximum length is greater than the actual length by more than

9 inches in piece-goods under 35 yards long;
18 inches in piece-goods 35 yards and up to 47 yards long;
36 inches in piece goods above 47 yards long:

Provided that no such piece shall measure less than the minimum stamped length.

II.—A trade description of width stamped on *grey, white,* or *coloured cotton piece-goods* shall not be deemed to be false in a material respect, unless the description exceeds the actual width by

half an inch in pieces stamped as 40 inches or less in width;
three-quarters of an inch in pieces stamped as over 40 inches or under 59 inches in width;
one inch in pieces stamped as 59 inches or more in width:

Provided that the average width of the goods in question shall not be less than the stamped width.

III.—A trade description of count or number, length or weight, applied to *grey,* or *bleached cotton yarn,* shall not be deemed to be false in a material respect, unless

(*a*) the described count or number is greater or less than the actual count or number by more than 5 per cent, provided that the average count of the whole of the yarn in question is not greater or less than the described count; or

(*b*) the average length of the whole number of hanks in a bundle is less than 840 yards; or

(*c*) in a bundle of yarn of any count under 50, described as being ten pounds in weight, the number of knots of twenty hanks each is not half, or the number of knots of ten hanks each is not the same as, and the number of knots of five hanks is not double, the described count for number of the yarn; or

(*d*) in a bundle of yarn of any count under 50, described as being 5 lbs. in weight, the number of knots of 20 hanks each is not a quarter of, or the number of knots of 10 hanks each is not half, or the number of knots of 5 hanks each is not the same as, the described count or number of the yarn; or

(*e*) in a bundle of yarn of any count from 50 upwards, the number of knots of twenty hanks each is not half, or the number of knots of 40 hanks each is not a quarter when the described weight is ten pounds, and is not a quarter or an eighth, when the described weight is five pounds, of the count or number of the yarn; or

(*f*) in the case of *bleached yarn,* the described weight exceeds the actual weight by more than

7½ per cent in counts from 1 to 8;
5 per cent in counts from above 8 to 18;
4 per cent in counts from above 18 to 30;
2½ per cent in counts from above 30 to 80.

IV.—A trade description of count or number applied to a bundle of *dyed cotton yarn* shall be accepted as indicating length only, the hank being taken to measure 840 yards, and it shall be deemed to be false in a material respect if the average length of the hanks in a bundle is less than 819 yards.

V.—A trade description of length applied to *thread of any kind* (of cotton, wool, flax or silk) shall not be deemed to be false in a material respect, unless it exceeds the actual length by more than 1 per cent.

VI.—The dimensions of goods on which their length or width is stamped shall be determined by measurement in imperial yards of thirty-six inches.

The grant of rewards is controlled by rules issued with Resolution No. 1088-S. R., dated the 23rd February, 1901, which are applicable generally to all cases under the Sea Customs and Indian Merchandise Marks Acts. The Resolution states that it is undesirable in practice to grant rewards to gazetted officers, but it was held in letter No. 4080-S. R., dated the 3rd August, 1901, to the Government of Madras that the prohibition does not apply to gazetted officers below the rank of Assistant Collector.

Part III.—Instructions for the Observance of Customs Officers.

Note.—The word "Act" when used in these rules, unless the contrary is apparent, is intended to include, in addition to the Indian Merchandise Marks Act, the connected provisions of the Sea Customs Act.

1. The following classes of goods are exempt from the operation of the Act:

(*a*) Goods not having applied to them any marks, trade descriptions, or other indications whatever of the nature contemplated in the Act, with the exception of piece-goods which require to be stamped under section 10 (*f*) corresponding to section 18 (*f*) of the Sea Customs Act.

(*b*) Goods imported for the personal use of individuals or private associations of individuals, and not for trade purposes. Thus, cloth imported by an individual for his own use or band instruments by a regimental band for the use of the members, are exempt; but not rails imported by a railway company, or cutlery and glassware by a hotel (see also paragraph 2, Notification No. 1430, dated the 6th April, 1891, as subsequently amended, quoted in Part II).

Exemptions from particular provisions of the Act are noted later in connection with the provisions concerned.

2. Goods affected by the Act may be classified as follows:

A.—Goods having applied to them counterfeit trade marks or other indications that they are the manufacture or merchandise of a *person* whose manufacture or merchandise they are not.

B.—Goods having applied to them false trade descriptions or other indications in respect of the *country* in which they were made or produced.

C.—Goods having applied to them trade descriptions that are false also in other respects.

D.—Piece-goods which have not the lengths properly stamped on each piece.

The importation of all such goods is prohibited by section 18 *(d)*, *(e)* and *(f)* of the Sea Customs Act.

It has been ruled that the indication alluded to in the words "any description, statement, or other indication, direct or indirect," in the definition of trade description, must be in the nature of a description or statement and does not include the "make up" of goods. The "make up" of goods does not therefore amount to a trade description in itself.

A.—Goods having applied to them counterfeit Trade Marks or other indications that they are the manufacture or merchandise of a person whose manufacture or merchandise they are not.

3. The indications referred to, in addition to (1) counterfeit trade marks, include (2) any such numerals, words, or marks, or arrangement or combination thereof, whether including a trade mark or not, as are or is, reasonably calculated to lead persons to believe that the goods are the manufacture or merchandise of some person other than they really are, or (3) any false name or initials of a person, that is, any name or initials

(a) not being a trade mark or part of a trade mark, and

(b) being identical with, or a colourable imitation of, the name or initials of a person carrying on business in connection with goods of the same description and not having authorized the use of such name or initials.

Items (2) and (3) of this rule incorporate section 4 (1) and (2) of the Indian Merchandise Marks Act. Without these clauses marks imitating another person's marks would only be controlled if they constituted a counterfeit trade mark, or happened incidentally to constitute a false trade description of country of manufacture, material or the like within the meaning of any of the clauses of section 2 (2). But two further classes of cases may arise:

A manufacturer's or merchant's marks may include many other marks or combinations of marks than a trade mark and goods may be known by such marks better than by the trade mark itself. For example, piece-goods are sometimes identified in the native market by their coloured labels or even by the manufacturer's or merchant's number impressed on them. Secondly, the merchandise of a particular firm may similarly be known by the firm's name or initials, which may not be included in the trade mark. The provisions cited are intended to meet cases in which such marks, numbers, etc., are used by other parties, or in which the use of such names or initials is not covered or condoned by the necessary authorization. In such cases the procedure to be adopted by Customs officers will be that prescribed below in rule 9.

4. The importation of goods having applied to them a counterfeit trade mark or any of the indications described is prohibited by section 18 *(d)* of the Sea Customs Act, read with section 4 (1) and (2) of the Indian Merchandise Marks Act. These provisions are intended not only for the protection of manufacturers and merchants against the piracy of their marks, but also for the protection of the public against the supply of goods of an inferior or unknown quality under cover of a well-known brand. Although therefore action will ordinarily be taken upon information received from the manufacturer or merchant aggrieved, Customs officers are not debarred from acting upon their own initiative.

5. When information of the nature referred to in rule 4 is received, unless it is in writing and supplies all necessary details, the informant should be required to furnish the Collector or Chief Customs officer with a notice in the form A appended. Upon arrival of the goods, if the Collector or Chief Customs officer is of opinion that there is clearly no reasonable cause for detention, he will permit delivery to the consignee. Otherwise he will detain the goods provisionally and require the informant either

(a) to furnish him with an indemnity bond in the form B appended within twenty-four hours; or

(b) to deposit security in cash or currency notes to the amount of 10 per cent on the estimated value of the goods to reimburse any expenses incurred or damages

awarded in respect of the detention, or of any proceedings consequent thereon, pending the execution of the bond, which in such cases should be furnished within four days.

Upon receipt of the bond duly executed the security deposit may be returned.

If the indemnity bond or the security, as the case may be, be not furnished within twenty-four hours, or if the bond following the security be not furnished within four days, the Collector will release the goods.

If the bond be furnished the Collector will detain the goods for one month from the date of the request for the detention in order to allow of the applicant filing a suit or taking other proper proceedings to have his rights in respect of them declared or ascertained, provided that if he institute a suit or take other proper proceedings for the purpose stated within the period named the goods should be detained until a final decree in the suit or order in the proceedings has been obtained, such decree or order in the case of an appeal being that of the highest Appellate Court to which the appeal is taken. If the applicant does not file a suit or take other proper proceedings as above stated within the period named, the goods will be released.

6. When an informant is not in possession of information of any definite case of importation or contemplated importation, but has reason to believe that his marks, etc., are being infringed and wishes to have Customs officers put on the watch for possible infringements, his application may be entertained if the Collector or Chief Customs officer is satisfied that it is *bonâ fide* and reasonable, and orders may be issued to Customs officers to take a note of the marks, etc., concerned with a view to taking action under paragraph 8 should occasion arise. Such orders should only have effect for three months, but may be renewed on the expiry of the period upon the Collector being satisfied that there are reasonable grounds for the renewal.

7. Any formal registration of marks, names, or initials in the Customs offices is prohibited.

8. The occasions on which Customs officers should take action upon their own initiative will naturally be rare, but will occur when upon an examination of the goods it is apparent that an attempt has been made to counterfeit some established mark or other indication, such as is well known to the officer concerned. In such cases the Collector or Chief Customs officer will cause

the goods to be provisionally detained for a period not exceeding four days, and send intimation to any local representative of the person whose name or marks appear to be counterfeited, with the request that he will take action if he wishes the detention continued as described in clauses *(a)* and *(b)* of rule 5 above. The subsequent procedure will follow that detailed above.

If there is no local representative the Collector or Chief Customs officer will pass the goods, but should send intimation by letter with sufficient particulars of the counterfeit marks or other indications to the person whose name or marks appear to have beeen counterfeited, describing the procedure to be adopted under these rules, should he wish to have any future consignments detained.

9. The powers of enquiry which the Collector possesses in regard to goods detained under the above rules are strictly limited and are only intended to enable him to satisfy himself that the counterfeit is plain and manifest and that there can be no real contest in the matter. For any purpose beyond this, his duty is to detain, under protection of an indemnity bond, the goods until the question of title is settled by a competent court. He should not therefore ordinarily take proceedings under the Sea Customs Act for the confiscation of goods detained under the above rules, or for the imposition of a penalty, upon his own responsibility, except in the following cases, namely, when the marks on the goods are admitted by the importer to be objectionable either as counterfeit trade marks, or as being of the description stated in section 4 (1) and (2) of the Indian Merchandise Marks Act; or when the Collector or Chief Customs officer is satisfied by the production of a duly certified copy of an order by a competent court that they have been declared by such a competent court either in British India or in the United Kingdom to be so objectionable, and provided that in this case no claim is made on behalf of the importer of a right to use the marks upon grounds not covered by the order cited. If such a claim be made the procedure laid down in rule 5 should be followed in respect of the importation.

B.—Goods having applied to them false trade descriptions or other indications in respect of the country in which they are made or produced.

10. Under this head three principal classes are to be distinguished:

(a) Goods made or produced beyond the limits of the United Kingdom and British India and bearing or purporting to bear the *name or trade mark* of any person who is a manufacturer, dealer or trader in the United Kingdom or British India.

(b) Goods made or produced beyond the limits of the United Kingdom and British India, to which is applied a *false trade description for indication (other than* the name or trade mark of a manufacturer, dealer or trader in the United Kingdom or British India) indicating that they were made or produced in the United Kingdom or British India.

(c) Goods made or produced in one foreign country, but bearing a *false trade description* indicating that they were made or produced in another.

11. The importation of goods falling under either of these three classes is equally prohibited by law under section 18 *(d)* and (*e*) of the Sea Customs Act and Customs officers should of their own motion detain goods falling under any of the three classes.

Note.—Samples or patterns readily distinguishable as such and valueless in themselves are not to be treated as subject to the provisions of the Act referring to the marking of indication of origin.

12. The law (section 13 of the Indian Merchandise Marks Act) also states that evidence of the port of shipment is *primâ facie* evidence of the country in which the goods were made or produced. This ruling, however, should be applied with discretion when the port of shipment is a place of transit from some inland country like Rotterdam or Antwerp with respect to Germany, or Trieste with respect to Italy or Switzerland. In the case of goods shipped from these ports, the statement that the goods are the make or produce of an inland country may be accepted if there is no reasonable ground to suspect the country of origin.

13. Although the importation of goods falling under either of these three classes is prohibited, the goods may yet be admitted if there is applied to them a counter-indication of origin accompanying

(1) the name or trade mark in the case of goods falling under class *(a)*;

(2) the false trade description in the case of goods falling under classes *(b)* and *(c)*.

14. In the former case, the nature of the counter-indication required to enable the goods to be imported is distinctly and specifically provided for by the law [see section 18 *(e)* of the Sea Customs Act.]

(1) The name or trade mark must be accompanied by a definite indication of the goods having been made or produced in a place beyond the limits of the United Kingdom or British India.

(2) The country in which that place is situated must, in that indication, be indicated in letters as large and conspicuous as any letter in the name and trade mark, and in the same language and character as the name and trade mark.

Where, therefore, goods made elsewhere than in the United Kingdom or British India bear the name or trade mark, being or purporting to be the name or trade mark of a manufacturer, dealer or trader in the United Kingdom or British India, the counter-indication must distinctly specify the country of origin or manufacture. In such cases the form "Made in ...." must be used; other expressions such as "Made Abroad," "Not made in the United Kingdom or British India," "Foreign make," "Foreign Produce" are not permissible.

15. The law does not, however, require a specific counter-indication in other cases. In the case of goods falling under class (*b*) or (*c*), the Customs officers cannot insist that the false trade indication should be corrected by a definite indication of the country of origin, and any indication negativing the implication that the goods were made or produced in another country is sufficient. In such cases, the following and similar expressions are admissible:

Goods falling under class (*b*)	Made in....................
	Made Abroad.
	Not made in the United Kingdom or British India.
	Foreign make.
	Foreign produce.
Goods falling under class (*c*)	Made in....................
	Not made in X (being the country in which, from the false trade description, the goods might be supposed to have been manufactured).

Note.—(1) Goods made or produced in the United Kingdom bearing the name or trade mark of a British Indian trader or dealer are not subject to the provisions of the Act referring to the marking of origin even when the marking is in, or includes, vernaculars.

(2) In the case of goods made or produced in the United Kingdom bearing an indication of make or production in any other country, a counter-indication of British origin should be required. Examples:—The expression "Munich Beer" on bottles containing beer made in England must have some such counter-indication as "Made in England" or "Not made in Germany." The expression "Amritsar" on shawls made in England must have some such counter-indication as "Made in England" or "Not made in India."

(3) In the case of goods made or produced in a foreign country, the trade description indicative of origin in British India or the United Kingdom which has been corrected by the use of such expressions as "Made Abroad," "Not made in the United Kingdom or British India," may still be false if the description contains an indication of origin in one foreign country when the goods were actually made or produced in another. As for instance, "Old Brown Cognac, Made Abroad," which was actually made in Germany. In such cases, a further counter-indication is necessary. This can be done in two ways. Either the name of the country of manufacture or production may be substituted for such phrases as "Made Abroad;" or the counter-indication must run "Not made in the United Kingdom or British India or X (X being the country in which the goods might be supposed to be manufactured)." Thus in the example given, "Not made in France" must be added to the description or the words "Made in Germany" must be substituted for the words "Made Abroad."

16. In the case of goods with distinguishable parts or constituents manufactured or produced in different countries, an indication of origin in any country on *one* part should be taken, in the absence of anything to the contrary, as applicable to the whole.

Example.—A British or German hall-mark on the case of a silver watch should be held to include the works and dial-plate also, and if the works and dial-plate are not of English or German make, as the case may be, a counter-indication should be required on the latter.

17. In the case of goods with indistinguishable parts or constituents made in different countries, a general statement such as "Produce of different countries" is permissible.

Example.—Brandy blended in the United Kingdom from the produce of France or Italy.

Note.—In the case of goods with indistinguishable parts or constituents made in the United Kingdom and other countries, the above counter-indication will be sufficient even when the goods bear the name or trade mark of a British or British Indian trader or dealer.

18. The names of provinces or towns may only be substituted

for those of countries if they are so extensively known that the Indian consumer, is not likely to be misled. Names such as Paris, Bohemia, Berlin, are permissible, but not Milan or Baden.

19. In cases where an indication of origin is required, the general rule is that the indication must be shown in letters as large and conspicuous as any letter in the name, trade mark or false description; it must be in the same language and character, and it must accompany every application of the name, trade mark or false description.

The size of the letters need not be rigidly insisted upon, provided that they are sufficiently conspicuous to catch the eye along with the name or trade mark.

The counter-indication should be adjacent on the same label, or part of the covering or goods, as the case may be, to which the name, trade mark or false trade description is applied: it should not be on a separate label, nor otherwise detachable from the application of the name, trade mark or false trade description itself; and it should be applied no less indelibly than the latter. It should be repeated for all applications of the name, trade mark or false trade description except when the latter are reproduced in such close proximity that one prominent counter-indication will suffice to cover all; and if different languages or characters, English or Indian, are used for the names or included in the trade marks, the counter-indication should be repeated in each language employed.

20. Customs officers should require the indication of the country of origin to be placed on the capsules and corks, as well as on the labels, of bottles of wine or other liquor produced or made beyond the limits of the United Kingdom or of British India whenever such goods are

(*a*) so described,

(*b*) or have applied to them British or British Indian names or trade marks in such a manner,

as to indicate or suggest that the wine or other liquor was produced or made in the United Kingdom or in British India.

Note.—Rules 21 to 24 below apply only to goods falling under class (*a*) of Rule 10.

21. The legal provision requiring that the name or trade mark of a British Indian or English manufacturer, dealer or trader, when applied to goods not made in the United Kingdom or Brit-

ish India, should be accompanied by a counter-indication, is not to be enforced in the case of

(*a*) Indian produce and manufactures imported by sea from foreign Indian ports into British India, and bearing the name or trade mark of a British Indian trader or dealer.

(*b*) Goods bearing the name or trade mark of a British Indian trader or dealer which are known or proved to be the produce of Africa, Arabia, Persia, or Turkey in Asia, with the exception of manufactured articles such as carpets, earthenware, shawls and silken or woollen goods. A list of such goods will be found in Appendix C.

The Local Governments are authorised to make additions to the list if and when it is found defective, but such additions are to be reported for the information of the Government of India.

(*c*) Coverings or labels [as defined in section 5 (3) of the Indian Merchandise Marks Act] made in a foreign country bearing the name of a British Indian manufacturer, dealer or trader, where the name is intended to refer not to the covering or label, but to the goods to be covered or labelled, and is the name of a firm who have ordered the covering for their own goods.

Examples.—Cardboard boxes made in Germany bearing the name, trade mark or advertisement of, and imported by, a British Indian Soap Manufacturing Company to hold soap of their own manufacture; labels made outside the United Kingdom or British India bearing the name of, and imported by, a British Indian chemist to be attached to phials, boxes, etc., for dispensing purposes; photograph mounts made in a foreign country bearing the name and imported by a photographer in British India to be attached to his own photographs.

22. Initials of manufacturers, dealers or traders in the United Kingdom or British India should not be treated as names requiring a counter-indication of the country of origin, unless they are so extensively known in India as to be indistinguishable in effect from the full names which they represent, or are followed by affixes distinctly suggesting a British firm as "& Co." (in the case of goods from Continental countries except Germany) and "Brothers" and "Bros."

23. If a manufacturer has a factory in a foreign country as well as in the United Kingdom or British India, his name or trade

mark requires a counter-indication, when applied to goods made in the foreign country. If a manufacturer having a factory beyond the limits of the United Kingdom or British India has only an agency or place of business within such limits, his name or trade mark of course requires a counter-indication whenever applied.

24. Such expressions as "imported by," "for sale by," "bottled by," and the like accompanying the names of British or British Indian dealers or traders do not render counter-indications less obligatory under the law although in connection with the general circumstances of a case they may justify relaxation of the provisions applicable.

Note.—Rules 25 to 37 below apply to goods falling under clauses (*b*) and (*c*) of Rule 10.

25. In these cases the offence consists in the use of false trade descriptions indicating that the goods are the produce or manufacture of a country in which they were not produced or manufactured.

26. A false trade description is defined in section 2 (3) of the Indian Merchandise Marks Act. It comprises any description, statement or other indication (including any numeral, word or mark which according to the custom of trade is commonly taken to be an indication) that the goods to which they are applied were made or produced in one country when such goods were really made or produced in another.

27. It is ruled by section 19A (3) of the Sea Customs Act that when any name on goods is identical with, or a colourable imitation of, the name of a place in the United Kingdom or British India, that name, unless accompanied in equally large and conspicuous letters, and in the same language and character, by the name of the country in which such place is situate, is to be treated as if it were the name of a place in the United Kingdom or British India.

Example.—Boston, in Massachusetts, should be accompanied by the name "United States," or by the initials "U. S. A." or by the word "Massachusetts."

28. A trade description which, in indicating a particular class of goods or method of manufacture, includes the name of a place, is to be held as naming such a place or country. Such expressions as "Kidderminster carpets," "Portland cement," "Egyptian cigarettes," "Balbriggan" on hosiery, "Windsor soap,"

"Shetland," or "Amritsar" on shawls, or "Conjeevaram cloth," though they might be held to be merely phrases descriptive of method of manufacture, are yet calculated to mislead as to place of origin and require counter-indications when applied to goods made or produced in countries other than those in which the places are situated. Similarly counter-indications are required on wine, not the produce of Portugal or Spain and described respectively as "Port" or "Sherry" (which words include the names of the places Oporto and Xeres); on brandy not produced in France and described as cognac (which indicates production in France); on liquors not produced in France and described as "Chartreuse," "Benedictine" (which indicate production at particular places in France); on beer produced in England described as "Munich Beer" (which indicates production in Germany). Where, however, as in the case of "Lancashire Swedish" on Swedish iron, the qualifying word follows the misleading name, the description may be admitted.

An exception must be made where such a description has become associated, as in the case of "Russian leather" with a particular class of goods in a manner practically to preclude any probability of deception.

29. The use in a trade description of a language which is not the language of the country in which the goods were made or produced usually requires counter-indication. An exception may be allowed in cases in which a particular language is so commonly applied to certain goods by the custom of the trade that there is no reasonable likelihood of the consumer in India being misled. Thus Spanish words applied only to colour, shape, size and the like, such as Reina, Fina, and Claro on the bands and boxes of German-made cigars, may be admitted without counter-indications, but any further indications of Havannah or other make, not being German, on the boxes should have a counter-indication applied to them.

30. The use of the English language in a trade description applied to goods not made in the United Kingdom or a British Colony is in itself to be regarded as indicative of British origin. This rule applies not merely to cases in which English words are used as trade descriptions, but extends to the use of descriptive terms or fancy names such as extra quality, gold medal, lever locks, bull-dog (on revolvers) and the like. The fact that words used in the English language are common to other languages also, such as Phœnix, Sardar, extra, patent, does not make counter-

indications less necessary in India where other languages than English or Indian are not generally known.

Note.—In the case of American goods bearing English words or descriptions, a counter-indication of origin should be required.

31. No counter-indication is required on marks consisting of English letters only, provided that they do not form words or a trade mark, or represent any initials so extensively known as to require a counter-indication under rule 22 above, or amount to a trade description. Thus a counter-indication is not required for letters such as K. S. on copper, which convey no indication of British origin, although it would be needed for letters commonly used in the United Kingdom to indicate description or quality, as described in rule 29.

32. The use of the English language on foreign made goods is admissible as parts of the goods themselves.

Examples.—English verses and texts on 'Xmas and birthday cards; words such as "Photographs" and "Stamps" on albums; "Tobacco" on pouches; "Gold," "Silver," "Stamps" on the divisions of a purse; the names of hotels or purveyors on crockery intended for use by the establishments or firms whose names it bears; "Fast," "Slow," on regulators of Swiss watches; regulating words such as "Blood Heat," "Boiling," "Freezing," on thermometers, or "Fair," "Rain," etc., on barometers; Christian names on handkerchiefs. The use on such goods, however, of names of makers, publishers, or dealers in this country, or of any description of the goods or address which would in any way suggest English origin, will involve detention. Expressions such as "Think of me," "For a good boy," on foreign goods must bear a statement of foreign origin.

33. Words in any Indian language, or letters or numerals in Indian character, or marks or devices, such as representations of Indian deities or emblems, which are reasonably calculated to lead persons to believe that the goods were made or produced in British India require counter-indications on the same principle when applied to goods made or produced beyond the limits of British India.

Note.—(1) An indication of the country of origin should not be insisted on when the only vernacular characters employed are the equivalent of numerals used as quality numbers.

(2) British goods, *e.g.*, piece-goods, bearing trade descriptions such as "Very good quality," "Best cloth," "Very best borders," "Fast colour," etc., in vernacular characters, or bearing tickets with represen-

tations of Indian deities and mythological scenes with their names in vernacular characters, in conjunction with the name or trade mark of a British or British Indian firm, should be passed without any counter-indication of origin. Such counter-indications should be insisted on only where such expressions as "Swadeshi," "Bande Mataram," "Cawnpore shoes," etc., are used, which apart from being in a vernacular character definitely indicate from their meaning that the goods were manufactured in India.

(3) No objection should ordinarily be taken to the application of tickets or designs representing Indian deities or emblems to British goods even when the name of the trader or the country of origin is not marked on such tickets or the goods. In particular cases, however, when there is good ground for considering that the use of such plain tickets or designs is specially designed to convey, and does in fact convey, the impression of Indian origin, they should be considered to be false trade descriptions. In deciding whether the use of a plain ticket or design constitutes a false trade description, regard should be had *inter alia* to priority of usage. For example, the subsequent application to British piece-goods of a ticket or design which has by usage become associated in the minds of dealers or consumers with Indian goods of a similar description should, in the absence of some counter-indication of British origin, be objected to; but a ticket or design previously associated with British piece-goods should not be objected to as indicative of Indian origin notwithstanding the later use of a similar ticket or design on goods of like description of Indian manufacture.

34. The use of the language of one foreign country on goods produced in another must be dealt with similarly.

Examples.—Chinese characters applied to French silk; French descriptions applied to German brandy and on German scents; Russian descriptions on French Kummel.

35. The same principles should be applied to indications other than words—such as pictures, pictorial indications suggesting a false origin.

Examples.—Counter-indications are required on foreign made goods bearing the British Royal Arms; on bottled Whisky made in Germany bearing the picture of a Highland gillie; on gold and silver goods made abroad bearing British assay marks; on bags of sugar bearing letters commonly used in the United Kingdom as indicative of description of quality.

36. The use of the name of a port or place of destination on mere packing cases or outer wrappers in which goods are clearly not intended to be sold or exposed for sale, or, if exposed for sale, then in an export market, will not involve detention. Address marks, when they are merely and manifestly such for purposes of carriage only, are not to be treated as subject to the provisions of the Act.

(2) Statements, descriptions or numerals on labels or tickets applied to boxes, cartons, parcels, or other packages, which are manifestly intended only for the purpose of identifying articles for the convenience of dealers and shopkeepers, and are not specially intended to attract the eye of the purchaser, are not to be treated as trade descriptions.

Examples.—On bundles of hosiery, "hose brown merino, size 10"; on shoes, "enamelled leather, men's No. 6"; on hats, "brown felt, hard, No. 7."

This instruction does not apply to a mark or description on the goods themselves, nor to a description of quality, nor to a description containing the name of a place, country, manufacturer or trader, nor to a trade mark.

37. When labels, capsules or the like are imported bearing trade descriptions of wines or liquors, and there is reasonable ground to believe that they will be applied to wines or liquors separately imported after passing the Custom House, and that when so applied they will amount to false trade descriptions, intimation should be sent to the Chief Excise authorities at the port of importation, in order that they may take steps to prevent goods bearing such false descriptions from passing into consumption.

C.—Goods having applied to them false trade descriptions that are false in other respects.

38. This class includes goods having applied to them trade descriptions that are false in respect of

(1) the number, quantity, measure, gauge or weight of the goods, or
(2) the time at which they were made or produced, or
(3) the mode of manufacture or production, or
(4) the material of which the goods are composed, or
(5) in respect of the goods being the subject of an existing patent or copyright.

It will be observed that a description of quality is not covered by this definition. Thus statements that goods are hand-made when they are actually machine-made, or that they measure 25 yards when they only measure 22, or that bottles have a capacity of 2 oz. when they have not that capacity, are false trade descriptions, but not, for instance, statements that a thermometer measures temperature in 1 minute when it really requires 5, or that a common watch is a chronometer, or which relate otherwise to the quality of goods.

Customs officers will detain goods falling under this class of their own motion.

The most important cases in the class affect yarn and piece-goods in respect of their measure, etc., under clause (1) and certain other goods in respect of the material of which they are composed under clause (4).

39. The standard of measure for yarn is the relation of length to weight, which is known as the count. The chief systems of count are (1) the British and (2) the metric.

(1) The British count may be defined as the number of hanks of a given yarn that weigh 1 lb. avoirdupois, equivalent to the number of yards that weigh 8·3 grains. The hank is 840 yards in length, and includes 7 leas of 120 yards each. The unit of count is 1 hank to 1 lb., equivalent to 840 yards to 7,000 grains, or 1 yard to 8·3 grains. The last formula is useful for calculating odd lengths.

The number of the count becomes higher in proportion as the length increases in relation to the weight. Thus if 2 hanks go to 1 lb., or 2 yards to 8·3 grains, the yarn is of count No. 2 commonly described as 2s. Similarly if 20 hanks weigh 1 lb., or 20 yards 8·3 grains, the yarn is 20s.

(2) The metric count for all yarn, with the exception of raw and prepared silk, represents a relation between metres and grammes, 1s being 1,000 metres to 500 grammes, or 2 metres to 1 gramme, equivalent to 1 yard to 7·0553 grains. Then length of the hank is fixed at 1,000 metres. Thus 20s by this count represents yarn weighing 40 metres to the gramme, or 40 hanks of 1,000 metres to 500 grammes.

The one system may be counted into the other by the following formulæ:

The English yarn No. $\times$ 0.847 = the metric No.
The metric yarn No. $\times$ 1.181 = the English No.

For raw and prepared silk, on the other hand, the count is the number of grammes weight in 10,000 metres. Thus 20s represents yarn of which 10,000 metres weigh 20 grammes.

40. If yarn is imported marked with the metric count, the

marking should be accompanied by the words "metric count," or other definite indication that it is packed on the metric system, as well as by the necessary indication of foreign manufacture if it has been manufactured beyond the limits of the United Kingdom or British India. These indications should be conspicuous and accompany every application of the count.

41. Yarn is ordinarily made up in 5 or 10-lb. bundles containing a certain number of knots, which in turn contain a certain number of hanks; and, as contemplated in paragraphs III to V of Notification No. 1474, as subsequently amended, reproduced in Part II, there is or should be a definite relation between the number of knots in a bundle and the count. Thus in a 10-lb. bundle in which there are 10 hanks to the knot, the number of knots is, or should be, the same as the number of the count. Similarly, if such a bundle is made up with 20 hanks to the knot, the number of the latter is, or should be, half the number of the count, and so on. But such a make up does not of itself amount to a trade description of the count: to constitute the latter, as mentioned in rule 2 above, there must be a description or statement applied to the yarn, or an indication, direct or indirect, of the nature of a description or statement, including the use of any numeral, word or mark which according to the custom of the trade is commonly taken to be an indication of the count. Thus the mark "20s" applied to the wrapper of a bundle of yarn indicates that the count is 20, and in the absence of the words "metric count" or other definite indication that the yarn is measured on the metric system, should be regarded as indicating further that it is measured by the British system.

42. Paragraphs 6 to 10 of Notification No. 1430 of the 6th April, 1891, as subsequently amended, reproduced in Part II, describe the conditions under which a test of yarn may be undertaken and the method of the test, and paragraphs III to V of Notification No. 1474 of the 13th November, 1891, as subsequently amended, reproduced in the same, declare what variations from the described length, weight, or count make trade descriptions false in a material respect.

In the case of Berlin wool, a trade description which shows an error in weight of less than 4 per cent, should not ordinarily be held to be false in a material respect, and, in the absence of any other reasons for suspecting fraud, consignments of this wool which show a shortage in weight of less than 4 per cent may be passed without a penalty after requiring the importers to remove the original marks and to stamp the packets with the correct weight as ascertained in the Custom House. If, however, it is found that this concession is being systematically taken advantage of, the importers concerned should be warned that they are liable to fine which will be imposed if deficiencies in weight are observed to be habitual.

43. For testing yarn the appliances chiefly required include a scale weighing up to one-tenth of a grain, a wrap-reel, a swift and a stove for applying the stove test. These appliances should be the same as those used in the testing house of the Manchester Chamber of Commerce, and may be obtained on indent through the Local Governments. The instructions in the explanatory pamphlet issued by the Manchester Chamber of Commerce to accompany the reel should be carefully observed.

44. The stove test need only be applied in cases in which weighment by the ordinary methods show the weight of the yarn to be short, or in which the feel and appearance of yarn indicate that it is abnormally moist or over-conditioned, or in which the importer demands the test. A fee of Rs. 5 (five) will be levied from an importer demanding the test, but will be refunded if the test fails to support the original determination of count and length by the Customs officers. If more than one application of the test is demanded, a further fee of Rs. 5 will be levied for each fresh test, the whole sum charged being retained or refunded according to the final result.

The *conditioning* of yarn is the term applied to the quantity of moisture a given yarn contains.

Under the stove test yarn is reduced to an absolutely dry condition and then weighed. In the case of cotton yarn a regain of 8½ per cent is next added, and the figure obtained is regarded as the actual weight under normal conditioning to be adopted for the purposes of determining whether a given length of yarn is of full or short weight. For the regains to be allowed in the case of silk, or woollen, or other yarns, a reference may be made to the tables of official standards supplied with the stove test apparatus.

45. The following is an example of the calculation to be made in respect of any hank tested in verifying the count of cotton yarn under these rules:

Declared count	30	
Weight of hank on being taken out of bundle . .	250	grains.
Length of hank ascertained by reeling	820	yards.

Weight after application of stove test	220	grains.
Regain at 8½ per cent.	18.7	"
Weight in corrected condition	238.7	"
Count in original condition $\frac{820}{250} \times 8.3 = \frac{820 \times 100}{100 \times 12}$	27.3	
Count in corrected condition $\frac{820}{238} \times 8.3$ . . .	28.63	
Difference from count declared	1.37	
Percentage of difference from count declared . . .	4.6	

The length of the hank tested is thus short by 20 yards, but the difference of count is within the 5 per cent margin allowed by Notification No. 1474 of the 13th November, 1891, as subsequently amended.

46. Trade descriptions of measure and the like applied to piece-goods include (1) the descriptions of length stamped on certain cotton and woollen goods in accordance with clause (*f*), section 18, of the Sea Customs Act, in respect of which rules 56 to 58 below may be consulted; and (2) other trade descriptions of number, measure, or weight applied to the above or any other piece-goods. Paragraph 4 of Notification No. 1430 of the 6th April, 1891, as subsequently amended, limits the occasions on which descriptions of length should be tested, and paragraphs I and II of Notification No. 1474 of the 13th November, 1891, as subsequently amended, prescribe the limits of variation beyond which descriptions, whether of length or width, on certain chief classes of piece-goods are to be deemed false in a material respect.

47. In testing for *length* the measurement should be made along the selvage. In testing for *width* the cloth should be measured by each of the following methods,—the mean of the measurements so taken being adopted—and care should be exercised in applying each method to select a portion of the cloth where the creases are fewest, and the warp and weft respectively as straight as possible:

(1) A double-fold of the cloth should be laid on the table and the creases stroked out, so that it may lie perfectly flat. The measuring rod should then be placed across the cloth, and the finger and thumb run down the rod on each side of it across the cloth so as to once more flatten the creases. Care should be taken in doing this to see that whilst the creases are

smoothed out, stretching is avoided and the warp threads remain perpendicular to the rod. The measurement should then be recorded.

(2) A fold of the cloth should be taken, and the doubled edge held between a finger and thumb at each end, and extended over the measuring rod which should be flat on the table. The extension should be sufficient to remove the creases, but not to stretch the warp out of the perpendicular.

48. In taking these measurements the peculiarities of the cloth under measure should not be lost sight of. Thus cloths, like grey shirtings, that are pressed but not folded gain slightly, but by no means uniformly, in breadth in the course of pressing; whilst those that are folded, like mulls, lose in the folding more than they gain in the pressing. These effects again are apt to disappear with goods that have been opened and handled in a shop. Loose cloths like mulls, especially if shrunk in the course of manufacture, are naturally liable to bag and stretch more than others, and owing to their flimsiness it is difficult to apply the first method of measurement satisfactorily: such cloths also are liable to drag in the weaving towards the end of a long piece, and the folds will sometimes not coincide with the weft. Due allowances should be made for these characteristics. If it is found difficult to determine a reasonable degree of tension for purposes of measurement, the mean between stretching to the full, and not stretching, may afford the best guide.

The influence of stretching for length on the width has always to be taken into account. A semi-circular appearance in the selvage across the end of a piece will show that the cloth has been stretched lengthwise in the making, in which case it must lose in length as the weft is straightened to measure the width. It may then have to be ascertained whether the trade description of length does not become false in the process of making that for width correct. To ascertain this a measurement along the selvages both lengthwise and across may be the best guide.

49. *(1)* In the case of *(a)* white zinc, red lead, white lead and similar substances, *(b)* linseed oil and *(c)* turpentine, which are described as such, no qualifying description need be required when the percentage of impurities is less than 5 per cent.

(2) When the percentage of impurities exceeds 5, but is less than 50, an adequate qualifying description such as "adulterated" or "reduced" should be required.

(3) When the percentage of impurities is 50 or exceeds 50, the actual percentage of adulteration must be marked in addition to the adequate qualifying description.

The marking where required under either of the two preceding clauses should be conspicuous and accompany every application of the description.

50. *(1)* In the case of white zinc, white lead, red lead and similar substances, the adulteration should be calculated on solid pigment alone and not on the solid pigment and oil together. In the case of these articles, a margin of 5 per cent may be allowed before requiring a description of marking already applied to be altered. For example, a keg of red lead is marked 50 per cent reduced and the chemical analysis shows 42 per cent red lead, 8 per cent oil and 50 per cent other matter. According to this analysis the keg should be marked 54·3 per cent reduced. As, however, the difference between this percentage and that contained in the description already applied is less than 5 per cent, the marking need not be objected to.

(2) In the case of turpentine this margin may be increased to 10 per cent.

51. The values declared for linseed oil, turpentine, white lead, red lead, white zinc, and similar substances afford a guide to the correctness of the marking. A list of prices should therefore be maintained at each port and periodically revised, showing the current rates for these goods in different degrees of adulteration or reduction. For goods adulterated to the extent of less than 50 per cent, samples should be sent for chemical analysis when the values declared are materially less than the current rates. For goods adulterated to the extent of 50 per cent or more, samples should be sent in all cases. But when any white lead, red lead, white zinc or any other similar substance of a particular manufacture has by previous test been found correct, a sample need not be sent for analysis on every subsequent importation. An occasional test will in such cases suffice.

Goods need not be detained pending analysis, unless from the invoice or otherwise there is good reason to believe that they are marked as genuine when they are actually reduced. In other cases they may be released on a letter of guarantee from the importers that they will not be delivered to purchasers without permission of the Collector or Chief Customs Officer.

52. Descriptions like "Star silver," "Art silver," "Potosi silver," "Aluminium gold," "Arcadian gold," "Real gold beads," and the

like, when applied to articles not made of silver or gold, should be treated as false trade descriptions. "German silver" and "Nickel silver" may, however, be passed without objection as these descriptions are well known to all classes likely to be affected, and have been in use for a sufficiently long period to render it improbable that a purchaser would be deceived by their use. No objection should be taken to the use of such marks as "Potosi," "Nevada," etc., provided the words "silver" and "gold" are omitted.

52A. The terms such as "Superfine," "Spanish stripes" and "Flannel" which denote pure woollen material should be treated as constituting a false trade description when used in connection with mixed or cotton fabrics made up in imitation of woollen goods unless accompanied by the words "Mixed" or "Cotton" as a counter-indication. No objection should, however, be taken to the application of the term "Merino" to hosiery or underwear made of cotton and wool mixed, or of the term "Velvet" or "Velveteen" to material made wholly or in part of cotton; nor should any objection be taken to the application of the description "All wool" on woollen hose of which the heels and toes are cotton and wool mixed, in cases in which the amount of cotton used is inconsiderable and is added only for the purposes of strengthening the heels and toes.

52B. Uncondensed milk should contain 3 per cent of fat, while condensed milk should contain at least 9 per cent of fat. In the case of condensed milk so described but which contains less than 9 per cent of fat, an adequate qualifying description such as "prepared from skimmed milk" should be required.

Note.—The percentage of fat in sweetened condensed milk should be calculated on the whole product, as in the case of unsweetened milk, and not merely on the actual milk constituents of the product.

53. In dealing with other false trade descriptions of material, or of number, quantity measure, etc., or under any other of the subheads specified in rule 38, due consideration should be given to the provision that a trade description to be false must be "untrue in a material respect."

54. When any indications that goods are of a certain standard composition accompany their descriptions such as the letters B. P. (British Pharmacopœia) in the case of drugs, the description should be regarded as false unless the composition is in accordance with the standard. The letters B. P., when applied to goods made outside the United Kingdom or British Possessions,

require a counter-indication of origin, even though the composition of the goods be correct.

55. Descriptions may amount to false trade descriptions although literally true; thus "Lavender water," "Kananga water," "Eau de Cologne" and "Florida water," or the terms "Extract," "Extrait," or "Essence" applied to an imitation of scent containing no spirit would amount to a false trade description, because spirit is one of the ingredients of these preparations in the ordinary acceptation of these terms. Similarly if the term "Bon Bons" were applied, in the Indian market, to tablets containing santonine or other worm medicine, so regularly as according to the custom of the trade to be commonly taken to be an indication that the tablets contained this drug, they would amount to a false trade description when applied to goods made up in imitation of such tablets, but containing none of the medicine in question.

D.—Piece-goods which have not the length properly stamped on each piece.

56. The importation of these goods is prohibited by clause (*f*), section 18, of the Sea Customs Act. The prohibition extends to "piece-goods such as are ordinarily sold by length or by the piece," and by Notification No. 1430, dated 16th April, 1891, as subsequently amended, reproduced under Part II, these are defined as including woollen goods, that is, woollen piece-goods of all kinds, and certain specified descriptions of cotton goods. The Notification defines the conditions under which goods should be examined to test the accuracy of the stamping, and exempts goods for personal use in the terms of the general exemption in rule 1 (*b*).

57. Under the definition quoted goods not being of cotton or woollen material, such as silk and velvet, are exempt. Alpaca should be treated as wool, and cotton mixed with silk, or wool mixed with silk, as cotton and woollen, respectively, provided that the cotton or wool is in each case a material constituent of the fabric. Shawls and blankets whether woollen or cotton are excluded, because they are sold by the unit and not by length or by the piece, whilst handkerchiefs, printed or plain, do not fall within the cotton goods specified for the reason that they are ordinarily sold with reference to the number of handkerchiefs, without consideration of the measured length of the piece in which they are contained. Fents, which comprise small pieces of cloth that are sold by weight, are also exempt, but cut lengths so long as they

are still sold by length or by the piece should be marked in the manner described below. Cotton *sarongs* when imported in lengths greater than 2½ yards should be stamped.

In addition to falling within the descriptions defined, goods, to be liable to stamping, must have been manufactured either beyond the limits of India, or if in India, then in territories beyond the limits of British India and on premises which, if in British India, would be a factory under the Factories Act. Thus goods manufactured in a factory at Bhavnagar, one of the Native States of Kathiawar, might be liable, whereas those manufactured on a handloom in the same place would be exempt.

58. In marking the length the stamping of numerals only is insufficient; the words "yards" or "yds." should accompany the numerals, and with cut lengths or pieces of the kind described above, the number of pieces should be marked as well as the yards on the front or outer face fold of the cut piece, the figures being presented in a way to show clearly what they are intended to mean; thus $\frac{\text{40 yards}}{\text{3}}$ would not suffice, but $\frac{\text{40 yards}}{\text{3 pieces}}$ or "40 yards, 3 pieces," or the like would meet the requirement.

Note.—This ruling should not be applied to ribbons, cotton embroideries, laces, trimmings and the like, which are not piece-goods.

The length must be in standard yards or fractions of a yard, and should represent the actual length of the goods as imported, and not the length before shrinkage or dryage, resulting from processes such as dyeing, or from atmospheric changes which can reasonably be foreseen. Marking in inches may be permitted on cloths of small dimensions and delicate make in accordance with the custom of the trade. The marking should be such as will not ordinarily be removable except by washing the fabric, or, in the case of goods that are not ordinarily washed, it should be of such a nature that it is not likely to be obliterated in the ordinary course of handling before the goods reach the purchaser. Marks, which are stitched on the fabric and are easily removable by cutting should not be permitted.

The marking should be conspicuous, in a different colour from that of the fabric, upon the fabric itself, not upon a removable label or ticket, and in a conspicuous place upon the fabric. It should not be upon an inner fold which cannot readily be seen, nor upon a wholly detached piece, but it may be upon a piece that is partly detached without being entirely severed. In the case of *sarongs* which are required under paragraph 57 to be stamped, the stamping may be permitted on the selvage in the innerfold instead of on the upper-most fold of the cloth.

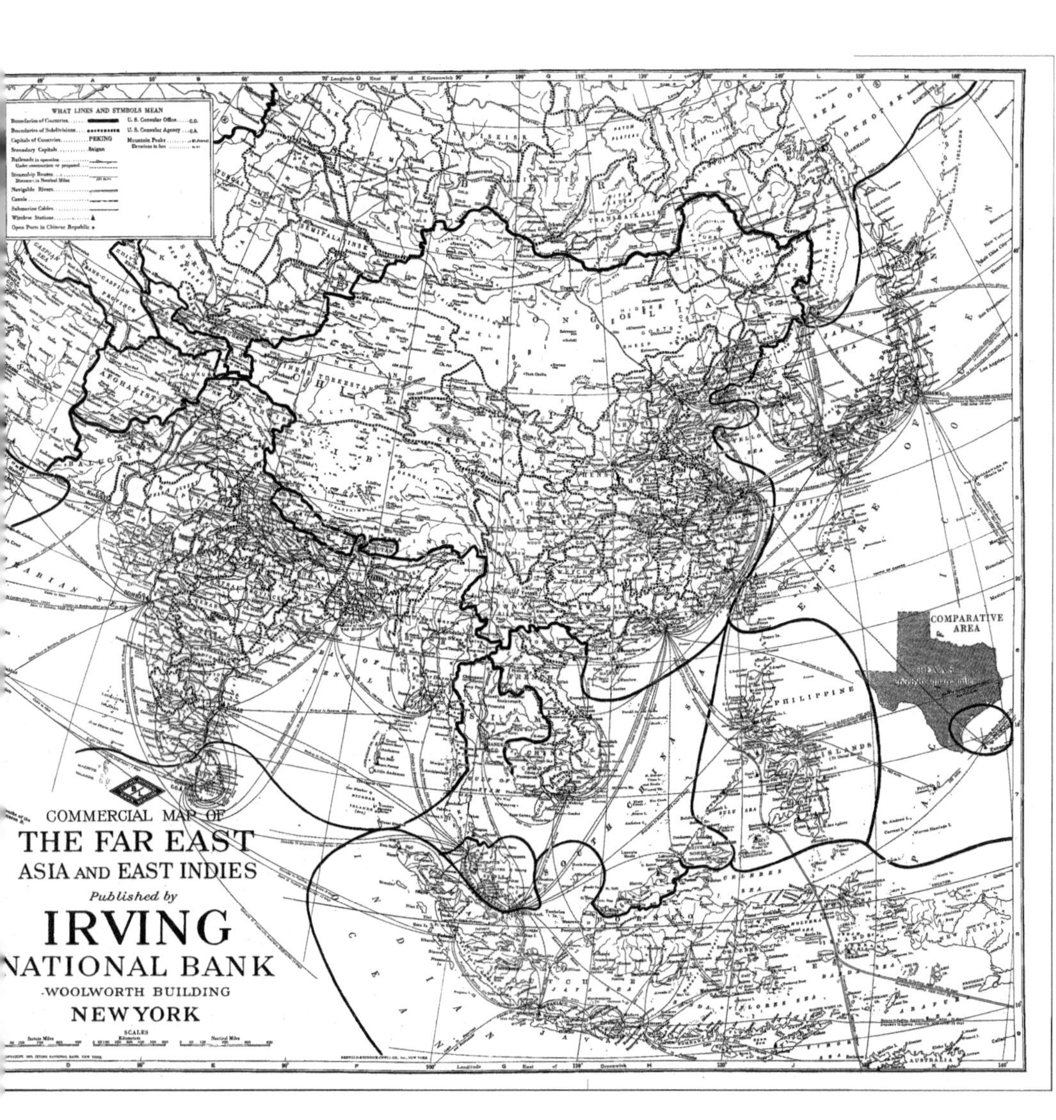
WHAT LINES AND SYMBOLS MEAN
Boundaries of Countries
Boundaries of Subdivisions
Capitals of Countries PEKING
Secondary Capitals Saigon
Railroads in operation
Under construction or proposed
Steamship Routes
Distances in Nautical Miles
Navigable Rivers
Canals
Submarine Cables
Wireless Stations
Open Ports in Chinese Republic
U. S. Consular Office C.O.
U. S. Consular Agency C.A.
Mountain Peaks
Elevations in feet
COMPARATIVE AREA
TEXAS
CASPIAN SEA
TRANS-CASPIAN PROVINCE
AFGHANISTAN
MONGOLIA
TIBET
PHILIPPINE ISLANDS
SEA OF OKHOTSK
INDIAN OCEAN
JAVA SEA
CELEBES SEA
COMMERCIAL MAP OF
THE FAR EAST
ASIA AND EAST INDIES
Published by
IRVING
NATIONAL BANK
WOOLWORTH BUILDING
NEW YORK
SCALES
Statute Miles
Kilometers
Nautical Miles

INDEX

F

N

U

V

W

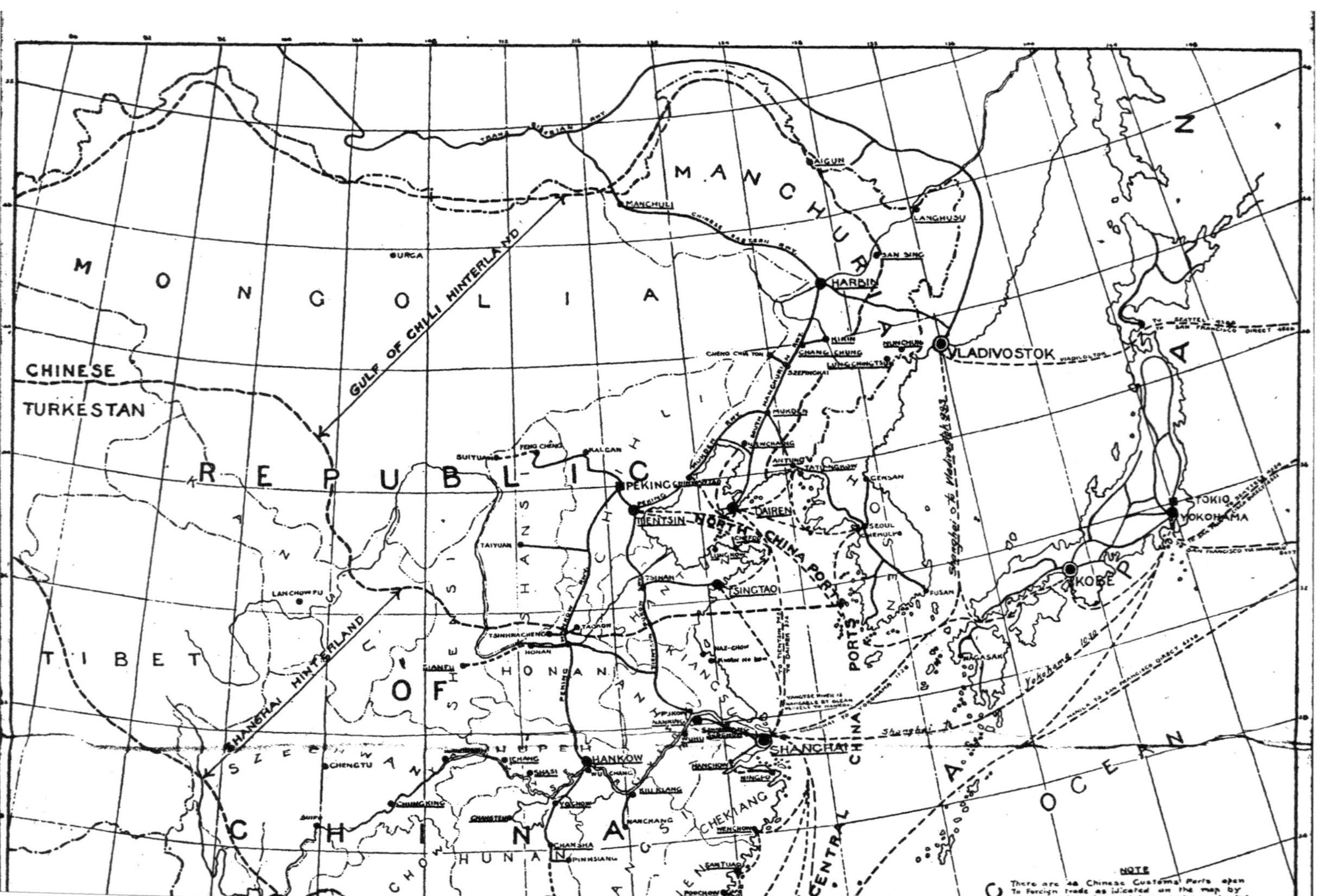

MONGOLIA
MANCHURIA
CHINESE TURKESTAN
TIBET
REPUBLIC OF CHINA
JAPAN
OCEAN
GULF OF CHILI HINTERLAND
SHANGHAI HINTERLAND
NORTH CHINA PORTS
PORTS
CENTRAL CHINA
TRANS SIBERIAN RWY
CHINESE EASTERN RWY
SOUTH MANCHURIAN RWY
MANCHULI
AIGUN
LANGHUSU
SAN SING
HARBIN
URGA
KIRIN
CHANG CHUNG
VLADIVOSTOK
MUKDEN
NEWCHWANG
ANTUNG
PEKING
KALGAN
FENG CHENG
SUIYUAN
TIENTSIN
DAIREN
SEOUL
CHEMULPO
GENSAN
FUSAN
TSINAN
TSINGTAO
TAIYUAN
LANCHOWFU
TSINHWACHENG
HONAN
SIANFU
HAI-CHOW
NANKING
SHANGHAI
HANCHOW
NINGPO
HANKOW
ICHANG
SHASI
KIUKIANG
YOCHOW
CHANGSHA
NANCHANG
PINHSIANG
CHUNGKING
CHENGTU
SUIFU
WENCHOW
SANTUAO
FOOCHOW
KOBE
NAGASAKI
TOKIO
YOKOHAMA
Shanghai to Vladivostok 983
Shanghai to Yokohama 1030
NOTE
There are 48 Chinese Customs Ports open To Foreign trade as idicated on the map by

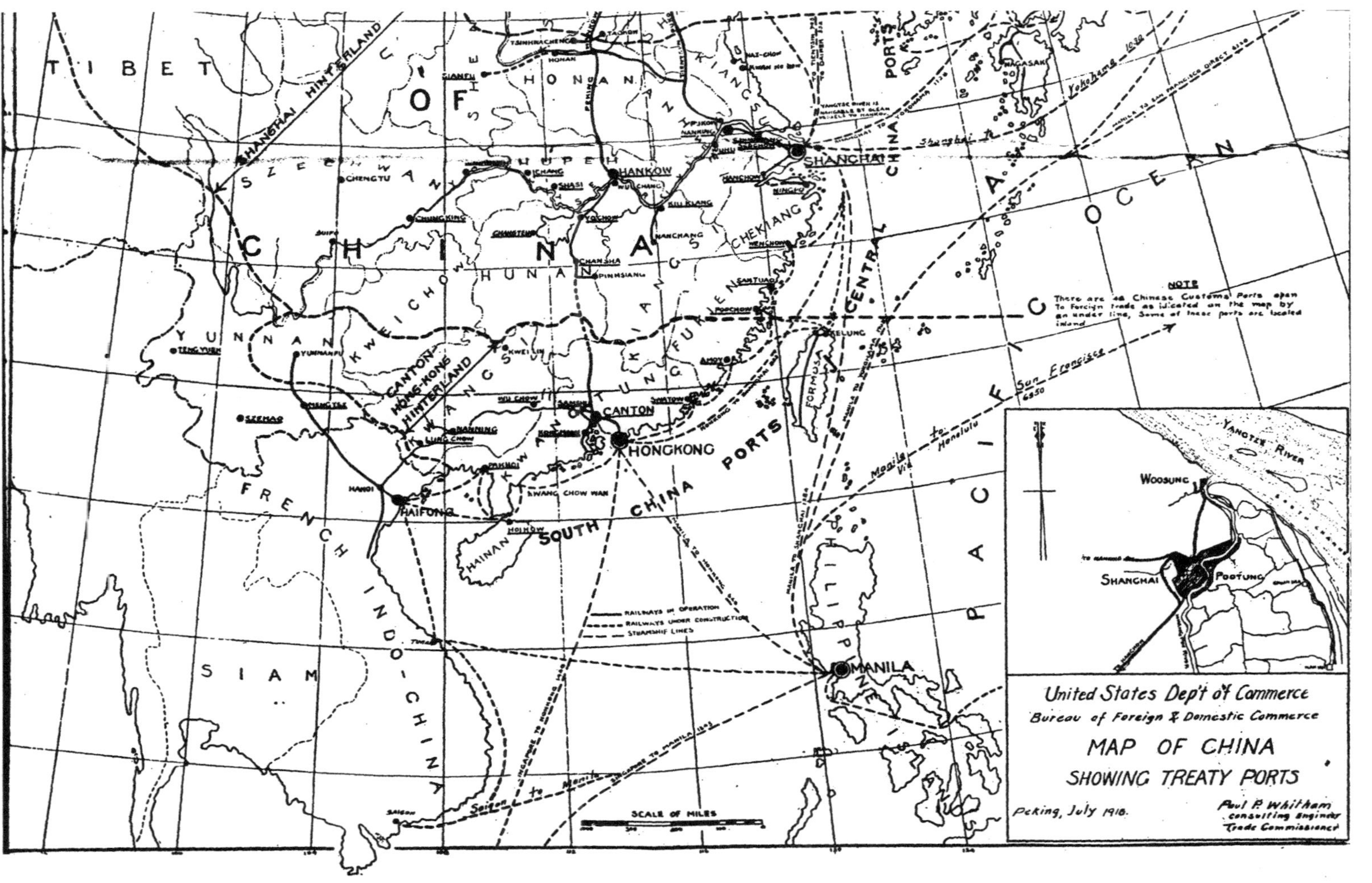

United States Dep't of Commerce
Bureau of Foreign & Domestic Commerce
MAP OF CHINA
SHOWING TREATY PORTS
Peking, July 1918.
Paul P. Whitham
consulting engineer
Trade Commissioner
NOTE
There are 48 Chinese Customs Ports open to foreign trade as indicated on the map by an under line. Some of these ports are located inland.
RAILWAYS IN OPERATION
RAILWAYS UNDER CONSTRUCTION
STEAMSHIP LINES
SCALE OF MILES
TIBET
CHINA
OF
PACIFIC OCEAN
CENTRAL CHINA PORTS
SOUTH CHINA PORTS
SHANGHAI HINTERLAND
CANTON-HONG-KONG HINTERLAND
HONAN
KIANGSU
HUPEH
SZECHWAN
HUNAN
KIANGSI
CHEKIANG
KWEICHOW
FUKIEN
YUNNAN
KWANGSI
KWANGTUNG
FRENCH INDO-CHINA
SIAM
PHILIPPINE IS.
FORMOSA
HAINAN
SHANGHAI
HANKOW
CANTON
HONGKONG
MANILA
HAIFONG
HANOI
CHENGTU
CHUNGKING
ICHANG
SHASI
YOCHOW
CHANGSHA
PINHSIANG
NANCHANG
KIUKIANG
WUCHANG
NANKING
HANCHOW
NINGPO
WENCHOW
SAMTUAO
FOOCHOW
AMOY
SWATOW
KELUNG
KWEILIN
WU CHOW
SAMSHUI
NANNING
LUNG CHOW
PAKHOI
KWANG CHOW WAN
HOIHOW
YUNNANFU
MENGTSZ
SZEMAO
TENGYUEH
SAIGON
NAGASAKI
Shanghai to Yokohama 1030
to San Francisco 6850
Manila to Honolulu
Saigon to Manila
YANGTZE RIVER
WOOSUNG
SHANGHAI
POOTUNG

www.ingramcontent.com/pod-product-compliance
Lightning Source LLC
LaVergne TN
LVHW011257110826
845149LV00001B/163

* 9 7 8 1 4 1 8 1 8 8 7 5 7 *